"Claude Debussy As I Knew Him"
and Other Writings of
Arthur Hartmann

Eastman Studies in Music

Ralph P. Locke, Senior Editor
Eastman School of Music

(ISSN 1071–9989)

"Claude Debussy As I Knew Him" and Other Writings of Arthur Hartmann

Edited by
Samuel Hsu, Sidney Grolnic, and
Mark Peters

Foreword by
David Grayson

 UNIVERSITY OF ROCHESTER PRESS

First published 2003
Reprinted in paperback and transferred to digital printing 2010

University of Rochester Press
668 Mt. Hope Avenue, Rochester, NY 14620, USA
www.urpress.com
and Boydell & Brewer Limited
PO Box 9, Woodbridge, Suffolk IP12 3DF, UK
www.boydellandbrewer.com

ISSN: 1071-9989
Cloth ISBN-13: 978-1-58046-104-7
Cloth ISBN-10: 1-58046-104-2
Paperback ISBN: 978-1-58046-364-5

Library of Congress Cataloging-in-Publication Data

Hartmann, Arthur, 1881–1956.
    "Claude Debussy as I knew him" and other writings of Arthur Hartmann /
    edited by Samuel Hsu, Sidney Grolnic, and Mark A. Peters.
        p. cm.—(Eastman studies in music; ISSN 1071-9989; v. 24)
    Edited from mss. in the Hartmann Collection of the Free Library of
    Philadelphia.
    Includes bibliographical references (p.) and index.
        ISBN 1-58046-104-2 (alk. paper)
        1. Hartmann, Arthur, 1881–1956. 2. Debussy, Claude, 1862–1918. 3.
Hartmann, Arthur, 1881–1956—Correspondence. 4. Musicians. I. Hsu,
Samuel, 1947– II. Grolnic, Sidney, 1946– III. Peters, Mark A., 1975– IV.
Title. V. Series.

ML418.H34 A25 2003
787.2'092–dc21   2003012641

A catalogue record for this title is available from the British Library.

This publication is printed on acid-free paper.

This book is dedicated with special thanks to
Regine Johnson and
William H. Roberts
and in memory of
James Reiber

Arthur Hartmann, 1916. Photograph from Hartmann Collection, Free Library of Philadelphia. Used by permission.

Contents

Photographs

Facsimiles

Music Examples

Correspondence

Note: Letters from Claude Debussy to Arthur Hartmann are identified throughout the volume by the abbreviation "CD" and a cataloguing number (e.g., CD-1) and letters from Emma Claude Debussy to Marie Hartmann and Arthur Hartmann by "ECD" and a cataloguing number. All letters from Claude Debussy and Emma Claude Debussy are included in Part 2, "Letters from Claude and Emma Debussy to Arthur and Marie Hartmann," and are arranged there by their "CD" and "ECD" numbers. Those Debussy letters which Hartmann included in his memoir are retained in the text (English translation only) and also appear at the end of the section with the other letters. Such letters are identified in the following list by their two sets of page numbers.

Foreword

David Grayson

There is no escaping the subjective element in biography, and, in Debussy studies, nothing dramatizes this fact more than the controversy surrounding the 1932 publication of Léon Vallas's landmark biography *Claude Debussy et son temps*. The *Revue musicale* was the site of blistering exchanges between Henry Prunières, this journal's founder and director, and the book's author, with charges, rejoinders, and countercharges stretching across three issues and covering no fewer than thirty-two pages. In contention were numerous points of fact and interpretation, but Prunières's essential objection was that Vallas's portrait was inconsistent with his own image of the composer. Vallas, he charged, had not known Debussy personally and therefore misunderstood the composer's character and misconstrued his motivations. Indeed he compared Vallas to certain "stendhaliens" with whom he was acquainted, "who develop a sort of hatred toward the great man to whom they have devoted their lives." To bolster his attack, Prunières enlisted support—and obtained considerable ammunition—from Robert Godet, a close friend of Debussy's during the last thirty years of the composer's life. Godet's contributions lent authority to Prunières's harsh critique, which, he declared, arose from a profound disappointment that their cherished image of Claude de France failed to shine through the great mass of documentation that Vallas had so laboriously assembled. Prunières further claimed the moral support of the composer's widow Emma Debussy, Charles Koechlin, Robert Jardillier, and "numerous admirers of Debussy."

While I value Vallas's book, I can certainly sympathize with Debussy's family, friends, and fans. I had a similar reaction a number of years ago upon reading a weighty scholarly biography of one of my teachers, Nadia Boulanger. I learned a great deal from this book but was unable to recognize in it the teacher I knew and loved. Like Prunières, I had the sinking feeling that the author did not particularly like her subject, even though Mademoiselle Boulanger had extended numerous professional and personal courtesies, granting the author interviews and access to her papers, and even permitting photographs to be taken of the two of them together.

I had a completely different experience reading Bruno Montsaingeon's *Mademoiselle: Conversations with Nadia Boulanger*. This relatively slim book doesn't purport to be a biography, but it seemed to me to capture her essence—her profound wisdom and inimitable personality. She came alive for me on every page. The irony is that, unlike the meticulously researched scholarly biography, Montsaingeon's book of "conversations" is partly fabricated. As the author readily discloses in a prefatory note, the conversations, as presented in the book, "obviously never took place" but were patched together from a variety of materials, and that certain links or missing "scenes" had had to be contrived on the basis of the author's identification with his subject. The resulting likeness nevertheless has the ring of truth—a human and artistic truth, if not an entirely scientific one.

These ruminations on biography, subjectivity, and truth were stimulated by a very different sort of book from the ones discussed above—the violinist Arthur Hartmann's reminiscences of his personal and professional encounters with some musical luminaries of his day, primarily Claude Debussy, but also Edvard Grieg, Charles Martin Loeffler, Joseph Joachim, and Eugène Ysaÿe. With the title of his Debussy essay, "Claude Debussy As I Knew Him," Hartmann openly announces the subjectivity of his memoirs, which are as much autobiographical as they are about their ostensible subjects. He clearly had a large ego, and many of his anecdotes are self-serving, as when Grieg and Debussy heap praise on his playing. His subjects and other supporting players do not always come off as well. Not surprisingly, he is especially critical of his far more celebrated violinist elders (one could hardly call them rivals)—Ysaÿe learned wrong notes in the Lalo Concerto; the Joachim Quartet's playing was lifeless, scratchy, and out of tune. But if he delights in the foibles of the greats and enjoys cutting them down to size, he does so not with malice, but with unconcealed admiration and affection. By divulging their imperfections he reveals their humanity.

Hartmann knew how to tell an entertaining story. These reminiscences were doubtless well rehearsed, told and retold countless times at post-concert dinners and receptions before being committed to paper. They are filled with the kind of human detail typically absent from conventional biographies: how Debussy talked, how he laughed, the nicknames he used, his fondness for blue clothing (suit, shirt, and collar), his painful hemorrhoids, and so on. Hartmann's anecdotes can even be revealing in ways he could not have imagined. In describing Debussy's dedication of *Le promenoir des deux amants,* he wrongly conjectures that the initials "p.m." which the composer appended to his wife's name stood for "petite Maîtresse." Hartmann was close. We now know that they actually stood for "petite mienne," but Hartmann's error shows us that Debussy truly wanted the meaning of these letters to remain a mystery, even to his close acquaintances.

How accurate was Hartmann's memory? How truthful are his memoirs? These are two completely different questions, and we will never know the answer to either. Nagging doubts are raised by Hartmann's sometimes conflicting accounts of the same events. Moreover, like many performing artists before and since, he took artistic license with his own publicity: he changed the spelling of his name, spoke with a phony foreign accent to conceal his American birth, and concocted a partially fabricated autobiography in order to create the proper image. Still, his stories have the ring of truth about them, and his subjects seem to come alive.

Skeptics who prefer to read their history through period documents rather than subsequent human memories can focus on the letters from composers (and their wives) with which Hartmann enlivened his reminiscences, and by the additional correspondence, documents, and photos that the editors have appended. Many of these have not previously been published, and they add richness and texture to Hartmann's engaging and insightful reminiscences.

In illuminating the unique personalities of some of the musical giants of his time and in offering precious glimpses of concert life at the turn of the century, Hartmann reveals a strong personality of his own: lively, generous, intelligent, and imaginative. It makes us wish that we could have heard him play the violin, a result which I think would have pleased him a great deal.

Preface

During the first quarter of the twentieth century, Arthur Hartmann (1881–1956) was celebrated as one of the world's finest violinists. He performed over a thousand recitals throughout Europe and the United States and consistently received critical acclaim for the sensitivity and passion of his playing. He also composed a respectable body of instrumental and vocal works and was particularly well known for the over two hundred transcriptions he created for violin and piano. Several of these became staples on the programs of such colleagues as Mischa Elman, Jascha Heifetz, Fritz Kreisler, Yehudi Menuhin, Maud Powell, and Jacques Thibaud.

Hartmann also wrote pedagogical articles on violin technique and was considered an authority on Bach's violin works, particularly the Chaconne. He was highly regarded as a teacher and was recruited in 1918 for the faculty of the DKG Institute of Musical Art, which became the Eastman School of Music in 1921. In Rochester, Hartmann led the Kilbourn Quartet, which performed weekly in George Eastman's mansion for his friends and guests. Leaving Eastman in 1922, he soon formed the Hartmann Quartet, which specialized in bringing to American audiences works by Frank Bridge, Alfred Casella, Ernst von Dohnányi, Eugene Goossens, and other contemporaries, as well as the standard repertoire.

His fellow musicians, from Leopold Auer to Efrem Zimbalist, valued his friendship and enjoyed his legendary abilities as a raconteur and musical mimic. Throughout his life, Hartmann was fascinated with meeting famous people, and his wit, talent, and ingratiating personality endeared him to such major figures as Eugène Ysaÿe, Edvard Grieg, and, above all, Claude Debussy. In a letter to Louis Laloy dated 5 January 1914, Debussy wrote: "[Hartmann] est intéressant et joue prodigieusement du violon" ("[Hartmann] is an engaging person and an extraordinary violinist").[1]

Up to now, little has been known about the relationship between Debussy and Hartmann, except for the fact that the composer accompanied the violinist in a program on 5 February 1914 that featured Hartmann's transcriptions of Debussy's *Il pleure dans mon coeur, La fille aux cheveux de lin,* and *Minstrels.* Now with the publication of Hartmann's memoir "Claude Debussy As I Knew Him," along with the letters from the composer and his wife, Emma, to the violinist and his wife, Marie, the richness of their relationship can be appreciated.

Shortly after his initial meeting with Debussy, Hartmann published a fascinating article in the form of a self-interview in the *Musical Courier* for 4 November 1908. Here he described Debussy's enthusiastic reaction to his transcription of *Il pleure dans mon coeur,* and quoted the composer at length regarding his plans for future operas.[2] After Debussy died, Hartmann published a memorial article in the *Musical Courier* for 23 May 1918. In 1941, he began to write a full-length memoir about his relationship with Debussy and incorporated much of the material from the 1918 article. Unfortunately, he left this work unfinished, so we have used the end of the 1918 article to round off the 1941 memoir.

Hartmann's relationship with Claude Debussy was unquestionably the most important inspiration of his life as an artist. During his retirement, however, he wrote other essays about famous musicians he had known. We include his writings on Loeffler (accompanied by an important letter Loeffler wrote to Hartmann in 1901), Ysaÿe, Joachim, and Grieg; the Loeffler and Grieg essays are published here for the first time, while the Ysaÿe and Joachim articles are reprinted with the kind permission of the Archives of *Musical America*. These four memoirs reveal many surprising facets about their subjects and function also as a kind of autobiography of Hartmann's youth and early career.

In order to provide a more complete understanding of Hartmann's essays on Debussy, Loeffler, Ysaÿe, Joachim, and Grieg, we have opened the volume with a biographical sketch of Hartmann. His memoirs are further enriched through additional related materials, including the twenty-three known letters from Debussy to Hartmann as well as the forty letters from Emma Claude Debussy to Hartmann and his wife Marie. Included with the Debussy letters is the facsimile of a Debussy musical sketch from a 1910 Christmas card, reproduced by kind permission of Karen Hartmann Kleinmann.

Facsimiles of part of two of the most important letters related to the relationship between Debussy and Hartmann also appear: Debussy's final letter to Hartmann, in which he reminisces about divers points in their friendship, speaks of his illness and the war, and assures Hartmann he is preparing to write the Sonata for Violin (24 June 1916, CD-23[3]); and a letter from Emma Claude Debussy to Hartmann in which she tells the violinist that she had not discovered any manuscript of Claude's that was intended for him (5 August 1929, ECD-37).

Two Appendices relating to Debussy appear at the end of the volume: the first documenting the transcription of Debussy's *Minstrels* and the second presenting three previously unpublished letters from Debussy to Pierre Louÿs which Hartmann had collected.[4] Also included are facsimiles of the *Minstrels* transcription: a Debussy autograph dated 17 January 1914 from the Sibley Music Library of the Eastman School of Music and an undated (circa 1944) Hartmann autograph from the Free Library of Philadelphia.

A catalogue of Hartmann's compositions and transcriptions rounds out the volume, documenting the extent of and providing a reference for his activities in these fields.

The impetus for the present volume came from the rediscovery of the Hartmann Collection of the Free Library of Philadelphia in 1995. Hartmann was clearly fascinated by his own life story and saved, it would seem, every program, review, and advertisement that in any way mentioned his name. Fortunately, he also saved every letter he ever received and thus provides us with glimpses of an impressive number of the musicians, artists, and literary figures of his time. Hundreds of these letters, along with his scrapbooks of programs and clippings, photographs, memorabilia, and manuscripts and publications of essays and music, were given to the Music Department of the Free Library of Philadelphia by his nephew, Alfred Bendiner, a few years after Hartmann's death in 1956.

After an initial sorting of this collection by librarian Frederick James Kent, the materials were stored away until an inquiry from Malcolm Gillies regarding Bartók's letters to Hartmann resulted in the reexamination of the collection by librarian Sidney Grolnic. Kile Smith, Curator of the Free Library of Philadelphia's Edwin A. Fleisher Collection of Orchestral Music, suggested that Samuel Hsu, Professor of Music at the Philadelphia Biblical University, evaluate the Debussy material. Hsu began the task of transcribing and translating the Debussy letters and soon recruited his former teaching assistant, Mark Peters (who recently received his Ph.D. in historical musicology from the University of Pittsburgh), to prepare Hartmann's memoirs for publication.

Many generous people have assisted the editors with the processing of the foreign language materials in the Hartmann Collection. Chief among these has been Regine Johnson, who translated over two hundred letters in French and German from the Hartmann collections housed in the Free Library of Philadelphia, the Sibley Library at the Eastman School of Music, and the State Historical Society of Iowa. Our debt to this indefatigable translator is incalculable. We honor also the memory of the late librarian James Reiber, who translated several important reviews, various Slavic language materials, and many letters by Emma Debussy. Others assisting with the foreign language aspects of the project have included Suzanne Baumeister, Stephen Henner, Jacques Iosti, Andor Kiszely, Aimée Lawrence, Mary Ann McNamee, Brenda Mellon, Marshall Taylor, and Chantal Vagassky. Throughout the volume we have attempted to standardize spellings (in all languages) in both Hartmann's text and all letters; any mistakes that do appear are the responsibility of the editors.

Those who advised or assisted the project in other ways include Roger Barclay, Russell Bird, Dorothy Black, Bonnie Blankenship, Julius Bosco, Thomas Broido, Graeme Burgan, Martin Canin, Samuel Cardillo, William Edgar, Alan Grolnic, Andrew Hui, Timothy Hui, Paul Jones, Sali Kaceli, Marion Kant, Michael Kennedy, Estelle Kerner, Keith Koch, Esther Lassman, Monica Lorusso, Harold McNiel, Candace Peters, Jared Peters, Philip Ryken, Geri Secrest, Elizabeth Shevlin, Gail Smith, Danièle Thomas-Easton,

Shana Tripp, Ken Van Horn, Gregg Wells, Matthew Werley, and Xiao-Fu Zhou. Jonathan Tripp compiled the initial catalogue of Hartmann's compositions and transcriptions and assisted the project in numerous other ways. Mervin Hartman, a cousin of Arthur Hartmann, and John Celentano, a pupil of Hartmann, provided valuable first-hand accounts of Hartmann's family life and artistry. Additional information about members of the Hartmann family was provided by George C. Hartmann, grandson of Arthur Hartmann. Special thanks to Camilla Cai, Ellen Knight, Charles Timbrell, Richard Wattenbarger, and an anonymous confidential reader, each of whom read various parts of the manuscript and provided valuable comments and corrections.

The editors had the privilege of consulting with Denis Herlin and the late François Lesure, who were glad to find additional letters for their complete edition of Debussy's correspondence. Herlin also discovered a letter from Debussy to Hartmann at the Bayerische Staatsbibliothek in Munich and brought the letter to our attention. We thank Sigrid v. Moisy and Ulrich Montag of the Bayerische Staatsbibliothek for the permission to include this letter in the present volume. Henri Thieullent, executor of the Debussy estate, graciously granted permission for the use of the *Minstrels* manuscripts and the letters of Claude and Emma Debussy. We also thank Jacqueline Leblond and Dominique Leblond of the Guilmant estate, Jerry Shaw Evans of the MacDowell estate, and Theo Erik of the Rummel estate for their permissions to reproduce letters related to Arthur Hartmann. Special thanks to Karen Hartmann Kleinmann, Arthur Hartmann's granddaughter, for access to her private collection from Arthur Hartmann's estate and for permission to reproduce materials from this collection, including a 1910 Christmas card from Debussy (CD-18) and a letter from Emma Claude Debussy, 21 April 1921 (ECD-28).

We are grateful for the assistance of David Peter Coppen of the Sibley Music Library; Ellen Sulser of the State Historical Society of Iowa; Gordon Hendrickson, State Archivist of Iowa; Dell Hollingsworth of the Harry Ransom Humanities Research Center at the University of Texas at Austin; Mary Devine of the Boston Public Library; Stephanie Challener, Associate Publisher of *Musical America*; the Archives of *Musical America*; and Karen Sherry and Fred Koenigsberg of the ASCAP Foundation. We further acknowledge the ASCAP Foundation's kind permission to publish materials from the Hartmann estate. We would also like to thank the staff of the Music Department of the Free Library of Philadelphia and the following Free Library of Philadelphia officials for many favors and considerations: Elliot Shelkrot, President and Director; Joseph McPeak, Head of Central Public Services; and Paul Savedow, Head of the Music Department. We thank them also for granting us permission to reproduce original material contained in the collection of the Music Department of the Free Library of Philadelphia, including Hartmann's essays on Debussy, Loeffler, and Grieg and many letters to Hartmann from various persons. We also thank the Sibley Music Library at the Eastman School of Music for permission to reproduce materials from their Ruth T. Watanabe Special Collections, including Debussy's *Minstrels* manuscript (transcription for violin and piano) and letters Hartmann received from various persons. Great efforts have been taken to secure all proper permissions, and we regret any omissions.

We are deeply grateful to David Grayson for writing the volume's Foreword and for recommending the project to Ralph Locke of the Eastman School of Music and editor of the University of Rochester Press's series Eastman Studies in Music. The editors note with deep appreciation the guidance of Professor Locke, Louise Goldberg, Timothy Madigan, and Molly Cort of the University of Rochester Press.

We extend special thanks to William H. Roberts, David M. Perry, and Krissy Anderson of Blank Rome Comisky & McCauley LLP for their generous and indispensable assistance with our requests for copyright permissions. Finally, the counsel of William H. Roberts was invaluable to the success of this project. His sagacity, perseverance, and extraordinary generosity of spirit inspired the editors to attempt to emulate his dedication and commitment. Indeed, he symbolizes the efforts of all the people mentioned in these acknowledgments; their selflessness, talent, and devotion have made this work possible.

Samuel Hsu
Sidney Grolnic
Mark Peters
Philadelphia, Pennsylvania
January 2003
Soli Deo Gloria

PART ONE

Arthur Hartmann

Arthur Hartmann, 1898. Photograph from Hartmann Collection, Free Library of Philadelphia. Used by permission.

Arthur Hartmann:
A Biographical Sketch

When I was a boy, my Uncle Arthur Hartmann was a famous violinist. He wore to his concerts a long velvet suit with half a dozen medals, and a yellow sash tied round his middle. He had his hair cut to look like the great Ysaÿe. After every concert he ate nothing but hothouse grapes—at least that was what I was told. We all worshiped and revered the great Uncle Arthur. Whenever he had a photograph taken, it was always in a soulful attitude with his index finger poking a hole in his cheek, and in his right hand a violin which my family insisted was one of the earliest and best Stradivariuses.

So Alfred Bendiner (1899–1964) wryly portrayed his once famous uncle at the beginning of his book of caricatures *Music to My Eyes*.[1] Bendiner's affection for his uncle is also evident in his *Translated from the Hungarian*, a nostalgic account of how his parents and their families established themselves in America after the long trip from Hungary.[2] In this memoir, Bendiner traces his family history by recounting amusing anecdotes but forgoes the accurate documentation of the daily details of births, marriages, divorces, and deaths. It is, however, one of the few sources of information about Arthur Hartmann's parents and childhood.

Family and Childhood

Arthur Hartmann's father, Sigmund Hartman, was born in the Hungarian town of Máté Szalka in 1843 and married Pepi Schweiger (also born in 1843) from the nearby town of Sátoraljaújhely in 1865. They became shopkeepers and produced nine daughters (three of whom, including one set of twins, died in infancy). In 1879, Sigmund's sister Rose in Philadelphia, the wife of Wilhelm Stern, sent the money to bring Sigmund and Pepi Hartman and their six daughters, Jennie, Gizella, Katie, Rachel, Bertha, and Rose, to America. Upon their arrival on 2 December 1879, Rose Stern put them up in the hotel and restaurant that she and her husband ran on tiny Duponceau Street (renamed Darien Street around the turn of the century) in the heart of Philadelphia.[3] Here Arthur Hartmann was born in the early morning of 23 July 1881.[4]

Arthur's talent was evident from a young age, and his father—himself a violinist of notable skill—dedicated himself to the boy's education. Sigmund brought Arthur's genius to an early flowering and soon to notice in Philadelphia's musical community. Sigmund's own account of Arthur's early education is related in an interview he gave to a reporter from the *Philadelphia North American* on 31 August 1903:

Because of [his pride, Sigmund] warmly resented some statements made in the published accounts. In these it was said that young Hartman, who, when a child, lived with his parents in very humble circumstances in Duponceau street, near Walnut, had been "discovered" and nurtured as a violinist by prominent men of this city.

Among those mentioned as his patrons were Frank Thomson, former president of the Pennsylvania Railroad, and George W. Childs. When the father read this he became angry.

"I will not be put before the world as a beggar. I myself educated Arthur until he was 6 years old. Afterward Mr. Van Gelder and Henry Hahn became his tutors.

"For every lesson I paid three dollars, and earned it with my own hands. And that, too, though I had eight children to support. Neither George W. Childs nor Frank Thomson ever helped me, and I did not ask them to, though they may have contributed to Arthur's concert to the extent of buying a dollar's worth of tickets.

"The only gentleman who took interest in Arthur's education was Simon A. Stern. He understood better than I did. He gave advice, and with his friends, Mayer Sulzberger, Simon Muhr, and S. B. Fleisher, paid Mr. Van Gelder for a full year's lessons.[5]

"Of course, both Jews and Christians in the best sense of the word interested themselves in Arthur's concerts. To them I am always thankful. With Mr. W. P. Clyde, of New York, and Mrs. Thomas Clyde, Arthur was a great favorite. And I was treated as an intimate friend. I often dined with them.

"Naturally, they honored Arthur very much. This, too, apart from the fact that when Arthur was studying in the New York College of Music in 1891 and wanted to go to London, Mr. William Clyde gave him a first-class free passage and more than enough money to maintain himself in the best of the hotels. . . .

"Since 1879 I have lived in Philadelphia—an immigrant—under my name Sigmund Hartman. That great name I inherited from my remote ancestors. I can neither tell a lie nor listen to one, so I shall be 60 years old the 19th of October coming. There are few days yet I do not attend for seventeen hours daily the little cigar store by which I live. Work never makes me tired. But I get nervous when I hear lies and bluffs, and am ready every minute to shake my fist under the nose, just as President Roosevelt does."[6]

Word quickly spread through the Philadelphia musical community that Sigmund Hartman's son was phenomenally gifted. The proud father must have arranged mini-recitals to show off his six-year-old genius,[7] and, before long, Arthur found himself studying with Martinus van Gelder, a violinist and composer who had himself been something of a child prodigy.[8]

Arthur flourished under van Gelder's guidance and even adopted "Martinus" as his middle name in tribute to his teacher. A "Hungarian Dance" (1895) for violin and piano shows how closely they worked together: the violin part, with its striking harmonics, is credited to Arthur, the piano accompaniment to Professor van Gelder. The cover picture of Arthur shows a frail, serious boy who holds his violin with obvious self-assurance.

Arthur studied at the New York College of Music during the 1891–92 academic year. In 1892, at age eleven, he began to tour Europe, playing recitals not only on board ship but also in the cities he and his father visited.[9] One goal of these excursions was for Arthur to perform for as many of the leading musicians as possible: he claimed to have played privately for Benjamin Godard and Ambroise Thomas in Paris, and in London, he so charmed Tivador Nachez that notwithstanding the twenty-two year difference in their ages they became close friends.[10] Nachez later dedicated his Second Violin Concerto (1908) to Hartmann.

Arthur played for Alexandre Guilmant in Paris in 1894, who, in turn, arranged an introduction to Camille Saint-Saëns. In a letter dated 4 June 1894 Guilmant addressed the "young violinist":

> I was very pleased to find your letter upon returning from traveling. I am pleased to hear that my friend Saint-Saëns has welcomed you warmly and has met you in London where, I hope, you let yourself be heard with success, as I have been very taken by your playing. You have the acumen, the rhythm, and other qualities of a virtuoso: hence, I most sincerely wish for the unfolding of a beautiful career for you. And if I can be of help in any way, I am at your disposal to recommend you enthusiastically.[11]

Saint-Saëns was not the only musician of import for whom Hartmann performed in London.[12] In that city on 8 June 1894 the conductor Hans Richter wrote the following testimonial for Sigmund Hartman: "I have listened to the playing of your son Arthur and believe him to be an exceptionally talented violinist; it is to be hoped that some day he'll become a master of this instrument."[13]

Arthur was also gaining valuable concert experience performing throughout America during 1894 and 1895. The *Boston Times* reviewer, C. L. Capen, wrote:

> Young Hartmann, though but thirteen years of age, has already awakened the enthusiasm of such world-renowned authorities as Sir Charles Hallé, Dr. Hans Richter, Camille Saint-Saëns, Guilmant, Paderewski, etc., so it would seem quite unfair to regard him solely as a phenomenon. His mastery of the violin is that of a mature concert artist, and . . . it is not at all impossible that he will develop into one of the most important musicians that the musical world has known. That he is already a virtuoso was demonstrated in his remarkably fine performance of the Second Concerto by Saint-Saëns. His interesting personality makes quite a suggestive impression at first sight. His countenance is one of the most frank and open that could be wished, and his face, if not exactly handsome, is very prepossessing, while his general appearance is fascinating, unique, and distinguished.[14]

In 1896 and 1897, Sigmund Hartman placed frequent advertisements in the *Musical Courier* proclaiming Arthur as "The Greatest Boy Violinist" and requesting that interested managers apply to him in regard to terms for a United States tour.

Boston, 1897–1899

Sigmund's attempt to manage his son's career came to an end when Arthur met a rich patron, Arthur D. Curran, who was willing to pay his expenses to move to Boston to study with Charles Martin Loeffler.[15] On 13 July 1897, a few days before his sixteenth birthday, Arthur obtained a Writ of Emancipation that freed him from the control of his parents and gave him the legal status of an adult.[16] The article "Arthur Hartmann's History" states:

> Like Josef Hofmann, Arthur Hartmann was fortunate in early finding a Maecenas who recognized the danger of exposing a tender musical blossom to the fierce white glare of public life. Hartmann's friend and almost father was a millionaire merchant of Boston who adopted the boy, nurtured his budding talent in the congenial field of the Hub, and had the satisfaction of seeing it flower into radiant maturity under the guidance of Charles Martin Loeffler, the violinist, and (since the passing of MacDowell's power) perhaps the greatest symphonic composer in America.[17]

The two years Hartmann spent studying with Loeffler proved to be incredibly stimulating for young Arthur. Loeffler was not only a marvelous violinist and an acclaimed composer, but also a sophisticated man of the world who knew "everybody" worth knowing. Arthur, still a teenager, was intimidated by this cosmopolitan teacher and, to judge by the essay he wrote four decades later, found Loeffler's personal mannerisms deeply annoying.[18]

No matter how unpleasant Loeffler might have been at times, he seems to have inspired Arthur in his own first attempts at composition. Arthur presumably attended many rehearsals and performances of the Boston Symphony, and it is likely that Loeffler introduced his pupil to his friends and colleagues, including, among Hartmann's later correspondents, the violinist Franz Kneisel and the critic Philip Hale. Loeffler inscribed a manuscript transcription for viola d'amore and piano of a Sarabande by Johann Mattheson to Arthur,[19] and he thought enough of Hartmann's abilities on the viola d'amore to ask him to play the solo part in his *La mort de Tintagiles* for European performances in 1906.[20]

While in Boston, Hartmann also took some theory, composition, and keyboard lessons from the organist Homer Norris. In the program notes for his Philadelphia Orchestra appearance in 1906, Hartmann's musical education is described as "of the strictest kind, his theoretical studies (harmony, counterpoint, orchestration, etc.) having been under Loeffler and Norris and finished later in Berlin and Brussels."[21]

Europe, 1899–1903

This Boston idyll lasted until 1899, when "an unfortunate mental malady manifested itself in Hartmann's protector and resulted in hopeless insanity."[22] Hartmann consequently decided to make a pilgrimage to Belgium to study with Eugène Ysaÿe. He gave recitals in Berlin and also in Budapest, where he met Béla Bartók, Jenö Hubay, and Zoltán Kodály. Eventually settling in London, where he lived with fellow violinist René Ortmans, Hartmann's network of musical friends and contacts continued to grow.[23] He had already met Edward Elgar and Alexander Mackenzie, and Ysaÿe gave him a letter of introduction to Joseph Joachim. Although nearing the end of his career, Joachim still made a powerful impression on young Hartmann.[24]

Hartmann mastered an extensive repertory, which he put to good use on his numerous European concert tours. His scrapbooks are filled with hundreds of enthusiastic reviews from Scandinavia, Germany, and the Balkans testifying to the precision, passion, and power of his playing. Hartmann was in high demand and spent much of his time traveling on trains with his piano accompanist (who included at various times Harold Bauer, Ernesto Consolo, Adolphe Borschke, and Alfred Calzin). He evidently enjoyed this kind of life, and, except for significant vacation breaks, kept it up from the turn of the century to the beginning of World War I. Some idea of the range of his activities and the reception of his talents can be gleaned from the 1906 article in *Violin World*:[25]

> Hartmann's fame spread rapidly throughout Europe, and tours were arranged for him from Madrid to Moscow. In Spain the then unmarried monarch Alfonso took a great fancy to Hartmann, and as they were of about an age, a great friendship sprang up between them, which Alfonso remembered on the occasion of his wedding, for Hartmann was one of the invited guests. In England, Hartmann toured the country with [Adelina] Patti, played at Queen's Hall several times under Wood's direction, and played second violin in a quartet headed by Ysaÿe. In Scandinavia, Hartmann toured with [Ernesto] Consolo, the pianist, and American newspapers told only recently how the two young artists played Grieg's C-Minor Sonata for Violin and Piano [*sic*] in the presence of that composer at Christiania, and moved him to say: "I have never really heard my work until tonight, though it has been performed for me very often." In Holland, Hartmann and Harold Bauer formed an artistic partnership, and were so signally successful that they have toured that small country profitably twice each year since their first monumental triumph there. In Roumania, Hartmann is persona grata at the court of King Carol, and his gifted spouse Carmen Sylva. The pair have showered honors on the young violinist, and have made him a knight, and decorated him with the highest order of the country. Carmen Sylva has dedicated several of her latest poems to Hartmann.[26]

Inventing "Hartmann"

In 1915, Arthur Walter Kramer headlined an admittedly laudatory article on the violinist "Enigma of Hartmann's Nationality." In it Kramer attempted to sort out some confusion that Hartmann had himself created:

There is a prize ready for the man who can determine the nationality of Arthur Hartmann. For years I thought that he was an American; in fact, I was certain that he was born in Philadelphia of Hungarian parentage. Yet when I talked to him a few weeks ago, I learned that I was incorrectly informed. There seems to be a real mystery in connection with the birthplace of this exceedingly individual musical personality. Mr. Hartmann related to me that if I would consult several dictionaries of music and musicians I would find that he was born in Berlin, Philadelphia, Chicago, Hungary, and Boston. It amuses him that this is so.[27]

Hartmann's veiling of his Philadelphia birthplace was part of his strategy for creating a mysterious and alluring public image. Hartmann's efforts to reinvent himself were central to his sense of professional success, targeting as he was an American concert-going public that expected artists to have long hair and foreign accents. Music journalists of the time frequently deplored the state of American culture and wondered if the nation would ever produce serious artists comparable to the European masters.[28] Hartmann had no time to wait for patriotism to overcome the fashion that favored European artists and therefore decided to pretend to be European. Although born in Philadelphia, Arthur instead claimed to be born in his father's home town of Máté Szalka, Hungary, while also adding the extra "n" to his last name to give it a more Germanic look.[29] Hartmann's obsession with his stateside image was reflected as well in the American advertisements for his concert tours: he was billed, for example, as the "Svengali of the Violin." While touring the United States, he often began extended interviews with an apology for his poor English. Reporters invariably remarked on how modest the great Hartmann was since he seemed to speak the language better than most Americans!

Hartmann also wrote many press releases and extended articles about himself, often in the third person. These usually represented a mixture of truth and fancy. The following flattering article, appearing in the 27 May 1903 *Musical Courier* (an issue that featured Hartmann's picture on its cover[30]), was characteristic:

It was in the South of Hungary, in the celebrated Nyir district, in the town of Máté Szalka, that Arthur Hartmann was born on 23 July 1881. There is a superstition among Hungarians that when a boy is born in a family after a long period, which has only been blessed with daughters, he is destined to be particularly gifted and very lucky—a tradition that seems likely to receive countenance in the case of Arthur Hartmann. He not only was the tenth child of his parents and the first son, but the first male grandchild among fifty-three of his maternal grandmother.

His musical talent, however, appears hereditary, for his grandfather was a violinist, though only an amateur, and often played duets with Liszt.

His father when a young man exhibited remarkable talent for the violin. He soon discovered the talent of his son, and began to instruct him when the little fellow was only three years and a half of age.

The family came to the United States and settled in Philadelphia. At the age of six years Arthur Hartmann was placed under the tuition of Martinus van Gelder in Philadelphia and almost simultaneously appeared in one of the important concerts in the Academy of Music.

At the age of nine, he created a sensation in London. The late Sir Charles Hallé, the world famous authority on Beethoven, the great conductor, the intimate friend of Bülow, Wagner, Liszt, hearing the boy play at the time, and being deeply moved by his talent, kissed him and exclaimed: "A genius! A star that rises but once in a century!"

When Hans Richter, the great Wagnerian conductor, heard him he declared him a master of his instrument. Three years later, at the age of twelve, on one of his trips through Europe, he gained a most valuable friend and ardent admirer in Alexandre Guilmant, the famous organist. At this age he played the enormously difficult concerto of Saint-Saëns, with Saint-Saëns, the composer, himself in Paris.[31]

Saint-Saëns was charmed with the boy's playing and took him to London, introducing him there to the Philharmonic Orchestra as "the infant genius, who played my concerto in a manner that no one could excel."

The following year Arthur Hartmann appeared in concerts in Vienna and Hungary. Yet with all the successes he still retained his unconscious charm and remonstrated urgently with his parents to let him withdraw from public life and devote himself to the furtherance to the fullest perfection of his gifts. He therefore withdrew to Boston, and for two years, under the guidance of Charles Martin Loeffler, the genial musician, the eminent violinist and composer, he worked arduously. Then followed a long period of introspection and trouble, during which time all of Europe, from Paris to Russia and around by Italy, was visited. Last year his success in the capitals of Europe was as instantaneous as it was unprecedented.

In Vienna Hartmann called to pay his respects to Leschetizky. This maestro of seventy-two years of age . . . played sonatas with Hartmann till the late hours of the night.

In Sofia, after a long and heavy program, the people insisted on encore after encore. The Prince of Bulgaria and the whole court attended this concert, and till the last were among the most enthusiastic plauditors. In London his success was enormous. Besides a half dozen recitals he appeared with Adelina Patti.

In Budapest Jenö Hubay, the world famous violinist and composer, gave him a banquet at which were present a large number of the nobility of Hungary, and Hubay himself acted as accompanist.[32]

It is with no little pride that America can say, "Here is the first man who, though a Hungarian, has received his entire musical education in America," and will undoubtedly, should he visit America, crown him with success as one of their own.

Arthur Hartmann possesses an Antonius Stradivarius instrument, one of the most extraordinary, as the master was in his ninety-second year when he made it. W. H. Hill & Son, in their new admirable work on the life of Stradivarius, comment on this Hartmann violin, for which he paid £1,050 sterling.[33] He also possesses a Jean Baptiste Guadagnini, one of this maker's best period, bearing the label "fecit Mediolano, 1752," and being most remarkable for beauty of varnish as well as tone. The workmanship of the scroll is particularly fine.[34]

Berlin, 1903–1908

Amidst all his concert activity, Hartmann found time to court and marry
Lutie Morrill Murray, the recently divorced wife of Charles Swift, heir to a
Chicago meat-packing fortune. Murray's alimony of four hundred dollars
a month enabled her to move to Berlin where she could indulge her passion
for concert-going. Her marriage to Arthur in August 1903 attracted newspaper coverage from Berlin to Chicago. Journalists sensed scandal in the
marriage of a lady of rather high social standing to a relatively impover-
ished "Hebrew violinist" ten years her junior.[35]

Arthur's marriage, meanwhile, only intensified the breach between him
and his father. An interview that Sigmund Hartman gave on this occasion to
the Philadelphia newspaper *The North American* reveals the father as a complex and emotionally tormented man, filled with a turbulent mix of justifiable
pride and irrational fear regarding his son's destiny. This front-page article
was headlined "Violinist's Marriage Sad Blow to Father / Elder Hartman Fears
Wedding to Mrs. Swift Will Spoil Boy's Career / All His Hopes in Son":

> There is a quaint little old man in a quaint little old cigar shop at the northeast
> corner of Eleventh and Spring Garden Streets who takes no joy in the marriage
> of young Arthur Hartman, the violinist, and Mrs. Charles H. Swift, divorced
> wife of the Chicago pork packer, who is ten years his senior.
>
> He is Sigmund Hartman, father of the boy, and the story he has to tell makes
> a strange and pathetic romance. . . .
>
> According to the cable dispatches, young Hartman, who is only 22 years old,
> and Mrs. Swift were married in Berlin last Wednesday, but the father of the boy
> has no knowledge of the fact beyond the statements in the newspapers.
>
> Divided between anger and doubt, he one moment declares that if the story is
> true he will cast the boy out of his heart and life, and in the next waves it all
> away with the exclamation that his "little son," who is evidently the apple of his
> eye, would never have done such a thing.
>
> The cigar shop, where the old man—he is just 60—spends his days, is a cubby-
> hole of a place, itself hardly bigger than a cigar box. Hartman the elder is short
> and spare, with a shock of white hair, a bushy white moustache and pale blue
> eyes that peer through old-fashioned steel-rimmed spectacles.
>
> A glance at his attire; at the paper collar without a necktie; at the soiled old
> suit of rusty black, tells the story of his circumstances in life.[36] He is a Hungarian
> Hebrew, speaking with an accent so marked that, in his agitation yesterday, he
> was often unintelligible, although he tried to tell all he knew of the affair. . . .
>
> Young Hartman has been in Europe about three years, and in the last year
> has lived in Berlin. He has been giving concerts in various cities, but his ambition
> seemed to be to accumulate money, if only to raise the fortunes of his old father,
> and relieve him from the drudgery of the cigar shop.
>
> Often he wrote that he meant to marry a rich woman, so that he could do
> this, and, as often as he did so, the old man warned, entreated, and pleaded with
> him not to take such a step.

"I said to my boy," the father told yesterday, "Your old Pop is all right. Don't you care for me. Keep away from the women—they are devils. I don't want to see you with a rich wife. I want to see my Arthur a great musician. You play music by Saint-Saëns and the masters, but I want you to have them play something by Arthur Hartmann. . . .

"I say nothing against her," he went on still in great distress. "I do not try to make her out a bad woman, but he had no right to get married."

"Was it because of the difference in their ages or because they are of different religions?" he was asked.

The old man waved his hands about his head, as he shouted:

"I say he have no right to get married. If he has done this I say to him: 'Go to hell!' I cut him in pieces. I never see him again."

Then, suddenly, he became calmer, his eyes grew moist. . . .

Above all his grief and alarm, however, the old man's pride in the lad, even though he might have deceived him, is a glowing beautiful thing.

"How will it all come out? With my son it is still uncertain whether he—me apart—reconciles himself with God and the people. I must wait. I am not lazy and have never smoked a cigar that my children's earnings have paid for. I have done more for my son Arthur than Moses did for the Jews who led them out of Egypt."[37]

The media furor soon subsided, and the couple set up house in Berlin.[38] Even Sigmund Hartman became reconciled to the match before too long and wished the couple well.[39] On 21 September 1905 Lutie gave birth to a son, Harold. Unfortunately, the relationship could not survive Arthur's frequent absences due to his concert tours. The couple separated in 1906 and divorced in 1907. Lutie remarried in 1909, and Arthur probably had little further contact with Harold.[40]

Despite the breakup of his marriage, Hartmann's years in Berlin seem to have been professionally fulfilling. He was constantly on tour and was the recipient of public adulation everywhere he performed. A high point of this period for Hartmann was his tour of Sweden and Norway in 1905, on which he played for and was enthusiastically received by Edvard Grieg. Hartmann's account of their meeting and friendship is related in his essay on Grieg in the present volume. Hartmann was also part of a historic political event on this tour, playing Grieg's music in Sweden on the very day Sweden recognized Norway's independence.

As a performer, Hartmann was particularly noted for his playing of the Bach Chaconne, and in 1904, he wrote an essay on this piece that targeted the alleged self-indulgence of romantic Bach performance practice. Hartmann offered his essay as a corrective, calling attention to "rational phrasing, proper polyphonic adjustment, and dynamic distribution of the voices, and the historically correct reading of the ornamentation." Hartmann condemned a kind of playing which disregarded the polyphonic nature of Bach's language, which, he argued, pervaded even his music for solo violin.[41] This essay was subsequently published in fourteen languages and prompted enthusiastic responses from Edvard Grieg and Claude Debussy. Grieg confessed in 1905, "I realize now the full meaning of the Bach Chaconne and why you play it so wonderfully."[42] Upon reading the essay in 1910 Debussy wrote to Hartmann, "It is regretful that J. S. Bach is definitely dead, because he would have thanked you for defending his 'Chaconne' against the interpretations of certain great masters of the violin!"[43]

But it was not Bach alone that occupied Hartmann during this period. Throughout his career, he was continually creating transcriptions for violin and piano.[44] Perhaps the most financially successful of these was *To a Wild Rose* (1907), one of ten transcriptions of music by Edward MacDowell. Hartmann generously assigned the royalties of this work for the support of its composer, who since 1905 had been slowly declining into helpless insanity and who would pass away on 23 January 1908. In a letter to Hartmann dated 25 July 1907, Marian MacDowell wrote, "It would be difficult for me to express my appreciation of your truly lovely interest, which has not taken the form of words but has been so active. I hear from all sides how beautifully you have played the little 'Wild Rose,' and I know the royalties will prove that, in a practical way. How I wish my husband could have heard you play it. He is much the same, a little more helpless, a little nearer the end."[45]

Also in 1907, the manager of the Victor Talking Machine Company sent a letter to Hartmann's managers inviting the violinist to come to its studio to make a test recording. However, it appears that nothing came of this offer.[46]

Despite his success as a performer during these years, Hartmann felt himself growing stale in the musical environment of Berlin. He sought a change, a renewal, a release from the repertoire that he knew so well and loved so much but had played so often that he experienced a sense of interpretive boredom. After the opportunity came to tour America again for the 1908–9 season, Hartmann left Berlin for a summer vacation in France before the tour would begin in October.

Claude Debussy, 1908–1914

Hartmann's memoir, "Claude Debussy As I Knew Him," begins with his search for renewed musical inspiration upon his arrival in Paris in June 1908. He was seeking a new style of music and quickly found it when he attended a performance of *Pelléas et Mélisande* by a composer of whom he had never heard, Claude Debussy. Hartmann was deeply moved by the experience, so much so that he parted company with a fellow musician who disagreed with his positive assessment of the opera. Having found that no further performances of *Pelléas* were scheduled, Hartmann decided to leave Paris for Finistère, the "end of the earth," in Brittany.[47]

Hartmann recalled in his later memoir that, toward the end of his stay there, he suddenly roused himself and "on impulse wrote a music publisher in Paris to send me any and everything that Debussy may have written for the violin." When he learned that there was nothing in Debussy's catalogue for solo violin, Hartmann asked the publisher to forward his request directly to the composer. In early September Debussy replied that he could not take advantage of Hartmann's offer to play his music on his upcoming American tour as he had written nothing for the violin.[48]

Not to be put off, Hartmann "immediately secured several of his songs and at once saw the possibilities of transcribing his exquisite *Il pleure dans mon coeur.*" He wrote to Debussy for permission to make the transcription, and, in a letter dated 17 September 1908, the composer granted his "full authorization."[49] Hartmann quickly finished the transcription and then asked the composer if he could show him the results before he left for America. The appointment was finally arranged for 6 October 1908.

Hartmann described his first meeting with Debussy in great detail, as recorded in his memoir of the composer in the present volume. Debussy's effusive commendation of the *Il pleure dans mon coeur* transcription stirred Hartmann's pride and excitement; the violinist had, after all, not only met, but also pleased, a man he regarded as a genius. Of course, Hartmann also found Debussy's friendship to be rewarding both professionally and personally.

The day following their meeting, knowing that his transcription would be published and that the composer wanted to be associated with him, Hartmann left for his American tour. On his Atlantic crossing, Hartmann prepared the parts for performance as an encore and wrote an account of his meeting with Claude Debussy. This article, in the form of a mock interview, provides a glimpse of how entertaining the 27-year-old Hartmann could be and of the sophisticated image he wished to present to an admiring music public. More importantly, it offers a portrait of Debussy that diverges significantly from the 1941 memoir:

> Arthur Hartmann, the violinist of the raven locks—prematurely streaked with gray—was seen by the *Musical Courier* interviewer soon after the artist's landing in America.
> "Would you—" began the man with the ink pencil.
> "I know," interrupted Hartmann. "You wish to know what kind of trip I had. Splendid, simply splendid, and not at all rough. I do not get seasick. My Stradivarius did not suffer from the voyage. There was a steamer concert. I did not play a violin solo, but acted as piano accompanist to Edward Tak, the new concertmaster of the Pittsburgh Orchestra."
> "Have you—"
> "Yes, I have played a great deal in Europe since my last American tour two years ago, and my travels have extended from Constantinople to Cork, and

from the Tweed to Tomsk. I believe that is the proper way to describe one's musical travels, is it not? I had the pleasure of meeting Grieg a year or so before he died, who came to my concerts in Christiania, and afterward invited me to his house, where I played his violin sonatas with him."

"Will—"

"My tour here will be a long one, including appearances with orchestra. My New York debut will be as the soloist of the Philharmonic concerts 13 and 14 November."

"I—"

"You wonder at my selection of the Saint-Saëns Concerto as my number, in view of the fact that it will have been played here three times publicly before my own appearance? The truth is, that the Philharmonic directors chose the work last spring, and therefore the reproach falls on the other violinists who rushed in to play it before I did. A few winters ago the Tchaikovsky Violin Concerto was utilized the same way in New York. Personally, I do not believe that such a beautiful work as the Saint-Saëns Concerto can be played too often, and I bear no grudge against my brother artists. However, I hope that the public and the critics will feel as I do in the matter, particularly as I am not to blame."

"You—"

"Yes, I met other composers besides Grieg. I spent a delightful day last summer with Guilmant, at his house in Meudon, near Paris. We played some of his works together, and he presented me with a number of them, inscribed most flatteringly. Guilmant is very fond of his gardens, and we passed some charming hours there. He spoke feelingly about William C. Carl, the American organist, whom he admires greatly,[50] and he also expressed his respect for the compositions of MacDowell. Guilmant wanted me to meet Fauré, but that gifted musician was away at the time."

"Were you—"

"I was in France all summer at a château in Finisterre, province of Breton. It is a marvelous country, full of natural scenic beauty, pastoral picturesqueness, and (owing to the historical and legendary associations of the locality) also full of quaint folklore, amounting in many instances to the weirdest superstitions. You know, Brittany was at one time part of Cornwall, before the English Channel broke through and separated France and England, and it was to an island where I lived this summer that Tristan was supposed to have been banished by King Mark. There are queer folk in Finisterre. I met a painter named Trondle, an impressionist of intense imagination. I saw his pictures and fell in love with a marine view of rare power and beauty. I am not rich, but I decided to buy that canvas at any reasonable price. 'How much,' I asked Trondle. 'For you?' he inquired. 'Yes,' I replied. 'Then take it as a gift,' he said; 'you are an artist, so am I. The fact that you admire the picture makes it yours.' 'What can I do for you?' I questioned, deeply moved. 'Play me the Chaconne of Bach on your violin. I admire that,' Trondle made answer. I wonder whether that sort of artist exists in America, too?"

"The Tristan—"

"An interesting story directly connected with that hero, but only indirectly with his island, is recalled by your mention of Tristan's name. You know Debussy is writing a *Tristan*. I have gone Debussy mad since my former visit to America.

Early this fall, in Paris, I heard *Pelléas et Mélisande*. I went there with my best friend, a well-known American composer. After the opera we quarreled and have not become reconciled since. It all started because of my friend's saying that he would like to hear *Pelléas et Mélisande* as orchestrated by Strauss. I studied the score of the work for weeks and became enamored of it. Then I procured the Debussy songs. Among them I found one, *Il pleure dans mon coeur*, which seemed to cry for violin transcription. In a fever of enthusiasm I adapted the piece, and sent it to Debussy for approval and permission to publish. I also asked him to let me play it for him."

"But—"

"I know what you would say, that Debussy is a recluse, never receives visitors, and is supposed generally to act like a bear. What was my surprise to receive a telegram from the composer of *Pelléas et Mélisande*, asking me to come post haste to Paris. I left that same day, and next morning I had the honor to shake the hand of Debussy, at his home in the Bois de Boulogne, a miniature palace, filled with exquisite art works and gold, white, and bronze decorations. A wonderful looking man, this Debussy, with a peculiarly shaped head and marvelous eyes, dreamy and illimitably deep. We smoked cigarettes and talked. I asked him whether it were true that he is composing three operas, according to report from New York. 'That would be too American,' he answered with a smile, 'I am writing only two.' 'And *Tristan* is one of them?' I asked. 'Yes,' was Debussy's reply.[51] 'There is Wagner's *Tristan*,' I had the boldness to observe. 'C'est bien, c'est bien,' answered Debussy in a tone that I would give worlds to be able to reproduce: 'I know it very well. But Wagner's Tristan was not our Tristan. Our Tristan is of that part of France from which you have just come. There are two Tristans, evidently a Celtic and a Welsh. Wagner's is a sighing and sentimental hero, who does nothing valiant and acts merely as the agent of a superior force. My Tristan is a doughty warrior, a man, every inch of him; in fact, he is the real Tristan of legend, with less idealism but more masculinity. I shall not use the Leitmotiv system of Wagner in my *Tristan*. The Leitmotiv reminds me of nothing more than a tonal visiting card. As each character comes on, he presents his thematic card and says, "Here I am."'" We drifted finally to the subject of violin music, and I asked Debussy why he had never written anything for that instrument. 'Because I do not understand it,' he answered, 'and also because, as a rule, I do not like the combination of violin and piano. Even the sonatas of the masters do not appeal to me. The only composer who seemed to be able to blend the violin with the piano was Schumann. My *En bateau* was not a violin piece originally. I did not even transcribe it myself for that instrument. The work was done by an orchestra musician.' We proceeded to play my adaptation of *Il pleure dans mon coeur*, with Debussy at the piano. Before we began I apologized for having incorporated some harmonies of my own and adding a new ending. 'It is an impudent thing to do,' I acknowledged, 'to the work of a man still living.' When we came to the harmonies in question, Debussy called out 'Bravo, bravo, quite in my spirit!' At his request we played the piece three times, and after each performance he grew more enthusiastic. I handed him a pencil with which to make excisions and corrections. 'Not one note different,' he cried. He immediately wrote to his publisher, Durand, asking that the transcription be issued at once. We spent another two hours together, discussing music and art in general.

That evening, Debussy came to the Grand Hotel, where I was living, and brought me his photograph, with his signature. When I called at Durand's, the publisher was dumbfounded, explaining that a miracle must have happened for Debussy to receive a stranger, entertain him for hours, and endorse a revamping of one of his own works. I replied that Debussy seems to be generally misunderstood, and that is my honest impression."

"It—"

"I know it is necessary for you to go, so do not apologize. I, too, must be moving, for I have a recital in Boston tomorrow and a Philadelphia appearance the day after. Good morning."[52]

In this 1908 account, Hartmann portrayed himself as a sophisticated man of the world who immediately won the composer's confidence and gratitude. By 1941, Hartmann presented himself as a nervous student confronted with a fascinating but thoroughly mysterious genius. The truth probably lies in some combination of these two depictions.

Hartmann's relationship with Debussy resumed in 1910, when the violinist returned to Paris with his new bride Marie (whom he had married on 21 December 1909 after a whirlwind shipboard romance[53]) and moved into a house around the corner from Debussy. Hartmann soon wrote a note to Debussy announcing both his proximity and his marriage. Hartmann's account of their second meeting, which likely took place in January 1910, suggests that Debussy felt quite relaxed in the violinist's company. Debussy found this natural-born raconteur and mimic entertaining and evidently opened up to him, coming early to trust the younger man.

Hartmann's next significant meeting with Debussy occurred on 21 February 1910, the day after the première of *Ibéria*. Upset by the mixed reception of his new work, Debussy solicited Hartmann's critical response. Hartmann was, however, reluctant to offer his opinion, which only angered the composer more.[54]

Hartmann then became acquainted with Madame Debussy, who soon thereafter struck up a friendship with Mrs. Hartmann, bestowing on her the nickname "Ma Grande Petite."[55] Social relations between the Hartmanns and Debussys also burgeoned: dinner parties became a staple in their routine. In April 1910, for example, Hartmann brought his violin along to avoid being forced to play cards. After dinner, he performed the Bach Chaconne, and then, accompanied by Debussy, his transcription of *Il pleure dans mon coeur,* followed by Bach's E-major Concerto. At another party, Hartmann's cook prepared a dessert that was so memorable that Debussy fondly recalled it in his last letter to Hartmann six years later.[56]

Despite Hartmann's assertion that they never discussed the music business, letters dated 10 and 17 March 1910 show that Debussy was using his influence with the conductor Gabriel Pierné to assist Hartmann's career in Paris.[57] Hartmann's performance of a Mozart concerto with Pierné on 18

December 1910 suggests that Debussy was at least partially successful. Later Hartmann returned the favor. Having discussed the pros and cons of Debussy undertaking an American tour, Hartmann arranged for the composer to meet with Marc Blumenberg, publisher of the *Musical Courier,* to explore the idea in depth.[58] This meeting took place on Saturday, 13 May 1910, but it did not go well. Blumenberg had quickly realized that the moody Debussy expected a large fee that was hardly commensurate with the composer's reputation in the United States. Debussy insisted on a guarantee of $15,000 for the projected two-month trip. He rejected the figure of $10,000 as entirely inadequate considering the "moral loss" involved in being away from his family for two months.[59] The composer struck Blumenberg as childish, petulant, and entirely innocent of any mature understanding of modern business practices. On 13 May 1910, Blumenberg wrote Hartmann explaining the reasons for his offer and expressing the hope that the violinist could get Debussy to accept the realities of touring in America. However, nothing more came of these talks or of the tour itself.[60]

One condition that Debussy laid down for the American trip was that Hartmann was to assist him in the American concerts and to play a new work, *Poème* for violin and orchestra.[61] In Hartmann's autograph book on 13 May 1910, the date of their meeting with Blumenberg, Debussy had jotted down the theme for this work and had enjoined the violinist to play it "every morning when you wake up."[62] Hartmann, enthralled by the idea of Debussy composing a violin piece especially for him, long flattered himself that the composer was actually doing so. Less than two months after the composer's death, his widow informed Hartman that she could not find a manuscript for such a work. Alas, just like the proposed American tour itself, it was not to be.[63]

On 21 May 1910 Debussy inscribed a copy of Book One of the *Préludes* to Hartmann. Three days later, Hartmann informed Debussy that he had transcribed *La fille aux cheveux de lin* from this collection. Debussy replied: "I request to hear 'the girl with the flaxen hair' play the violin, for I do not doubt that she has considerable talent!"[64] The composer was indeed pleased with Hartmann's second transcription of one of his works.[65] For his part Hartmann not only valued this transcription highly, but also appointed himself a defender of the piece against the interpretive license he discovered in performances by Fritz Kreisler.[66]

The Hartmanns returned to the United States in 1911 and resided on a little farm that Marie owned in Houghton, New York. On 25 May 1911, Marie gave birth to Gregory Kemenyi Hartmann. During this period back in America, Arthur dedicated his time to playing recitals, composing and transcribing, teaching private students, and writing pedagogical articles. The Hartmanns returned to Paris in the fall of 1913 and quickly resumed their friendship with the Debussys.

The high point of Arthur Hartmann's career came on the evening of Thursday, 5 February 1914, when he and Claude Debussy performed together on the stage of the Salle des Agriculteurs for a large and appreciative audience. The program was advertised with a handsome red and yellow poster on which Hartmann's name appeared in type three times as large as Debussy's.[67] In addition to works by Bach, Corelli, Geminiani, and Paganini (for all of which Hartmann was accompanied by Eugène Wagner), the recital included the Grieg Violin Sonata in G Major and Hartmann's transcriptions of *Il pleure dans mon coeur, La fille aux cheveux de lin,* and *Minstrels* (accompanied by Debussy).[68]

In his memoir, Hartmann asserts that the composer, for financial reasons, asked him for permission to publish the *Minstrels* transcription as the work of Claude Debussy. While it may seem incredible that Debussy would make such a request, the evidence points to Hartmann as the original author of the transcription. Although the poster, the program, and the reviews of the 5 February recital all credit Hartmann with each of these transcriptions, the *Minstrels* transcription was published by Durand a few months later under Claude Debussy's name.[69]

The Hartmann/Debussy recital, and the *Minstrels* transcription in particular, won critical acclaim. The following review by Louis Laloy with introduction by Émile Vuillermoz in the latter's column entitled "La Musique au Concert" appeared in *Comoedia,* 9 February 1914:[70]

A concert of very particular character captured the attention of musicians anxious to defend a poet of harmony presently persecuted by the peasants. Louis Laloy has emphasized the importance and timeliness of the action of Claude Debussy affectionately lending his two helping hands to Edward Grieg at the very moment when a formidable suffragette overwhelmed the dear little old man with blows from her umbrella. My tenderness for the oppressed one and his defender makes it a duty for me to hereby let Louis Laloy speak, to allow him to harmoniously conclude his fine article of last Thursday:

"Mr. Arthur Hartmann is a master whom the violin obeys without debate. His bow when it gets hold of a string adheres to it as if it were magnetized; his fingers strike the neck with a clear patter, the sound, from the depths of the fourth string all the way to the dizzying heights of the highest string, retains its density and its caliber. The strokes and chords never give way to the least hesitation. One would think that the instrument belonged to him like a part of his body which he uses at will, that the varnished body is an elongation of his chin, and that the strings are the last branchings of his exposed nerves. The Chaconne of Bach, where the most formidable problems of technique are aggravated by the requirements of style, finds, thanks to him, the sublime purity of the thought which inspired it. Like Paganini, who, by the way, he resembles through some asymmetry of his person, he is a bit of a magician.

"Mr. Claude Debussy, who accompanies him as a special favor, is magical. This is not the place to deduce the differences between sorcery that fools the spirit and magic that wins it. The power of the magic will be understood by all those who have ever heard this supernatural piano, where the sounds are born without hammer impacts, without touching the strings, and rise in a transparent air that joins them without confusing them and they evaporate in iridescent mists. Mr. Debussy tames the keyboard with a charm which is out of reach of any or our virtuosos. Like one of his spiritual ancestors, François Couperin, he could write an *Art of Playing the Piano*,[71] which, none the less, would not betray his secret to the layman.

"Grieg's G-Minor Sonata did not disappoint my recollection: I still love its grace, freshness, tenderness, its bravura interspersed with nostalgic refrains, and, finally, its always pleasant and clear tone. Of the three pieces by Mr. Debussy which that evening were split up between the violin and the piano, the one which comes through the process the best was the third, *Minstrels,* where the violin surrenders to the most burlesque capering, and particularly to gliding pizzicati where the whole dark continent is held in miniature."[72]

The relationship between Debussy and Hartmann continued in Paris for several months after the 5 February recital. However, the Hartmanns were forced to flee Paris in late August 1914 due to the war and the only contact between composer and violinist after this point was by way of letter.[73]

Bartók and Webern, 1914

During the summer before his departure from Paris, Hartmann had contact with both Béla Bartók and Anton von Webern. On 24 April 1914 Hartmann wrote to Bartók:

> During last night's concert of our compatriot Szántó, I heard one of your compositions, Rumanian Dance, for the first time in my life. I was greatly amazed at the quite enormous technique and modern style of composing, and I therefore take the liberty to write to you, provided you didn't forget me, and to ask you for an opportunity to become acquainted with some of your other works. Of course, anything you might have composed for the violin would be of great interest to me. But otherwise just about anything.[74]

Bartók replied from Budapest on 22 May 1914 that he would be coming to Paris the following month and would be pleased to meet with him.[75] On 23 June 1914 Bartók sent Hartmann a note informing him of his arrival in Paris,[76] and on 26 June the two old acquaintances renewed their relationship. On that day, Bartók signed Hartmann's autograph book and scribbled out a musical example.[77]

Hartmann also wrote to Arnold Schoenberg around this time to request violin works. Schoenberg wrote back saying he had nothing suitable but strongly recommended the music of his student, Anton von Webern. Hartmann then wrote to Webern and eventually received a professionally copied manuscript of Webern's *Four Pieces* for Violin and Piano.[78] Hartmann wrote back to request explanations for the unusual notations and directions in the *Four Pieces*. Webern replied at length, supplying technical illustrations of what he intended.[79] No evidence exists, however, to suggest that Hartmann ever performed these pieces publicly.

New York, 1914–1918

Hartmann described thus how he and his family escaped from a Paris in panic as war exploded in Europe:

On Sunday, Aug. 30 at 12:45 (noon) the first German aeroplane flew over Paris, dropping three bombs, which killed seven people and slightly damaged some houses. I thought it was time to act, especially as the War Department gave out practically no news and very little even of favorable events.

Since the middle of August I had been trying to get passage to America for my wife, baby, and self, and found there was no possibility of getting away before the end of September. On Monday, 31 August, I spoke to the American Ambassador at Paris and was told that if I was to leave Paris at all, I should do so at once—the same day—before night! The Germans were less than 40 miles from Paris.

I flew to the steamship office, in despair of a means of leaving for America, and was told that I could still get on the *Patria*, sailing from Marseilles, 3 September—I to share a cabin with three other gentlemen, my wife and baby to be in a cabin with three other ladies. However, I was first to go to the Gare de Lyon to get my railroad ticket; and if the trains could not get me out of Paris, there would be little use in buying the steamship ticket. Just then I was told that the steamship company had that day been able to get twelve places out of Paris on the train to Marseilles, and having the money with me (which I had carefully hoarded since the early days of mobilization, for the banks would pay only 250 francs of one's deposits), I secured the steamship and railroad tickets and bolted for my home at Arteuil.

I rushed into the house at 6:30 P.M. and told my wife that we must leave at once, that we were allowed but sixty pounds of baggage, that if we were taken it would have to be left on the station platform—and that everything must be ready by nine o'clock.

Where to begin? What to take first? All our furniture, silver, paintings, rugs, manuscripts, decorations—and books, scores, and music worth several thousand dollars? I hastily threw into my trunk the forty odd pages of foolscap size of a work on Bach and his violin sonatas which I was preparing and the priceless manuscript of six unknown and hitherto unpublished sonatas for the violin by Felice di Giardini on which I was working out the rather complex musical ornamentation and supplying accompaniments after a figured bass.[80]

The dinner on the table and the house just as we inhabited it, we closed the door and walked out! For the coming season I was booked in all Scandinavia, Belgium, Holland, France, and in Paris.

Never shall I forget the terrible moments I passed on the streets, now in total darkness, vainly looking for a conveyance of any kind to get us to the station—

a good five-mile run from our house. Paris, 'la Ville Lumière,' was in total darkness on account of the nearness of the enemy and the danger of their aeroplanes.

I had despaired of everything and was almost hysterical when a military wagon came by, and I prevailed on the soldiers, for a good bribe, to come to my house and fetch my wife, my baby, and my trunk.

We finally got seats in a third-class compartment which we occupied with eleven other passengers. For two nights and almost two days—to be exact, for 37 hours—we traveled thus, and there were people who slept on the floors and in the corridors. At last we reached Marseilles—only to learn that our trunk was lost![81] At the last moment we were obliged to buy the necessary linen, etc., for the trip, and after 15 days at sea, we reached America, via the Azores.

It is my intention to settle in New York, where I shall teach and from whence I shall make concert tours.[82]

And so he did. After setting up a studio, Hartmann quickly acquired a number of private students and also a faculty position at the Von Ende School of Music at 44 West 85th Street.[83] The March 1915 issue of *Musician* sported a story entitled "Arthur Hartmann: Violinist and Thinker," in which the violinist spoke at length about his approaches to teaching and performing:

People may think a violinist is a man who lives in halls and on trains, and does not care to teach. I *do* like to teach, and am curiously conscious that my great mission lies really in teaching, teaching those who will come after me. I take myself to be [the pupil's] guide and adviser in learning how to study; in becoming more and more *self-reliant*; in being *brought out individually*. We exchange ideas. Bad style and taste I correct from experience. For every pupil I play the accompaniment myself, making him *hear* the harmony. Suppose I have an advanced pupil for repertoire: First of all I play from beginning to end the concerto which he will take up in study, playing or whistling the solo violin voice with the accompaniment. After a general impression of the work I dissect it; disclose what the form is; which parts are going to be prominent; the first and second themes of a movement; the development of the motives, and then the figures, memorizing the solo part before the instrument is taken up. By this time I have it fixed musically in my mind. Then I work out a fingering that is reliable. I teach him the harmony of the work, and at the same time am careful of every technical detail linked with it. When the concerto is memorized and studied along these lines comes the interpretation. As I play along with him, I strike with my fist on the piano, and say, for instance, 'This is a horn'; then when he comes to a trial with orchestra nothing startles, he knows exactly what accompanying instruments he may expect. Otherwise the whole instrumental web will seem floating away like an illusion when he comes to play for the first time with an orchestra.

My plan before appearing in concert is to sit quietly alone and think on my program in every single detail, with all the concentration I own. To use the fingers is unnecessary; it is mind, not muscle, that makes main reliance in such moments. Being something of a composer, things are to me more real in that way, capable of a greater concentration than when actually performed. Public playing is abnormal, perhaps at times almost unreal, done as it is under great stress and strain. One is always called upon to do the unexpected; conditions are never twice the same. On tour, weariness, lack of opportunity to practice, a general physical state upset by change of life's routine must all be faced. Then, as I insist once more, the sole reliance to save one lies in a preparation in advance which brings unshakable authority in the crucial moment.[84]

Hartmann was a well-regarded member of the musical establishment and was an object of continual attention in the major music periodicals. *Musical America,* for instance, published a facsimile of his handwriting as the fiftieth in its "Autograph Album" series on 29 January 1916. The same magazine then published an anecdote recounting how the six-year-old Hartmann had bowed to his offstage father instead of the audience after a performance of a concerto by Pierre Rode.[85] On 4 March 1916 *Musical America* published an article by Hartmann, "The Subtleties of Violin Art," and followed this with a photograph on 25 March 1916 of the child Hartmann playing his fiddle in a "Famous Prodigies—Who's Who?" column. Leonard van Noppen's sonnet, "Haunted," dedicated to Arthur Hartmann, appeared in the 24 August 1916 *Musical Courier* along with a group of photographs showing the violinist's visage in sculpture, painting, etching, and "in life." The *Musical Courier* also noted on 9 September 1916 the birth of his daughter, Helen Elizabeth, on 21 August 1916 at his wife's farm in Houghton, New York.

Hartmann continued to appear in concert as opportunity arose. One notable such event came on 20 February 1918 when he performed Henry Huss's Violin Sonata in Aeolian Hall with the composer at the piano. The large audience included Eugène Ysaÿe and Albert Spiering, both of whom had played the sonata. The *New York Evening Post* reported: "[Ysaÿe] doubtless wanted to hear how Hartmann would play [the sonata]. He must have been hard to please if he didn't like this performance."[86]

Hartmann also resumed his activities as a composer and transcriber and prepared various works for publication and performance. On 23 December 1917 the New York Orchestral Society premièred Hartmann's *In the Orient: Two Symphonic Sketches.* On 13 April 1918 Hartmann was joined by Constance Purdy, contralto; David Bispham, reader; and Clarence Adler, piano, in presenting an evening of his own compositions and transcriptions at the MacDowell Club.[87]

Arthur Walter Kramer's article, "Enigma of Hartmann's Nationality," paints a flattering portrait of Hartmann as a composer at this point in his career:

I know few living composers who have shown themselves masters of all forms as has this singularly gifted man. He has written everything, from short violin pieces, through symphonic poems for orchestra to choruses for mixed voices with orchestra. When I first made the acquaintance of some of his songs—it was at a recital given by the American baritone, Charles W. Clark, at Mendelssohn Hall, five years ago—I expected to hear music such as a violinist whom I knew to be a good musician might write. Well do I remember my surprise at listening to very individual modern music in these songs. Many fine songs has he given us, among the best of them a setting of Stevenson's Requiem, a grim Ballade, *A Fragment*, *A Child's Grace*, *In a Gondola*, and *Sleep Beauty Bright*. A symphonic poem, *Timar*, after Maurice Jokai's once popular novel *Der Goldmensch*, lies on Mr. Hartmann's desk.

He assured me recently that he actually wrote it at seventeen and that the revision has been slight. Beautiful music is this, modern and vital. In it he has contrasted the two elements, which stand at opposite poles of the story, by the keys B Major and C Minor; and he has obtained a uniquely calm and thrilling effect by placing these two triads one after the other and modulating enharmonically on the D-sharp, which becomes E-flat, of course. The scoring is masterly, the writing for the instruments, though very difficult, idiomatic in every instance. Then there are superb choral compositions, taxing to sing, to be sure; yet is this not true of mostly all music that is worth while?

I asked Mr. Hartmann what he had been doing in composition since he had returned to America, and I learned that he had been working on a new edition of the Six Solo Sonatas (or Suites) for the violin by Bach. Of rare interest also is a set of six sonatas for the violin by Felice di Giardini, an Italian composer, who flourished in 1716, which Mr. Hartmann has virtually reconstructed. They were brought to his attention in Paris by his friend, Walter Morse Rummel, the composer.[88] Mr. Rummel found them and, knowing Mr. Hartmann's rare gifts, entrusted him with them. There was nothing but the violin part and a bare figured bass for him to work on; he wrote complete piano accompaniments for them, as well as editing the violin part and bringing it up to date by subjecting it to the possibilities of modern violin technique. The set will be published in the near future. And only a month ago Mr. Hartmann's *Suite in Ancient Style* for violin with piano accompaniment was published. In it he displayed a remarkable gift for writing in the Bachian manner, yet providing a constant interest, so that the person hearing it does not get the impression that he is being served with the dust of old masters. During this coming season, Mr. Hartmann's *Preludes* for Piano will be played by Frances Moore, Alexander Raab, and Ethel Leginska.[89]

On 25 March 1918 Debussy died. Hartmann soon set to work on an article about the composer, and the *Musical Courier* published "Claude Debussy As I Knew Him" on 23 May 1918. Although long expected, the composer's death deeply affected Hartmann. The loss of Debussy symbolized for Hartmann the loss of that happy prewar world in which he had achieved so much fame and success—now he would have only his memories to sustain him in the decades ahead. Hartmann had received an undated letter from Walter Morse Rummel that described Debussy's last days:

I was glad to get news from you. Yes, the death of Debussy is terribly sad and terribly sad the way he was buried. He was going down for a year, and his memory and his vitality had been diminishing gradually. Happily, he died without suffering and very peacefully. I had not seen him for many weeks. He died at a terribly anguishing moment. Happily, that afternoon the bombardment, by some good luck, stopped, and the funeral procession which from his house proceeded all the way to Père Lachaise past the danger zone came off quietly although the weather was terrible and the people few, so few that at the entrance to the cemetery you could count them on your fingers. I have seen Madame Debussy since several times, and it has been terribly sad to be there without him. I don't think, had he lived, he would have created much new music, for many years he had not done anything great (in the line of *Pelléas et Mélisande* and *Saint-Sébastien*). He spoke often of you and your playing, and although I am sure he wasn't a good correspondent, he thought of his friends often.[90]

Hartmann's connection to Debussy did not go unnoticed in the press: in his column of 4 April 1918 Byron Hagel noted:

[Debussy] very seldom took any active part in concerts, but one of the exceptions was the evening in which he appeared in joint recital with Arthur Hartmann, the violinist, who has made some violin transcriptions of Debussy works which are fine examples of what transcriptions ought to be. Together they played a Grieg Sonata, and Debussy played a group of his own works. It was evident that the piano technic of other composers had long been strange to the Debussy fingers. The spirit was there, but the flesh was not always willing; but as a player of Debussy, the palm for excellence must certainly go to Debussy himself. Hearing the mystic, ethereal, original effects in tone color which he drew from the instrument, one understood thoroughly why he had remained true to his own style of composition, once it was discovered.[91]

Hartmann began in 1918 to consider other approaches to his own art. He knew that the roving life of the concert artist was becoming increasingly difficult due to wartime conditions. He also could easily foresee that circumstances after the war would not permit a return to Europe for years to come.

Eastman, 1918–1922

In his unpublished essay on George Eastman, "The Real George," Hartmann described his plight:

The summer of 1918 found me living with my family in an obscure village in the upper part of New York State [Houghton]. America too was in the war and all my eligible pupils had by now either been drafted into service or had escaped to South America or Mexico. There were about a dozen concerts booked ahead for the coming season, and my managers, too, had been conscripted.[92]

At this time Hartmann received a telegram from Alf Klingenberg of the DKG Institute of Musical Art requesting that he come to Rochester, New

York. In light of his circumstances, Hartmann accepted the invitation and moved to Rochester in 1918. This Institute of Musical Art had been founded by the violinist Hermann Dossenbach and the Norwegian pianist Alf Klingenberg in 1913; Oscar Gareissen, a voice teacher, joined the staff the following year. From that point on, the school was known as "DKG" after the initials of the last names of its directors. It was this school that George Eastman purchased in April 1918 to form the core of what would become in 1921 the Eastman School of Music. Hartmann's essay on Eastman describes the very fluid and confused activity involved with organizing this new conservatory, on whose faculty he served until 1922. In addition to his teaching responsibilities, Hartmann played first violin in a quartet (eventually known as the Kilbourn Quartet) that performed in George Eastman's mansion on "Sunday evenings for 100 to 125 guests, culled from a rotating list of 1500 friends and acquaintances, Kodak employees, university and Eastman School faculty, and distinguished visitors."[93]

Elizabeth Brayer's biography of George Eastman describes Hartmann's impact in Rochester: "He would shortly personify the ecstasies of electrifying music and agonies of financial and personal difficulties that Eastman would face in this new breed of European musician coming to conservative Rochester. The town would be alternately amazed, diverted, and scandalized by Hartmann and his ilk."[94]

For his part, Hartmann not only grew to view with contempt the "tone-deaf" George Eastman (who, Hartmann felt, had no true appreciation of either music or musician), but also soon wearied of Rochester itself. His only consolations were his students and his friends on the faculty, notably Christian Sinding, who came to Rochester in 1920 to teach theory and composition.[95]

When Hartmann left the Eastman School of Music in 1922, he also left behind an assortment of letters and souvenirs that are now housed in the Sibley Music Library. Included in this collection of over seventy letters or postcards are items from Leopold Auer, Béla Bartók, Frank Bridge, George Chadwick, Walter Damrosch, Claude Debussy, Arthur Foote, Ossip Gabrilowitsch, Alexander Glazunov, Leopold Godowsky, Alexander Gretchaninov, Alexandre Guilmant, Philip Hale, Vincent d'Indy, Franz Kneisel, Zoltán Kodály, Fritz Kreisler, Charles Martin Loeffler, Tivador Nachez, Ole Olson, Maud Powell, Arnold Schoenberg, Richard Strauss, Jacques Thibaud, Anton von Webern, and Leo Weiner.

Concert Tours, 1922–1925

Upon leaving Rochester, Hartmann again dedicated himself to concertizing, beginning with an extended tour of Germany in the fall of 1922. On 21 October he performed both the Tchaikovsky Concerto and the Saint-

Saëns B-Minor Concerto with the Berlin Philharmonic, conducted by Richard Hagel. On 26 October he performed a recital in Leipzig that included Bach's E-Major Concerto, the Paganini "Moses" Variations, the Bach Chaconne, and several of his own transcriptions of works by Corelli, Vivaldi, Poldini, Gretchaninov, and Tchaikovsky. He performed the same program in Munich on 2 November, Dresden on 5 November, and Vienna on 22 November.

Hartmann was horrified by the gross inflation that was then raging in postwar Germany. César Saerchinger reported from Berlin on 19 October 1922:

> Arthur Hartmann dropped in on your correspondent a few days ago. "Conditions" here have upset poor Hartmann terribly. Handing out thousands to a cabman, waiting in line for a new paper-supply at the bank (where they were "out" of everything but ten-thousand mark notes at the time) are symptoms of a fearful upheaval to him. We, who have watched street battles with hand grenades, smile superciliously at this.[96]

Any nostalgic hopes Hartmann had of returning to a Europe that resembled the prewar civilization he had once enjoyed proved illusory. Leonard Liebling, Hartmann's friend and the editor-in-chief of the *Musical Courier,* had advised Hartmann not to go to Germany and printed one of Hartmann's personal letters in the 8 February 1923 issue as a warning to others:

> First of all, old man, I can hear you crowing, all the way over here. The whole of Europe has been a frightful disillusionment to me, and we will soon be on our way back to l'Amérique. However, I am quite content, for I simply had to experience things for myself. You see there is so much "old" interest here, that one has to remind one's self that we are seeing History repeat itself—the revulsion, the back-wash from murder, from social chaos. I cannot see it otherwise but that America has the best of it in all ways. I have become disgusted with the local and the national chauvinism—and the worst is that instead of the all-embracing, far-reaching universal brotherhood of man, people are more distrustful of each other, hate each other more today than during the times when they could bury their knives in each other's hearts. My experiences—dishonesty, corruption, and, what is for me as an artist more vitally immoral, mediocrity all over enshrined, applauded, upheld. Mediocrity and conceit and inefficiency. . . . I feel sure that all Europe is cracking and that damn soon.[97]

Hartmann returned to America exhausted and took a long sabbatical before resuming a routine of private teaching (at his New York studio, 315 West 79th Street), occasional recitals, and pedagogical publications. Theodore Presser and G. Schirmer featured his transcriptions in their advertisements, and Hartmann continued to produce new ones during the mid-twenties. He proudly kept track of who was programming his works, a list that included Fritz Kreisler, Jascha Heifetz, Mischa Elman, Renée Chemet, and Andre Polah.

In the spring of 1924, Hartmann began to advertise in all the major music magazines that he would be returning to the concert stage for the next season. He did play a few of his standard programs during 1924–25 (including a joint recital with the pianist Marie Mikova on 19 February in Boston's Jordan Hall which utilized the services of Arthur Fiedler as accompanist for four of Hartmann's transcriptions), but could not put together a full concert tour.

The fact that Hartmann was still a musician of importance is evidenced by Aaron Copland's request on 17 April 1925 for a letter of recommendation for a Guggenheim Fellowship. Hartmann complied, and on 24 April 1925 Copland thanked Hartmann for his gracious recommendation and invitation to call on him.[98]

Between 1923 and 1925 Hartmann and Bartók corresponded regarding the possibility of joint recitals and then of a joint concert tour.[99] On 25 January 1925 Hartmann wrote to Bartók:

> I was happy to receive your letter but its subject, of course, didn't give me any joy since I had hoped for improved conditions overseas. Sincere thanks for the included photo.
>
> Please excuse my delayed answer. I was busy moving (from the village to the city) and immediately started to work here. I have just returned from Canada, where I gave some concerts. While there, I had determined to finally write to you.
>
> I am looking forward to your visit to America, and to answer your question, yes, I'll be here during the coming season. It would be a great honor and joy should you wish for me to publicly perform with you here. In that case, you would have to communicate your desire to your agency here. I am on very good terms with Varèse and Salzédo, and both of them have tried several times to find a work I could première at the "International Composers' Guild."[100] Do compose something for me, maybe a new sonata, and then, by God, nobody else but I will play it for the first time.[101] So, as you can tell, I only ask for the best, and if you want Hartmann you just have to request Hartmann through the management which is sending you over here. All is in your hands.
>
> Did you see Ravel's *Tzigane*? Should gypsy music once again become popular, then God knows, you could compose a fabulous work with Hungarian motives for me between now and January 1926. And I shall perform it! I transcribe for Universal but find it impossible to transcribe your Rumanian Dances due to the intricate harmony. I don't suppose they could be simplified? I suppose they would be rather banal sounding and also be less interesting. My wife and I send our most sincere regards to you, your wife and the young gentleman. Your old Arthur Hartmann.[102]

Hartmann and Bartók did not, however, play recitals together at any time in Europe or tour America during the 1926–27 season. Bartók's first U.S. tour took place December 1927 to February 1928 and featured recital appearances with Hungarian violinist Joseph Szigeti.[103]

Hartmann String Quartet, 1925–1929

After his difficulties organizing a solo concert tour in 1924–25, Hartmann formed his own string quartet in 1925 which led to a renewal of his concert career. The other original members of the quartet were Bernard Ocko, second violin; Mitja Stillman, viola; and Lajos Shuk, cello. The *Musical Courier* announced on 12 November 1925 the formation of the Hartmann Quartet and printed its statement of purpose:

> The string quartet, because of the absolute purity of its part writing, represents that which is the most clarified, most beautiful, the loftiest in musical form. As a rule, the greatest composers have cast their most profound utterances in the strict austere mould of four-part writing, and it is a generally conceded fact among musicians that even Beethoven did not attain the sublimated heights, did not reveal himself to the world in his immortal symphonies as he did in some of his string quartets. The string quartet is therefore the aristocrat of music and represents the perfect blending of four individualities, each at times subservient to the others, each cooperating in the logical development of its own personal voice for the achievement of the art ideal. The culture of chamber music is not yet as widespread as the huge repertory and nobility of the works merits. The Hartmann Quartet will endeavor, with the aid of the public, to sustain and spread the influence of this miniature art, to reverence all that is beautiful in the old masters and with equal interest welcome the living composers.[104]

The first concert of the Hartmann Quartet at Town Hall on 16 November 1925 featured the Quartet in G Minor by Frank Bridge and the Quintet in E-flat Minor, Op. 26, by Ernö Dohnányi, with the composer at the piano. The evening concluded with Beethoven's Quartet in E Minor, Op. 59, no. 2. The *Musical Courier* reviewer wrote on 26 November 1925:

> The Hartmann String Quartet made its bow to the public on the evening of November 16 at the Town Hall. . . . The program was far removed from the trite and tiresome groups of overplayed classics that one is usually condemned to hear at chamber-music concerts. . . . The playing throughout the entire evening was of the masterly character not usually associated with quartets making their initial bow on the concert platform. There is a tradition that such organizations cannot reach perfection merely by means of careful rehearsing but must attain it through several seasons of actual performance. Mr. Hartmann thoroughly disproved this tradition. His quartet showed none of the uncertainty of newness. It was quite evident from the beginning that the men had felt out their interpretations in rehearsal and had arrived at perfect unity. The playing displayed astonishing dash and verve. It was as if four fine solo artists were playing each his own part in complete freedom, yet the result was perfect blending, completely satisfying balance, and an ebb and flow of dynamics that expressed the highest emotional content in the music. It was a splendid performance, and places the Hartmann Quartet on a par with the world's best.[105]

The *Musical Courier* further published a compilation of other critical response on 17 December 1925:

> Said F. D. Perkins in the *Herald Tribune*: "Their playing belied the shortness of their association. It was notably spirited and expressive, thoroughly unified, with that effect of mental as well as mechanical unity which marks the best quartets." Olin Downes wrote in the *Times*: "This is the first season of the Hartmann Quartet, yet the performances were not those of an organization in the formative stage. There was balance, euphony, warmth of tone and feeling. The members did not play as if they were still finding each other out or undecided in regard to this or that nuance or sonority." The *Evening Post* critic said: "There were warmth and breadth in its playing. Its ensemble work was excellent, always displaying a fine sense of the composer's writing."[106]

On 27 December 1925 Hartmann joined Alfredo Casella, Dane Rudhyar, and a small group of the leading players of the New York Symphony Orchestra conducted by Fritz Reiner for the first concert of the fifth season of the International Composers' Guild at Aeolian Hall. Hartmann and Morris Tivin premièred Arthur Lourié's Sonata for Violin and Double Bass.

On 4 January 1926 the Hartmann Quartet presented its second Town Hall concert featuring Eugene Goossens's Piano Quintet, Op. 23, with the composer at the piano, Mozart's D-Minor String Quartet, K. 421, and Leo Weiner's first String Quartet.[107] On 31 January 1926 the Hartmann Quartet played at the University Club in New York, performing Reinhold Glière's Quartet in A Major, the slow movement from Tchaikovsky's Quartet in D Major, Percy Grainger's *Molly on the Shore*, and Schumann's Third Quartet, Op. 41.[108] They performed the Glière and Schumann quartets again on 8 March 1926 at their third Town Hall concert. Alfredo Casella also accompanied Hartmann and the cellist Shuk in his *Siciliana Burlesca*.[109]

The Hartmann Quartet premièred Casella's Concerto for String Quartet at Aeolian Hall on 14 February 1926. This work appeared in an International Composers' Guild concert that featured the American première of Stravinsky's *Les Noces*, which was performed both before and after the Casella Concerto. Although the concerto was overshadowed by *Les Noces*, it met with critical acclaim and provided valuable exposure for the Hartmann Quartet.[110]

In 1927, Walter Edelstein replaced Bernard Ocko as second violin and Naoum Benditzky replaced Lajos Shuk as cellist in the Hartmann Quartet, and the group began to play outside of New York City. Bookings for the quartet continued to increase, and the ensemble went on an extensive American tour in 1928. Despite this success, the quartet disbanded early in 1929 (Edward Kreiner, viola, having by then replaced Mitja Stillman).

The year 1929 also brought the breakdown of Hartmann's marriage of twenty years. Upon their separation Marie took the two children to California, and on 5 September 1930 Arthur and Marie were divorced in Los Angeles.[111]

Illness and Retirement, 1929–1931

Hartmann decided to go on vacation in the spring of 1929, but this, too, proved a disaster:

> The year 1929 brought me, at one stroke, every tragedy that I think can befall man—loss of health, home, family, money—and with little hope of change, this situation endured for a decade! I arrived in Paris literally bent in two with pains and within two hours after registering at a hotel, I got glimpses of the city that once was my home from the inside of an ambulance. In the wonderful American Hospital at Neuilly, to which I always look back with emotional gratitude for their great efficiency and kindliness, I lay for three months, after an operation, and when I came out, the world had changed for me thenceforth and forever. I was too tragically sad to see or even want to communicate with Debussy's wife, who since some years had had to retrench, leave the luxury of the villa at "no. 24 Square" and was inhabiting a small apartment at 24 rue Franklin at Passy.[112]

Hartmann's misfortunes continued when, arriving in England, he had to have his gall bladder removed. Returning to America, Hartmann convalesced in California, during which time he presumably stayed with Marie and the two children.

By the end of the year, he felt well enough to teach again, and placed ads in the January 1930 issues of *Pacific Coast Musician* announcing his availability as a teacher "during his visit in Hollywood." Hartmann also returned to the concert stage on 20 February 1930, performing the Bach E-Major Concerto with the Women's Symphony Orchestra of Los Angeles conducted by Arthur Alexander. Elizabeth Alexander accompanied him in a set of his own transcriptions on the same program. By the summer of 1930, Hartmann was back in New York, planning to open a studio in Steinway Hall in October.

But Hartmann's misfortunes soon began again. On 1 February 1931 the following article appeared on the front page of the *Philadelphia Record*:

> Arthur Hartmann, internationally known violinist and composer, is seriously ill at Temple University Hospital, it was learned last night. Physicians said he had been operated upon Thursday for an abdominal ailment. He came to Temple after previous operations in Dresden [*sic*] and Paris failed to cure the ailment. His condition last night was reported as "fair," but it was added that he was "a very sick man."[113]

Hartmann was not only in serious medical condition, but serious financial straits also. On 28 February 1931, Leonard Liebling, editor of the *Musical Courier*, printed the following in his "Variations" column:

> Apropos, does anyone wish to purchase a genuine Maggini violin, in fine condition, and with a glorious tone? The instrument belongs to a well-known violinist

who is ill and in need. He is willing to sell also several original manuscripts of Debussy, including that master's famous *Minstrels*. Anyone interested in immediate purchase may address the writer of Variations.[114]

Hartmann sold the precious *Minstrels* manuscript to the Sibley Music Library at the Eastman School of Music for $600 later that year. By then, he was finished convalescing at the home of his nephew, Alfred Bendiner. On 30 May 1931 Leonard Liebling printed the following about Hartmann in the *Musical Courier*:

> Arthur Hartmann, having fully recovered from his series of illnesses, will concert-ize from now on under the direction of Betty Tillotson. Between times he will do a limited amount of teaching. Mr. Hartmann has been absent from the concert field since June 1929. While in Paris he was stricken almost on his arrival and taken to a hospital where he underwent a serious operation. Later, en route to America following his supposed recovery, he stopped off in London only to be stricken the second time and taken to another hospital. Returning to America, he underwent his third major operation in Philadelphia. At times hope for his entire recovery was rather doubtful, but when he met with a railroad accident and escaped with a scratched wrist, Mr. Hartmann came to the conclusion that he was destined to live.[115]

Later Life, 1931–1956

Despite his announced return to the concert stage, Hartmann did not in fact continue his performance career. His later life was dedicated primarily to composition and to writing.[116]

In 1931 the International Society for New Music premièred Hartmann's String Quartet, Op. 18, in Berlin. The slow movement of this quartet was published in 1932.[117] On 12 November 1931, Hartmann conducted the Syracuse University Symphony in performances of his *Timar* (1899) and *Impressions from the Balkans* (1905–1908), which were highly acclaimed by audiences and critics alike.

Hartmann also conducted a performance of Ernest Chausson's *Poème* with his friend Andre Polah as violin soloist. Shortly after this concert, he set up a studio in Toronto, hoping to take over the students of the late Luigi von Kunits, who had died on 8 October 1931. He commuted from New York to Toronto until February 1933, but his attempt to establish himself there was not successful.[118]

On 12 May 1932 the Sigma Alpha Iota sorority at Fort Hays Kansas State College presented an entire concert devoted to Hartmann's songs, violin pieces, and piano pieces.[119] Two concerts by the Grand Rapids Symphony also featured compositions by Hartmann: *Impressions from the Balkans* on 15 and 16 January 1932 and *Caprice on an Irish Poem* (1931) on 16 and 17 December 1932 (Hartmann also performed the Tchaikovsky

Concerto on this program). His tone poem *Timar* was performed by the Syracuse Symphony on 7 January 1933.

On 4 February 1933 the *Musical Courier* reported that Ernö Rapee had conducted the Radio City Symphony on 29 January in the first "air performance" of Hartmann's *Impressions of the Balkans.* This work, along with *Timar,* received fairly frequent performances by the smaller orchestras throughout the rest of the decade.

Beginning in the early 1930s, Leonard Liebling hired Hartmann to write frequent reviews of new violin publications for the *Musical Courier,* as well as longer articles from time to time. These include "Woodstock and the Woodstockians," 5 December 1931,[120] and a commentary on Saint-Saëns's *Au courant de la vie,* 5 March 1932, which opens with the following comparison to Debussy:

> Debussy, in his Monsieur Croche series of writings, was caustic, impish, sometimes cruel. A perusal of Saint-Saëns' essays, with their constant honeyed praise of his colleagues, inclines one to term him "le grand benisseur."
> Truly critical, Debussy had not, however, either the erudition or the polished literary style of Saint-Saëns. Polish, indeed, was the chief characteristic of the Saint-Saëns nature—in his music he is always the uncanny artisan, often the artist, and unceasingly the polished gentleman and *l'homme du monde.* And therefore when Saint-Saëns' writings treat of his French contemporaries, everything is "perfectly lovely" and for the best. Those who knew Saint-Saëns personally will recall his maximum expression of delight—"C'est la perfection; c'est comme Gounod!"[121]

Hartmann's literary ambitions were further stirred by news of George Eastman's death on 14 March 1932. He began work on his essay, "The Real George," which portrays the philanthropist as a boor and all those around him as terrified sycophants.[122]

Two more positive literary efforts from this period were related to Debussy. In *Musical America,* Hartmann contributed a two-page article on Debussy, "La Plus Que Lente," which contained in miniature some of the anecdotes that he would elaborate and expand in the 1940 memoir.[123] Memories of Debussy also arose in an interview that Hartmann gave to the *Toronto Daily Mail and Empire,* 4 February 1933. Again, most of these are repeated in the memoir but one is unique to this source:

> Debussy took it into his head to ask Hartmann to play the Kreutzer Sonata with him, reading it off, as Mr. Hartmann said yesterday "as easily as you or I would smoke." Finally Debussy stopped, made comical burlesque of buzz of many notes here and there, and said, "It's stupid."[124]

Hartmann became increasingly interested in the traditions and histories of the great violinists. In the *Musical Courier* on 15 June 1935, he published an "Homage to Henri Wieniawski" which evaluated the music and influence of Wieniawski and traced his position in the Franco-Belgian school of violin playing. Hartmann published essays on Joachim, Ysaÿe, and Sarasate in *Musical America* in 1940.[125]

By 1940, Hartmann had decided to make one last attempt to memorialize the most important artistic relationship of his entire career, that with Claude Debussy. He wrote to Leonard Liebling, explaining that he wanted to base the new work on his 23 May 1918 article. The editor assured him that the *Musical Courier* granted him permission to use "any or all parts" of the previous essay. Liebling, in a three-page letter dated 11 February 1940, strongly encouraged Hartmann: "I am not laughing at your plan to publish a booklet on Debussy. Very little inside stuff exists about that elusive man and personality. I don't know how well Vallas knew him, but as for Thompson, he never even saw or heard him."[126] Hartmann worked on the memoir through 1940 and into 1941. Despite the encouragement of such friends as Joseph Szigeti,[127] Hartmann never completed the work for publication.[128]

Liebling published Hartmann's essay on Paganini in the 1940–41 edition of *Who is Who in Music*.[129] Hartmann also made his own transcription of Debussy's *Beau Soir* during the war, which was published by G. Schirmer in 1943. Ernest N. Doring published articles on Hartmann and his various violins in the September 1946 and December 1946 issues of *Violins and Violinists*.[130]

During this period Hartmann developed a particularly close relationship with Jean Riegger (1902–1946), the sister of composer Wallingford Riegger (1885–1961). She was a singer with various choral groups in New York and was a devoted admirer of Arturo Toscanini. When she died in 1946, just short of her forty-fourth birthday, she left her small estate entirely to Hartmann, including a typed manuscript of over 300 pages detailing her experiences as a choral singer.[131] Hartmann composed a piece for orchestra in her memory, *My Jean* (1949), which was performed on WNBC on 7 November 1949 by Donald Vorhees and his Orchestra.

In 1950 Edition Musicus published Hartmann's 1943 revision of *Il pleure dans mon coeur* in arrangements not only for solo violin, but also viola, violoncello, and flute. He sent a copy to Gregor Piatigorsky in March 1950 but evidently wrote an impatient letter in May that caused the indignant cellist to send the music back to him on 20 May.

Hartmann's lifelong fascination with meeting famous persons continued in his later years. He used some of his free time to write letters to people whom he admired, often receiving lengthy replies. One example is the letter from Albert Schweitzer dated 13 May 1950 from distant Lambaréné. The organist thanked Hartmann for his thoughts on the state of Bach research and promised to send him his treatise on the bowing of Bach's solo violin works.[132]

Hartmann lived alone with his many memories until he suffered a stroke during Easter Week in March 1956. He died very early on Good Friday, 30 March 1956. His nephew, Alfred Bendiner, arranged for his cremation and for the eventual burial of his ashes in the Artists' Cemetery in Woodstock.[133]

PART TWO

Claude Debussy

Poster announcing Hartmann/Debussy recital, 5 February 1914. Hartmann Collection, Free Library of Philadelphia. Used by permission.

Claude Debussy As I Knew Him

Introduction

My first purpose in writing about this extraordinary artist and creator is to show the *man* as *I* knew him, regardless of how he appeared to others. My next reason is that for some years past, I have been urged by friends to record my experiences. They reminded me that I too shall pass and that my anecdotes (which with good wine and among the right kind of listeners, I would pour forth, together with imitations of voice and gestures) would otherwise vanish with me. Added to all this, it deserves passing mention that some of the Debussy biographers did not have the privilege of a friendship, let alone an intimacy, with him, and in one case, the biographer had never once seen or met Claude Debussy.

In order to show what steps finally led me to his door and to a friendship of unmatchable beauty and integrity, from the first day of our meeting to that of his deeply lamented passing, it will be necessary for me to become autobiographical for a brief time. I shall have to speak of my years of residence in Berlin (after the turn of this century) when Germany had her "Glanzperiode" [Golden Age], when she stood at the apex of her cultural and cosmopolitan achievements. In view of present world conditions, it must not be thought I am writing with personal hatred and prejudice, for what immediately follows is largely taken from my Memoir on Claude Debussy which appeared (in the *Musical Courier* of 23 May 1918) scarcely two months after the demise of the great poet and which, I am pleased to say, was carefully preserved and utilized in parts by subsequent writers of Debussy biographies.[1]

Music and Maps

Every intelligent person, including the present-day enemies of Germany, will readily acknowledge that country's imperishable gift to mankind in the music which German composers bestowed on all humanity, and I am certain that every living musician, of all nationalities, races, and colors, would gratefully endorse this. As for me, being neither politician nor even a diplomat, I must briefly state my Credo, and it is that MUSIC is God's greatest benefaction, next to the sun! All Art is universal and is removed from racial, political, or national boundaries, considerations, and prejudices, and in that sense the artist too belongs to the world and not to any one people or nation. That people proudly claim those who—after crucifixion—have proven Messiahs, is in line with human and nationalist feelings. Ultimately they learn to know those names which have brought glory and recognition to their country, and they love to boast of it. Knowing music as I do, living for it since infancy and humbly adoring its endless meanings and the unsolvable mystery of its Source, I can affirm that Music is the one art in which a lie is very quickly paid for and where insincerity carries its own revenge.

Life and Music in Germany Prior to 1914

On an early morning in June of 1908,[2] I returned the keys to my Berlin apartment to the proprietor and boarding a train for the French frontier left the city which had been my home for several years. I knew this was no mere recreational trip, for I had already placed my belongings in storage. I had at last decided that after completion of another, impending, concert tour of America, I would not again return to that city which I had called "home." It meant a farewell to Berlin and very possibly even to all Germany.

Germany, at that time, was a good, clean, and cheap country to live in, and practically every musician of note, of all nationalities, had domiciles there. Everything was organized admirably, nor had I, at first, any complaint with the orderliness and regulation of civilian life in the Prussian capital. Gradually however, this "system" began to be an irritant and in time began fomenting poison into my nature. Everywhere methodical adjustment, metrical and symmetrical arrangements of everybody and everything, but to me all imagination was dead. "Why," I argued, "should everyone when giving his own concerts have to play three concertos with orchestra? Are we artists or athletes? Is the fine line, the delicacy of nuance and color, the grace of bowing, and appreciation of musical phrasing and breathing to be branded as 'perfume' or 'superficiality and affectation' and only the brutal quantity to be bowed to?" The colorless interpretations of Bach that I heard had for me an exterminating tedium. Such impersonal tone ("objective" was the worshiped word), such deadly slowness of tempi, were these really a substitute for "profondeur" [profundity] and had to be swallowed as a traditionally correct interpretation of "Classicism" and of the music of a man who had had a score of children? Yet all this was stamped as authoritative, was taught thus and played and applauded by the people who considered themselves the most musical on earth. The playing of Brahms I almost invariably found to be extremely irritating through the brusqueries and coarse heaviness which were always in the fore, whereas to me, already then, he had become a true lyricist and what is more (also worse) one who often reveled in cloying sentimentality. Again I argued, "Why do concerts have to begin at 7:30 (in some German cities even at seven in the evening) when the people then go to the cafés and stay out the greater part of the night?" In more than fifty years, could Germany point to one great violinist, the product of Joachim's way of teaching the violin? True, the Germans were a musical people and Joachim's influence had been an enormous one, extending in wide directions. But my contention was—and is—had what the entire nation called "The German Method," exalted in Joachim and his numerous subteachers for over one-half of a century, had this produced one, only one, great violin artist?

The bookstore windows were always crowded with the works of Goethe and pictures of Frederick the Great, and many times had I been thoroughly grounded in learned conversations on "objectivity and subjectivity" and the great national faith: "Deutsch sein, heißt *der Sache wegen!*"[3] Nor could I view with any sympathy the gluttony of the people, for this too was carried on with "German thoroughness" ("mit Deutscher Tüchtigkeit") also of course, "der Sache wegen," and I found this quantitative indulgence extended from their boards to music itself. Dinner parties too were not to my liking, for no matter how rightly one entertained one's guests, and they left after midnight, they steered "en masse" to the lighted café at the nearest corner and had to have a final beer "to keep all the rest down," as they explained it.

German Thoroughness in Music

Of course I knew and valued what Germany had contributed to the world in Science, Literature, Philosophy, and Music, that is, to be specific, up to Wagner and Brahms. And surely the greatness of wealth of Bach's and Beethoven's humanism and revelations need not even passing mention. Every musician surely kneels in humble adoration and gratitude to his musical heritage.

But my argument in 1908 was that the monumental and (to me) indestructible music of earlier times was a thing of the past. Where, I kept asking and seeking, are or were the composers and the artists of that time, the world of the then-today, and of the future? Were there composers of real personality? The formulae of musical science had become so thoroughly within the control of any German musician, academically trained, that to write a symphony was very much like putting the meat and vegetables into the pot, fixing a slow or fast fire for just so long, and the stew would be ready. It was, furthermore, a mastery of technic and craftsmanship that was marvelous and practically without parallel. The phenomenon was that such equipment was so widespread and of almost uniform excellence. Decidedly, this training and thoroughness are exemplary and laudable, and should, in a measure, be emulated by other nations. Yet nowhere did I feel an individual voice or an expression for the future. However excellent it may have been, it was yet uniform. Music, I felt, was dead, for quality had been buried under quantity. Methods which had perfected it all had put the machinery of system above the value of spontaneity, individual expression, poetry, and art. Inspiration, I felt, was dead.

Richard Strauss the Giant

There was of course the outstanding giant of those days, Richard Strauss, and his music I heard applauded almost nightly. But there too I was making my own analysis: gigantic dressing-up of things so often banal, bourgeois, vulgarities, all dished up with a great daring and with an original orchestral virtuosity. There is, of course, much good music in Strauss together with much bad music. And then I debated (with myself), "Is there such a thing as 'bad music'? If it is bad, does concededly great virtuosity make music of great verbosity?" More important to me then was: is this the music of today and tomorrow, or did it, most decidedly, point back to Liszt and Wagner? Has Strauss ever discarded one of his hundreds of vulgar little tunes, cadences, and cheaply conventional modulations? This was my estimate then, and I have not yet been able to alter it. Strauss to me is a giant, an almost-genius, who can overwhelm and talk you down. Perhaps his strongest elements are the bombastically heroic, the burlesque, and the buffoonery.

The German language was the one in which I felt, thought, spoke, and wrote. I lived the German life there, associated with German musicians and writers on terms of intimacy, and worked assiduously to make their viewpoint the plane on which my life's basis must henceforth be laid. I absorbed great and lasting benefits, and I carry unchanged feelings of gratitude for the many and great opportunities which the cultural life of the Prussian capital at the time offered. Berlin's magnificent opera houses and almost two score theaters presented a daily variety in the classical and modern repertoires then unrivaled anywhere in the world. A publishing house in Leipzig issued books costing but five cents apiece, which gave German translations of the world's literature of all times and tongues, and I was never without at least two or three dozen such volumes. I read the plays and novels by contemporary authors of the Finnish, Japanese, Icelandic, Russian, and exotic languages; works which at that time were not yet obtainable in any other translation!

Though I was extremely young, my intelligence was sufficiently alert to not let me permit indulgence in the self-delusion that I was completely right in my opposition to an "art" which an entire nation upheld. I could carefully argue my opinions with Germans up to certain points, but I, obviously, could not discuss my feelings as well. One could not justly expect sympathy for antipathy, and my apparent defects were argued by them as evidences of my not being properly attuned. Fortunately, I had some friends among Hungarian and Polish painters and writers (Frenchmen never were travelers, and none studied in Germany), and there I found my greatest sympathy and understanding. Notwithstanding, my yearning and unhappiness kept growing more and more. Was there not a different Art somewhere and a place where I could find people and thoughts that were more congenial to my temperament?

Having reached the decision to leave Berlin forever, I set out for Paris without knowing anyone in France and without a single letter of introduction. I wanted to see whether I would find a living art there and not dead formalism. I was thoroughly familiar with the entire output of French music and French literature up to those times and had heard nothing newer than *Louise,* which I had seen in Budapest some years previous to its reaching the German stages.[4] As for Debussy, even his name was totally unknown to me. Perhaps he had been played in Germany, but it is certain that I must have been somewhere on a concert tour, for I had never heard a note of his music.

Rameau and Chabrier I loved, as also a dozen or so of the songs by Gabriel Fauré. These I could play from memory, and those four volumes are yet in my possession. I had great admiration also for the latter's two piano quartets, that by d'Indy and his *Istár,* and a few, a very few, scores by Saint-Saëns, most notably his Third Symphony. The often lachrymose melodies, coupled with "bouche-amère" ["bitter-tasting"] mysticism of harmonies and a certain religious passionateness of Franck's music had an exalted meaning, only if taken in small portions. In this Franck, as the kin of Bruckner and like him and all musicians up to and including Debussy in the earliest stages of his development, was influenced by Wagner.

Wagner's works I knew forwards and backwards and, of course, from the orchestral scores. Concurrently, I was equally familiar with all literature, mythology, letters, etc. relating to the growth of this extraordinary genius. My Bible, however, was the *Faust Symphony* by Liszt, and this I played, to the best of my ability, on the piano and of course from the score, at least twice weekly! My adoration for this work and its importance to all music—to Wagner and all musicians who have since created, including Shostakovich and Miaskowski (in my judgment)—burns with undiminished fire. Yet only last year when I casually said to a refugee conductor, and who (one might as well say of course) got appearances with the leading orchestras here, that I love the *Faust* of Liszt, he looked at me with amazement and with freezing politeness said, "Aber mein lieber Herr! Wir sind doch jetzt in 1940!"[5]

Dream Music

I hoped and dreamed that somewhere, some day, there may be a creator with the power to seize and fasten onto paper those shy, sensitive vibrations, the tenebrous and unseizable and receding. So sensitive that even the slightest approach of an analysis would frighten it back to its fabulous origin! A music which would immediately evaporate, vanish, at an attempt to penetrate that which should eternally remain unsolved, a music so quivering with lovely frailty and transparence of purity, of a timbre so clairvoyant yet fleeting that would reveal glimpses of the eternal beauties of life's most poignantly poetized sorrows as in a spirit of reincarnated mysteries, and which might vaguely suggest the sources of its being as in the very roots of mythical glory and classical loveliness.

Paris and Its Make-Believe

Thus I arrived in Paris. The city charmed me at once, and I took it to my heart thenceforth. With peculiar intuitiveness I recognized its odors and sounds from a dimmed past, for as a child I had lived and played there. Happily I recognized that here a highly cultured people were playing at "make-believe" in all the problems of the seriousness and drabness and tragedy and struggle of the thing called "living." "This," I thought, "is the first sign of wisdom, of intelligence and civilization, and of individuality."

The little "toot-toot" of the conductors' tiny horns of the huge motor buses; the excitability of the people; their hot-blooded argument, in which, however, they or some passer-by would inject some humorous comment; the disorderliness; the laissez-faire of the police; the gossiping or wrangling of the concierges, at times with excessively polite phrases and pronounced in the best Comédie-Française manner; the goats in the streets being milked a pint at a time by the vendor of such milk; the crooked streets and tumbledown little hotels—all, all was to my liking. The declamation of the language was a welcome interest to my inner ear. And to be placed at the head of all, no matter where one went, good food, excellently prepared, and the choice of perfectly cured wines. Was it then to be wondered at that I concluded that right here, in every way, was the best philosophy of living?

I had been in Paris as a child and had played there with Benjamin Godard, Ambroise Thomas, Alexandre Guilmant, and with Camille Saint-Saëns his enormously difficult and now obsolete First Concerto. It is a miserably poor work, in C Major, tediously long and vapid.[6] Even then it was little known because unplayed, and by now has become extinct. My copy of it reposes in the Congressional Library in Washington.

Encountering some American friends, we decided to dine together the following evening. Attired in "tails and white tie" with collapsible high hat, but without topcoat in the summer evening, we began the homage to Paris and French dining in a swanky restaurant in the Bois. Later in the evening we came to a well-lighted pavillon which seemed to offer distractions. On a long, elevated platform were about twenty women in a row.

They wore the large hats and fluffy long skirts of those days. These they lifted high, revealing the old-fashioned round garters and the full bloomers over the kneecap. Raising one leg, they dangled their knees, while the band played on, and this, I think, was called the can-can. After a mere glance I commented to a lady of our party, "How stupid and boresome! I had really expected something more of the women of Paris!" Following the crowd of well-dressed and perfumed pleasure-seekers, we came to another pavillon. The "fun" there seemed to be in sliding down a wide, wooden chute. More correctly, however, the fun lay at the bottom of the chute where the slide precipitated men and women, amidst screams and shrieks of laughter, into a pêle-mêle of flying skirts and hats, and a topsy-turvy jumble of arms and legs in the air. We each paid one franc (twenty cents in those days) to sit on that sliding board and presently we too reached the bottom in great disorder and with plenty of screams. As soon as our party had climbed back to the top (or perhaps there was an escalator) I, completely disregarding them, rushed across the platform to the ticket office, flung down my franc and lifting my coat-tails was again on that slide. For the third time, as I again ran to deposit my franc, my friends seized me and warned me that I was wearing out the seat of my best trousers at the rate of twenty cents a slide. They bantered me on my "running after women" and "falling among them easily," while in great exhilaration I kept repeating, "Oh, *this* is the place for me! I'd love to live in Paris for the rest of my life." As they dragged me away, soberly adjusting that rarely worn high hat which ill became me and in which I never was at ease, I turned on them. "Poof!" I exclaimed, "so you think it was getting jumbled up with women down there that made me take all those slides, do you? Well, listen! Out there in the garden is a small kiosk, and on its roof are four horn players. FOUR HORNS, vous entendez, and in the night, and in the woods, and they played (and here I sang) do you hear *that*? Do you? D Major with an augmented fourth! Ah mon Dieu, *this* is the place for me! What charm . . . what color . . . augmented fourth in D Major on a summer evening in Paris . . . with champagne and as I slide, that refrain," and imitating the sound of the horn, I sang, again and again:

Example 1. Hartmann imitating four horns in Paris

On First Hearing *Pelléas*

And thus it happened one morning, while strolling on one of the lower Boulevards that my eye caught the announcement of the Opéra Comique—

Pelléas et Mélisande. The title arrested me for I had seen its première as a play, and in German, at the Kleines Theater, *Unter den Linden,* perhaps a year or two previously. I had thought it unseizable as a play, mystifying with its endless scenes, rapid curtains, half-suppressed sighs, and vague, incompleted mutterings—hesitant, retreating, perhaps symbolic or mystical or Heaven knows what! "Allons-y," I muttered aloud, for, after all, I had always made it a point to be a Roman when in Rome and my ears were sharply and critically registering and correcting nuances in the spoken language. I went to that performance with something slightly differing from my usual indifference or blasé interest, for there was an element of curiosity to see what a composer could have found possible of dramatic action in such a "libretto."[7] Remembering that in Germany and Italy almost everything excepting the railway guide books had been set to "music," I assumed this "Claude Debussy" was another youngster who had gotten a chance at being performed, just as I had known of cases in Germany where an opera was studied, mounted, and performed exactly once! True, this was certain no "première" but it assuredly was the first time my eyes encountered the name . . . CLAUDE DEBUSSY.

It is utterly useless and impossible for me to even attempt a description of my feelings, of my transport at having at last realized that for which I had yearned, that which, in exalted moments, tormented me with a fleeting vision and with a prescient expectancy. When the full contemplation of beauty clutched my heart with a painful ecstasy which was akin to the contemplation of a great grief, and I murmured humbly, "Great God, how lovely!" I knew it was le coup de foudre [the lightning strike], love at first sight!

Returning very slowly toward my small hotel in the old Latin Quarter, I strolled, dream-laden, toward the Panthéon and feeling sleep impossible, returned to the Raspail and there, seated on a bench under the quietly soft shadows of that picturesquely gaslit Avenue, I became lost in my impressions, dazed in my emotions.

In the small hours of the morning, I finally awakened the portier, got my key and a bit of wax taper and crawled three or four flights to the little room I had taken. I slept but little and that feverishly, and after a few hours arose. Something strange had happened to my life, and I was eager to breathe more of that air, to know more of that soil which could produce such impressionism (and that was the exact word I thought of) in music as it had done long ago in painting. The mood was upon me but not the idiom—I wanted to again *hear* those harmonies and sonorities, those things which ever surprised me by their voluptuousness and sensuousness, an orchestral palette so new, a music that "came from I know not whence" and had gone, away from this globe and vanished—perhaps for ever! At this point I became startled! "Gone? Even from Paris? No—no, this must not be! This cannot be! I must hear it again. I must bring it all back again," and impulsively I added, "There *is* something that can bring it back! I've never tried it, yet, after all, now is the time."

Returning to the Opéra Comique, I inquired when the next performance was to be and was told perhaps between such and such dates, weeks removed, and Paris was not exactly the place to spend one's summer, if even in a larger hotel room. I wanted to hear no more of the other kinds of music. I had heard plenty of bad music everywhere. I knew orchestral scores upside down! I knew the formulae: but *this* kind I had never heard, and I wanted nothing to divert me from what filled my brain and heart, and my soul! I did not want to lose the vision, I wanted this thing that possessed me to continue, and for the first time in my life, at eleven of the forenoon, I sat down at a café table and ordered an absinthe! After all, why not? "When in Rome," and thus forth. I expected some hashish-like results and began to observe myself inwardly. I drank another, and yet the Magi did not appear. With the third I expected my yearning would bring the exquisitely misunderstood Mélisande to my side: with the fourth I wondered how those effects had been gotten with such small instrumentation, and with the fifth I was trying to figure just what sort of person that "Claude Debussy" could be? What could he look like, and *where* could he have come from? I felt myself quite wooden, with a peculiar, licorice-wormwood taste all through me, quite numb and ill, but no visions came! I continued in this deadened condition for some hours and suddenly bethought me of friends who had repeatedly urged me to be their guest at their villa in Dinard, on the Coast of Normandie, and in the state in which I then was, thought myself capable of overcoming my horror of being together with strangers and accepting hospitality and kindnesses which I abhorred doing and hated to have to thank for. I dispatched a letter and at the same time went to a travel bureau and made inquiries, not only about Normandie but also the Côte d'Azur and other parts of a country that was totally new to me. Suddenly my eye fell on a word: "Finistère!" "What is that?" I exclaimed, "Finistère? The end of the Earth? That is the place for me," and began requesting information regarding it. "Are there mountains?" "O, mais bien sûr, Monsieur, and bathing in the Ocean." "Then I go, that's the place . . . Finistère in Brittany," and suddenly I decided to go to the Bon Marché [the name of a department store] and buy me a pair of sandals! "And I'll wear a fisherman's blouse and cut me a limb from a tree, and hatless, like a Trappist monk, I'll find the hills and the woods and like Tannhäuser will make the pilgrimage to . . . to . . . why of course, to the end of the earth! But what does it matter, as to where? For there *is* a new music," I exulted," and *that* is all that counts. *That* makes the world different!" Thus I arrived at Douarnenéz, my sandals in my high hat, my trunks full of books but, as yet, minus the sailor's suit.

I did not find the little town to my liking, with its canneries near the quays which worked at odd times, occasionally even through the night,

when the boats returned with a catch. Alas, I too was to learn that sometimes they did not return at all. . . . After a few days there, I heard of a
place, directly across the Bay of Douarnenéz, called Tréboul. It too was a
fisherman's village, yet contained a half-dozen or so excellently built villas,
and a neat little hotel with the attractive name Hotel des Sables Blancs . . .
Hotel of the White Sands. I installed myself there, expecting to stay several
months, but immediately on the first night, I found sleep impossible! I had
not experienced what effect the restlessness of the Ocean would have on
me, and I could not banish the "swish-sh-sh" of the waves, even at low
tide, from my consciousness! It was useless for me to plug my ears, to
count sheep, or to put my watch under my pillow and concentrate on its
even tickings. The quiet "swish" of a roll would make me count, "(swish)
2–3–4–5," only to have an irregular interruption, let us say at 3½ or 5¼,
whereupon I would start again. Whether I tried to get an even two or a
three rhythm (and so far as I know, these are the only rhythms there are in
all Nature and music, despite the complications of modern "music" where
I have encountered even a 6/2 and 1/8 tempo-indication) it all was exasper-
atingly hopeless. I tried this for the better part of a week and decided I must
leave there too.

On making inquiries, I found that farther back, on the hills on the main-
land, were about one dozen "propriétaires" with well-built eighteenth- and
nineteenth-century villas, surrounded by little gardens, and that some of
these could be had for rent "for the season," which meant until the snow
came. I found one desirable villa, with about one acre of fruit trees and
shrubs, all carefully walled in, and an independent part of the villa yet
available. This I rented for the sum of five hundred francs ($100) including
"two sea-side cabanas."

It was a stone house, two stories high, with a granary on top, was named
"Chalet St.Yves," had about nine rooms (all furnished, of course), a kiosk in
the garden (where I later drank mint tea in the afternoons), commanded a fine
view over the Bay of Douarnenéz and there, directly in front of me, in that
bay, stood L'île Tristan . . . the island to which Tristan had been banished
(according to Wagner). This Île Tristan is so small that even the guide books
giving the information which I now quote, have it not jotted on their maps:

> The origin of Douarnenéz (specialties: sardines, tuna, mackerel) dates back to
> the founding of a priory in the Island of Tristan. During the League, the little
> town was destroyed by the Chief of the bands of Fontenelle who solidly estab-
> lished himself in the Isle Tristan and who could not be dislodged thence until
> after many years of efforts by the troops of Henry the Fourth. This Isle owes its
> name to the Knight of the Round Table whose memory is inseparably linked to
> that of Isolde.[8]

The owners came very often and always at unexpected times, not even
ostensibly on a friendly visit but to see that the pebbles in the walks of the

garden had not been pushed out of place and the bordering ivy trampled on; and once when these two old, retired misers stopped in front of a pear tree and excitedly called to me, "Monsieur, M'sieu, there is a fruit missing on the pear tree," I was fortunate in being able to find that miserable, little, shriveled, gnarled wind-blown among the vines, and understood that those plums, pears, and apples were to be admired but not eaten by the tenant. However, as I was given permission—and voluntarily—to pluck a leaf of mint, here and there "and, of course, not every day," I contented myself with sipping mint tea in "my" little garden house while I contemplated the remains of a small turret on a small "castle" on the Island of Tristan and which was out there in the sea less than one hundred yards from my Chalet!

Brittany is famous for its roads, its tides, and its treacherous quicksands at ebb, and to these I would add the practically unique store of its superstitions.[9] I might have, at low tide, actually walked the ocean's bottom to reach the rocks and climbing them enter the former asylum of that legendary hero who so yearned for an Irish beauty, yet instead I spent the months in inward questioning and in dream-lost staring at that sea at which he too must have long gazed . . . but I never once went or rowed over to L'île Tristan.

One day I suddenly roused myself and on the impulse wrote a music publisher in Paris to send me any and everything which Debussy may have written for the violin. Receiving the reply that as yet Debussy had created nothing for my instrument, I wrote Debussy himself, in care of that publisher, meekly begging to be allowed to see some of his violin compositions, as I should love to play them and if possible introduce them to American audiences on my forthcoming tour. After a considerable lapse of time, I finally, and to my delight, received the appended answer from which it becomes evident that I must have written him twice, perhaps to addresses of two different publishers:

Monday, 6 November 1908 [i.e., 6 September; CD-1][10]

Dear Sir,
    Having been away from Paris, I have read your two kind letters only today. Unfortunately, I have written nothing for the violin and cannot therefore take advantage of your offer.
    If you come to Paris, it would give me great pleasure to shake your hand. Warm regards.

Claude Debussy

Thereupon I immediately secured several of his songs and at once saw the possibilities of transcribing his exquisite *Il pleure dans mon coeur.* I wrote him this at once and asked if he had any objections to my attempting this. His answer, which follows, shows that he was not paying much attention to the calendar, for he could not have written the first letter in the eleventh month and then have answered my letter in the ninth month. The days and dates too are incorrect.

Thursday, 17 September 1908 [CD-2][11]

Dear Sir,

Forgive me, but I do not always have the time to write as I wish. You may certainly transcribe *Il pleure dans mon coeur,* and this letter gives you full authorization to do so.

Warm regards.

Claude Debussy

True to my instincts and convictions, I set to work to transcribe this for the violin, changing where I deemed it necessary in order to make it more idiomatic. Early in October I was to sail for another American concert tour, and so I once again wrote Debussy that I had his preciously poetic song ready for the fiddle and craved the privilege of showing it to him, at the same time indicating the two days that I expected to be in Paris ere embarking. To my great joy, he answered immediately, saying it would give him pleasure to have me call at 11 [*sic*] in the morning of the date suggested in my letter [see letter CD-3].

My First Meeting with Debussy

Arrived at the appointed hour, I was shown into his workroom and left in a silence which, in the high tension in which I was, seemed to be without termination. I had ample time to note everything, the immediate first of which was a huge table, at least five feet long and three feet wide, and which served as his desk. It must have been especially made, of nice light-colored wood, and like a carpenter's worktable had wide cross-boards upholding it at each end.

There was not an inkspot on the enormous blotters, and pens were piled in an orderly manner. There were quite a few Japanese ornaments and sword-tops and an exquisite Chinese parrot in porcelain, and on the wall a picture of Kipling among two or three French authors. The few bookshelves contained a number of books by Kipling (in French translation of course) and some by Lafcadio Hearne and Poe, besides a goodly number of French novels in their typical paper bindings. Repeatedly I looked at my watch and finally noted that I had been there for over ten nerve-wracking minutes. Approaching the window which overlooked a small fenced-in garden, I heard a door open noiselessly behind me and turning round, there stood Claude Debussy! He was slightly taller than myself, I should say about 5 ft. 7 in., was a heavy-set man and with extremely broad shoulders. There was an air of intense nervous energy about him, and he was a striking and magnetic individual, "and very handsome, I should say," I added mentally. What struck me immediately, besides his strange, dark, burning eyes and his sensitive and voluptuous mouth, was the extraordinary peculiarity of his head. Never had I seen such a skull on a mortal, for it had an extremely high "front" (as the French say) and the top of his head sloped down with startling suddenness. Immediately I bowed very low while I further noted his coal-black hair and beard, the moustache and beard slightly curling, the unusual eyes suggesting the physiognomy of a Japanese. He in no manner recognized my greeting, but puffing at his cigarette was with half-closed eyes studying me quizzically.

It surely was a strange meeting, for from the instant he had entered, his eyes had fastened into mine and without a bow or sign of recognition, he continued standing there, concentratedly studying me. He was breathing heavily, his left hand in the pocket of his double-breasted coat, in his right a burning cigarette, and he was completely attired in blue. I was fascinated by this strange personality and felt at once a sympathetic attraction, and as this peculiar situation continued unchanged by sound or gesture, I bowed again. But suddenly my sense of fun rose to the top and ere I had stopped to think what I was going to say or do, I blurted, smilingly, "Eh bien, est-ce que l'on ne dit pas bonjour?" ["Well then, doesn't one say 'How do you do?'"].

He gave a quick, low laugh and retorted smilingly, "Justement . . . bonjour!" ["Exactly . . . how do you do!"].

A brief pause followed another bow I made him, and smilingly I made another attempt at conversation. "Alors vous êtes Debussy! Maître Claude Debussy! Vous êtes donc celui qui a créé *Pelléas!*" ["So then, you are Debussy! Maître Claude Debussy! You are he who created *Pelléas!*"].

"Oui," he answered in a peculiarly timorous voice, "ça . . . ça c'est indiscutable . . . ," and after a light pause, whimsically added, "et tout seul!" ["Yes, that . . . that is indisputable . . . and all by myself!"]. I chortled and felt that I loved him at once for the termination of that sentence! I had already noted some peculiarities of timbre, of his speaking voice, and the hesitant, playful, almost petulant manner of speaking, as if interrupting himself, and then the sudden jets of several words together. This time, however, he continued and in a tiny crescendo added: "And furthermore, as well as I know that my name is Claude Debussy, I know perfectly well that you are Mr. Arthur Hartmann," and of course like a good Frenchman, he did not pronounce the "t" nor aspirate the "H" in my surname.

It was now my turn to say, "Ça . . . ça c'est indiscutable," and as one glance showed me that he too relished the humor of the mood I immediately added, paraphrasing his words, "And what is more, as I know perfectly well that my name is Hartmann, so do I know that you are the first and the greatest musician since Wagner, and I, for one, am grateful to you for this!" Another pause seemed imminent, so I commented with casualness, "I see that smoking does not bother you?" and to which he returned with caprice, "Oh, not in the least." As he continued smoking, without offering me a cigarette, neither of us having yet taken a step from where we were at the opposite ends of the room when he had entered, I took out my cigarette case and bowing toward him asked, "So, may I?"

"Please do!" he chuckled cordially.

Surely never had I had or even heard of a more strange reception, I thought as I went to deposit the burnt match in one of the small Chinese vases I saw on his table, when suddenly, he flew at me and with rigidly outstretched forefinger stopped me, exclaiming, "Not there! There . . . this one is for the ashes," and then, in a milder voice and kindlier manner, "Now this one, you see, this one is for the matches." Thus, it would seem that I had picked the wrong vase, for one was for the burnt matches whereas the other was destined to receive the ashes.

By this time I knew that I not only loved him for his whimsies and drolleries but I also felt that he too liked me—just a little bit—and much amused, I felt less strange at being there, a stranger, all alone with that unique poet . . . Debussy! Impulsively I followed my own moods while I keenly noted his voice, looks, that most strange head, and suddenly I commented: "How strange!"

"What do you mean?" he asked in his strange timbre with its quivering, low richness, "Eh bien, c'est drôle, n'est-ce pas?"

I answered, "Que de voir deux hommes complètement vêtus en bleu, du pied jusqu'au nez et qui se regardent en face." ["Well, it is strange, isn't it, to see two men, completely attired in blue, including shirts, collars, and socks, and looking at each other"]. "Do you know," I added, "my family has never been able to understand me at all—in anything—and even down to that peculiarity of mine—blue, even down to my writing-paper."

"O, ça," he answered with some vehemence and making a wry face, "let's not talk about families . . . neither did mine understand me. . . . But I see that you have brought your violin. May I ask you to please play your manuscript for me?" In spite of our whimsical talk, I was almost trembling with nervousness as I approached him at the piano and asked for the A. He gave me a handful of dissonance, somewhat like the following:

Example 2. A "Tuning Note" from Debussy

and glancing at me sideways, he laconically knocked the ashes from his cigarette while I "picked" an A from that offering.

Still dreading to play for him, I exclaimed almost helplessly: "What a pity that you are here and that I have to play this for you, for, do you see, if you were *not* here, I could have this published as it is, for I was obliged to make some changes and these, of course, you won't like! But, you see, the violin is such a confoundedly exacting animal and so long as I stick to her, I want to do the best by her that I can. Thus to really transcribe, or transfer from one medium or color to other media requires many changes; that is to say if I want your song to sound like a violin piece and not appear a monstrous or maltreated thing."

He observed me very intently and then with his vibrant yet hesitant manner said: "Monsieur, I do not know you, and I have never heard you play, but I have a peculiar feeling that your ideas will not find me unsympathetic or displease me. Would you now have the goodness to kindly play this manuscript with me." Immediately I was ravished by the exquisitely modulated sounds he produced in the opening measure, such perfect roundness and evenness as in the soft monotony of a quiet rain, or tears falling silently. After we had played it through, he remained silent for a full moment and lighting a fresh cigarette said to me with grave politeness: "Could I ask you to do it again, one more time please?" I could not tell from this whether he was pleased or pondering something, and thus we played it right through again. Once again, the piece terminated, he remained in thoughtful concentration and then said abruptly, "One more time, I beg of you!" and this time I was in a panic! Three times in succession, straight through and without interruption, and no comment of any kind. Thoughtfully turning toward me he said: "There is only one little place," and pointing to it continued, "You see this? Well, this is yours and you put it in the violin, and this is mine, and in the piano part, and instead, I would ask of you to permit me to change that so that *I* become the violin and *you* the piano, this way, we will become more . . . this way," and he made a gesture of clasping his hands tightly, with fingers interlaced, and then he impulsively held out his hand to me in our first and long handclasp!

I am, today as always, profoundly moved when I recall the poetically beautiful manner in which he had shown sympathetic understanding and proffered me his friendship . . . "thus" . . . with his hands tightly clasped and his fingers interlaced, "that we may become more like this," and gave me that handclasp which endured to the day of his death!

While I was replacing the violin and bow in its case, he inquired casually at which hotel I was staying and my reply was, "At the Grand Hotel yet this one night, for early tomorrow the 'boat-train' leaves and I embark at Cherbourg." I also slipped the manuscript under the canvas cover of my double violin case and prepared to take my leave.

In that peculiarly hesitant, timorous voice of his and as was his manner of completing a sentence by a full gush of words after many broken bits of phrases and disconnected words, he said: "I do not know what your intentions are with regard to that manuscript but I assume that you would like to see it in print?"

Bowing my assent, I said, "Naturally, cher Maître, only if it has your approbation."

"That," he answered with sudden intensity, "it has completely . . . entièrement . . . but it is that . . . you see . . . I don't know how to say this . . . but I have no relation with those people. . . . I must tell you that publishers are very hard . . . they are hard people . . . and on my part, I regret to tell you that I can have nothing to do with the transaction. However, if you are so disposed as to take the time and trouble to go see l'Éditeur [the Publisher] Fromont, you may tell him that you do so at my suggestion and with my full approbation." I thanked him profusely and while studying his strange face and oddly shaped head with an inner intensity by which I knew I was engraving it within myself for all time, I told him in simple words that I would never forget him and that morning! Holding my hand in his strong, warm grasp he answered simply: "Merci, and for having heard you, for you have something in your playing . . . something in your tone . . . how shall I express colors? . . . well, how the Devil does one say! Well, it's . . . it's Poetry." I returned to the Grand Hotel to there deposit my violin and in an exalted state took a cab to the publishing house of Debussy's early works.

On entering the store, I approached a clerk and asked to be allowed to speak to the proprietor. To him I duly gave my name, telling him I was a violinist, that I had made a transcription of a certain Debussy song, that I had come from Brittany to Paris to play the manuscript for the composer, when I was interrupted by his exclaiming, "Who? Debussy? But he will not see you Sir . . . never!"

"Mais je vous demande pardon, Monsieur," I answered, "I just came from his house."

"And he received you?" he exclaimed incredulously.

"Most charmingly, I assure you Monsieur, and with beautiful warmth!"

"Who—that 'bourru,' that rude, gruff, ill-bred grouch!"

It was my turn to exclaim in a tone of resentment, "But indeed Sir, I beg of you! Debussy, I tell you, welcomed me so warmly that I was absolutely charmed, Sir!"

With a gesture, he hastily retorted: "Just a moment, please Sir, excuse me while I find someone, and I would ask if you could tell them what you just told me," and disappearing to a nearby office, he issued thence dragging a lady by the hand. He introduced me hastily: "My wife, sir, Mister . . ." and I supplied the name. Then, in a state of great excitement he admonished his wife: "Now Rosalie, listen carefully, this is an incredible story!" and I proceeded calmly to give the exact details, from beginning to end, whereupon the gentleman folded his arms in exasperation and again asked, "Has one ever seen such a thing! And he received you politely . . . that hot head with his brusqueries!" I didn't know what to think for I was meeting this gentleman for the first time, even as I had Debussy but a few hours previously.

Coming to the question of the publication of the manuscript, he said: "First of all I must tell you that I am not very much in favor of issuing arrangements," and in that regard he was very much like the French publishers of those other days and totally unlike all American publishers of those times and all times. "Secondly, were I to persuade myself to accept it," he continued, "I am not sure that I would care to pay you anything at all, for, you see Monsieur, I own the rights to the original and if I do not choose to print your arrangement, transcription, or whatever else you like, you cannot get it issued anywhere else," and in this he was not unlike some of his American brethren.

"Bon, bon, bon Monsieur," I interrupted impatiently, "I am not discussing any price with you. I am only trying to ascertain whether you *will* publish this, for I am leaving tomorrow for a concert tour of America, and if I knew you are to print it I would yet include this piece on programs, wherever possible, for programs have gone out in advance some weeks ago."

He reflected for some moments and said, "If you give me your assurance that you *will* play this piece, I'll print it and pay you fifty francs outright for your manuscript."

"Agreed," I said, delighted and relieved, and signed the necessary papers. On returning to the hotel I was surprised to find a small package and, on opening, it struck in my heart with dumb amazement and humble gratitude. As if he had read the wish which my lips dared not utter, Debussy had, unasked, driven by and left an inscribed photograph of himself![12] I spent the evening on a letter to him in which, in abominable and misspelt French, I attempted to describe my exultation over his remembrance and also to give an account of my transactions that afternoon with "those hard men the publishers." Next day, on board the steamer, I delved among my manuscripts and finding the sketches to *Il pleure dans mon coeur* I recopied it neatly and on arriving here programmed it wherever yet possible, as I did later years in Europe, despite which it has yet remained unnoticed by the thousands of fiddlers.

How I wish I might have dared beg Mme. Debussy to give me that letter which her husband wrote her when on one of his few concert appearances in Europe, and which she read me one afternoon while taking tea with us during Debussy's absence. From Budapest he wrote her: "And then came a singer who among things sang *Il pleure* and which has become insufferable to me as a song, since Uncle Arthur redid it for the violin." His exact words were: "qui m'est devenu insupportable depuis que l'oncle Arthur l'a fait pour le violon."[13]

My Second Meeting with Debussy

Returning to Paris about eighteen months later, I married and for a very short time lived in the same "Square" where Debussy occupied the house (or as the French call it, the Villa) at No. 24.[14] After a few weeks, I ventured to send him a note, merely mentioning the above changes in my life and adding that if ever he felt like losing a few moments of his time, I would be honored to call, assuring him that I would not be tedious or boresome. The next morning's early mail brought his reply. He said that he had gotten my letter "avec les nouvelles stupéfiantes" [with its stupefying news] and that any forenoon, toward eleven, whenever I felt like passing, "j'aurais plaisir de vous voir et de vous serrer la main" [I would be happy to see you and shake your hand]. Delighted with the whimsicality of that reply, I did not await the dawn of another day but donning my best blue suit and renewing a dash of perfume behind the coat lapel, I ran around the little grilled garden which was encircled by twenty-four houses and yet was called a "Square" by the French, and rang the bell to Debussy's villa. The butler took my card and asking me to wait in the antechamber, returned in a moment and led me to Debussy's room. He received me cordially, and as we shook hands, I at once felt those eyes fasten into mine while again I was aware of that burning intensity in him, that vital, nervous magnetism and also of the scent of perfume on him and on his glossy hair. Again I noted the warm, sensual mouth, the tenderly curling beard and moustache, and a certain heavy-gaited way of moving about. Recollections of some sentences in good form, from the days of my youth when I began struggling with the French language came to my aid, and I started with, "I am very flattered by the honor which you have been good enough to accord me in deigning to reply to my letter, and in your so charming reception of me," when he interrupted with a "pffouff" and a shrug. Immediately I became myself and exclaimed, "God damn! This French language is so difficult!" And we both laughed. Immediately I had to take out my cigarette case while I asked "Vous permettez?" and suddenly every detail of our first meeting flamed in the subconscious, and almost mimicking his voice and gestures, as I approached one of the small Chinese vessels to deposit the burnt match, I admonished myself, "Not here! This is for the ashes and this . . . this is for the matches!" He watched and followed me amusedly and when I commented: "You see, I have not forgotten—but I ask you, would you have recognized me?"

"Why not? You have not changed at all."

"Oh but I have, a lot 'o très beaucoup,' as the Americans say, I am now a married man. But you still think I look myself anyway?"

"Yes, all things notwithstanding," he answered playfully.

Presently I said, "You know it is not easy for me to always speak in French, and you must have noticed that I have not improved while I was away from here," and to which he retorted, "Obviously, even in this regard you seem like yourself!" I loved his entering my moods of the moment and I felt myself getting "wound up," and I knew that at such times nothing could stop the lightning-like rapidity of my imagination or the torrents of words and ideas unimagined in the preceding second.

"However," he quickly added, with characteristic French courtesy, "you speak French very well and better than I know any other language."

"Oh, oui et merci," I returned mockingly, "even though I know you must speak Italian much better."

He looked at me amusedly and asked, "Italian? I? But tell me, please, who told you this?"

"But no one, but after all, you were Prix de Rome, were you not?"

"So?" he asked.

"Well, after all, during your years of sojourn in Italy, you . . ."

He broke me off by shaking a finger at me, in a horizontal motion of meaning "no" and said, "I will recount to you that after I had been there quite a while, I one day noticed in the window of a book shop one of those little books which claim to be 'self-teachers of French-Italian.' Eh bien, I bought it and when suddenly, some weeks later, I found myself in need of some correspondence paper, I started out with it. Having twisted my tongue around with trying to pronounce the sentences which I found on certain pages dealing with shopping, I entered a store with this book in hand. When with greatest difficulty I tried to read off that first sentence, I found that the clerk spoke much better French than me myself." Laughingly he continued, "So, since that day, I have never tried to understand any language, for after all, tout le monde parle français, n'est-ce pas?" ["everybody speaks French, don't they?]

"Evidemment" ["Of course"], I answered, while I reflected that in this particular attitude, he was no different than the majority of the intelligent and even educated Frenchmen, at least prior to the World War.

"Tell me please," he continued, "why did you get married," and with a voice which tried to conceal his fun, "all this without telling me?"

"Well, dear master and grand master," I said with mock solemnity and taking a pose of penitence as David before Hans Sachs, "I got drunk, that's all! My God, I was so drunk, and here I am, suddenly married! I don't know how, but I was in a train car on the way to Versailles all alone with my new young wife, and I was so drunk I started singing an aria to her, the way they do at the opera: 'Oh my beloved, let me rest my poor head on your capacious breast and let me sleep' like the dragon says in the opera," and with a pretended yawn I chanted, "Lass mich schlafen," and made a big glissando on the last word.[15]

He gurgled with delight and then in a sudden turn of anger he exclaimed, "Oh! That one! That Wagner, with his endless motifs at every moment that go on forever! As soon as they start one of those endless stories on the stage, in the orchestra they start showing their calling cards as if they were committed to taking a long journey! Oh God, he is such a bore, that one! I saw Wagner once at Bayreuth,"[16] and covering one side of his face and eyes as if to shut out a horrible vision, he continued, "ah ... he had eyes ... my God ... ferocious eyes ... horrible ... terrible ... but Liszt," (which he as a Frenchman of course pronounced Litz), "ah Litz," and here his face became all-beaming and warm, "Liszt was ... how would I say it," while with arms outstretched he was seeking adequate expression, "Liszt was goodness itself!"[17]

I seized both his hands in mine and exclaimed, "Ah, words now truly fail me! To tell you that I could hug and embrace you is nothing at all. Do you know, savez-vous, Liszt ... Liszt ... I love him ... I adore him ... oh thundering name of God, this makes me so happy!" There was exultation, warm sympathy, and fire in that room, and I felt I had found something which stolid German musicians had never been able to share with me ... my great, unreasoning, and limitlessly enthusiastic love of Liszt!

We smoked continually, he a black, abominable cigarette which I afterwards learned was the "Maryland roulé," and I my favorite Sultan Flór tobacco which I spent hours in making into cigarettes. I was entirely unconscious of self in his delightful company. He presently, with great delicacy, apologized for taking unto himself the liberty of commenting that every time I rose to deposit matches or the ash of the cigarette, I had a rather ginger and careful way of reseating myself, and he was curious to know, without meaning to be offensively familiar, as to whether this was a personal peculiarity or due to some sort of physical annoyance? In answer I told him that it was strange he had noticed it, for no one else had and that I was, up to that moment, unconscious of this unusual awkwardness when seating myself. Beginning a long tirade, I said, "Vous savez ... the life of a concert artist is not easy and I never pay any attention to myself or to the instrument. I have played concerts when I could have counted the hairs in the bow, I had neglected the rehairing for so long, or had not the time, or was not in a place where I'd hand my bows to any carpenter. We have to rush for a train, or, all overheated and perspiring, dressed in our one full-dress suit, and which even the headwaiter in fine hotels wears all day long, we have to stand in the rain, or on snow-covered docks, in thin patent leather pumps, awaiting embarkation. We eat badly and when the train schedules permit a stop long enough for some cod fish and Smørgåsbord with Arrac or Aquavit, and do not sleep in a bed for more than two nights out of ten and seldom in the same bed for two consecutive nights! Always and forever harassed, physically exhausted, nervously overworked, pestered by accursed autograph hunters and others wanting testimonials for violin strings and violin 'methods,' and at the end of such travels, it has often come upon me, oh, many times, that I feel annoying things ... down there. Look here, just this season, I started a tour of all Scandinavia, on 1

September, and played every country, including the Islands of Jutland night after night . . . fifty-nine concerts in sixty-seven days!" I repeated this with great emphasis. "Imagine . . . every night on a small steamer, or shaken over the mountain tops of Norway in a wagon-lit. Oh, I assure you, I arrived in Paris quite emaciated and all I now care for is cognac and cigarettes. It will all right itself, in time, it always does, for I have never seen a doctor in all my life, excepting a dentist, and . . ."

"There you are completely right," he interrupted vehemently, "for those people don't know anything except what you tell them! Never go near them! I hate all doctors and preachers, yet I must confess that at least I have more regard for the former than the latter, for you see, if a person, and let us say an intelligent person such as yourself, tells one of those so-called doctors something about himself, he at least knows something then, n'est-ce pas, and, if need be, you can show him the spot where he can verify things for himself. But those people who stand in pulpits and take upon themselves de vous raconter des histoires, stories of things which they have never seen, fabrications and at that, not even good fables, and similar stupidities. What I should like to know, has anyone ever returned from that boresome place called Paradise and recounted his experiences or tried to describe that huge, stupid Void? Avoid those people. Doctors, like preachers, know nothing, nothing at all."

With happy laughter at our concordance with everything, I added, "Tenez, take for example what these camels, the doctors, tell one. They tell one that wine is not good, that coffee and tobacco are injurious! Why, those are the most beautiful things, the most flagrantly poetic benefactions of le bon Dieu lui-même . . . that is to say, after music, n'est-ce pas?"

"Bah!" he exclaimed, "Does anyone understand music, even among those who make it! Take for instance Monsieur Brahms. He has to have first of all a first theme which is at least sixteen measures long, for that is proof of profondeur. The second theme as a consequence should be thirty-two and if possible sixty-four measures long and very, very slow, for that shows feeling. And as to the development, mon Dieu," (making wide, wide gestures with both arms) "you can't find space enough for it in this room!"

I roared with him, and he at once resumed, "And take again as an instance the stupidity of the so-called doctors who tell you that wine is bad for you when what is really bad, that is to say bad for you just now, is alcohol, for you will kindly permit me to tell you that you have what we call in French hémorroïdes, and . . . la, la . . . do I know what they are!" He covered his eyes while shaking his head and leaning his elbow on his desk, let his cheek rest on his hand while he continued, "No, no, just live your own life, but drink wine instead of cognac even though I always have about one-half pint of whiskey every night. That is one thing that one must concede those English, *that* they know how to brew, and fortunately we now have a domestique ("We," I thought, "then he too is married?") who has known how to find the most charming little 'bar' not far from here and whence he fetches me this whiskey every night." In answer to his query as to whether I had ever tried to do anything with regard to that condition, I answered that perhaps I might apply some of the things described in the fifth chapter of Rabelais's *Gargantua,* and feeling exhausted with all the excitement and laughter of that long visit, I prepared to leave. He accompanied me all the way, out of the house, into the small garden, and to the grilled gate.

I felt his mood change; there was that aura of the dream-world around him, and I felt a hidden sorrow somewhere in his being while he said to me gravely, "Take care of yourself. I would like to tell you something in confidence . . . that is . . . with me the hemorrhoids have become hemorrhages, and believe me it isn't nice when it happens to you, especially when you have important things to do." He opened the large outside "grille" and warmly squeezing my hand said, "Don't delay—come and see me whenever you want. It will always be a pleasure to see you." I was in a delirium of exultation. I had a friend now, as well as a loving wife, and this friend was none other than that great genius, the man people spoke of as brusque and rude and insulting: the unapproachable and impossible and elusive Claude Debussy!

Exultantly I ran around the little garden and entered my temporary home exactly one and one-half hours after I had left it and found my wife consumed with eagerness to hear every detail of my visit. Her questions came in torrents and, naturally, I was too excited to be able to tell her very clearly just how all that time had gone. "What is he like? Did he tell you what he's working on now? What does he look like? Did he ask you about me? How is the inside of his home? What did he tell you of his ideas about music? Oh, how I wish I might have seen him and heard all the wonderful things he must have told you!" Bit by bit I began to describe his appearance, to mimic his voice, his brief spurts of almost goat-like laughter and told her there was no talk of music, certainly not of his work or plans or anything that I could seize upon excepting that he seemed to like me and that he was quick in repartee, very witty and that we had fun, just bantering, quite simply, and arranging the universe to our own tastes. Incredulous, crestfallen, and disappointed, she exclaimed, "Oh but that's impossible! Or, rather, what I mean to say is, I understand all that, but what I mean is, just what was the main subject of your conversation?"

"That," I answered, suddenly shy, "that, my dear, I'm sorry, but that is something that I cannot talk to you about: it was just a little thing between him and me."

"Oh, but my darling," she retorted, "surely you cannot have any secrets from me, can you?"

"No, of course not, but you see that I hesitate to talk and that it would be rather awkward, and besides he told me something, well, not exactly as a secret, yet just the same, he confided it to me."

As can be imagined, things were taking a turn as if a quarrel were in the brewing, and when I heard, among other reproaches, "Is this the way we are starting out on our life together?"

I lost my temper and hurled back: "Oh, very well, if you must know, we spent the time talking about hemorrhoids." "Hemorrhoids!" Marie almost screamed, and I yelled back, "Yes, hemorrhoids! He's got 'em and so have I!"

As may be imagined, I did not abuse the kindness of his cordiality but dropped in on him at intervals of about ten days to a fortnight. Always mindful of the extraordinary person in whose presence I was, I felt with each visit a growing intimacy. He read my moods with instinctive sympathy and immediately, while greeting each other, he would murmur, "Qu'a-t-il aujourd'hui, qu'est-ce qui se passe?" ["What's wrong with him today, what's going on?"]. I had many times noted his playfulness at certain times when he rather "babied" me, and in trying to read my thoughts or sense my moods would interrogate himself aloud and speak of me in the third person and as if I were not standing there before him. Unaware of the fact that Debussy's private life was the exact parallel of my own but with every situation reversed, he seemed to sense the many difficulties essential to the adjustment of a new life and the delicacy which forbade my confidences as it did any intimations on his part. Though he was then the established and sought-after world celebrity, he was also the most fiercely disputed composer of his era and was regarded by some as the leader of a new music and by others as a disintegrating and extremely dangerous element, if such things as what he projected were to be taken at all seriously and allowed to infiltrate music to the extent of becoming an actual influence. Though he was in years one generation removed from myself, I never once felt this difference in years but only that this man had ready sympathy and helpful understanding and seemed to have pleasure and delight in my company. It must furthermore be remembered that my ability to express myself in his language was as deficient then as it has since remained, yet curiously enough with him I could talk in a terrific flow and jumble of words and gestures whereas I yet become totally mute before "la jeune fille bien élevée," the American girl who spends years in Paris, in private schools, and acquires the correctness of the rolling "r"s in pronouncing, "une robe rose ravissante." Understanding needs no explanations or detailed expressions, and if I did not call on him with the purpose of formally commenting on the weather or attempting discussion on "world problems," I also did not bring in the subject of music or venture to probe his ideas or theories . . . if he had any.

Ibéria

One Sunday afternoon Piérne conducted Debussy's *Ibéria* at the Châtelet.[18] It met with hisses, protests, and acclamations, for the French, like the Italians, are very natural and follow their impulses. Apart from all scholastic questions, Debussy was still a hard pill to swallow, and whatever the conservatoryists or the stylists found in this or that, the fact remains, the composition was hissed, or as I prefer to say, "protested." Fortunately, I was in town and of course would not for worlds have missed the première of a new work by my great friend. I had not seen Debussy for quite some time, and I daresay he was under the impression that I was concertizing somewhere. Monday morning, as if by hazard, I dropped in at 24 Square du 80 de l'Avenue du Bois de Boulogne.[19] To ring meant to follow the butler, and I often wondered how he announced me to his master. In my neighborhood, I had succeeded in running monthly bills with the butcher, baker, and milkman, after I had given sufficient documentary proofs that I am the son of my father and am capable of paying a small trust of a few dollars monthly. As no Frenchman is capable of aspirating the "H," I always pronounced my name by first blowing the "H" very hard and distinctly separating the two syllables.

"Ah," said la boulangère, starting to write, "Monsieur Art . . ."

"Non, non," I objected, "asch Hartmann."

"Parfaitement Monsieur," says she, continuing to write "Arth."

"*Non,* Hartmann," and it became "Arthe man." I gave up all further efforts and my bills came simply to "Mons. Arman" or even "Mo. Herman."

Through the opened door I saw Debussy pacing back and forth. He paused a moment to shake hands with me while the butler closed the door. Smoking his "éternelle cigarette" he stopped in front of me, and with a backward gesture of his hand asked, "Eh bien?" There was that in the sound which written language cannot possibly convey. I understood its full implications, for he was not making use of a vacuous comment. He was not merely saying, "Well?" he was demanding: "Now then, tell me!"

"Eh bien quoi? Well then what?" I said. "Eh bien! I was passing and took the liberty of dropping by simply to wish you good day."

"Oui!" he exclaimed, stubbornly planted in front of me. "Sans doute and all that's très bien but," very suddenly, "you were there yesterday?"

"Bien sûr," I said, "of course I was there, voyons!"

"Exactly and bien sûr and voyons," he mimicked, his tension at the breaking point. "Eh alors!" he demanded.

"Eh alors," I said most respectfully, "well, then, dear master, nothing more to say. It was marvellous, magnificent, and that's that!"

I made a pretext of looking at the ashes on my cigarette, as if they required depositing in that one Japanese vase, but no, not even his eyes would release me while he further cornered, "'Eh bien' and 'cher Maître' and 'merveilleux' and *I,* who am asking *you,* were you there yesterday? 'Yes'? Well then, eh bien!"

"Ah, écoutez," I begged soothingly, "what do you want of me, my opinion? Who am I? I hear your work for the first time . . . I speak French very badly . . . I don't know enough about music, and after all, who am I to express an opinion to you?"

"Listen to me," he said very positively, "I know you! I know you, in fact, very well. Forget all this chi-chi. I asked you: 'Were you there?' 'Yes'? Eh bien, talk! Crénom de Dieu, God damn it, talk! It is I who demands, my friend!" This was all too much, and just then I wished I might have vanished into space. There was no evasion, no circumlocution.

With an apologetic gesture I said slowly, "Eh bien, la première partie, the first part, you understand without any question that I am perhaps wrong, but the first part, for me, is more photography than painting."

"Umph," he grunted, "continuez!"

"Mais non, mais non," I protested, "it's already enough for you."[20]

Meeting Madame Debussy

As my first visit to him had been around eleven of the forenoon, I imagined this was the time he preferred to receive visitors and thus when I dropped in on him it was at that time or within a half-hour after. Invariably I was received as soon as the butler apprised him, and the full appreciation of this always warmed me with grateful affection. On each visit, as soon as I entered, I made my deductions anew. Always I thought him terribly handsome, and I loved the fierce sincerity of his character. His eyes burnt with an intensity that told of too much indulgence. He breathed in a short, quick, nervous manner, and his terrifically concentrated, nervous intensity revealed all too plainly overstimulation and great mental excitement. Outwardly he was relatively calm (even as is my nature when wracked by the deepest emotions), and during the time we were talking, as also in the lapses of silence, I always felt that great dreamworld around him and kept saying to myself, "I wish I knew something about him, about his life. I wish I knew what is that great sorrow that I feel in him, that quivering, indefinable thing that is silently weeping in the depths of an exquisitely poetic being, in a heart so solitary!"

At about the sixth visit (within a few months) while he and I were chatting, the door opened and Mme. Debussy entered. It doubtlessly was prearranged between them, for as soon as she entered, and ere Debussy could present me, she said (in French, of course, for though I had never heard her converse, I understood she also spoke English), extending her hand: "Bonjour Monsieur. My husband tells me so much about you that I thought it time at last to see this interesting man myself, and all the more so as Claude tells me you have recently married. Yes but tell me, why do you hide your bride and why couldn't we have a little dinner here, at your pleasure, informally and in private?" Within the next few days a letter came from Mme. Debussy to my wife, inviting us to dinner and giving the choice of several evenings. Marie, who knew French—the comm'il faut [proper] French—much better and more correctly than myself (even if I spoke the language with greater rapidity and "boulevardier" [street talk], with the fluency of cusswords and argot), seemed to be as sympathetic to the Debussys (and more particularly to the Madame) as myself, and thus our reunions became strengthened.

Among individuals of what the world might call supersensitive and aesthetic affinities, there soon developed an intimacy between the older and the younger wife and, very possibly, their confidences remained as unrevealed to me, by my wife, as mine with "Claude" were largely unknown to her. I could very easily assume that some intimations gathered during talks had been made known to Mme. Debussy as also that some of the tête-à-tête exchanges between Marie and Emma-Claude were perhaps better known to Debussy than even to myself.

The exchange of letters was always affectionate, those of Debussy's wife to mine invariably having the greeting, "Ma chère Grande Petite" (for Marie was quite tall), and his to me, "Mon cher ami," with terminations of "En toute amitié," or "Votre affectueusement dévoué ami."[21]

The Personality of Chouchou

One afternoon we were expecting the Debussys to tea and were surprised to find that instead of the three "Claudes" there were but two: Mme. Emma-Claude (as she called herself) and little Claude, the adorable, only child of Debussy who was called by them "Chouchou" (Tiny Cabbage). The French have peculiar terms of endearment, for when Debussy was not angry at his wife, he called her "Mon chat" ("my cat," and masculine at that) and she affectionately addressed him as "Mon chou." At the side of this might be mentioned that to the Hungarian the greatest possible expression of his love for his wife is when he calls her "My sow." Chouchou was a perfect miniature copy of her father, with his peculiarities of appearance, the odd forehead, the black hair, warm eyes and mouth, the sturdy little body, and also the amazing independence of spirit. She spoke English quite neatly, for they always had an English governess for her who, in various lines of succession, appeared to have no other name than "Miss." We had scarcely more than greeted them when the Madame started in, "Excuse me, it's rather embarrassing but, after all, we are friends and n'est-ce pas this will remain strictly entre-nous for Claude does not want it known, but you must know my husband suffers from a most annoying thing. You must have noticed his rather peculiar gait, a sort of awkward way of walking .. . it is because he is obliged to wear a rubber pad. Whenever he is under great excitement or things upset him emotionally, this thing might overtake him at the most unexpected times and places and he has, quite simply, a hemorrhage. Today was a very bad one for him, much chagrin and emotional upsets, and so, on the way over, he had one of his accidents, and I had the chauffeur take him home while Chouchou and I took a taxi the rest of the way. Excuse it, won't you please? It won't take him long to change his clothes, and he'll be here, perhaps within a good half-hour from now."

We of course made a fuss over the little girl who, however, remained quite self-possessed and had a certain aloofness about her. When I, in an aside, whispered to the Madame how much Little Chou was like her father, she retorted, "If you only knew her positiveness in likes and dislikes! For instance, at one of the rehearsals of *Pelléas* at Covent Garden, she sat in the darkened auditorium with Claude and when 'La Scène de la Grotte' began, she slipped her hand into Claude's and said to him quite angrily: 'Tu sais, papa, je n'aime pas ça!' ['You know, Papa, I don't like that!']."

Presently Debussy arrived in a quiet and saddened mood. There was that silent sympathy between us all and his face showed much suffering. He was particularly affectionate to Chouchou and after a while asked her to sing something "pour l'Oncle Arthur," but the child answered, "I don't want to . . . I am not in the mood," and he began to coax her. However, in a perfectly calm manner the little girl said that she wanted to assure her father that she was perfectly all right and was having a fine time, only "you understand, papa, yes?" it just happened that she did not feel like singing. He held her close and while caressing her curled locks, said to me, "C'est tout ce qu'il y a de meilleur dans ce monde!" ["It's all that is best in this world!"] and he kissed her little hands. We had more tea, bon-bons, and chocolate for the baby, and presently Chouchou said, "Papa, if you still want me to sing for Uncle Arthur, I am now disposed to do so." I took her in my arms and held her to me. She put her little arms around me and kissed me on both cheeks while Debussy painfully seated himself on the piano chair. I expected she would sing some little French nursery rhymes or perhaps even English ones. My amazement will be understood when I say that Debussy started off with Fauré's *Les roses d'Ispahan,* which little Chou, with hands calmly folded, sang through in the most adorably natural manner and followed it with three or four songs by Fauré, Chausson, and Duparc. This baby of five or six could not be treated as a child, and I am very sure that the bond of love and understanding which Debussy had for an equally individualized entity, yet so much a part of himself, was what made this rare little being suddenly follow her adoring father, within one year after death brought him release from years of cruel torture and from a long-lingering and deeply gnawing horror! Unfortunately I am not in possession of the heart-breaking letter in which, in words of wild pain wrung from a shattered heart, language that would wrest and twist tears from out of stone itself, she told of Chouchou's having been torn from her suddenly, without any preliminary illness, a "stupide diphthérie" which, within three days, robbed her of all she had of Claude Debussy and all that life held for her.[22] Claude-Emma (Chouchou) was born in October 1905 and died in 1919. She lies buried with her father in Passy.

Performing for Debussy

Ere taking their departure we of course had to agree on a date for dinner at their house. A bit fearful of the "imprévu," I was wondering how an entire evening would be spent with them. Of course I had no intention of continuing to sacrifice my love for wonderfully prepared dishes, and I considered my behavior had sufficiently retaliated for the experience of the time when we were their hosts at dinner.[23] I had heard the Madame comment that they had recently had two old friends to dinner and afterwards played a foursome of whist (or possibly bridge) and, "as always the evening ended by Claude's being in a high temper." As I did not know one card from another, instinctively I felt that musicians can always have the joy of making music together, but was at once seized by a nervous panic at the very thought of playing before Claude Debussy! Immediately there sprang to its side the matter of what to play, for I could not presume to ask a Debussy to play sonatas with me, and even if I were capable of such tactlessness, I knew that the formalism of the Teutonic Sonata could be only an irritation or a piece of boresome stupidity to the musician whose originality expressed itself in the essence and with amazing revelations even in the adumbrative: one who surely could not much admire or respect the willful tortures of an idea through the manifold machinations of contrapuntal devices. Be it here noted that in speaking of "Teutonic formalism" I am not verging on political boundaries but purely accrediting the development to the highest achievements in the sonata form to the composers of Austria and Germany, even if Haydn was of the Croatian race and Beethoven of Dutch ancestry. There is no "Chauvinism" either implied or intended, for Debussy was singularly free of this trait, as further episodes will prove. My wife urged me to take my violin along, for apart from that first time, some 18 months previous, when I had played him his *Il pleure*, Debussy had never heard me play. It was equally impossible of thinking to ask him to play mere accompaniments, and I knew the virtuoso repertoire could scarcely be to his liking. Nonetheless, as the day arrived, I decided to take my box with me and leave it, unnoticed, in the antechamber in the event the evening should drag, and should my courage then not fail me, I'd play some unaccompanied Bach. In the eventuality he may ask for other things, I slipped his *Il pleure*, long since in print, into the cover, and finally also the Bach E-Major Concerto which I thought might be as good as any to play with piano.

Dinner over and the first bottle of champagne gone, I asked if he would mind if I played something for him. "What?" he asked, "something for piano?"

"No," I answered, suffering with "nerves" and too much "dining and wining," "I've taken the liberty of bringing my violin—though you understand, I have the jitters now, and have left it outside in the ante-chambre." He ran ahead of me to fetch it, and I played the entire first sonata of Bach. After expressions of "merveilleux" and thus on, from the Madame, I continued with the Fugue in A and, as he yet demanded more, the Ciaconna!

As I replaced the instrument, I ventured to slowly pull out my copy of *Il pleure*. As soon as he got a sufficient glimpse of the title page, he sprang to the piano most happily, while he said to his wife: "Now you are going to hear something." Amid the shower of those exquisite French expressions: "C'est ravissant . . . de toute beauté . . . c'est inouï . . . bis . . . bis . . . O encore une fois, je vous en supplie," he kept saying to his wife, "N'est-ce pas, n'est-ce pas?" We played it again, and he asked: "Haven't you brought any other music?" and with the *élan* of enthusiasm, he put both hands on my shoulders and exclaimed, "Ah, this man! Ah my God, I would willingly make music with him my whole life long!" I produced the Bach Concerto, and we played it, or rather, he played it as if *he* had worked out every section and bowing and nuance! As soon as we had finished, he exclaimed "du champagne!" and walking back and forth while we all talked and I mopped my wet face, he kept repeating almost as if in a challenge—"N'est-ce pas? N'est-ce pas?" while he made abrupt gestures and threw his hands wildly, "Il n'y a que lui," he kept saying emphatically, "Il n'y a que lui!" ["He's the only one!"] and once more planting himself before me he said with that burning intensity of all his nature—"Oh Lord! Good God, he is the only one! What a man he is, and what a musician. What a gift from God! I am not talking about the violin, that is a game for him, but with him I will make music *my whole life long!*"[24] With a large gesture, extending from his shoulder, he flung his arm with outstretched hand wide, while with greatest emphasis he repeated "Toute ma vie!" Debussy was a "positivist" in everything he did and every action of his life proved that he was either completely for or against. Exalted as I was by his enthusiasm, his burning eyes, and his gestures which were almost defiant, I noted his peculiarity of speaking directly to me yet in the third person, as if he were fighting for me with someone else.

It was now our turn to agree on an evening for dinner at our house, and these exchanges recurred thenceforth at intervals of three or four days, during the times I was in Paris and not absent on concert tours. For that first dinner at our house, I engaged a first-class cook, just for the day. She was a real "cordon bleu" for the simple reason that she was a highly intelligent and big-hearted person, had been Réjane's maid and had traveled with her extensively.[25] She begged to be allowed to make one of her "specialités" for dessert, a thing that she called "nègre en chemise,"[26] and to insure her good will, I agreed to that experiment. I myself bought the wines, and between us we knew how to temper the reds, cool the whites, and get the champagne to beyond the point of any feeling. Everything was succulent and the "negro"—a miraculous concoction of chocolates and pumpernickel and spices of which only the good old Madame Thérèse knew the abracadabra, and with a white "chemise" over it—made such sensational success with Debussy and myself that I became Mme. Thérèse's friend for the rest of her days. Occasionally I paid her a visit on a Sunday, and often shared "pot-luck" with her—a thing which gave her almost as much joy as it did myself. Grateful and affectionate thoughts to her memory!

A Proposed American Tour

With the arrival of Spring, Marc Blumenberg, owner of the *Musical Courier,* arrived, as usual, at his Paris home, and I told Debussy that if he were still favorably considering an American tour, I would seek an interview with Blumenberg in his behalf. Thanking me he added, "It would be amusing if we met there for a brief time."

"We?" I asked, "Did you say 'we'?"

"Mais naturellement—bien entendu. You didn't for a moment imagine I'd go without you?"

"How charming," I laughed, "and what am I to do—interpreter?—valet de chambre?"

"Pouf," he emitted with a brusque gesture—"nous irons là-bas pour faire de la musique!"

"Wonderful! But what—a sonata by yourself?"

"Never!" he snapped emphatically.

"Yes—but the programs would be of your music only, and so how else could we—Seigneur mon Dieu, if it were really to be ever true!—how else could we appear in a concerted number except in a sonata of your own?"

"Never!" he snapped again—"I shall never write a sonata!"

Somewhat perplexed, I mildly shook my head from side to side and murmured, "Bon—bon—but why not?"

He drew himself up haughtily and addressing me with cold formality said, "Monsieur—for the last time—never—mais jamais de la vie—shall I write a sonata! That I leave to the good boche carpenters—comme Monsieur Brahms and his clique!" There was no mistaking his defiantly determined attitude as he stood there before me, rigidly contracted with anger as he glared at me! I daresay I dropped my eyes or looked past him at the floor or the walls during an unpleasant moment, for presently he said, "I have projected something else—I am going to write a Poème for violin and orchestra—that is to say for you and you alone—and that we will play in all concerts, except of course, not at *Pelléas* if they should mount that in a few cities and where I might perhaps conduct the performance." I skipped around the room in such wild happiness that I used every cussword I knew in French while he chortled with delight, when suddenly I pulled up before him and making a sharp sound with my lips, I cried, "Halte-là!" ["Stop!"].[27]

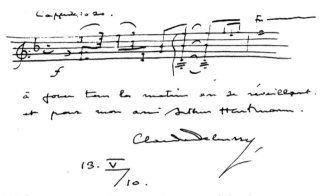

Example 3. Debussy's entry in Hartmann's autograph book

To be played every morning when you wake up
and for my friend Arthur Hartmann.

Claude Debussy
13 May 1910

Three Debussy Songs

One morning, strolling along the Avenue du Bois de Boulogne, I impulsively decided to drop in at "No. 24" and, as always, was immediately received. His mood was quiet and sad, and we sat in long silences and smoked. The only thing that broke the mood was when the train of the "ceinture" issued from the tunnel right by his house, the little garden became covered by black puffs and white steams of smoke. He just sat there, dreamily looking into it until the garden became cleared of the clouds, "just as in *Nuages,*" I thought as I shared in that mystique *al fluidum* of the moment. In that silence we suddenly became aware, and offensively, of someone's whistling in the room adjoining. Involuntarily and panther-like, he had jumped from his chair, torn the door open in a gust of fury, and there stood the butler, caught too suddenly to have stopped the tune, a large duster in hand. Debussy's anger struck with unrestrained force, and the servant was dismissed on the spot! Banging the door shut, he turned to me and apologized for "these little scenes of domesticity." Almost pathetically he began telling me of some of the difficulties they have in getting good servants, adding, "This one came but recently and was recommended by a person whom I've always considered a friend, even if a bad musician, but now I know him, hélas, to be also un mauvais collègue."

Gradually he became calmer and fully forgetting the disturbance said, absent-mindedly, "Ah, what was it that I wanted to show you? I know there was something that I wanted . . . oh yes . . . tenez . . . here it is, just received from the publishers." I glanced at the title-page: *Le promenoir des deux amants,* three songs to texts by Tristan Lhermitte. "Would you mind if I sang these for you?" he asked with peculiar timidity.

I bowed while I answered, "Please do," and in baffled wonderment asked myself whether I had heard aright "sing"?

He seated himself at his piano and turning to me said, while he made room for me at his side on the piano bench, "You would be kind enough to come turn pages for me."

His almost indefinably beautiful piano tone always ravished me immediately, and in a small voice, replete with vibrant tenderness and emotional expressiveness, he sang the first and the second of the songs. I could do no more than look at him, and he understood I could not express my thoughts and emotions. He started on the third and I had partially turned from him so as to better listen to *that* quality which was so marvelously his own as a Being, a Creator, in his piano touch, even in his singing voice! I shall never be able to describe it nor can anyone who has not heard him have any understanding of its peculiar pathos and warmth. It was as if tears of blood dripped from a soul anguished by the tragic greatness of Beauty itself and I thought, "You are the Blessed Damsel, you are Mélisande herself, that so beautiful spirit, coming from Antiquity, not knowing whence or whither bound, the reincarnation of Beauty and Loveliness and of heart-breakingly eternal loneliness and yearning." Resting my elbow against the music rack, I leaned my cheek on my hand while he was terminating the third song. Sitting thus beside him, in silence, he read my emotions and saw I was struggling to find expressions, and what is more, to gather these emotions and impressions suffficiently together as to begin to formulate them.

Suddenly I jumped from the piano bench exclaiming, "Nom de Dieu!"

Still in the mood of his music, he asked me, "Then . . . it's all right?" and it might have been little Chouchou standing there.

For answer I gave him, with blazing eyes, "Nom de Dieu de nom de Dieu!"

"So then," he said with quiet smile, "will you allow me to give you this folio as a gift," and he inscribed it: "Pour Arthur Hartmann, de son ami, décidément Claude Debussy."[28]

But here I must speak of the most extraordinary and sheer unbelievable experience and coincidence in my life! When Debussy showed me the music, I noted it bore the dedication, "à Emma-Claude Debussy . . . p.m. . . . de son mari, Claude Debussy." "Tiens! C'est incroyable!" I exclaimed aloud, almost reeling in my startled surprise!

Nonplussed he looked at me and asked, "Quoi-donc?"

"Might I beg of you," I answered, gathering my wits, "to divulge the secret, to reveal the meaning of those letters 'p.m.'?"

He looked at me in an indefinably amused way and said, "Oui, c'est très curieux . . . mais c'est . . . c'est un secret."

"That," I retorted smilingly, "I never for a second doubted," while I felt his eyes trying to read the meaning in mine. It may appear indelicate, though certainly not far-fetched, if I comment the interpretation I gave those letters, or more correctly interpreting my meaning of them, I thought of them as initials. While trying to think of something to say to extricate myself from a situation which touched another's life too intimately, I mused, "How few are the women on earth who have the happiness of being called 'petite Maîtresse' by their own husbands," while aloud I said, with a mock sigh, "Ah! Yes, the little secrets of love. Only, you know, in English, p.m. means in the afternoon?" He relished this with his short, goat-like chortle.

However, I have progressed but midway in my explanation of this incredible coincidence, for it was not the "p.m." that had actually made me jump, but the fact that I had used a similar dedication myself more than seven months previously! Debussy never knew that I had attempted compositions in various forms and for instruments from the full orchestra down to the cimbalom and the viola d'amore, and I would rather have run away from him forever rather than mention this, not to speak of showing him any of my attempts. Thus, shortly after my marriage, I found among my papers a poem of no particular value, authorship not given on that newspaper clipping, but the point is, the title was "Closer." Hence what more natural than for a young honeymooner to set verses which wove around "nestling closer to my heart" and "dear one" and "love's raptures" as for voice and piano? When I had completed the manuscript I gave it to my then young wife, with this dedication written on it: "For Marie Arthur Hartmann . . . my wife," and those who may have seen that kind of dedication on one of my Preludes for piano must, doubtlessly, have thought I was aping the Great Debussy, but the irrefutable facts are exactly as stated!

It was time that I take my leave, but he said, "there was something else too," and walking painfully to another part of the room, there took another small volume of music from a package, and as he passed me he said: "And this too." Seating himself with some difficulty, he took a pen and inscribed it to me, "en toute amitié."

It was the First Book of *Préludes*![29]

The Art of Transcribing

As soon as I reached the Avenue, I opened the large envelope and began to read these compositions, with their poetic or bizarre titles at the end and on the bottom of the page. Scanning page after page of these *Préludes*, my eye chanced upon that simple line, the opening of *La fille aux cheveux de lin.* Immediately I thought, "This could be played on the fiddle," but at exactly the twenty-fourth measure struck a snag, a slight and momentary one, for in the same instant its solution "appeared" to me and this solution I should like to explain.

To put it concisely: anything can be arranged from one instrument to another, such as playing a song on a violin, or arranging a piano composition as a violin solo with piano accompaniment. But the point is, was the operation performed without leaving a scar, or perhaps even without a trace of one, and, most important of all, has a thoroughly *idiomatic* (violinistic) piece been created onto which an equally complete piano part has been supplied? Or did the original piano piece remain as it was, with the exception of one voice, its top or melodic line, removed and transferred to a totally foreign medium? This process I should term "scalping," for it is not complete decapitation. Or again—to illustrate another type of arranging—has it resulted in two thoroughly hostile, unrelated, and maimed pieces trying to "blend" when colors, like ligaments brutally severed, are hopelessly seeking each other, when the elbow is protruding from the shoulder blade and one hand lacks several fingers? On the other hand, the true transcription can become an artwork only when one artist is capable of approaching the personality of another with that complete understanding of his individualistic expressions in music, timbre, and sensibilities, and can so transfer a piece that in its new garb it produces the effect of having been originally conceived in that form and none other.

Thus, I mused from measures 24 to 27, "This is nothing, nothing at all but 'color' or 'atmosphere' . . . something typical of Debussy. I know how he would produce this. It is to be blurred exquisitely, receding, vanishing somewhere between the strings of the piano and both pedals and, most surely, not to be pedestrianed [*sic*] by reinforcement, by doubling the top note on the violin! Heavens, the very thought is too horrible, revolting in its heavy crassness! Right here, against that Carrière-like background, I shall trace with the lowest-available mysteries of harmonic sounds, that long line of this maiden with flaxen but not hempen hair, and she will remain 'exquise,' 'ravissante,' 'délicieuse,' and become 'a child of the sun' according to my old 'faiblesse' for the women of the Scandinavian countries." Immediately on entering my home and ere starting to work on the idea, I despatched "un petit bleu" to Debussy in which I said, "The girl with the flaxen hair asks the privilege to come over and play the violin for you," and at once received the adjoined reply [CD-9[30]]:

> My dear friend,
>   It is absolutely true . . . I will be playing the piano (4 *Préludes*) tomorrow evening at Erard's. I will do everything possible to send you tickets tomorrow morning.

I request to hear "the girl with the flaxen hair" play the violin, for I do not doubt that she has considerable talent!

Cordially yours,
Claude Debussy

The next day, sans cérémonie, I took a cab with my fiddle-box and manuscript and was received by Debussy at once. Immediately he was at the piano and I with violin in hand. I stood slightly in back of him, reading the notes from over his shoulder, and when he reached the measures from 24 to 27, he turned to me smilingly (while continuing to play "the accompaniment" from memory) and made the impish remark, "That's not stupid . . . that . . . not at all!"

Credo

There are artists who attain a certain vogue where the public accepts everything they do without the slightest critical appraisal and whose performances in time become "tradition" and one which may have even pernicious and long-lasting influence on the younger and musically more ignorant generation. One such artist is Fritz Kreisler, even if I count myself among the first to accord him merited homage for his extraordinary gifts as a violinist and his interpretative and artistic powers. However, I am now concerned with the discussion of Kreisler's way of playing this, my transcription, and also his making changes, without authority or reason to do so, and because of his eminence the matter deserves detailed analysis.

Himself a master transcriber, he is prone to too easily make changes in the compositions of others, sometimes even of standard works, be the change so "slight" as the insertion of that by him innately beloved Orientalism of a grace note, turn, or brief trill, but which is more than questionable taste because of being foreign to the creation of that specific composition or the style of its composer. Kreisler, like all highly developed individuals and artists, possesses certain virtues, characteristics, and mannerisms which may be termed typically Kreislerian. I am not referring to external mannerisms which of course everyone has in varying degrees, but to those which in musical interpretation differentiate one artist's playing from that of another. One of the strongest characteristics of Kreisler is his nervous intensity and a vital, rhythmic feeling which, at times, tends to overaccentuation. Thus a virtue may grow into a defect through abuse or malapplication, for instead of presenting the long line, in one breath, at the opening of this exquisite composition by Debussy, Kreisler breaks it into jerky groups of three notes, and were he playing the piano, I would expect those accents to be indicated by the head, wavering between short nods of "no-no" and "yes-yes" until the last group when it is "yes-yes-yes-definitely." But it happens that the naive and blonde little maid whom I know does not possess this particular whimsey, for though she is elusive and capricious, she is not jerky.

His substituting closed notes for where I have placed harmonics and harmonics where I have closed notes, or playing it vice-versa, as also adding the theme at the end, on the violin, instead of leaving it in the piano-part where "we" put it, I find without raison d'être and also not gratifying. I have to take this means of protesting my displeasure because of the widespread influence of such a famous artist and because it is here appropriate to make detailed criticism. By the time I heard Kreisler play this transcription publicly, he had not only recorded it some years previously, but on a world tour had played it in many countries and continents. Thus it was futile and too late to do anything about it or even to inform Fritz that with fiddle in hand, I had suggested all the things which he does and even yet others to Debussy, leaving the choice to the composer, and that Debussy had rejected them all, finding them distasteful and not according to his ideas of that composition, and that the manuscript I played to Debussy was exactly as is the printed copy of today. Several world-famous violinists have asked me whether I approved the changes which Kreisler permits himself to make, and my invariable retort was, "Most certainly not, nor would have Debussy. But I am not the composer, and by the time Kreisler took this piece up, Debussy had joined the Immortals."

And finally, for those who hear artists on records only, I would advise listening to the recording of this transcription by Heifetz, who plays it exactly as it should be and beautifully, of course.

It is my conviction that all real artists and especially those few who have attained world-importance must and should never lose sight of their own realization of their service to a Divine Art which is not only greater than their triumphs of the hour but also greater than they themselves and all their ilk are! Then would performances, in the highest sense of interpretations, be entirely freed of the slightest taint of concession to a falsity and not be subject to the censorious reproach of having introduced any foreign and most often vulgar "effect," that cheap catch-for-applause.

A Concert Attended by Debussy, 2 June 1910

The early summer was for Paris "la haute saison" for concerts, and with my pianist we announced two recitals at which we intended to play two (of the five) programs which we had already played over eighty times in the Scandinavian countries. I was to open with the Bach E-Major Concerto and end with the Paganini Concerto (in my version), and in between the pianist was to have a solo group. About ten days before the first recital, the billboards were pasted all over Paris, and presently my wife commented, "Of course you're going to ask the Debussys, and I suppose they had best sit with me?"

"Whiewhh," I whistled, "you are sick . . . even worse than that, you are crazy!" She somehow thought it best to drop the matter, yet about five days later, she again asked, with more emphasis, "*Aren't* you going to invite Debussy?"

"Listen, Marie," I begged, "you know perfectly well that I'd die if I had him sitting there under my nose. I'd be simply paralyzed. I wouldn't be able to forget him at all!"

"Aren't you strange?" she answered languidly, "You know perfectly well that he loves your playing and when you are in the room with him, you've often played together and . . ."

"Yes, I know, I know," I interrupted impatiently, "but that's quite different. That's a mood: good dinner, wonderful wines and champagnes . . . then I'm different. But a public concert, at a fixed hour and on a certain date, all the lights on and he with those eyes of his fastened on me? Oh, là-là, but I would rather die than have him there!"

"Yes, but," she argued gently, "don't you think he'll think it strange, for you know he goes around in his automobile and perhaps by now has even seen the posters himself. In any event, sooner or later, he's bound to hear about it and don't you think he'd consider it rather rude that you haven't even asked him, even if he does not come, has a previous engagement or something?"

I let myself be persuaded that perhaps she may not be entirely wrong and forthwith dispatched a letter. I told him I was writing under duress and only because my wife wished me to, that she feared it might be discourteous if I did not invite him and Madame to one of my concerts. Therefore I was taking the liberty of enclosing two tickets and hoped very much he would *not* do me the honor of attending for I would rather die than to have him there, "right under my nose, however big it is." With characteristic truthfulness and according to his mood, he answered: "Thanks, my dear friend, for sending me two invitations to the approaching recital. In spite of my horror for that type of music-making, I'll drag my wife along with myself on Thursday. In devoted friendship, Your Claude Debussy" [CD-10[31]].

We had just terminated the first movement of the Concerto when Debussy and his wife entered, and as the usher started them toward their seats, this sensation threatened to disrupt the concert. From all sides, heads were stretched and fingers pointed, and as one person whispered his name to another, there was a quite audible hiss in so many saying "Debussy-Debussy" at the same time. He kept his eyes on me, as they came on that long trip down the aisle, and when he had seated himself (next to my wife), I bowed to him and gave the pianist a sign to begin. I squeezed my eyes shut tight and with the most intense concentration I was capable of, gave all that I had, in the slow movement.

Then came the final movement, which is a Rondo. It is a form in which a little tune recurs three times. Separating each return is a melody or idea of a different nature and never twice alike. Despite my tightly shut eyes, I could not rid myself of the picture of Debussy sitting down there in the fifth row . . . and suddenly, something happened. Instead of my presenting the second little tune for the second time, I had skipped to the third time! My pianist, perceiving the change, had jumped after me, but in that split second I had become aware of my lapse and had jumped back to the place where I should originally have been. This resulted in a tiny hitch, but I went determinedly on my way, and the pianist soon found the place for his backward jump. Debussy, immediately aware that "something had happened," gave my wife a vicious dig with his elbow (so she later told me) and fiercely whispered, "I'll bet he could kill that animal-of-a-pianist!" There was of course no actual stopping, and the performance was greeted with the ususal applause. These things occur in less than two seconds of time, yet the jolt often remains inexplicable and in bad cases, may become a fixed aberration.

Hardly had we left the platform when my pianist, with hands folded in a gesture of supplication, excitedly implored, "Master! I don't know how you can ever forgive this! Voilà, fifty times that we have played this together and exactly tonight, oh I don't know what seized me, mais que je suis malheureux, ah mon Dieu, cher Maître, je ne suis qu'un misérable! Oh, my God, what a miserable wretch I am!" And with patronizing kindliness I patted him on the shoulder and said, "My boy—let's not say any more about it. Those things happen . . . as you see, they can happen to anybody."

The next day, Debussy sent me the following, delivered by his chauffeur [CD-11[32]]:

> Dear friend,
> You are a very great artist. I do not know if the persons who heard you yesterday evening had that impression? In any case, I did not wish either to accompany them or to hear them congratulate you in "all the tongues."
> I preferred to keep within myself the strong remembrance of your art which, for the moment, transcends all music!
>
> Thanks, cordially,
> Claude Debussy[33]

TOS–CA–nini[34]

One afternoon I strolled over to call on Claude Debussy. As usual, I was immediately received. Even if I say it lightly, I had deep realization of what this meant, and I never abused this privilege. I had not forgotten what had occurred on an earlier visit, some months previously. He and I were in his little garden, chatting and smoking incessantly, when suddenly the bell to the outer "grille" was pulled and ere I knew how it had happened, Debussy had seized me by the scruff of my neck and shoved me behind a bush. He hid himself behind another and winked at me while we heard the butler telling the caller, "Sorry, but Monsieur is not at home." But this afternoon's unpremeditated drop in on him convinced me that he must have instructed his butler to admit me whenever I called, as all my visits, heretofore, had been in the forenoon.

Debussy was generally known as a "caractère un peu difficile" or "pas commode," which means in other words, a "crank" with whom it was not easy to get along. Well, for my part, I'm willing to let everyone judge things according to his own experiences, and mine with the Immortal Claude were nobly beautiful and unforgettable. Debussy then was the world-famous personage, a man whose music was being fought over, and he had made himself inaccessible to the world. Though I knew and appreciated all this at the time, yet I was never in all my life more my own self than when I was with him. I loved the exquisitely sensitive and poetic nature of that man who as a being was appealingly solitary! I also found his outbursts of temper perfectly natural, for I had (and yet have) a goodly sized lump of hellfire within me. And if he abominated certain kinds of cooking, I could only love him the more, as I too had the same hatreds in me. If I had the good sense to not ask him his opinions in music, it was because his company was far too delightful to be dragged to the level of one-sided musicians, however famous some of those egoists were. I think I agreed with all his tastes, including perfumes and wines, but not with the kind of cigarettes he smoked. His preference was for the "Maryland" and mine for the delectable Greek, Turkish, and Balkan tobaccos which I balanced and of which mixture I made my own cigarettes. He advised me often to switch to his kind, "roulée à la main" [hand-rolled], but I told him I had more confidence in what my own hands prepared and the tobaccos which I bought in small cartons directly at the *Ottoman Régie*. What I tactfully withheld was the picture, at the back of my head, of numerous shabby men, strolling the Boulevards, a thin long stick under their arms. At the end of this yardstick was a small, sharp nail, and as soon as these jobless folk perceived a cigarette stub which had been thrown away, they'd seize it by jibing the sharpened end of that nail into it and then remove the stub to their pockets. There was quite a trafficking in these stubs, resold to some tobacco jobbers who had some means of cutting off the burnt ends and reworking the tobacco into other cigarettes. I am not implying that these were the only kind of cigarettes manufactured in France or the reason for my not caring for Maryland or Caporal. It was, of course, a matter of difference in tastes and earlier breeding. If Debussy was a "volupté" and a gourmet for the sensuous and ecstasies of Life, I flattered myself that as a second fiddle, my tentacles did not reach so very far behind.

He greeted me with warm affection. As I felt my hand in his warm grasp, I studied the peculiarity of his forehead with almost the same curiosity as when I first beheld it. There was always a burning intensity about him. It showed in everything he did and said, though he was generally terse and epigrammatic. There was a concentrated strength in him, both mental and physical. A high-tension nervousness was stimulated, or more correctly, aggravated, by his various indulgences in alcohols, foods, and ceaseless smoking, and usually he was short of breath and inclined to be choleric. Again I looked at his warm, dark eyes and his sympathetic mouth, surrounded as it was by a softly curling moustache and beard, doubtlessly the virgin growth.

Each time I saw him, I immediately felt his warm magnetism and attractiveness and then too, I knew that if he didn't like me, there would be no reason for him to see me at all. Of course we started smoking at once, while he reseated himself at his "desk." This was an enormous table, about five and one-half feet long which, doubtless, some expert carpenter had built for him. The home of the Debussys was furnished with many an exquisite and beautiful thing, but this "desk" of his was a regular carpenter's work table with cross-beams at its ends. There seemed to be good reason for a composer to have a large desk, for when a man has finished a page of an orchestral score, it's not such a bad idea to have a small music stand, right there on the desk, on which to place that completed page and yet have sufficient room to be able to compare lines as the continuation on the new page progresses. The world little realizes that the man who, in silence, is writing an orchestral score is constantly, in his subconscious, balancing colors and sonorities against each other. It has to be architecturally constructed too, for if a mere dot were placed on the wrong line, it might result in a blast on the trombone or a landslide on the bass drum. Often had I dropped in on Debussy, à l'imprévu, yet never found him at work on any music. Nor was there ever a single inkspot on his vast blotters. I had had the eerie feeling as if some great mystic spirits helped him over his work, even if I am sure that in those days neither he nor myself had heard of the "ghost-writers."

We chatted for a while when he suddenly said, "Tiens, il y avait un drôle de type qui est venu me voir hier." A Frenchman could designate almost any individual, or bizarrerie of trait or character, by the exclamation "Quel type!" Hence I was intrigued when I heard him say, "There was a queer sort of guy who came to see me yesterday." He continued, "Il s'appelle . . . TOS–CA–nini." He pronounced the name exactly thus: the first two syllables very slowly and widely spaced and the last two jumbled together in a manner scarcely discernible or audible. I smiled as we exchanged glances. "Do you by any chance know him?" he asked.

"Alas, unfortunately not," I retorted, "for I admire him immensely."

"Quel drôle de type," he repeated with evident amusement, while he regarded the burning edge of his cigarette. I knew Debussy's ways well enough to know that all I need do is to wait. If there is to be any further comment, he will make it. And if not, it is something he does not care to talk about. Usually, he started in his timid, hesitant manner, a few detached words, a sentence seldom completed. At other times the termination would come in a sudden spurt and generally with considerable heat, for he was easily roused to anger. "Eh bien, comment dirai-je?" he continued after a pause. "Enfin voilà toute l'histoire, and it is that yesterday this drôle de type came to see me and at a certain moment he started telling me about *Pelléas*.[35] Very soon I found myself getting into an argument, for ce TOS–CA–nini-là claimed that at a certain point in the text where they say so-and-so there is this-and-that-kind of a chord! 'Mais non, mais non,' I answered, 'there is no such chord if you mean the exact spot where they are saying so-and-so.' 'Mais si, mais si,' protested ce drôle de type and proceeded to not only name the chord but every instrument which had a note in that chord, a fa-bécarre [F natural] here, a do-dièse [C sharp] there, the horn on this note, the fagott on another and thus on. I found myself getting angry and finally said to him, 'It is futile to carry this discussion any longer, for after all Monsieur, it seems to me that I ought to know the work. You know, perhaps, that I wrote it . . . and quite by myself!'" I joined his goat-like chortling as he proceeded, "Eh bien, ce type-là answered by no-no-no-no-no, repeated about fifteen times on end, and subitement he said, 'Regardez! It is bien simple, that which I now propose to you! Have you, by any chance, a copy of the score of *Pelléas*?'" Painfully Debussy rose from his chair and going to the bookshelf in the corner of his room, drew forth the miniature edition of the work and brought it over to me. Continuing his narrative, he said, "Eh bien, ce type de TOS–CA–nini soon turned the pages to the exact spot in discussion and," with a burst of laughter and throwing wide his arms, Debussy concluded, "and he was right, il avait raison ce drôle de type!"

Debussy and the Cimbalom[36]

It was midsummer [1910]. The concert season was practically over, it was "la saison morte," as the French called it after the "Longchamp" had taken place. A new work by Debussy, eagerly expected by his followers, mildly hissed at its première chez Colonne, had again started the many discussions as to whether Debussy had found new paths for the expression of his genius or whether this last work, *Ibéria*, only documented his exhaustion. There were many who argued and believed that with *Pelléas* he had not only fully expressed himself, but had built a ring around himself from whose confines he could never escape: that all the newer compositions, songs, and piano pieces were evidences of a growing sterility and but poorer expressions of an earlier Debussy. If it must readily be conceded that thirty years ago there were considerably fewer people who understood him than are now, it is nonetheless startling to think there are yet uncultured musicians who think that Debussy's "originality" lay in his use of the five-tone scale (a thing so limited in itself as to be very hemming) whereas it required all the Greek Modes to paint the Art of this profoundly great and unique musician and to interpret the depths and the poesy of his exquisite fervor.

Thus I found him, many times, at work on what was growing into a considerable pile of closely written blue paper, and one morning I had the temerity to ask: "What is that you're doing? Compiling a new tourist's guide of Europe?"

With characteristic gesture, pointing his index finger rigidly and suddenly at the stack of papers, he asked, "What? That? That's the libretto to a new opera I am writing on a story by Poe," which he, of course, pronounced "Po-aye." "It is called," he continued, "*La chute de la maison Usher.*"

"And you are writing the libretto yourself?!" I exclaimed, and he answered slyly, "Oui, moi-même . . . tout seul" ["Yes, quite by myself"]. Whether he achieved the story or not, I do not know, but it is certain that he left no music behind to this projected work.[37]

The frequent interchange of visits and evenings spent together, dining at his house, at mine, or elsewhere, continued, and he had suddenly become enthusiastic about a new kind of sonority and a music, evidently unknown to him. In the newly opened Hotel Carlton, in Paris, he had discovered the Hungarian Gypsy band . . . the Cimbalom, the high E-flat clarinet which played along in the altitudinous regions of that of the "Primás" or Leader, the original raspiness of the double-bass player, and delightedly he told me that all the players wore richly ornamented red jackets! Time and again his thoughts reverted to those Gypsies, and he would sigh, "Ah, ces Messieurs qui portent l'habit rouge!" ["Ah, those Gentlemen who wear red jackets!"]. Summertime and in a happy Paris, the "Fashionable World" crowding all attractive places for "The Five o'clock," the Gypsies playing their wild and melancholy rhapsodies and making of everything, from *Ave Maria* to a German waltz, an unrecognizable, exotic Ragoût tziganesque [Gypsy stew], while a carefree world loved and laughed and flirted. Nothing would do but that I must fix upon an afternoon and agree to go with him (at about *four* o'clock, of course) to "feevoclockay" with him at the Carlton and admire the virtuosity of ces Messieurs qui portent l'habit rouge. The ladies were of the part, and ere we broke up, the Debussys had again fixed on a date for dinner together, at their house within the next few ensuing days, and would not hear of it otherwise.

Once again, after dinner, we went into his study where, as usual, two bottles of champagne added their spirits, when suddenly Debussy arose and said, "And what if we all went into the other room, into the Salon where there is a grand piano, and I played something for you?" And he played, played with such ravishing beauty of tone, technique, and dynamics as I have never heard surpassed and equaled by only three pianists in all the galaxy of famous instrumentalists whom I have known or heard in the last thirty years. On his part, he never spoke of himself as a pianist except in a deprecating and mocking way, yet I who have known some of the world's greatest pianists and in an intimacy which gave me countless, unforgettable opportunities to watch them at very close quarters, hear them practice by the hour while I sat beside them on the piano bench, I reaffirm that not one surpassed Debussy in sheer beauty of tone and tone-colors, in the command of the technique of the keyboard, as well as in those of nuances of expressiveness. It must be understood that I never heard him play any other music than his own, and if my praise of his so highly individualized pianism may seem exaggerated, I think his contributions to the literature for the instrument corroborate my judgment. For it should not be forgotten that although he never, never practiced, Debussy *played* his own works, and that these reveal his profound understanding of the piano and its possibilities and are as original in their pianism as those by Chopin and Liszt, a triumvirate of distinct yet inseparably related creators, of innovators in the arts of piano technique and expressiveness.

He played a few of his compositions and with such magic that, at will, I can again evoke the colors and hear those shy revelations of beauty and sound. We murmured our admiration when, suddenly, his mood changed and he said, "And now I'll play you my latest," and I thought I detected a faint smile of derision on the face of his wife. Without an instant's loss of time, he started that composition which, as I afterwards learnt, was to be called *La plus que lente*.[38] For those who would torture a rose to try to find where its fragrance is hid, some of Debussy's titles must present puzzles which no logic or dissecting can ever solve, for the titles perhaps came later or were suggested by a nuance of nature or a bit of color, not to list ebullient or morbid moods. However, I noticed that he played this piece with considerable amusement and ere long, judging by its quality as well as his manner of playing it, I had the feeling that Debussy had attempted a "bestseller."

Hilariously I exclaimed, "By jingo, oo-là-là, isn't that stylish, altogether ripping . . . but what's its name?" and while he turned to fetch his glass, Mme. Debussy in a voice inaudible to him, answered, "the production of an entire summer," and then, smilingly and with expressive gestures she added, "*La plus que lente*." Only a few weeks previously we had dined together at the Cascade, in the Bois; and he had roared, actually roared until with tears running from his eyes he begged me to desist, merely because I had made my retorts in all the slang words I knew at the time, or when words failed me I interrupted, him or myself, by a sharp whistle through my front teeth and showed him how I could produce harmonics: those whistled between the front teeth as differentiated from those blown from the back of my cheeks. This was one of my reprehensible mannerisms at the time, but it was a habit which always threw him into spasmodic laughter. Evidently that summer, they were going around a good deal and thus the sinuous voluptuousness of chic "Five o'clocks" had gotten into his blood and he, perhaps they, had named this willowy, salon-like effusion *La plus que lente,* which may mean "the-more-than-slow," "the-most-than-slow," or any indescribable and untranslatable affectation which some salon players would enjoy interpreting with their nods and eyebrows for "Society." Musically, to me the piece, notably in its middle section, is an excellent Chaminade and nothing more.[39]

Flaunting my perfumed handkerchief around, I floated from one to the other while I sighed, "Oh, I love you . . . ah, embrace me again, chérie!" Wiping the perspiration from his brow and almost weak from laughter he said to me, "Eh bien mon cher vieux, my greatest ambition would be to hear this played par ces Messieurs qui portent l'habit rouge," and forthwith, unasked, he played it over again, keeping up a flow of amusing comments as to the instrumentation he would plan for "les habits rouges." He played it capriciously and by no means slowly, and when, finally rising from the piano, he again sighed, "Ah those gypsies, with their red jackets!"

I asked, "Do you mean that seriously?"

"Absolutely!" he said with emphatic earnestness, "Only I don't know how to write for their instrument, the what did you call it . . . cembalo?"

"Cimbalom," I corrected, "but if you mean it all in earnest, there is nothing easier, for I have one and in fact, at one time was quite a proficient player myself. I'll tell you what I'll do, if you permit me. I'll make an exact copy of its resonance box and this will give you not only its range but show you exactly where every note and every bridge is." He thanked me with warmest profusion and enthusiastically shook my hands. Within a few days, I called at his house with an enormous roll of wrapping paper on which I had made the drawing in actual size, inserting between each "string" a stave on which I had given the actual note, with clef, which it represented. Once or twice thereafter, when dropping in on him unexpectedly, I found him standing over his large table, with my plan of the Cimbalom fully stretched before him, and with two penholders in hands, he was "practicing" arpeggios.

Some twenty years later I was recounting this anecdote to a circle of musicians, and to my surprise, one of them commented "C'est exact! It's absolutely true, for Debussy himself scored that piece for small orchestra with cimbalom." I lost no time in obtaining a copy of that score and found he had scored it for such groups of players as might obtain in small cafés only and to be found only in France, I think, for I doubt whether elsewhere.[40] It calls for one flute and one clarinet only, a "piano-conducteur," quartet of strings plus double bass, besides a "cymbalum" ("if obtainable," I think he should have added). He changed the opening of the piece, extending it by six measures with an introductory Cadenza optional for either flute solo or one of a different kind, optional for the "cymbalum," either of which, quite honestly, is of a caliber which not even an ordinary musician would have employed! As for his treatment of the cimbalom, it is not only bad, totally ineffectual, but also incorrect, for by no stretches in the tunings of those wire strings, in both directions of the limits of that string box, could certain notes at all be procured, for they simply do not exist on the cimbalom! I daresay that one fine day my roll of wrapping paper went into the furnace and when the mood to orchestrate returned, two years later, it would seem according to the copyright, he had remembered its approximate range but, unfortunately, with not too great accuracy.

I repeat, my first impression was the correct one: Debussy had attempted a best-seller, and, in my judgment, failed utterly. And when I hear violinists, the best and most famous of them, playing *La plus que lente* "with emotion," slowly, gravely, and taking it so seriously, others playing it with that abomination which has helped vitiate the art of violin playing and which today seems to be generally known as "schmalz," my wistful memories linger on those days when Debussy could gurgle with happy laughter when I emitted those short, sharp sounds "the flageolet-tones through the front teeth" and on his naive delight when he had discovered "ces Messieurs qui portent l'habit rouge!"

A Fragment for Violin

Paris, at the time, was having a number of prizefights, and Debussy knew that, occasionally, we attended them. It was something of a novelty, in those days, for ladies to accompany their husbands to these exhibitions. Properly speaking, these "fights" were more of the "fashionable" kind, attended by "le haut monde" and took place in not too large theaters and casinos. I used to amuse him by referring to the "catégorie . . . poids lourds . . . catégorie . . . léger," and mimicking the antelope-like manner of some French boxers, as also the polite phrases of the announcers and the inexact manner in which referees stretched the time between seconds and often prolonged the time by slow and hesitant ways of drawing out the words of the count. So it happened that one day he sent his chauffeur to me with a few lines of music, to which he had pinned a torn bit of paper with merely this scrawled on it: "Est-ce faisable?" Obviously it was for violin and he wanted to know whether "can it be done?" It was not only impractical but utterly impossible of execution, and on an equally picturesquely torn bit of paper, I scribbled merely: "Non . . . et de *toutes* catégories," meaning, "I'll take on all comers . . . regardless of weight and size."

This impersonal way of answering his traceless query I put into a copy of my article on the Chaconne of Bach which had just appeared in a French translation and gave the chauffeur, together with D's bit of manuscript. His sense of humor was delicious, for he answered [CD-14[41]]:

Dear friend,

Thank you for the "violinistic" information. It did not fall on deaf ears!

It is regretful that J. S. Bach is definitely dead, because he would have thanked you for defending his "Chaconne" against the interpretations of certain great masters of the violin!!!

You are decidedly a rare man, because you have found a way to be a great virtuoso as well as a sensitive and intelligent artist.

It appears that we are having dinner tomorrow evening at the "Majestic." I will immediately have my beard trimmed to look more American.

Until then, let us shout: "Long live America, Long live Hungary, and even, Long live France," since these various charming nations will be gathered around the same table.

Your friend,
Claude Debussy

The termination, of course, referred to that memorable dinner party, as his last letter to me will reveal!

A Dinner Party

We had been their guests twice, and despite my arguments and urging, my wife could not bring herself to the point of inviting them to a dinner at our house, for our simple and modest ménage could in no way be compared to that of Debussy, whose cook, or perhaps chef, was truly a "cordon bleu." I was fully sympathetic and shared my wife's nervousness about having the Debussys for dinner and an entire evening at our house, but I in no way upheld her about making any pretenses at sumptuousness and having dinner at one of the large restaurants on the Champs Elysées. Always hating sham and pretense, I argued that it was our home, incidentally located in one of the best sections of Paris, and that it contained the best among interesting furniture, rugs, paintings, bibelots, and thus on. The only point I was willing to concede was that our little "bonne à tout faire" was scarcely qualified to cook, not to speak of serving, a dinner for such guests, and I was quite willing to engage a professional cook for that day. After all, on the Avenue Victor Hugo I could purchase as fine wines and champagnes as does Debussy elsewhere, and I can even supply him with his abominable cigarettes. However, Marie won out and insisted we invite them to dine at the Hotel Majestic which then was one at the head of swanky-swank and where they served an excellent dinner for Frs. 10. ($2.00) and which was considered quite high enough, even in Paris. That my instincts were right is sufficiently proven by a letter which I find among my papers from Mme. Debussy and written on *her* blue paper [ECD-2[42]]:

Tuesday [2 August 1910],

Dear Madame,
     It is very kind of you to invite us to dinner. It will give us great pleasure, but my husband asks why the "Majestic"? He dreads the obligatory evening dress in places called "Majestical." Tell him whether it is essential, then 'til tomorrow. Wednesday at 7:45 wherever you like (because Thursday we are not free). Forgive my questions and accept our affectionate remembrances for you and Uncle Arthur.

Emma C. Debussy
     I think upon your return Chouchou will begin violin lessons! Poor us!! Happily *her* teacher will be our reward.

Debussy's response to that invitation I quote, for it is indicative of his opinion of the hotel in the Av. Kleber: "It appears that we are having dinner tomorrow evening at the 'Majestic.' I will immediately have my beard trimmed to look more American. Until then, let us shout: 'Long live America, Long live Hungary, and even, Long live France,' since these various charming nations will be gathered around the same table."[43]

The day of that dinner, Marie suggested that we go to the hotel in the forenoon, just to ask to see that evening's menu. Innocently, I fell in with her plans only to learn, when she stood before the Major Domo, that she had planned a typical American dinner. "Now, to start with, we'll have grapefruit, well iced."

"Oh my God," I groaned, doubled over and seizing my stomach as if in cramps, "Are you insane? Grapefruit? That awful, bitter stuff and iced! The first thing on an empty stomach? A shock that will give him cramps . . . sour fruit and always that damnable ice and ice-water!"

But it was useless for she was trying to continue ordering. "Listen, darling," I said as I gently drew her away, and then fiercely hissed into her ear, "Listen! You'll drive me crazy . . . grapefruit in Paris! Why you know as well as I that in the few stores where they are obtainable, they cost sixty-five cents a piece . . . sixty-five cents! Have you forgotten 'M'sieu Dame? Trois francs vingt-cinq M'sieudame et merci,' and after all, YOU don't know Debussy! I'm telling you, he is just like me and he'll *hate* that stuff just as I do . . . and fruit, in the evening, first thing on an empty stomach . . . he'll go mad!"

But it all was without avail, and she returned to the head waiter and continued: "Grapefruit, followed by consommé, just clear consommé."

Again I groaned and implored, "Don't, please don't make it a thin soup with nothing in it. I tell you it must be a potage and a thick, heavy one!"

I was swept aside with, "And then I'd like some nice roast chicken with good stuffing, but not too much sage. Then some artichokes, then, perhaps a mince pie and an ice and . . ."

"And what about wine?" I interrupted heatedly.

"Oh yes, then a bottle of white and a good *dry* champagne."

"And what about bread!" I almost screamed in fury.

"Oh yes, some saltines and olives and celery, and some nuts before each plate, you know." We left and I raved against the dry wine, the hard "goût américain champagne," at her "et bien sec n'est-ce pas," as she had said, and at the bill, which thus à la carte, had reached cataclysmic figures. To top it all, as evening arrived, she decided to wear evening clothes, and I had to wear my "smoking" which I abominated.

Arrived at the hotel, the Debussys finally appeared, the Madame well dressed and he in his blue suit and blue shirt and blue collar, and I accepted this first faux-pas of the evening as a considerable solace. As soon as we were seated I hastened to explain that nothing put me in a greater temper than wearing a "smoking" and that it, together with this idiotic dining at an hotel was completely my wife's idea and not mine; that, after all, if I could not afford the luxury that they were used to, well, after all, "I was no Debussy . . . eh bien, quoi . . . n'est-ce pas, après tout . . . quoi!" He kept up a steady making of approbative interruptions, "mais naturellement . . . bien sûr . . . ouf pourquoi pas . . . mais qu'est-ce que ça fait," while my wife kept apologizing for my bad manners and my bad temper. I insisted on telling them that the first time we had the honor of having them as our guests, to dinner, we should have had them Chez nous . . . whatever our little home is like, and not this glaringly lighted hotel dining room, when suddenly I became aware that, with mixed expressions of amusement and irritation he was watching a waiter deposit one-half grapefruit before each of us. Scratching the beard on his cheek, as if in amused perplexity, he stared at the grapefruit as it sat there, perched high in a container filled with chipped ice, each of its scalloped edges so cunningly ornamented with a very thin slice of maraschino'd cherry, and began to turn it around and critically examine it. I had already detected his ill-natured glance at the glasses of water with small cubes of ice floating in them, and ice too was a rarity in Paris, obtainable only in small quantities in drug stores and only for use of invalids. However, with great "gentillesse" he turned to Marie with: "I should like to ask you Madame, si vous voulez bien me le permettre, what is *that*? What *is* that thing, and has it a name?"

Marie told all she knew about "that" and he tried several times to pronounce its name but could not get beyond making it sound somewhat like "crrropfroo." Marie tried to tell him yet more about it, but he interrupted with, "Oui, tout cela c'est très bien. Mais je voudrais savoir . . . does one *eat that*? Cet animal-là . . . does one, seriously, *eat* it?"

I felt his growing irritation, and I was gloating inwardly while Marie answered, "Taste it, and you will see," applying her best charms.

Alas, if *sounds* could be conveyed and not attempted to be described by words! It is impossible to more than try to imagine his exasperation, the expressiveness of that rigid finger, his eyes ready to jump from their sockets, the words almost a choked scream as he repeated, "*Ça* . . . on mange *ÇA?!*" He bristled as the cat's back is arched when it is about to spit at its enemy, and I felt recompensed for my annoyances and quarrels during an entire day. "Ah non Madame," said he, pushing that "animal" further from him, "that, Madame, you may keep for yourself for as long as you like. Me eat it? I? Moi? Never, mais jamais de la vie, Madame, would I *eat that*!"

"Mais Claude, Claude," remonstrated his wife, "Voyons, Claude! But one does not do that," and he gave her the full blast of his temper.

"Do what? Eat that? That? O mais jamais . . . ah bon Dieu . . . jamais de la vie!" It was a brilliant opening, and while I gloated inwardly I reflected, "He's even worse than I am. What's next, I wonder?"

Then came that clear, thin consommé at which he gave one vicious glance but was quickly admonished by signs from his wife—signals which even I, with my eyes on the cup before me could see. However, he did not lift his spoon to taste, but turning to Marie a face that by now was comic to behold for he was in a bad temper and trying hard to dissimulate, said to her in a voice of measured and restrained mildness, "Madame, might I ask of you the extreme kindness to be good enough to have one of those waiters go get me some bread? Have him fetch me just simply bread, Madame, good, simple bread if you please, Madame, and I beg of you?" He began to sit sideways at the table and suddenly noticing the celery and olives and saltines on the plate to his left, he pushed it from him while we all found it difficult to light on something that might help us until the next blunder arrived.

Presently the chicken was brought in, carved and served, and I saw him looking helplessly dejected. I caught a waiter's eye and demanded, "Et le vin donc!"

Debussy started on the chicken, and I knew he found it dry, despite the "giblet-sauce," but when he encountered the stuffing, he commented, dans l'air, without addressing anyone in particular, "What curious people ces américains! After all, there are things which, frankly, I do not understand. First that animal of a crrropfrooo, then a soup which ran through water, meals without bread, and bread they take and stuff into the back-side of a chicken." This met with indignant protests from the ladies while I agreed with him boisterously and to the greater discomfort of us all.

· I now raised my glass, and as he tasted his wine, his face contracted and he hastily put the glass down and stroked his throat. Immediately, in hopes of saving a bad situation, I caught a waiter's eye and asked him to uncork

the champagne which had been standing in its container at my side. I drank
to them and thanked them for the great honor they had shown us in coming, and so on. But when Debussy swallowed his champagne, there was no
mistaking his displeasure, and as I had had a day of arguments and then
the chagrin of such a "dinner party," I suddenly found that nothing on
earth could restrain my anger, and turning to him, in a white heat of fury, I
said, "Would you perhaps prefer to order your own dinner?"

"Ah, I could not ask for better!" he answered without the slightest hesi-
tancy and in a temper which equaled mine!

Disregarding me completely and looking into the vast dining room, he
attracted a waiter's attention by a "pst" sound and holding his arm up,
asked for a menu and called after him, "And bring me the wine card as
well." He ordered a complete dinner: a potage, agneau, a half bottle of a
good French red wine, a salad, a soufflé, and a bottle of champagne (of
which I had a few glassfuls with him). I need add nothing more except that
with good food, he gradually became mollified and toward the end, very
good-natured, so that at parting, he said, "Let's see, this is Wednesday . . .
how about Thursday evening at my house?"

"Mais non, mais non," I answered unceremoniously and irritated to the
bursting point.

"Mais pourquoi pas?" he asked.

"No, no, no, there is no hurry!"

"Very well, then what about Friday, dinner at our house?" But I was too
ill-natured to give any other answer and repeated a series of no, no, no. He
insisted, "I am not going to ask about Saturday and put it off into next
week! What do you say, Thursday or Friday?"

I wanted to burst from that hotel. I never wanted to hear about "dining
out," and so I said unrestrainedly: "No, no, no! And I had to wear this
stupid high hat and to which I am so little accustomed that when we took
a taxi to get down here, I bumped it against the roof of the cab, in stepping
in, and turning around found it lying in the street behind me. Ah, sacré bon
Dieu! No, no, no . . . no more 'diners' for me . . . j'en ai mangé, moi, ce
soir."

Fortunately for me, instead of his resenting the insult of my vulgar play
on words (the approximate English of which might be: I've eaten my cud
this evening), he chortled, apparently amused at my familiarity with French
colloquialisms, and turning to Marie said: "Voyons Madame, it's *your* husband and where you accept he'll be obliged to go—so I ask of you un bon
p'tit 'oui,' and to choose. Voyons, which shall it be, Thursday or Friday?"
She chose and we parted, good-naturedly of course and as friendly as ever.

But in the cab I started all over again: "Sour fruit . . . ice-water soup . . .
ridiculous chicken which chokes one . . . no bread . . . a half-dozen waiters
to tip . . . a couple of hundred francs spent . . . thrown away . . . a hideously
spoilt evening . . . my stomach soured . . . absurd evening clothes . . .

'smile,' smile and be polite when everyone wants to be at each other's throats
. . . all that wine left there . . . the food uneaten . . . and I'm hungry," and I
found myself as furious against Debussy as I had been against my wife! I
swore I would never . . . but never-never! . . . have dinner with him at his
house. "He might be Debussy and God himself," I shouted, "but when it
comes to temper, I play second fiddle to nobody, not even to Old Jehovah!"
I raved and my wife heard torrents of blasphemy in one half-dozen languages. "Never mind, never mind, dear," she soothed, "we'll find something, some scraps at home, and raid the ice-box." This was truly more
than a figure of speech, for there were no ice-boxes in France and the most
modern and expensive apartments of those days boasted a "glacière," a
metal or nickel-plated box, large enough to hold about 1,000 cigarettes,
and which was fastened to the outside of the kitchen window.

After a while, my anger subsided, and I declared I'd agree to have them
at our house, after the approaching Friday, but only on one condition: I
shall have the concierge come upstairs and cook a good ordinary ragoût de
mouton, with plenty of garlic, for that is one dish which every janitress in
any part of France can cook in a manner to make one lick one's chops. "No
outside professional cook!" I yelled, as all the outrageous things of the
evening welled before me, "just the janitor's wife!" Marie agreed with me,
anything to be able to terminate such an evening, and thus I extracted the
promise that at that next time, *I* select the wines and not my well-meaning
wife with her "goût américain."

Friday evening we arrived for dinner, and seemingly even the memory of
our last unfortunate evening together was effaced, nor was there, of course,
any allusion made to it throughout the evening. But inside me it still rankled,
and after one marvelous meat course (for Debussy was also a rare gourmet) the butler approached with a tantalizingly savory ragout of another
kind. I suddenly could not squelch the imp who reared his head within me
and looking up at the butler, I said on the impulse, "Non, merci." At that
instant I detected Mme. Debussy pulling the napkin across her mouth in an
attempt to hide a smile as the man proceeded to Debussy. With outstretched
finger, he motioned to him to return to me and serve me first. I pretended
to become aware of the man's presence only after a few instants and then,
again looking up over my shoulder and inhaling the divine aromas of this
mysterious ragoût, I said quite casually, "Non, merci, je ne mange pas de ça."

Suddenly, to my right, Debussy's temper had gotten under full sway and
in his broken way he began: "Inasmuch as I am a man of intelligence" (and
furiously) "or at least I think I am and what is more, I shall persist in that
belief, je me demande, in fact I should like to know, mon cher ami, how it
is possible that a man as intelligent as yourself, enfin, how is it possible that
you do not eat that?"

"Quite simply because . . . because I don't eat that," I answered suavely
and could feel that the wives were relishing this little tilt.

"Yes but," he insisted, again directing the butler with his oblong covered dish in which those intriguing sauces were playing havoc with my very being, "you have not even tasted it, cher ami, and so how do you know you don't eat it?"

"I taste with my nose, as every intelligent person does," I replied, tapping my proboscis vigorously, "and I concede that the sauces look finer than Correggio and Michel-Ange but . . . tout simplement . . . je ne mange pas ça et merci beaucoup, c'est merveilleux vous savez, mais c'est que comment dirai-je, c'est que je ne mange pas ça!" Mentally I added, "For every dish you'll sniff at hereafter, I'll sneer at yours, even though I might be longing to eat it." I am no longer quite sure, but I think just then Marie requested an extra helping . . . and furiously I started to fill the gap by drinking while I had to endure the agony of her exclamations of wonder and enjoyment. However, I well knew there would yet be a soufflé and a bombe glacée with choice of dessert wines, coffee, and, as usual, two bottles of champagne, later in his room.

Those days I had not yet broken myself of the habit of the demi-tasse after dinner and though my passion for coffee seems inalterable, it is matitutinal and my hunger sonambulistic-nocturnal. Thinking myself a connaisseur of things such as wines, teas, tobaccos, woods (though not of violins), and perfumes, I had always found it difficult to obtain really good coffee in Paris, even though I searched the most exclusive and luxurious stores. However, the Debussy ménage knew where to find excellent coffee and the cook knew how to brew it and thus I drank it, of course without sugar or cream. At a previous dinner, Debussy, at whose left I always sat and thus on the right of Madame, reached for a block of sugar, while my head was turned in conversation with her on the subject of good coffee, and dipping into my cup "schlirrrpt" it with a long and not exactly agreeable sound. Involuntarily I turned quickly and saw he was quite serious about this while he, rather timidly commented, "I hope you don't mind, but you see . . ."

"Not a bit," I interrupted, "mais, je vous en prie! Except of course I have already been drinking out of it," "which does not matter in the least," he continued, "for you see, coffee is forbidden me at night and yet, je suis comm' vous, so that just a few tastes, just on a few pieces of sugar, satisfy me . . . that is, if you don't hesitate to drink it after that." Thus it became a customary thing, when the butler had brought me *my* demi-tasse, for "Claude" to eat his loudly while I drank silent mouthfuls in between. That particular evening I placed the demi-tasse—as usual—between us, for it also amused me to observe, out of the corner of my eye, the canine and feline-like manner in which he got his lump of sugar and then into my cup.

These intimate little dinners (with a little framed menu on the table), each course a masterpiece of a "cordon bleu," the sauces which made me exclaim, "Ah! à côté de ça Beethoven n'est qu'un," completing it by a sound with my lips, or, holding the plate sideways and in many directions, I'd rhapsodize, "and luthiers claim that the secret of Stradivari's varnishes are lost or that Tintoretto was a great artist," and thus on with each wine. These things, always irrepressible in my nature, came to expressions only when with entirely sympathetic people, and what could one ask for more than a genius and poet who seemed to find delight in everything I said or did? When champagne was served in this atmosphere of exquisite perfection of tastes, with finely clothed and tantalizingly perfumed women, the luxury was of the kind that almost suffocates. At such moments I'd sit back in a deep chair and observe Mme. Debussy, who was rather petite, vaporously gowned, and always affecting a little "moue" and who had one, just one, short exotic white curl in a head of short, curly, *golden* hair! I was so little concerned with the arts and wiles of womankind that it never occurred to me that women dyed their hair. Thus, one night at the opera I noticed a gorgeous creature with a head of *blue* hair, my comment was, "She is wearing a wig." Twenty-five and more years ago, women did not paint and rouge as they now do, and, as my wife employed none of those things, I was entirely unconcerned with the subject. Furthermore, as I had begun to turn gray very early and before I was twenty-five had a white streak extending from my forehead straight back through the middle of my head (to anticipate the thoughts of my colleagues, "just like the white line on a skunk's back"), I would muse on the bizarrerie of Mme. Debussy's having a small white curl so closely resembling the fancifully cut little papers one sees wrapped around the bone of a broiled lamb chop. Like Debussy, the Madame had a keen gift for cryptic comments, a love for subtle, sly, and not entirely unmalicious humor, and thus I placed her on a par with her husband and, quite honestly, considered myself among excellently congenial spirits. Furthermore, I had often had the feeling that "Claude" may have played some pages, finished or otherwise, after a period of work and in moments where understanding and rare wines were unforgettably drawing them closer, and what more natural than to have a person of such "raffinement" and exquisiteness of taste for the exotic, the sensual, and voluptuous to make a comment somewhat like the impossible-to-translate, "C'est comme la terrasse des audiences du clair de lune."

Return to Paris, Fall 1913

Returning to Paris, this time as a family man, the immediate problem was to find an apartment, in a desirable neighborhood and within my means, where music-making was at all permitted. Time and again, when arrangements were about to be concluded, the concierge would say, "Might I be permitted to inquire what is the profession of Monsieur?" and I would reply vaguely,

"Artist."

"Oui, Monsieur, ça se voit—one can see that—but what kind? Artist-painter or artist-musician?" and my being obliged to admit the musician part of it, I was treated to "Mes regrets—tout mes regrets" and the door held open for my departure.

On one of these quests, on a street in Passy, I encountered my old friend W. Morse Rummel, whom I had known in Berlin practically since the days when he donned his first long trousers. Surprised at seeing me thus suddenly in Paris after an absence of a few years, Walter said excitedly, "Only yesterday I saw a great admirer of yours."

"Yes?" I queried without particular excitement or curiosity, "Who?"

"Hm—one who speaks of you with the greatest enthusiasm—he chortles when he recalls some anecdote or experience or other—he always speaks of you as 'Quel type' and 'Quel original.'"

"Caro Walter, per l'amore de Dio, give me his name—who is it?"

"Claude Debussy."

"Claude Debussy!" I exclaimed, elated by his remarks, "and *that* 'type' and 'original' says that of me?!"

"Not only that," continued Rummel, "but when I started to speak of your violinistic art—you know everything of what I think, for haven't I written you enough letters?—well, as I was praising you, he almost blew my head off with the vehemence with which he exclaimed—'When it is a question of the violin—there is no one but him! Oh my God, what a character—what an original—How I would like to know where he is at this moment!'"

Thus began that chain of never-ending visits, exchange of dinners and squabbles, fits of ill nature as of clowning or bantering, and of practically no allusions to matters musical, not to speak of musical discussion. How time passed I do not really know, except that I was completely myself with him and was able to speak French well enough to all purposes to be able to banter with him for a few hours at a stretch—or be silent and moody with him for moments which have remained suspended in time and space.

Conception of a Concert

Once upon a time (for I do not remember whether it was in the early days or toward the end), I rang the gate-bell and left a large envelope with the butler, to be given to Debussy. It was the manuscript of an arrangement I had made of *Golliwog's Cakewalk,* a composition which, quite honestly, I had never thought very much of. Several days passed and no word from him regarding it. In the course of the ensuing week or fortnight, an invitation to dinner, but as the evening passed in the usual manner, with never an allusion to Golliwog, I had to assume that my manuscript had gone the way of other things he did not care for . . . the wastebasket.

Thus, in mid-January of 1914, I took him my transcription of his *Minstrels,* and it was a bizarre and daring one, for it was literal (to the original) only in spots and was more an attempt to interpret, on the violin, the spirit of a minstrel-*show* and not Minstrelsy. Abominating the tone color of the mongrel banjo as also its lack of adaptability to anything but "strumming," I had hoped to introduce a new effect (and, as I still believe, for the first time in violin-writing), namely that of a glissando-pizzicato (plucking the strings while at the same time sliding with intensity, as on the guitar) with, incidentally, a type of hitting—literally hitting—the strings with the bow and hair, and not entirely with the stick alone.

I told him all this briefly, and he, seizing the manuscript, immediately took it to the piano while I prepared to unpack my instrument. "You know, it's curious, nevertheless," I said, almost over my shoulder.

"What's that?" he asked over *his* shoulder, for he had spread the music on the piano rack but, naturally, as a real musician *would* do, was studying it in silence. Of course I had for a long time been perfectly aware that I never addressed him personally for I felt that we had long passed the point where I would call him "Monsieur" (a thing which, in his case, would have been beneath good form to do) and yet I knew that were I to always call him "Maître" he probably would have said, "How annoying you are," or more likely, "Is my beard as long as the tedium of some of those deadly bores at the Conservatoire?" In writing him I always addressed him "Mon cher Maître et ami Debussy," and on his part he never . . . never once, except in his last letter to me . . . addressed me in any manner other than "Mon ami" or "Mon cher ami," though I had noticed that his wife, often remonstrating with me, would say, "Voyons Hartmann!"

"You know, it's curious," I continued. "On the way over, in the taxi, I had a curious idea. It wasn't exactly an idea—it was, well, let us say a vision or a sort of premonition. You had written a piece for the piano . . . remarque bien, pour le piano et pas pour le violon! . . . but which, in its limits, did not go beyond the limits of the violin. In other words, it would probably be no more 'pianistic,' let us say and without meaning any offense to you, than some of the piano music of Schumann . . . but it would be entirely *violin-technique* . . . with G as its lowest note, full of violinistic arpeggi, widely dispersed chords, imitation saltando, let us say imitation-pizzicato and who knows but that *you* could do it, even flageolet-tones and . . ."

While I had gone on chatting, at the same time rosining my bow, he had drawn his small pocket-memo from his vest-pocket, written something, and approaching me said, "Ça-y-est! I have it!"

"Quoi donc?" I asked, and pointing to his scribbled words, I read, "Paganini-Hartmann." He then shook hands with me as if thanking me for something!

As in former experiences, we went over the manuscript many times and the places he did not like we experimented with: here an octave higher, there a single note of pizz., here a fuller chord, there some notes omitted from a chord or a run. The spirit and the idea of it all pleased him immensely and after a thoughtful moment or two he said to me, "What if you gave a concert and I played your three transcriptions with you?"

I was speechless with amazement, and as I tried to thank him for his wonderfully generous offer I repeated, "Vous voulez dire that you yourself would play . . . *accompany* . . . these three numbers? That is wonderful, epoch-making, inconceivable, but it is also 'énorme' . . . for *you* cannot appear merely in the role of *accompanist* and, Dieu sait that I do not know how to dare suggest that you play a group of your compositions."

"Ça . . . non!" he retorted categorically, "mais, en réfléchissant, if I could play well enough to give you satisfaction, I would play a sonata with you. There remains then only the question of whose?"

"La vôtre?" I ventured to indicate by pointing my finger at him, yet scarcely believing what a wonderful run of good fortune I was in!

"Mine?" he asked, interpreting my gesture, "a *sonata* by me? That never! Mais jamais de la vie!" There was no mistaking this emphaticness, and his tone was not very amiable.

"But why not?" I asked coaxingly. "Look . . . when you appear, the entire affair is yours anyhow. You offer me the great honor of accompanying your compositions in transcriptions. It is an event of historic importance and, naturally, all the receipts are yours . . ."

"Pouff!" he interrupted, "nonsense! It is not a question of money at all, but not at all. Pas un sou, vous entendez! It is, tout bonnement, that we are friends, and apart from my admiration for you as an artist and musician, you have made possible for the violin some of my things . . . Vous savez, it is a long time that people are expecting things from me, but I find it always more and more difficult to work and to terminate things . . . and so I took the liberty of suggesting, of saying that I thought these transcriptions should be presented in a public concert, and that if you cared to do this, I would give you my collaboration, and all that is, tout bonnement, all there is to it. L'affaire est donc bien simple. On top of it, I am agreed to play a sonata with you, but not one by me, for not only have I none but also because I shall never make one . . . never . . . for that je laisse aux Boches . . . and Teutonic formalism . . . which is completely contrary to my nature."

I noted that he said "make" emphatically and that his temper was in a rapid ascent. I reflected a moment and then said: "Voyons! This concert, which is of monumental value to me, it can wait, can it not? So long as you do me the honor to say you will play a sonata with me, what is more natural than that you, Debussy, should play a sonata by Debussy and to which I have the honor, la gloire, of giving its first performance?"

His mood changed completely and my blood turned cold at his first-uttered word, for drawing himself up he said with great formality, "Monsieur! I have already told you that I shall *never* make a sonata! That kind of *manufacture* . . . je laisse aux Boches!"

From head to heel he was a bristling protest, and as I murmured "Bien, bien" and tried to smile, I thought, "Now you've done it. You've spoilt something that was too wonderful to be true. His mood is gone and now he'll think you tried to get not only a sonata but also its dedication!"

Pacing before me for a few moments, he resumed, "There remains only the question as to which one, and in those matters you know better than I do."

Thinking to be tactful I immediately said, "A French sonata," to which he snapped unequivocally, "There isn't one!" "How about the César Franck?" I suggested, meaning to imply that perhaps in this case he would consider him Belgian, which of course Franck, at all times, was.

Suddenly his face contracted as if in a spasm of pain, and clapping the palm of his hand to his cheek, he rocked back and forth while he moaned, "Oh, mon Dieu . . . ouch . . . oh but what a terrible tooth-ache I have . . . and what a sudden tooth-ache," and then we both roared.

Becoming serious again, he reflected for a while and then, "No, my dear friend, there is only *one* sonata," and I waited in tense curiosity and eagerness for him to name that fortunate composer, "it is Schumann's!"

"Which one?" I asked with ill-concealed disappointment.

"Which one?" he echoed, "then evidently there are more than one?"

"Two," I informed.

"Then it will not be difficult to decide . . . either one or the other . . . at your choice. Il n'y a que Schumann," he continued with warm enthusiasm, "though, apparently you do not care for either of them? And, no doubt you have your reasons?"

"It is that they don't sound," I retorted, "they remain within the fiddle and never come out of the box. Besides, in my opinion, they are too subdued for public performance . . . too intimate, so to speak . . . 'chamber music' . . . true room-music and not for the platform. But now that we have gone over to les Boches, may I ask, why not a Beethoven, even if I would hate to play a Mozart or Händel?"

"Bzzzz!" he exclaimed, scratching the beard on his cheeks with both hands, "quelle barbe . . . ah mon Dieu, quelle Barbe!" Thus again we were in an impasse. After his retort to my suggesting a French composer I could not mention Saint-Saëns, Fauré, d'Indy—and on my part I had no great loves among the German sonatas, with the exception of three by Beethoven, one by Brahms, and six by Bach. In perplexed thinking we smoked, each one trying to hit upon a work that would be mutually sympathetic. Jumping from his seat, he exclaimed: "I have it! Il y a une sonate . . . *Ondine!*"

"*Ondine?*" I echoed casually, "connais pas. Never heard of it!"

"Mais si, mais si," he took it up enthusiastically, "*Ondine—Ondine—*et c'est par Monsieur REI-necke." He pronounced the name as if it were of two words, and running the last two syllables (with the "n" incorrectly attached) together.

"Reinecke," I exclaimed incredulously, "that's curious, for I've never heard it nor even of it," and withheld my opinions of other compositions by him. "Oui-oui, vous verrez. Try to get it immediately and if you like, we'll agree on an appointment for, let us say tomorrow, at four o'clock, with your violin. We'll read it together and afterwards we'll feevoklockay here, chez moi, and the concert can be for as soon a date as you like. It must be about twenty-five years ago that I heard it . . . *Ondine* . . . and it is by Rei-necke."

In a delirium of joy I jumped into a cab and went to the store of my old friend Max Eschig and on entering asked if I might see him personally. I tried to control my excitement and not shout as I informed him that Debussy had just offered to accompany me in three transcriptions and to play a sonata with me, the *Ondine* by Reinecke. Jumping from his desk, he swung open the doors to his bureaux and running below, called to everyone: "It's incredible! Incredible! My friend Mr. Hartmann just tells me that Debussy is going to play a public concert with him and wants to play a sonata by Reinecke . . . vous entendez? . . . of all people, by Reinecke!" This was greeted with loud laughter and various comments by his clerks, and after Eschig had gotten over gesticulating and exclaiming "C'est fantastique! C'est fou! C'est incroyable!" he turned to me and said, "But are you sure, Monsieur Hartmann, that he said, *Ondine,* for that is not even for the violin? It is a sonata for flute."

"Ça m'est égal," I said, waving my hands, "flute . . . violin . . . just so it's by Monsieur Rrrrei-necke, as Debussy pronounces it."

"Very well," said Eschig, "I'll see if we have it, for we don't sell a copy of that old stuff once in a thousand years!" So even a publisher and his clerks knew it was "old stuff," and though I had misgivings, I yet hoped it might be that Debussy remembered a little gem by a "composer" whose tons of notes may have buried a composition with the weepingly poetic title of *Ondine.* The clerks reported that it was out of stock, but Eschig assured me he had some copies in some crates of music in the stock rooms in the cellar and would require a little time to get at them. I told him of my appointment for the following afternoon, and he promised to make the search early in the morning and then send me the copy by one of his clerks, for I told Eschig that I did not much relish sight-reading a work when the musician at the piano was no less a personage than Claude Debussy. However, when two o'clock of the following day had arrived without a sign of a messenger, I had the concierge telephone Eschig, for I would have no phone in my apartment and, as a matter of fact, there was very little need of one. Never a friend of anything mechanical, however much I recognize the indispensability to all mankind of most of these inventions, I found also that every country has its specialties in procedure. One previous call that a party had made for me was carried on with the most formal courtesies and a language of the purity of the Comédie Française. "'Allô? 'Allô? Ah, bonjour Mademoiselle. Auriez-vous la bonté de bien vouloir me donner le numéro: Centrale 5–2658 deux-fois quatre," and I mused at the strangeness of custom in repeating the last number requested and confirming an "8" by saying "twice four." I was told that a copy had "just been found," but that, unfortunately one of the clerks of the store could, just then, not be spared (Europe was not America) and that as I needed the music so urgently I had best come for it myself. Which I did, taking fiddle-box along and going thence straight to my appointment. I knew I'd be on my toes until I saw what kind of music by Reinecke it was that Debussy remembered pleasurably, and after a mere glance or two I determined to let nothing betray my feelings, if at all within my control.

To my surprise, I found Emma-Claude sitting in his music room and knitting, for he had not included Marie in his invitation of the day previous. We started in at once, and it did not take me long to know that all this Leipzig "manufacture," bearing the echoes of a pre-Mendelssohnian-Gade imprint, was maddeningly insupportable to me. Immediately at the termination of the first movement, he expected I might tune, but as I remained silent, looking right at the notes before me, he asked, "We continue?" "O, je vous en prie," I replied, bowing to him. In the second movement, I glanced over the music at Emma-Claude sitting directly before me, and we exchanged a few derisive smiles.

This ready sympathy made me feel sure that by this time, Debussy too had thoroughly felt what we all had felt in that room, and as I again smiled at Emma-Claude and she replied with a scornful twist of her mouth, Claude, glancing up saw this pantomime and turning on her with fury, he asked scorchingly: "Je me demande, je voudrais bien savoir pourquoi est-ce que tu ris dans ta barbe!" which in English is something like, "I'd like to know why you're laughing in your beard!" It was evident that his irritation was against himself, but so long as he was too obstinate to give up (for he surely did not need to play the entire work), and I questioned whether his sense of "justice" compelled him to continue. But continue we did, without comments or even smiles, for we all felt the certainty of accord and as soon as the last measure had been played, he turned toward me, with outstretched hand, and said, "Eh bien, my dear friend, I was wrong. I made a mistake, tout simplement. Excuse it, will you please, and now we must think again for, after all, nom d'un chien, there must be a good sonata to be found somewhere!"

"What about Grieg?" I asked spontaneously.

"Grieg? Perhaps . . . yes . . . pourquoi pas? I don't know it. I've never played it. You have the music? Oh well, so much the better! Why not jump over to your house and also bring Mme. Hartmann with you, and then we will all have tea together." Entering home, I informed Marie of all this while I grabbed the two good Grieg Sonatas, the ones in G and C, and hoping this time he'd choose and decide on one, we flew back over to the Debussys.

A New Tradition Is Born

The biographers of Debussy have created a most bizarre interpretation of this event and the fact that he was playing a Grieg Sonata with me. That Debussy should at all appear with a violinist, partially as accompanist in his own music, rearranged, was sufficiently sensational to start all tongues wagging. I realized all this and knew that day would become historically noted. Today I am humbly proud of the fact that it has remained unique in Debussy's life history as in mine, if I may at all link myself in this manner. Up to that time, he had not made more than perhaps one-half dozen public appearances both as pianist and as conductor, and naturally, always in his own music only.[44] Apparently there seemed to be some necessary reason or justification in Debussy's appearing thus as pianist and in "his" choice of a work by Grieg and none other. How it happened to fall on Grieg has just been recounted by me, yet it became turned into a "gesture to rehabilitate Grieg," to a "championing of his music." Thus Laloy, the critic, made of it a polemic with supposed insinuations against certain "scholastics" in his article "Debussy Holds Out His Hand to Grieg."[45] And thus again, we have an instance of traditions being created whose ludicrous foundations wobble in the risibles! There was, furthermore, another implication, and it went back to the time when Grieg, with one utterance, sacrificed his popularity with the French public.

"L'affaire Dreyfus"

What strange people lived in those days when a writer like [Émile] Zola, at the risk of his life, property, and position, after being mobbed and finally succeeding in escaping to London, whence, in secret hiding, he carried on the fight; when France's outstanding barrister, Maître Fernand Labori, who also survived an attempt at assassination, undertook to fight against their own Government to vindicate a man, a Jew whom they had never seen, but of whose innocence they were sure! What more tragic irony could exist in the world of today than to briefly recall this case which now seems incredible and probably is unknown to most people? There always was, there always will be, anti-Semitism, and about forty years ago, when an innocent man, a French Jew, Captain in the Army, Alfred Dreyfus, was made the scapegoat of French military traitors, it stirred the people of two continents.[46] How incredible that a musician, Grieg the Norwegian, could so deeply resent an injustice to a man of different race and nationality, as to refuse an invitation to appear (at the Paris Châtelet) as conductor in a concert of his own works, before a people (this time, the French) who were capable of such an act. Years after the Dreyfus case had passed on, but was by no means forgotten, the invitation to Grieg was repeated and this time he accepted, only to be greeted by violent hisses and equally tumultuous applause.

Debussy himself was at no time concerned with politics. He was the most unchauvinistic individualist one could desire to know. Completely removed from racial hatreds or nationalistic prejudices, even during the war of 1914, and despite the "Musicien français" which, somehow, became appended to his name.[47]

Minstrels and Its Authorship

Having gone to a concert agency to obtain a desirable hall at as early a date as possible, I went straightway to Debussy to see whether this fitted in with his plans or moods. It was in the afternoon, an unprecedented thing for me to do. As the butler excused himself for preceding me, asking me merely to follow him, I needed no further proof to know that the servants must have had instructions to always admit me, whenever I may call. This is one of the most cherished of my memories and a souvenir of which perhaps only four individuals could have boasted! Following a knock, the butler opened the door and there sat "Claude" at his enormous table, bare as always of any manuscript paper. He rose painfully and coming toward me pressed my hand warmly but in silence, and turning from me started to pace the room. One glance showed me that he was in great torment of a kind peculiarly akin to my own nature and experiences. He was suffering in silent, but not subdued, agony. It was the torture which wracks by its fury; the rage at one's impotency not to be able to destroy the conditions, to break the chains ere the brain—whence there seems no means of escape—burst. He smoked furiously as he took a few rapid steps before me, turning with sudden vehemence from one direction to the other until finally, planting himself in front of me, he cried, throwing wide his arms, with characteristic violence, "Oh, God damn it, God *damn* it!" He stood there, panting heavily, his face showing the struggle of intense anger and the hideous bitterness of trying to "writhe" a smile in mocking disdain of it all!

My heart responding at once, I said sorrowfully, "Ah, oui! Ça, oui! And note well one thing . . . in that, I do not dispute you. I am completely d'accord . . . Nom de Dieu de nom de Dieu!" My mood too was bitter, and after a moment's pause, I added, "And now, if you want me to, vous n'avez qu'à dire, you only need say so." After all, why analyze, why try to philosophize, why wait for explanations, who wants to probe? Is it not all summed up in understanding, even that of which one knows nothing, but in knowing the same agonies or burdens? Who cares to know details, causes, and results?

The point was, he was in revolt as I have been countless hundreds of times, and we understood each other. Rising to go, I held out my hand as I said wearily, "Eh bien, je m'en vais, I'm leaving!"

"Mais non, mais non," he remonstrated briskly, "quite the contrary! Why don't you sit down? Sit down, I beg of you!" I did, and he continued pacing in silence, his hands clasped behind him. I lit a cigarette while I watched him getting calmer, that bitter exhaustion born of an agony which has already half crushed one. "Ah mon Dieu! Ah, how I would like to escape it all . . . de m'échapper du milieu . . . de mon milieu . . . et de moi-même aussi . . . and from myself too!"

"How well I know that too," I sighed heavily.

"Do you know," he added after a pause, "c'est curieux . . . c'est même très curieux . . . it's curious just the same, but you seem to have been sent to me, and just now." He re-seated himself and we continued to smoke in silence. I expected no confidences, but I knew that what so thoroughly arouses hate, anger, bitterness cannot be explained . . . and need not be! I knew nothing of his life and did not even ponder what sorrows or problems wracked my cherished friend, besides his physical aggravations. We sat thus, each turned away from the other, and as the moments went by, I could sense the anger receding, and as if my presence had calmed him, I saw the expression of a mutely enduring sorrow settling even deeper, and I might have expected to hear him say, quietly, "And now, please go home." Instead however, he said, "C'est que . . . I don't exactly know how to say it . . . but it is . . . ," and as he broke off his hesitant words, I said gently, "Try two words, will you please? Just two, I beg of you, and I'll try my best to meet you and see whether I understand, will you?" "It is," he resumed, "it is that . . . enfin . . .," then in a furious outburst, "it is that I find myself in an embarrassed position." And I knew that when a Frenchman uses the phrase, "Je me trouve dans l'embarras," it means a pecuniary difficulty.[48] In answer, I started to open the top button of my vest to reach for the bill-folder in the inner pocket, gently saying: "Listen, you know I haven't great shakes with me but whatever . . ." He held up his hand in sign of protest and said, "It isn't that . . . it isn't that at all. This is not what you can do for me . . . it is something else!"

"Soit!" I exclaimed, "so be it and *whatever* it is, it is already done! I'll give you *anything* that I have! That you know without my saying so. And as for money, I haven't much, but I'll give you every last penny, down to the last *sou*." "Eh bien mon cher ami, here is the situation. Voyez-vous . . . I have never written for the violin for I felt I did not know how to treat it as a solo instrument, and voilà bien des années that people are asking me for something else . . . for I find it always more and more difficult to write. Eh bien, that manuscript which you have made . . . that *Minstrels* . . ."

"By all means, by all means!" I exclaimed, gesticulating with both arms as if I were throwing it at him, "don't mention it! Good God, why did you bother tormenting yourself? If you had merely indicated . . . why, I beg of you . . . most certainly," and suddenly remembering something, I interrupted myself, so to speak, "But wait! What about the bill-boards? It's already announced under my name on the bill-boards" (les affiches) to which he replied temperamentally, "Moi, je m'en fiche des affiches." He had made the almost inevitable pun, but it was not humorously done. The English equivalent was, "What the hell do I care a damn about the bill-boards!" He proceeded: "Published under your name, it brings you nothing and me, eventually, a bit of royalty. Published under my name, as my first violin piece, I could sell it outright, and it pulls me out of a hole!"

"Tant mieux, à la bonne heure," I said, waving my hand at him several times and rising to go. He accompanied me out of the house and into the garden. Suddenly we heard the outer bell ring, and ere I realized what had happened, he had seized me by the scruff of my neck and had pushed me behind a small bush, while he hid himself behind another, close to me. He winked at me as we both heard his servant answer, "Sorry, but Monsieur is not at home." We looked at each other heavy-heartedly for a moment and shook hands in silence, and he closed the gate after me. In a saddened mood I strolled homeward, but I told my wife nothing about my afternoon's experience.

The Concert—5 February 1914

In keeping with a life-long habit, I never practiced on the day of a concert nor even played so much as a scale. I would open the fiddle case several times a day and see whether the E string had given way any more. In that case, I would first relax it, by tuning it down, and then slowly bring it back to the required pitch. In those days we all played on gut strings, which required about two days to get stretched to pitch and stay there. For this reason, all concertizing violinists had double cases which contained two violins, as gut strings often broke during performances and the artist had to make use of his "reserve fiddle," in my case a J. Guadagnini. In the afternoon, with time dragging heavily, I stretched out so as to completely relax, and to darken the room, I let down the outer iron shades. By some inexplicable malchance, the iron curtain folded suddenly and caught the first joint of the index finger of my left hand, and I spent an hour putting cold compresses over it. As a small boy I had once wanted to cut the crust end of an enormous rye bread, and as the big carving knife slipped off, I had severed a tendon of my "first" finger, violinistically speaking. I yet bear that scar! Furthermore, this finger remaining weak, had later suffered a bone fellon, had twice lost the nail, and had often played concerts with a finger cut out of a white glove covering that joint. Thus I had sufficient reasons to be uneasy, besides facing the nervous ordeal with Debussy in the evening ahead of me. A hundred times had I raised and lowered those "jalousies," yet exactly on that day of all days, and just once in my life, did I have to meet with a stupid accident which jammed my weakest finger. I mention this only as an incident to show that scarcely ever does an artist appear publicly except under an abnormal strain or combination of nervous and physical complexities, when not influenced by a mishap, however slight.

When the concert got well under way, I glanced over the top of my music stand at times when Debussy had phrases for the piano alone, and noted quite a few people, in different parts of the hall, leaning aside the wall and making sketches of him. When we returned to play "my" transcriptions, I—of course—stood aside at the termination of each and would take no part of the applause.

The concert terminated, the "greenroom" became jammed with people, and in the midst of compliments, hand-shaking, and signing programs and autograph books, I heard Debussy's voice repeating, "Never! Absolutely never!" I knew its inflections so well to at once recognize that he was in a state of great exasperation. Turning around I saw that he was "cornered," literally crowded against the wall by a mob of autograph hunters, some of whom having come with a stack of three and four books under their arms. In perfect fury I pushed and elbowed to the right and left, and rescuing him from the corner said, "And now that you are saved from those camels . . . que c'est déplorable . . . let me tell you that I had hoped we'd have a little supper together!"

"Naturally," he interrupted, "I had counted on our being together afterwards, cher ami."

"And so," I continued, "if you will indicate the place of your preference, you have your car, down below, so please whisper in my ear and we'll join you as soon as the room clears of some of these who, for lack of a better one, will accept my autograph."

He laughed at my innuendo, playing on a French saying, "for lack of anything better, one sleeps with one's wife," and putting his arm around my neck he said into my ear, "chez Prunier."

"On the wing already," I exclaimed exultantly as I called after him, "and Sapristi but you smell good!"

"So do you," he answered from the door-way, "toujours!"

I see him before me, warm, intense, and overstimulated. "How he played!" he kept repeating. "Ah mon Dieu, how I wish this were only the beginning. I'd like to make music with him toute ma vie!" Two bottles of champagne had not yet exhausted his mood of the evening. He did not speak much or often. He was reliving an evening, one so strange to him, and as tiny figurations in Grieg's writings, sometimes pianistic and at others the contrary, came to him, he would comment and illustrate them with his fingers on the table.

"How he knew how to find all the fine little nooks and crannies!" he repeated. Finally he said, "You play that Grieg as if you had composed it . . . Sapristi, you play it as it you had the devil in your belly . . . le diable au ventre!"

"Exactly the words that Grieg said to me," I exclaimed, ordering more champagne. And for another hour or so I recounted my experiences with Grieg and raved about Norway.

Grieg's Widow's Opinion of Debussy

I sent the widow of Grieg one of the programs, and it is interesting to quote her answer:

Hotel König von Dänemark, Copenhagen, 7 March 1914

Dear Mr. Hartmann,

Many thanks for your friendly letter, which actually came into my hands when I was in Kristiania for a few days. Immediately afterwards I had to go to Berlin, which is why my reply is unfortunately so late getting to you. I had already heard from the Swedish composer, Emil Sjoegren,[49] the cheerful news that Claude Debussy had performed the C Minor (*sic*)[50] with you magnificently, but it brought me much joy to hear it from you personally. I had already heard earlier from Percy Grainger that Debussy loves Grieg, and it can also be heard in his compositions, which are very dear to me. With repeated thanks, your devoted

Nina Grieg.[51]

"That Debussy loved Grieg," wrote Nina Grieg, "I had already heard through Percy Grainger . . . for that matter, one can also hear this in his works."[52] Well, perhaps, and again, perhaps not. But in contrast to this I have another experience to relate.

The Widow of Edward MacDowell on Debussy

It was in a large studio in New York City, in 1940. There was a semipublic concert to which about 150 people had paid to hear a recital of music for voice, piano, flute, and clarinet. The purpose was to raise more funds for the MacDowell Colony, and the program was quite international. There was a "tradition" present in the live widow of the American composer.

About mid-way in that program, a pianist played a miscellaneous group in which was a single composition by Debussy. Hardly had he completed it when Mrs. MacDowell arose and said: "It might interest you to know that Debussy and my husband were fellow students at the Paris Conservatoire, when they were little boys, and that in those days, Edward MacDowell was considered by *far* the greater iconoclast of the two."[53]

A Visit by the Debussys

In the early afternoon of a certain day in June his chauffeur brought me a note which read, "Dear friend: will you be 'at home' (these two words in English) this afternoon? If yes, I would have great pleasure in coming to see you. Affectionately your friend, Claude Debussy." There was also a post-script—"It is understood, n'est-ce pas, that we will be alone?" In reply I thanked him for a visit I was looking forward to with great pleasure and in a postscript assured him we would be quite alone. At about four o'clock, however, all three Debussys arrived, he entering first. He came in timidly, and nervously glancing around asked, "We are quite alone?"

"Quite," I answered, "except for my wife, who is in her room."

"In that case," he said, "we will leave the ladies to get acquainted, and I will sit with you. Where is your room?" By this time he was halfway down the corridor and according to my directions preceded me to my room, while I called to my wife to come and greet our guests.

I was considerably at a tension to know what the object of his announced visit could be, and when he suddenly led me toward my own room, leaving the two women and the little girl alone in the antechamber, I must say I was perplexed by his peculiar behavior. I felt an unusual tenseness about him, a concentrated absorption, but which was quite natural to a man of his gifts and equipment, yet noted withal that he was not ill-natured that day.

He at once ensconced himself at my desk and as he started to quietly examine one object after another—my curious penholders, inkstands, and bibelots, then the pictures on the walls, and finally my books—he seemed to become calmer, and again I began to sense that dream-like aura about him. Thus I watched him, and in silence could hear his heavy breathing, while I knew that when he wishes to break this silence, he will do so and then, who knows, it might be with some picturesque quip, quirk, or a po-etic quiver. He looked at me thoughtfully every once in a while, and gradu-ally I began to understand that however I sought the motive or explanation for this curious visit, it was none other than that he felt a desire for my company and he, quite simply, came over to see me.

There was always a sympathetic warmth between us (and I now realize I was never more myself than with him), and that instinctive understanding which defies analysis and which, furthermore, makes it superfluous, and finally the great tribute, the beauty of such feeling of the older for the younger man brought me the full realization that this wonderful man liked me, that when he wanted to be with me—and in silence—he, in all simplic-ity, came to me, and in silence let me feel and understand it all!

Reseating himself at my desk, he absent-mindedly opened the top drawer and extracting therefrom a sheet of my writing paper, placed it on top of the desk. Looking at me, while silently smoking, he finally said, heaving a deep sigh, "Eh bien, c'est comm' ça," ["it's like that"], and he made a dot on the large blank page. With great emphasis I retorted, "Ah oui, c'est certain que c'est comm' ça!" ["Oh yes, it surely is like that!"] whereupon he added another dot. After a slight pause, he made another dot and using my words, commented, "Ah oui, c'est certain que c'est comm' ça," pointing to the dot, and to which I returned, with but ill-concealed restraint in imitating his voice and gestures, "Ah ça . . . ça c'est indiscutable! C'est certainement comm' ça!" ["Oh that . . . that's incontestable! It's certainly like *that*!"] and I pointed with great positiveness to his last-made dot while we both chuckled at this unanimous philosophical consummation.

Impulsively I bethought me of the set of ancient Norwegian buttons which I had collected with unimagined difficulties on that last tour. They were hand-wrought, of a sort of silver thread, wound round and round and raised to the height of about one half inch and resembled nothing more than a miniature wedding cake. I had begged and bribed these heirlooms and paid and even played for them, from various individuals in Norway, some coming from modest peasant abodes, some from small coastal towns, hundreds of miles apart, and as far north as Tromsö! When I had, at last been fortunate enough to have gathered four of these beautiful though primitive handmade ornaments, my first intention was to give this set to Debussy after I shall have had them connected by links, to serve as cuff buttons. But when I had finally corralled six of them, I decided to keep them for use on a double-breasted evening vest, for *that*, I was very certain, no other mortal could duplicate! However, on the impulse, I decided to give this unique set to Debussy, and as I handed them to him, gave the story of their rarity and the difficulties I had experienced in getting them. Silently he took the set and after a mere glance put them into his pocket without a word, and rising suddenly he rang for the maid. On her appearance, he peremptorily stretched forth his hand and commanded "To tea." Deeply hurt and disappointed, I preceded him to our little salon (as the living room is called), and immediately my wife detected that something must have happened that had changed my mood for I was "making the long nose," as we called it when an emotional slump precipitated into a sudden melancholy. Questioning me with a glance, I said sadly "the buttons!" while Debussy, who had just noticed some music on the piano, instinctively and rapidly approached the instrument.

Charles Martin Loeffler

In a former existence I had innocently loaned some of my rarest books and scores to some of my "best friends," who somehow managed to never return them. In time I learnt to know that one may lend money (which is never repaid), but a book? Not to my best friend. However, the rare does happen, as I found, after marrying in Paris and when some of my boxes, left in storage in Germany arrived, for to my great surprise I found some songs by Loeffler which some guilty conscience must have dropped onto the stacks of music which were always on the piano and my shelves, in my home in Berlin. Thus many, many years later, I was to see in print those very things which I'd hear him "tinker" with, bit by bit and snatch by snatch, on his piano. For, as I used to say, that great and morbid anomaly Loeffler, when he was in the Boston Symphony Orchestra and with whom I practically lived at a period of my adolescence, had the honor of being my teacher, and it was a thing which he, seemingly, never forgave. This, of course, merits deeper analysis, and perhaps someday I may write about that man as he was when I knew him.[54]

I have often wondered what Debussy liked in my company, for music was the one thing we never talked about! It could not possibly occur to me to ask his views on any musician, living or dead, and whatever was commented was the aphorism of the moment, with characteristic brevity or parody on his part, and if I may add, or on mine. Thus it just fitted that I should, quite casually, have those Loeffler songs on the piano rack when he announced his intended visit. As I said, as soon as he saw music, he approached the piano, lit a cigarette, and tilting the piano chair forward, began to play the compositions of Loeffler, sight-reading them flawlessly and at the same time "solfègging" the voice part! On reaching the end of the first song, he remained silent for a full moment and then slowly, very slowly, turned the page. He thoughtfully lit a fresh cigarette and proceeded with the next song in like manner. I think there were three songs, during which we all sat in utter silence while we heard him sing and play and he turned pages for himself.

When he had finally terminated, he turned to me, lit another cigarette and after yet another pause, he asked, "Who is this Monsieur?"

"Eh bien quoi,'" I said non-commitently, "he's Loeffler . . . that's all!"

"Yes, of course," he retorted, "that I see for myself. But what I mean is, who is he?" adding, after a slight pause, "Do you, by any chance, know him?"

"Mmm, mnyes," I answered in a manner as nearly as I could to be noncommittal. "Hm," he grunted, "but then, how old is he?"

"Mmm . . . about your age," I replied with a bowing gesture toward him (Debussy then was about 52–53 years old).[55]

"Tiens," he said indifferently, "that amazes me!"

"But why?" I asked quickly, for I knew that if, up to now, he had been quiet and indifferently perplexed, now would come the explosion and I'd get his real opinion. And it came, with those sudden spurts and hesitancies and in a voice of exasperation. It always started slowly and then was gotten over with in a rushing climax.

"This bothers me," he repeated, "because . . . well . . . I don't know how to say it . . ." (then in full anger and rapidly) ". . . we can all see perfectly that this is a man that cannot write!" And with a furious gesture of his left hand, he brushed it all away while he emitted a sound like "Fffouff."[56]

We went to the dining room where the tea and chocolate were awaiting, and presently Debussy produced the buttons, saying to his wife, "Tiens, mon chat, a present," indicating me with his eyes. In full wretchedness I gazed at those regretted buttons while my wife gave accurate accounts of the places and circumstances under which I had gotten them, for there had been places where the good, honest Norwegian would say that he could not take payment for them because he had not purchased them himself but had inherited them from his father's vest and I saw the least I could do was to give him as nice a gift as was possible to buy in such small towns! The Madame went into ecstasies over the unusual carvings, the almost unde-tectable evenness in the pattern of the various buttons, and showing these to Chouchou kept repeating how kind it was of l'Oncle Arthur to bring such a gift to Papa besides having brought those charming little fur boots to "Chou" and herself. Debussy merely assented with a, "Oui, n'est-ce pas," but made no other remark. Finally it was time for them to take their departure, and, standing in our little ante-chambre, fully dressed, he turned to me very suddenly and said, "Mon cher ami, you have something in this apartment which I should very much like to have!"

Chagrined over the loss of "my" buttons, I said with a flourish, trying to dissemble my hurt, "Ah, at last! Let me see . . . you doubtlessly wish my photograph, n'est-ce pas?" to which he retorted with a sharp "Ffouff" and an abrupt gesture as if brushing a thing aside. "Charming," I drawled, as I made him a mock curtsy, "you really mean my photo *with* my autograph on it, do you not?"

"Non plus," he answered brusquely, but honestly.

"Eh bien," I said with impatience, "you know perfectly well that all you need do is to mention it, or am I supposed to divine?"

Impatiently seizing my arm, he dragged me back to my room and ap-proaching my desk, he rigidly extended his arm and pointing to an object he said, with the greatest emphasis, "That!" It was an oddly shaped stone, about the size of a twenty-five-cent-piece, of a kind of black marble, with a few large white patches at its sides, and which must have rolled for ages down the unique Svartisen . . . the Black Ice Mountain in Norway.[57] An octogenarian in Bergen had presented it to me, telling me he had picked it up, on the Svartisen, on his bridal tour a full half-century ago. Faintly smiling, I waved him toward it and he, seizing the large pebble, immedi-ately pocketed it with the greatest delight. His effusions and joy over it were simply incredible and as he repeatedly squeezed my hands and thanked me over and again, he kept repeating, with one hand on my shoulder, "Oh, isn't he nice! Ah mon Dieu, quel amour d'un homme . . . what a lamb!"

while inwardly I was inconsolable over the buttons. I must add that ever after, the curious pebble kept its place on his writing table, alongside of precious Chinese ceramics and Japanese oddities, and that never again did I see a single specimen of those antique buttons, either in Norway or elsewhere.

Debussy's Last Letter to Hartmann[58]

I could quote from scores of letters, but they would only speak of deep affection and the assurance of an unalterable friendship. Instead, I shall quote a part of the last letter I had from him and which, to make sure that it reach me, he both registered and sent "express." It consists of four very large pages and written in that minute script of his, scarcely legible. When we remember that it was a moribund writing, and mention that a simple tea at Debussy's was as lavish as most dinners, while a dinner at his house was nothing short of sumptuous, his allusions to the repasts we had had together seem all the more touching. I well recall a bizarre dinner at his house when everything was in red, from the tablecloth and napkins to the champagne (mind you, red champagne, if you please, and not sparkling Burgundy!).

The last time I saw him was on his birthday, 22 August 1914, when I took him a few blue cornflowers and teasingly asked him how he was relishing his plate of lentils or macaroni at noon. Dukas, the composer, was there, and I well recall Debussy's characteristic comments about the Germans and their music. "Ouf," he said with disgust, "those people drink whether they are thirsty or not! Everything with them is 'en gros.' A theme must be long, regardless of its contents or value; the longer the better. Then another interminable episode and then another endless theme. Then, after sixteen quarts of beer, they begin a development so long, so long that there is scarcely room in this house to hold it. Take, for instance, the symphonies of Mahler" (which he, of course, pronounced Mal-air) "with its thousand voices and whips, submarines, and what not. Or Monsieur Strauss, who is clever in that he knows how to write nothingness itself. Well, my friend, with it all, their noise does not sound any louder than the finale to Beethoven's 'Fifth,' produced by a small orchestra with but the addition of a contra-faggot!"

In answer to my apprehension that the Germans might pass Namur and head for Paris, he whistled and winked several times, and, as I insistently reiterated that this might become a possibility, he put his hand over his heart and solemnly said, "My friend, I assure you on my word of honor that the Germans will never come to Paris. Do you believe it now?" And, offering him my hand, I told him that I believed him fully, to which he blurted in fury, while his eyes bulged almost out of their sockets, "Besides, let them come and you will see something that you overlooked in your reckoning, for do not forget, dear friend, that every concierge woman in Paris would go out and fight them with knives and forks. Do you hear me—with knives and forks, thus, piff pouff, one in each eye. Voyons, you forget what the women of France are, my dear friend."[59] And now for his letter [CD-23[60]].

24 June 1916

My dear Hartmann,

The principal theme of this letter should be: *I am guilty.* But it is also due to circumstances, because I was first stretched to the limit, and then came the sickness. Ask a doctor what a "rectitis" is . . . then let me know. To be blunt, it's as if one was tearing your rectum out with red-hot pliers. This has been going on since December 1915, and it is not over yet!

Of course, this sickness came after a period of good work.[61] Oh my friend, I have shed tears for it! Add to all these horrors four months of morphine shots that turn you into a walking corpse and eliminate all will power—No matter how much you want to go right, you go left, and other such nonsense.

Anyway, if I gave you the detailed account of my misery, you would begin to cry, and Mrs. Hartmann would think you were crazy.

I had worked like a whole plantation of slaves and was preparing to write the sonata for violin and piano, for which you must be quite impatient. Now I no longer know when I will regain my creative energy? There are times when I feel like I never knew music.

You will never understand what it means to have to make a living. The editors here have become very hardened. And unfortunately I have exhausted all my credit with Durand . . . I cannot count on him anymore! I have threatened to commit suicide, but he acted as if I were speaking about his great-grandfather.

I was very touched by the picture you sent. It seems to me that Gregory has changed a lot?

What are you going to do with this nice young man? I hope you will dedicate him to music? Don't you owe this good goddess at least that?[62]

I don't know if you are aware that my poor aged mother died? During the last days of her life I passed by the house where you lived almost every day, and knowing that you were so far away was of no comfort to me.

The Rummels still live in that strange apartment that you know where there are so many hallways that one thinks he needs a guide to get around. Walter has made tremendous progress on the piano; I have no information about his other regimens.

Do you remember the Grieg Sonata? Dinner at Prunier, how long ago is all that, and how distant from us is this past with so many pleasant moments!

And "Le nègre en chemise"?

And this animal called "Grapefruit"?

Writing to you evokes in me thousands of memories, and I would need even more paper to write them all down!

You must believe that musically, Paris no longer exists . . . except for military music, alas! which is not worth much.

Concerning the Hungarians, I will agree with you, but I don't understand why they did not take the opportunity to separate from the Austrians, whom they hate anyway. Besides you, whom I love with all my heart, I have some friends in Hungary who are absolutely wonderful. Indeed, I will never forget their warm welcome.

War does horrible things, for it separates people for no worthwhile reason, people that we love a great deal.

As for the Viennese, let them all die. They dance like madmen. I will not speak of the Germans for there are no words to describe them.

And now, I will leave you, having been called by those insufferable bandages; and besides, the longest letters are not always the best ones! It would have almost been enough to tell you that I have never forgotten you. Nobody can forget a man like you, dear friend.

You speak of Miss Hartmann as if she were already there? And your confidence in her gender troubles me.

Any time you want to send me some news about yourself, it will be welcomed, believe me, as you believe in my devoted friendship.

Best regards to your wife, of whom my wife speaks often.

Regards to Gregory.

Your old
Claude Debussy
Madame Debussy sends her love to your wife and Gregory.

And when, on a recent tour, I accidentally ran across the news of his death in a morning paper, and after realizing the grief it meant to me and the loss to art, I cabled his wife and child a few words of sympathy. I recalled with bitter sorrow that but a few years ago he, on learning of the birth of my son (the little chap whom he remembered even in his last words to me), had cabled me congratulations and best wishes.[63]

Letters from Claude and Emma Debussy to Arthur and Marie Hartmann

Letters from Claude Debussy to Arthur Hartmann

CD-1

Lundi: 6 XI 08 [i.e., 6 IX 08]

Cher monsieur,
    Ayant été absent de Paris je lis seulement aujourd'hui vos deux aimables lettres. Malheureusement je n'ai rien écrit pour le violon et ne puis par conséquent profiter de votre proposition.
    Si vous passez par Paris, j'aurais grand plaisir à vous serrer la main et je vous prie de croire à mes sentiments de sincère cordialité.

Claude Debussy

Monday, 6 November [i.e., 6 September] 1908

Dear Sir,
    Having been away from Paris, I have read your two kind letters only today. Unfortunately, I have written nothing for the violin and cannot therefore take advantage of your offer.
    If you come to Paris, it would give me great pleasure to shake your hand. Warm regards.

Claude Debussy

CD-2

Jeudi: 17 IX 08

Cher monsieur,
    Excusez-moi, mais je n'ai pas toujours le temps d'écrire comme je le voudrais. Vous pouvez naturellement faire la transcription de *Il pleure dans mon coeur* et cette lettre vous en donne la pleine et entière autorisation.

Croyez, cher monsieur, à mes sentiments de sincère cordialité.

Claude Debussy

————

Thursday, 17 September 1908

Dear Sir,
Forgive me, but I do not always have the time to write as I wish. You may certainly transcribe *Il pleure dans mon coeur,* and this letter gives you full authorization to do so.
Warm regards.

Claude Debussy

CD-3

2 X 08[1]

Cher Monsieur,
Je vous attendrai mardi matin à 11h ½.

Cordialement votre
Claude Debussy

————

2 October 1908

Dear Sir,
I will expect you on Tuesday morning at 11:30.

Cordially yours,
Claude Debussy

CD-4

17 III 10 [*sic*][2]

Cher monsieur,
Le Conservatoire est l'endroit le plus inabordable qui soit à Paris, et, je vous avouerais franchement que ma recommandation auprès de Messager ne serait pas d'un grand poids. En outre, le public de ce con-

cert est terriblement traditionnel—dans le sens le plus étroit du mot!—
La lettre pour Pierné est prête, et partira sur un signe de vous?

En toute sympathie votre
Claude Debussy
    Merci pour l'Amérique!

---

7 March 1910 [*sic*]

Dear Sir,
    The Conservatoire is the most inaccessible place in Paris, and I will
admit frankly to you that my recommendation to Messager will not
carry much weight. And besides, the audience for this concert is terribly
traditional—in the narrowest sense of the word! The letter to Pierné is
ready, and will be sent upon your direction?

Sincerely yours,
Claude Debussy
    Thanks for America!

CD-5

10 III 10 [*sic*]

Cher monsieur,
    Enfin, j'ai reçu la réponse de mon ami Pierné à ma demande. Il prétend
qu'il est trop tard pour cette année, et vous conseille de "solliciter une
audition en octobre!" Vous en ferez ce que vous voudrez; quant à moi
cela ne me satisfait nullement et répond mal à ce que j'avais demandé
pour vous.
    Croyez à mon regret de ne pas avoir mieux réussi, et à mon affectueuse
cordialité.

Claude Debussy

---

10 March 1910 [*sic*]

Dear Sir,
    I have finally received an answer from my friend Pierné to my re-
quest. He claims it is too late for this year, and recommends that you

"ask for an audition in October." You can make of this what you wish, but it does not satisfy me at all and is not what I had requested for you.

Be assured of my disappointment at not having succeeded better. Warm regards.

Claude Debussy

CD-6[3]

Cappriccioso [*sic*]
à jouer tous les matins en se réveillant.
et pour mon ami Arthur Hartmann.

Claude Debussy
13 V 10

———————

Cappriccioso
To be played every morning when you wake up
and for my friend Arthur Hartmann.

Claude Debussy
13 May 1910

CD-7

15 V 10

Mon cher ami,

Que l'affaire d'Amérique réussisse ou ne réussisse pas, je tiens à vous dire toute ma sympathique reconnaissance, pour ce que vous m'avez montré de dévouement.

En y réfléchissant, votre dernier conseil est excellent! Il faudra toujours mieux attendre que de partir dans des conditions qui ne sont bonnes qu'à la surface . . . étant donné la perte morale de deux mois et demi sans pouvoir travailler, la somme de $10.000 n'est certainement pas suffisante.

Mes respectueux souvenirs à votre femme et pour vous, mon affectueux dévouement.

Claude Debussy
P. S. Tout bien pesé, mon dernier mot est *$15.000* pour *24 concerts— pour les deux mois!*

15 May 1910

My dear friend,

Whether the American project succeeds or not, I would like to express my heartfelt gratitude for the devotion you have shown me.

Your last suggestion, after I've given it some thought, is excellent! It is always better to wait than to go under conditions which are good only on the surface . . . given the emotional loss of two and a half months without being able to work, the sum of $10,000 is certainly not sufficient.

My best regards to your wife and for you, my warm devotion.

Claude Debussy

P. S. All things considered, my final word is *$15,000* for *24 concerts—for two months*!

CD-8

27 VII 10 [*sic*][4]

Mon cher ami,

Voici les conditions dans lesquelles j'accepterais d'aller faire une tournée en Amérique:

I°. $15000 pour janvier-février 1912. Frais de voyage payés. Paris—retour. (Frais d'hôtel à ma charge).

II°. Le nombre de concerts ne dépassera pas 24, à raison de trois semaines. Dans ces concerts je dirigerais l'orchestre [dans] un opéra de ma composition, ou jouerais du piano.

III°. Il est bien entendu que mon ami A. Hartmann me prêtera son concours dans ces divers concerts, il jouera mon Poème pour violon et orchestre.

Votre ami,
Claude Debussy

27 July 1910 [*sic*]

My dear friend,

Here are the conditions I will accept to tour America:

I. $15,000 for January to February 1912. Traveling expenses paid, Paris—round trip (I will pay hotel expenses).

II. No more than 24 concerts in the space of three weeks. In these concerts I will conduct the orchestra in an opera that I have composed, or I will play the piano.

III. It is understood that my friend A. Hartmann will assist me in these various concerts. He will play my Poème for violin and orchestra.

Your friend,
Claude Debussy

CD-9

[24 May 1910][5]

Mon cher ami,
C'est l'exacte vérité . . . je joue du piano (4 *Préludes*) demain soir chez Erard. Je vais faire tout le possible pour vous envoyer des places demain matin.
Je demande à entendre "la fille aux cheveux de lin" jouer du violon, car je ne doute pas qu'elle n'ait un considérable talent!

Amicalement vôtre,
Claude Debussy

My dear friend,
It is absolutely true . . . I will be playing the piano (4 *Préludes*) tomorrow evening at Erard's. I will do everything possible to send you tickets tomorrow morning.
I request to hear "the girl with the flaxen hair" play the violin, for I do not doubt that she has considerable talent!

Cordially yours,
Claude Debussy

CD-10[6]

30 V 10

Cher ami,
Merci pour *La fille aux cheveux de lin*. Re-merci des places pour le concert, où, malgré mon instinctive horreur pour le genre, j'entraînerai Mme. Debussy.

Mes respecteux souvenirs à votre femme et pour vous, ma sincère amitié.

Claude Debussy

———————

30 May 1910

Dear friend,

Thank you for *La fille aux cheveux de lin.* Thank you also for the tickets to the concert, to which, in spite of my instinctive horror for this kind of affair, I will bring Madame Debussy.

My respectful regards to your wife and for you, my sincere friendship.

Claude Debussy

CD-11

[3 juin 1910][7]

Cher ami,

Vous êtes un très grand artiste. Je ne sais pas si les gens qui vous écoutèrent hier soir en ont eu l'impression? En tout cas, je n'ai pas voulu les accompagner, ni les entendre vous féliciter dans "toutes les langues."

J'ai mieux aimé garder en moi le souvenir puissant de votre art qui, par instant, va plus loin que toute la musique!

Merci, et amicalement votre
Claude Debussy

———————

]3 June 1910]

Dear friend,

You are a very great artist. I do not know if the persons who heard you yesterday evening had that impression? In any case, I did not wish either to accompany them or to hear them congratulate you in "all the tongues."

I preferred to keep within myself the strong remembrance of your art which, for the moment, transcends all music!

Thanks, cordially,
Claude Debussy

CD-12

22 VII 10

Cher ami,

J'espère que vous avez de meilleures nouvelles de votre mère, de mon côté, la santé de mon père m'a inquiété ces derniers jours![8]

Croyez bien que vous m'avez "manqué" aussi, et, de ne plus voir votre "chère vieille figure" m'a semblé quelque chose d'extraordinaire! Donc, à bientôt et avec tous nos souhaits pour le complet rétablissement de votre femme,

Soyez sûr de l'amitié de votre
Claude Debussy

———————

22 July 1910

Dear friend,

I hope you have better news of your mother. As for me, my father's health has worried me recently!

Be assured that I "missed" you as well, and, not being able to see your "dear old face" seemed strange to me! So goodbye for now, and best wishes for the complete recovery of your wife.

Cordially,
Claude Debussy

CD-13

Copy of letter—5 Villa Victor Hugo, à porter. Original presented to Edwin Bachmann.[9]

23 VII 10 (6^h)

Cher ami:—

Je rentre et Chouchou me montre la trace charmante du passage de "Uncle Arthur." Je regrette infiniment d'avoir été obligé de descendre dans Paris et j'espère bien vous voir demain.

Comment va votre femme?

Nous voudrions vous avoir à dîner, mais la cuisinière est un monstre d'empoisonnement redoutable et farouche. Soyez tranquille, elle s'en ira et je vais la recommander à un de mes confrères!

Votre ami,
Claude Debussy

---

23 July 1910 (6 o'clock)

Dear friend:—
I returned and Chouchou showed me the charming trail of "Uncle Arthur's" passing through. I'm terribly sorry that I had to go to Paris, and I certainly hope to see you tomorrow.
How is your wife?
We would like to have you to dinner, but the cook is a ferocious and frightful master of poisoning. Don't worry, she will be leaving and I am going to recommend her to one of my colleagues!

Your friend,
Claude Debussy

CD-14

3 VIII 10[10]

Cher ami,
Merci pour les renseignements "violonistiques," cela n'est pas tombé dans l'oreille d'un sourd!
Il est dommage que J. S. Bach soit définitivement mort, sans cela il vous aurait remercié d'avoir pris la défense de sa "Chaconne" contre les interprétations de quelques grands maîtres du violon!!!
Vous êtes décidément un homme rare puisque vous trouvez le moyen d'être un grand virtuose en même temps qu'un artiste délicat et compréhensif!
Il paraît que nous dînons ensemble demain soir au "Majestic." Je vais immédiatement me faire couper la barbe pour avoir l'air américain.
En attendant crions: Vive l'Amérique, Vive la Hongrie, et même, Vive la France! Puisque ces diverses et charmantes nations vont se trouver réunies à la même table!

Votre ami,
Claude Debussy

―――――――

3 August 1910

Dear friend,

Thank you for the "violinistic" information. It did not fall on deaf ears!

It is regretful that J. S. Bach is definitely dead, because he would have thanked you for defending his "Chaconne" against the interpretations of certain great masters of the violin!!!

You are decidedly a rare man, because you have found a way to be a great virtuoso as well as a sensitive and intelligent artist.

It appears that we are having dinner tomorrow evening at the "Majestic." I will immediately have my beard trimmed to look more American.

Until then, let us shout: "Long live America," "Long live Hungary," and even, "Long live France," since these various charming nations will be gathered around the same table.

Your friend,
Claude Debussy

CD-15

27 VIII 10

Cher ami,

Je pense qu'il serait pénible que vous partiez tous les deux sans être venus dîner avec nous. Voulez-vous venir demain dimanche?

Un bon "oui" et les meilleures pensées de nous deux pour vous deux.

Claude Debussy

―――――――

27 August 1910

Dear friend,

I think it would be sad if you both leave without having dinner with us. Would you like to come tomorrow (Sunday)?

A good "yes" and best wishes from both of us to both of you.

Claude Debussy

CD-16[11]

Merci, cher ami d'avoir pensé à moi le jour de votre départ. Vous pouvez être tranquille, je n'oublierai pas votre "pale et mélancolique figure," et votre amitié a toutes les raisons de m'être précieuse.
Mes souhaits d'heureux voyage et ma sincère amitié.

Claude Debussy

Thank you, dear friend, for thinking of me on the day of your departure. You can rest assured, I will not forget your "pale and melancholy face," and your friendship is precious to me in every way.
My wishes for a happy trip. Cordially,

Claude Debussy

CD-17

15 IX 10[12]

Mon cher ami,
Nous voudrions bien suivre le conseil que nous donne votre carte postale, mais, hélas! On ne nous remue pas aussi facilement, et nous sommes condamnés par les circonstances à rester à Paris. Il y fait d'ailleurs un temps abominable! Pluie, vent, ciel gris comme un cor-anglais. Le soleil a mis la "sourdine" jusqu'au prochain printemps . . . si vous croyez que cela vous excite à faire de la musique! C'est beaucoup plus fait pour le suicide.
Naturellement je travaille beaucoup, parce que j'ai besoin de faire de la musique, et que je serai très embarrassé pour construire un aéroplane; mais la musique est quelquefois méchante, même pour ceux qui l'aime le plus! Alors, je prends ma fille et mon chapeau, et je vais me promener au Bois de Boulogne, où l'on rencontre des gens qui sont venus de très loin pour s'ennuyer à Paris!
Je pense à vous, je pourrais même dire que vous me manquez . . . ! (Prenez s'il vous plaît, l'air inspiré et saluez!) Quant au poème pour violon, soyez sûr que je l'écrirai. Seulement en ce moment je suis tout à *The Fall of the House of Usher*. On m'en parle trop, il faut que je finisse, sans cela je deviendrai enragé. Encore une fois, je tiens à écrire, surtout à *cause de vous*; je crois bien que vous serez seul à jouer ce poème. Les autres essaieront et reviendront très vite, au concerto de Mendelssohn.
Nous sommes très contents que votre femme supporte joyeusement le voyage, à tous points de vue c'est une bonne chose et puis qui, mieux

qu'elle, pourra essuyer votre front ruisselant; bercer votre tête fatiguée par le bruit de la gloire?

Allons! Du courage . . . je ne peux pas vous dire, à bientôt puisque vous voilà absent pour de longs mois . . . c'est très mélancolique, mais c'est la vie, qui n'est pas toujours drôle, pourtant elle vous donne (la vie) de temps en temps, l'occasion de rencontrer un véritable ami, doublé d'un grand artiste, c'est assez pour qu'on la remercie.

Dites à votre femme tous nos affectueux souvenirs et croyez à la sincère amitié de votre

Claude Debussy

Miss Chouchou, n'oublie pas Uncle Arthur, elle a même cassé le petit arrosoir, probablement en signe de deuil!

---

15 September 1910

My dear friend,

We would like to do what you suggest in your post card, but unfortunately, we do not move so easily and are bound by circumstances to remain in Paris. Besides, the weather is horrible! Rain, wind, gray sky like an English horn. The sun is "muted" until next spring . . . if you think that this inspires you to make music! It is more conducive to suicide.

Of course, I'm working hard, because I need to make music, and I would be so clumsy for making an airplane; but music is sometimes mischievous, even to those who love it most! So I take my daughter and my hat and go for a walk in the Bois de Boulogne, where one meets people who came from far away to be bored in Paris.

I think about you, and could even say that I miss you . . . ! (Please look inspired and wave). I will surely write the poem for violin. But right now, I am absorbed with *The Fall of the House of Usher.* Everyone talks to me about it, and I will go crazy if I do not finish. Once again, I want to write, especially *because of you*; I think you will be the only one to play this poem. Others will try but will quickly return to the Mendelssohn Concerto.

We are pleased to hear that your wife cheerfully tolerates the trip. It is a good thing from every point of view, for who could better wipe the sweat from your forehead, cradle your head made weary by the sound of glory?

Come now! Take courage . . . I cannot say I will see you soon, since you will be gone for many months . . . it is depressing, but that's life, which is not always pleasant, but occasionally gives you the opportunity to meet a true friend, who is also a great artist. And that's enough for me to be thankful.

Give your wife our best wishes. Cordially,

Claude Debussy
   Miss Chouchou doesn't forget Uncle Arthur. She even broke the small watering can, probably as a sign of mourning.

CD-18[13]

[printed card in English]
   Ye Olde Time Greeting

   Christmas steep you in its sunshine
   Christmas charm away all care—
   And the year that follows after,
   Only smiling aspects wear.

   A Merry Christmas
   From [signed] Monsieur et Madame C. Debussy
   25 XII 10

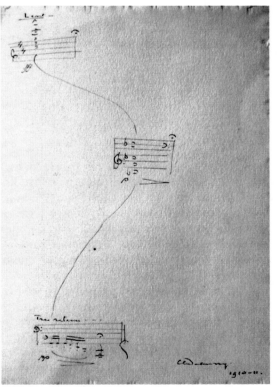

Debussy sketch in Christmas Card, 25 December 1910. Private Collection of Karen Hartmann Kleinmann. Used by permission.

CD-19[14]

Bu 56 M 13
Paris, 7 June [1911] Vic Fch.

Arthur Hartmann
The Waldorf 1110 Main St, Buffalo NY

Affectueuses félicitations des trois Debussy.
3:48 P.M.

Bu 56 M 13
Paris 7 June [1911] Vic Fch.

Arthur Hartmann
The Waldorf 1110 Main St, Buffalo NY

Affectionate congratulations from the three Debussys.
3:48 P.M.

CD-20

29 novembre 13

Mon cher ami,
    Votre lettre m'a fait un grand plaisir, croyez-le bien. Et, si votre amitié vous entraîne à me donner une importance peut-être imméritée, je ne puis tout de même pas vous en vouloir. Comme je vous l'ai déjà dit, l'impression d'un grand artiste tel que vous me sera toujours infiniment précieuse. Ne vous inquiétez donc jamais de penser qu'une amitié comme la nôtre puisse faiblir . . . c'est quelque chose qui est au-dessus des petites comédies humaines, parce que cela est basé sur un commun amour de l'art!
    Vous savez que nous ne pouvons pas venir chez vous samedi soir? C'est particulièrement idiot de manquer une soirée où vous êtes décidé à jouer du violon! Je peux bien avouer que j'ai une espèce de nostalgie de vous entendre. C'est donc comme si l'on m'avait privé de boire pendant des mois, et, qu'au moment où l'on me tend un verre d'eau pure comme le cristal, le verre se brisait! Il y a dans la vie des petits drames comme celui-là, on n'en meurt pas, mais c'est très désagréable.
    Heureusement que cela n'est pas irréparable et j'espère que nous retrouverons des occasions meilleures.

Au revoir, cher ami, si je ne vous vois pas avant mon départ je vous serre amicalement la main et suis comme toujours votre très amicalement dévoué

Claude Debussy

---

29 November 1913

My dear friend,

Your letter gave me great pleasure, believe me. And if your friendship leads you to give me perhaps unmerited importance, I cannot hold that against you. As I have already told you, the impression of you and your great artistry is infinitely precious to me. Do not ever worry that a friendship like ours could fade . . . it is something above petty human comedy, for it is based on a mutual love for art!

You know we cannot be at your place Saturday evening? It is really foolish to miss an evening when you will play the violin! I must admit that I long to hear you. It feels as if I had been kept from drinking for months, and when I was handed a glass of crystal clear water, the glass shattered! There are small tragedies of life such as this. One does not die from them, but they are most disagreeable.

Fortunately, this loss is not irretrievable, and I hope we will have better opportunities in the future.

Good-bye, dear friend. If I do not see you before I leave, please accept my friendship and know I am still your dearly devoted

Claude Debussy

CD-21[15]

[Paris, lundi] 29 décembre 13

Mon cher ami,

On doit toujours avoir le temps de voir ses amis, surtout quand il s'agit de Arthur Hartmann. Je vous attendrai donc mardi et vous prie de me croire toujours votre ami.

Claude Debussy
L'ours russe a été tout à fait aimable pour moi![16]

[Paris, Monday,] 29 December 1913

My dear friend,
   One should always have time to see friends, especially when it is Arthur Hartmann. So, I am looking forward to seeing you on Tuesday.

Cordially,
Claude Debussy
   The Russian Bear has been very kind to me!

CD-22

Lundi, 2 janvier 14[17]

Cher ami,
   Vous pouvez compter sur moi le 5 février prochain. Pour *Minstrels* j'y travaille en ce moment, aussitôt terminé je vous préviendrai.[18]

Amicalement,
Claude Debussy

———————

Monday, 2 January 1914
Dear friend,
   You can count on me for next February 5. I am working on *Minstrels* right now, and as soon as it is finished I will let you know.

Cordially,
Claude Debussy

CD-23

24 juin 1916

Mon cher Hartmann,
   Le motif principal de cette lettre devrait être: *Je suis coupable*. Pourtant il y a aussi la faute des événements, car j'ai commencé par être embêté jusqu'à la gauche, puis est venue la maladie. Demandez à un médecin ce que c'est qu'une "Rectite"[19] . . . et vous m'en direz des nouvelles—Sauf votre respect c'est comme si on vous arrachait le rectum avec des tenailles rougies—Cela dure depuis le décembre 1915 et ce n'est pas fini!
   Naturellement cette maladie est arrivée après une période de bon travail. Ah! mon pauvre vieux, j'en ai pleuré! Ajoutez à toutes ces horreurs, 4

mois des piqûres de morphine, qui font de vous quelque chose comme un cadavre ambulant et supprime toute espèce de volonté—Quant on veut aller à droite, on va à gauche, et autres imbécilités du même genre.

Enfin, si je vous faisais le récit détaillé de mes misères, vous vous mettriez à pleurer, et Madame Hartmann vous croirait devenu fou.

J'avais travaillé comme toute une plantation de nègres et me disposais à écrire cette sonate pour violon et piano dont vous voulez bien être impatient. Maintenant je ne sais plus quand je retrouverai mon élan? Il y a des moments où il me semble que je n'ai jamais su la musique.

Quant à avoir besoin de gagner de l'argent c'est une question dont vous ne vous figurerez jamais assez l'importance. D'abord, ici les éditeurs sont devenus durs comme pierre, et malheureusement j'ai épuisé tout mon crédit chez Durand . . . il ne marche plus! J'ai été jusqu'à agiter le spectre du suicide du suicide [*sic*], mais c'est exactement comme si je lui avais parlé de son arrière grand-père!

La photographie que vous nous avez envoyée m'a beaucoup ému . . . il m'a semblé que Grégory a beaucoup changé?

Qu'est-ce que vous allez faire de ce gentil petit bonhomme? J'espère que vous le consacrerez à la musique? Vous devez assez à cette bonne déesse pour cela—?

Je ne sais si vous savez que ma pauvre vieille maman est morte?[20] Pendant les derniers temps de sa vie je passais presque chaque jour devant la maison où vous habitiez, et de savoir que vous étiez si loin n'était pas pour me consoler.

Les Rummels habitent toujours cet appartement bizarre que vous connaissez où il y a tant de couloirs que l'on pense qu'il faudrait un guide pour le bien connaître.[21] Walter a fait d'immenses progrès sur le piano, sur d'autres gymnastiques je suis mal informé.

Vous rappelez-vous la Sonate de Grieg? Le souper chez Prunier. Comme c'est loin tout cela, et comme cela nous éloigne d'un passé où il y a eu tant d'instants charmants!

Et "Le nègre en chemise"?

Et cet animal de "Grappe-fruit"?

De vous écrire fait remonter en moi et mille et mille souvenirs, il me faudrait du papier encore plus considérable pour les noter tous!

Vous pensez bien que musicalement, Paris n'existe plus . . . si ce n'est de la musique de guerre, hélas! qui ne vaut pas grand chose.

Pour les Hongrois, je veux bien être de votre avis, mais je comprends mal pourquoi ils n'ont pas profité de l'occasion pour se séparer des Autrichiens qu'ils ont du reste en horreur? À part vous que j'aime de tout mon coeur, j'ai en Hongrie des amis tout à fait gentils. Certes, je n'oublierai jamais l'affectueuse manière dont ils m'ont reçu.

Le sort des guerres est abominable, car il éloigne pour des raisons qui n'ont pas de valeur personnelle, des gens que l'on aimait beaucoup.

Letter from Claude Debussy to Hartmann, 24 June 1916. Hartmann Collection, Free Library of Philadelphia. Used by permission. Page 1, top.

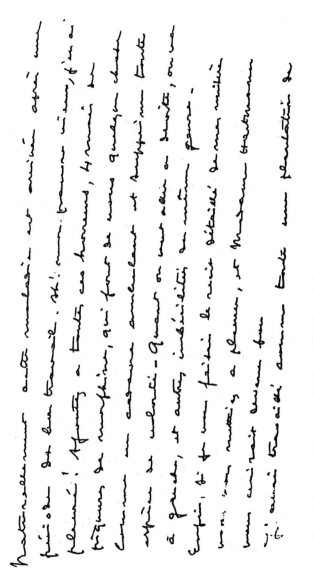

Letter from Debussy to Hartmann, 24 June 1916. Page 1, bottom.

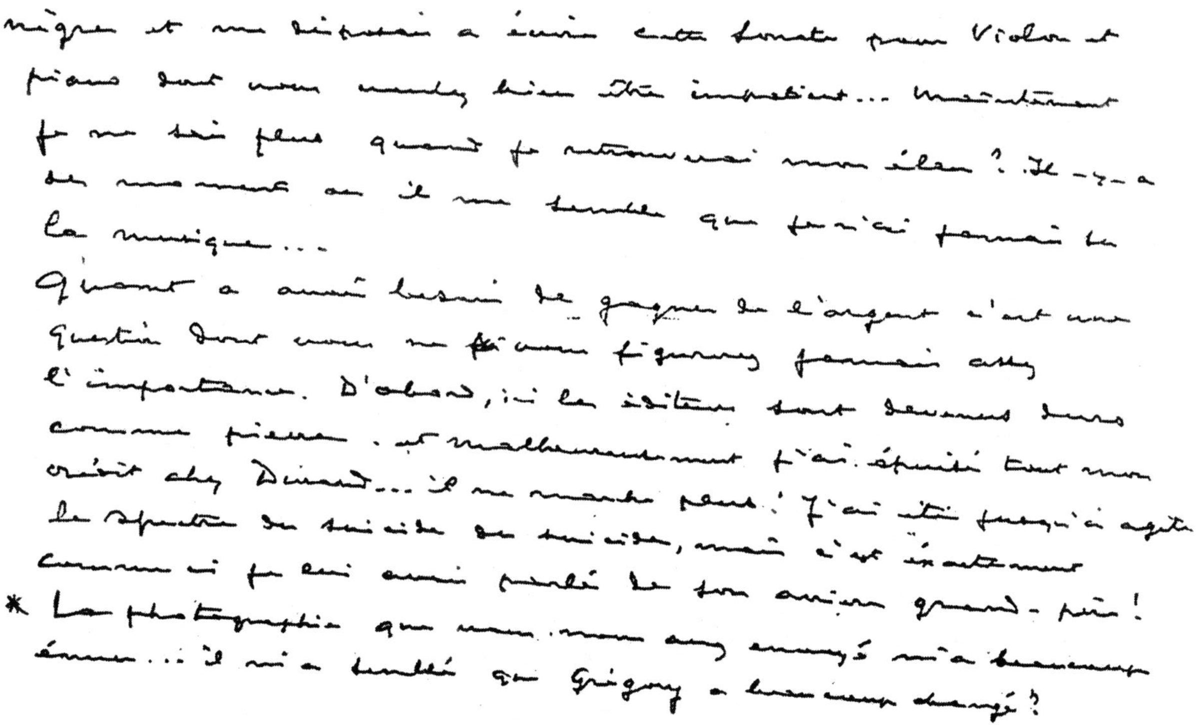

Letter from Debussy to Hartmann, 24 June 1916. Page 2, top.

Quant aux Viennois ils peuvent tous mourir. Ce sont des danseurs maniaques.—Je ne parle pas des Allemands parce qu'il n'y a pas de mot pour cet emploi!

Et maintenant, je vais vous quitter, appelé par d'impérieux pansements, et puis, les lettres les plus longues ne sont pas les meilleures! Il suffisait presque de dire que jamais je ne vous ai oublié. On n'oublie pas un homme comme vous cher ami!

Vous me parlez de Mademoiselle Hartmann comme si elle était déjà là?[22] Et votre assurance sur son sexe n'est pas sans me troubler?

Toutes les fois que vous voudrez me donner de vos nouvelles elles seront les bienvenues, croyez-le bien, comme à ma vieille amitié dévouée.

Mes affectueux souvenirs à votre femme, dont la mienne parle très souvent aussi.

Respects à Grégory.

Votre vieux
Claude Debussy
Madame Debussy embrasse votre femme et Gregory.

––––––––––

24 June 1916

My dear Hartmann,

The principal theme of this letter should be: *I am guilty.* But it is also due to circumstances, because I was first stretched to the limit, and then came the sickness. Ask a doctor what a "rectitis" is . . . then let me know. To be blunt, it's as if one was tearing your rectum out with red-hot pliers. This has been going on since December 1915, and it is not over yet!

Of course, this sickness came after a period of good work. Oh my friend, I have shed tears for it! Add to all these horrors four months of morphine shots that turn you into a walking corpse and eliminate all will power—No matter how much you want to go right, you go left, and other such nonsense.

Anyway, if I gave you the detailed account of my misery, you would begin to cry, and Mrs. Hartmann would think you were crazy.

I had worked like a whole plantation of slaves and was preparing to write the sonata for violin and piano, for which you must be quite impatient. Now I no longer know when I will regain my creative energy? There are times when I feel like I never knew music.

You will never understand what it means to have to make a living. The editors here have become very hardened. And unfortunately I have exhausted all my credit with Durand . . . I cannot count on him anymore! I have threatened to commit suicide, but he acted as if I were speaking about his great-grandfather.

I was very touched by the picture you sent . . . it seems to me that Gregory has changed a lot?

What are you going to do with this nice young man? I hope you will dedicate him to music? Don't you owe this good goddess at least that?

I don't know if you are aware that my poor aged mother died? During the last days of her life I passed by the house where you lived almost every day, and knowing that you were so far away was of no comfort to me.

The Rummels still live in that strange apartment that you know where there are so many hallways that one thinks he needs a guide to get around. Walter has made tremendous progress on the piano; I have no information about his other regimens.

Do you remember the Grieg Sonata? Dinner at Prunier, how long ago is all that, and how distant from us is this past with so many pleasant moments!

And "Le nègre en chemise"?

And this animal called "Grapefruit"?

Writing to you evokes in me thousands of memories, and I would need even more paper to write them all down!

You must believe that musically, Paris no longer exists . . . except for military music, alas! which is not worth much.

Concerning the Hungarians, I will agree with you, but I don't understand why they did not take the opportunity to separate from the Austrians, whom they hate anyway. Besides you, whom I love with all my heart, I have some friends in Hungary who are absolutely wonderful. Indeed, I will never forget their warm welcome.

War does horrible things, for it separates people for no worthwhile reason, people that we love a great deal.

As for the Viennese, let them all die. They dance like madmen. I will not speak of the Germans for there are no words to describe them.

And now, I will leave you, having been called by those insufferable bandages; and besides, the longest letters are not always the best ones! It would have almost been enough to tell you that I have never forgotten you. Nobody can forget a man like you, dear friend.

You speak of Miss Hartmann as if she were already there? And your confidence in her gender troubles me.

Any time you want to send me some news about yourself, it will be welcomed, believe me, as you believe in my devoted friendship.

Best regards to your wife, of whom my wife speaks often.

Regards to Gregory.

Your old
Claude Debussy

Madame Debussy sends her love to your wife and Gregory.

Letters from Emma Claude Debussy to Marie Hartmann and Arthur Hartmann[23]

ECD-1

Samedi [3 juin 1910][24]—

Que de regrets, chère Madame, de n'avoir pas eu le plaisir de vous recevoir hier tous les deux! Je vous avais quittée si brusquement la veille au milieu de cette foule "en délire," sans vous avoir dit toute la profonde admiration que le merveilleux talent (et ce n'est pas assez dire) de votre mari m'inspirait. Aucun artiste jusqu'au présent ne m'avait causé une impression aussi humainement vibrante. Vous lui direz tout cela mieux que moi, voulez-vous? Et avant votre départ, puis-je vous demander de venir dîner sans cérémonie avec nous mardi ou mercredi?

Pour vous et Monsieur Hartmann, je mets ici l'expression de ma sincère sympathie.

E. C. Debussy

———

Saturday—

Such regrets, dear lady, for not having had the pleasure to see you both yesterday. I left you so abruptly the night before in the middle of that "delirious" crowd without having told you of the profound admiration which the wonderful talent (and this isn't saying enough) of your husband inspired in me. No artist up until now has provoked such a humanely rousing impression in me. You will tell him all that better than I, won't you? And before your departure, may I ask you to come to an informal dinner with us Tuesday or Wednesday?

For you and Mr. Hartmann, my cordial regards.

E. C. Debussy

ECD-2

Mardi [2 August 1910]

Chère Madame,

C'est très gentil à vous de nous vouloir à dîner, ce qui nous sera un grand plaisir. Mais mon mari demande pourquoi "Majestic"? Il craint beaucoup l'habit de rigueur dans ces endroits "Majestiqueux" [sic]. Dites-lui si cela est indispensable et alors à demain Mercredi 7h.¾ où vous voudrez (car jeudi nous ne sommes pas libres). Pardonnez mes questions et recevez pour vous et Oncle Arthur nos très affectueux souvenirs.

Emma C. Debussy
Je crois qu'à "votre" retour Chouchou commencera le violon! Pauvres nous!! Heureusement que *son* maître sera notre récompense.

―――――――

Tuesday [2 August 1910]

Dear Madame,
It is very kind of you to invite us to dinner. It will give us great pleasure, but my husband asks why the "Majestic"? He dreads the obligatory evening dress in places called "Majestical." Tell him whether it is essential, then 'til tomorrow. Wednesday at 7:45 wherever you like (because Thursday we are not free). Forgive my questions and accept our affectionate remembrances for you and Uncle Arthur.

Emma C. Debussy
I think upon your return Chouchou will begin violin lessons! Poor us!! Happily *her* teacher will be our reward.

ECD-3

Vendredi

Chère Amie,
Voulez-vous venir tous les trois demain samedi à 4h ½ prendre une tasse de thé avec nous!

Tendres souvenirs,
E. C. Debussy
Si votre mari m'a pensée "beautiful" au concert l'autre soir maintenant il va s'évanouir!

―――――――

Friday

Dear friend,
Won't the three of you please come tomorrow, Saturday, at 4:30 to have a cup of tea with us!

Best wishes,
E. C. Debussy
If your husband thought me "beautiful" at the concert the other evening, now he is going to faint!

ECD-4

Jeudi

Chère Madame,
Voudriez-vous nous faire le très grand plaisir de venir ainsi que votre mari dîner sans cérémonie samedi prochain à 8 heures?
"Le veston de travail est de rigueur."

Veuillez croire chère Madame à mes sentiments les meilleurs,
Emma C. Debussy
Mille mercis de la part de Chouchou pour le bel arrosoir.

Thursday

Dear Madame,
Would you please do us the great favor of coming—along with your husband—to an informal dinner next Saturday at 8 o'clock?
"Work clothes are compulsory."

My best wishes,
Emma C. Debussy
A thousand thanks from Chouchou for the pretty watering can.

ECD-5

28 novembre 1911

Vous ne savez pas, chère grande petite, combien votre lettre m'a fait plaisir—Il faudra donc si vous m'aimez un peu, être moins avare de vos nouvelles.
Ce bijou de fils m'intéresse infiniment et je vous serai très reconnaissante de m'envoyer n'importe quelle photo m'indiquant sa chère petite trompette qu'il me pardonne cette familiarité affectueuse!!
Et les mois se succèdent sans que vous nous annonciez votre prochain retour. Je sais bien que le temps n'est guère confortant ici, mais votre amitié nous réchaufferait tous de son mieux!

Nous nous sommes absentés un mois seulement—très heureux de regagner notre logis—mais maintenant si nous avions pu nous éloigner un peu pour rechercher un soleil plus fréquent nous l'aurions fait avec joie—Malheureusement nous ne pouvons pas bouger! Dans quelques mois je serai grand'mère! Jusque-là je vais passer par mille angoisses.

. . .

31 décembre!

Je suis dans mon lit—j'ai une petite congestion du foie—
Je souffre beaucoup mais je vais mieux—
Je pense tout de même à vous trois que j'aime bien et auxquels je souhaite tous les bonheurs et tous les succès—

Votre amie,
Emma Claude Debussy

Aujourd'hui vendredi 19 janvier je retrouve votre ou plutôt "ma" lettre non expédiée!! Excusez-moi je vous en prie—mais vous voyez que je n'ai cessé de penser à vous—et qu'aussi je n'ai cessé d'être souffrante. En ce moment même j'en suis à ma troisième congestion du foie depuis le 1er janvier!! Malgré cela je tenais absolument à vous écrire pour vous remercier et de votre affectueuse lettre et de la délicieuse photo de l'amour de Gregory—riant un peu comme vous à qui il paraît ressembler tout en ayant le front si beau de son papa! Il va rougir—mais c'est vrai—Vous avez deviné mon désir—je souhaitais tant ce portrait! Vous m'avez fait le plus grand plaisir—merci mille et mille fois—je vous écrirai bientôt—cette lettre est "enchantée"—Finira-t-elle par partir, cette fois?

Toute mon affection très sincère,
Emma

---

28 November 1911

You have no idea, dear grande petite, how much pleasure your letter gave me—If you love me at all you must be less miserly with your news.
I find this jewel of a son infinitely interesting, and I would be most grateful if you would send me any picture—no matter which one—pointing out his dear little button nose, if he'll pardon such an affectionate familiarity!!
And the months pass one after the other without any announcement from you about your next return here. I well know that the

weather here is not very comforting, but your friendship would warm us all the more.

We were gone only one month—very happy to return to our home—but now if we could have gone away for awhile in search of more frequent sunshine, we would have done so with joy—Unfortunately, we cannot budge!! In a few months I will be a grandmother! Until then I am going through a thousand anxious moments.

. . .

31 December!

I am in my bed—I have a slight inflammation of the liver—
I am in misery, but I am doing better—
All the same, I think of you three of whom I am so fond and to whom I wish all happiness and success—

Your friend,
Emma Claude Debussy

Today (Friday, 19 January) I found your, or rather "my," letter that was never sent!! Forgive me, I beg of you—but you see that I have not stopped thinking of you—and that I have also not stopped being ill. At this very moment I am enduring my third inflammation of the liver since January first!! Despite this, I absolutely had to write you to thank you for your affectionate letter and the delightful photograph of that little love, Gregory—laughing a little like you whom he seems to resemble while still having the handsome forehead of his father! He will blush—but it's true—You guessed my desire—I so wished for this portrait! You have given me great pleasure—thank you a thousand, thousand times—I will write you soon—this letter is "under a spell"—Will it end by actually going this time?

All my sincere affection,
Emma

ECD-6

Mardi—

Chère Amie,

Excusez ce crayon—mais je suis criblée de *rhumatismes* dans la main droite (et ailleurs aussi!) et à l'encre je suis tout à fait illisible—

Vendredi je dois conduire Chouchou chez Mme. Rummel pour qu'elle rencontre sa petite amie *Denise*[25]—Mon mari était invité aussi mais il n'accepte *aucune* invitation en ce moment parce qu'il a beaucoup à travailler et qu'il a été mis très en retard par près de 4 mois de maladie.

Tous nos regrets et à bientôt, tout de même, j'espère!

Affectueusement à vous trois
Emma Claude Debussy

Tuesday—

Dear friend,

Please excuse the pencil—but I am riddled with *rheumatism* in my right hand (and elsewhere besides) and write totally illegibly with ink—

Friday I must drive Chouchou to Mme. Rummel's to allow her to see her little friend *Denise*—My husband was also invited, but he is not accepting *any* invitations at the moment because he has so much work to do and he was set back by close to four months of illness.

All our regrets, and we will see you soon in any case—at least I hope so!

Affectionately to the three of you
Emma Claude Debussy

ECD-7

Samedi—

Chère Amie,

Je ne savais plus ce que vous étiez devenue (moi hélas j'étais dans mon lit!!). Mais ne nous attendons pas—

Voulez-vous venir prendre une tasse de thé vendredi 2 janvier [1914] à 5 heures? (*tous les trois!*)

Mes tendres souvenirs
Emma C. D.

Saturday—

Dear friend,

I don't know any longer what has become of you (I alas was in my bed!!). But let's not wait—

Would you like to come for tea on Friday, 2 January [1914], at 5 o'clock? (*all three of you!*)

Yours fondly
Emma C. D.

ECD-8

Jeudi soir

Chère grande petite,
    Merci pour vos jolies cartes et vos voeux affectueux pour le nouvel an—Je souhaite tout le bonheur et toute la réussite de vos désirs et toute la santé nécessaire pour jouir de tout cela.
    Cette semaine et la prochaine sont très encombrées à l'heure du thé. Quel soir voulez-vous nous faire le plaisir de venir dîner? Sauf mercredi, nous sommes libres tous les soirs pour le moment (je parle, bien entendu de mercredi 7 [1914], qui est pris!).
    Un mot de réponse vous serez gentille et tous mes regrets de ne pas vous avoir demain.

Tendrement,
Emma C. D.
    Des caresses (s'il les tolère) à Gregory de ma part s'il vous plaît.

Thursday evening

Dear grande petite,
    Thank you for the beautiful cards and your affectionate wishes for the new year—I wish you great happiness, every success, and the good health to enjoy it all.
    This week and next are very booked up at tea time. What evening would you give us the pleasure of coming to dine? Except for Wednesday, we are free every night so far (I mean Wednesday the 7th [1914], which is taken!).
    Would you kindly let me know? And all my regrets for not having you tomorrow.

Fondly,
Emma C. D.
    Embraces (if he'll tolerate them) to Gregory from me please.

ECD-9

Entendu pour mercredi—4h ¾—nous vous attendons avec grand plaisir
tous les trois, tous les trois—

Affectueusement vôtre
Emma Cl. Debussy

Understood for Wednesday at 4:45—All three of us look forward
with great pleasure to seeing all three of you—

Affectionately yours,
Emma Cl. Debussy

ECD-10

Mercredi—

Quel dommage! Nous ne sommes pas libres dimanche! Indiquez-nous
vos jours libres la semaine prochaine et le maître choisira—
Je retourne voir "le roi" que j'avais lâché pour vous—(Samedi)

Toutes nos amitiés fidèles,
E. C. Debussy

Wednesday—

Oh what a shame! We are not free Sunday! Let us know which days
you have free next week and the master will choose—
I am returning to see "the king" whom I had dropped for you—(Saturday)

All our faithful regards,
E. C. Debussy

ECD-11

31 janvier 1914 [postmark][26]

Samedi—

Désolée de vous savoir souffrants—Chouchou va beaucoup mieux,
merci. Merci aussi pour les programmes. Envoyez-moi 4 ou 6 billets.
Pourquoi ne vous mettez-vous pas à côté de moi?

En hâte, tendrement
Emma

---

31 January 1914

Saturday—

So sorry to find out you are ill. Chouchou is doing much better, thank you. Thank you also for the programs. Send me 4 or 6 tickets. Why don't you put yourself next to me?

In haste, tenderly
Emma

ECD-12

Mardi soir

Chère Amie,
Voilà tout ce que je puis avoir pour demain soir—Si vous n'en voulez pas, soyez assez gentille pour me les renvoyer le plus tôt possible.

Affectueusement à vous
Emma Claude Debussy

Tuesday evening

Dear friend,
Here's everything that I have for tomorrow evening—If you don't want them, be kind enough to send them back to me as soon as possible.

Affectionately yours
Emma Claude Debussy

ECD-13

Mercredi—

Chère Amie,
Vous seriez très aimable en m'envoyant le plus tôt possible une vingtaine de programmes.

Affectueusement et très en hâte
Emma C. D.

————————

Wednesday—

Dear friend,
    It would be most kind of you to send me twenty or so programs as quickly as possible.

Affectionately and in great haste
Emma C. D.

ECD-14

30 mai 1914 [postmark]

Vendredi soir

Chère Amie,
    Voulez-vous venir demain soir nous rejoindre au Théâtre des Champs Elysées, loge 18—avec votre mari bien entendu! Répondez-moi le plus tôt possible.

Très affectueusement votre
Emma
    j'ai une écriture d'alcoolique parce que j'ai un rhumatisme au doigt.

————————

Friday evening

Dear friend,
    Would you be so kind as to come tomorrow evening and join us at the Théâtre des Champs-Elysées, loge 18—with your husband, of course! Let me know as soon as possible.

Affectionately yours,
Emma
    I have the handwriting of an alcoholic because I have rheumatism of the finger.

ECD-15

Dimanche—

Vous êtes trop gentille chère grande petite de me demander de mes nouvelles. Malheureusement depuis que j'ai eu l'imprudence d'aller samedi soir à Auteuil étant aussi souffrante, je n'ai cessé d'avoir la fièvre, puis une petite angine. Je vais un peu mieux je crois, mais je suis toujours aphone. Je viens m'excuser d'avoir été aussi encombrante et triste chez vous, cela m'apprendra à rester chez moi lorsque je serai dans un pareil état.

Un bon baiser à votre grand garçon pour vous et votre mari, mes meilleurs souvenirs.

Emma Claude Debussy

———————

Sunday—

You are too kind, my dear grande petite, asking how I am. Unfortunately, since I was imprudent enough to go to Auteuil Saturday evening ill as I was, I haven't stopped having a fever, then a little sore throat. I'm doing a bit better, I think, but I am still voiceless. I come to apologize for having been so burdensome and sad at your place. That will teach me to stay home whenever I'm in such a condition.

A big kiss to your big boy. My best thoughts for you and your husband.

Emma Claude Debussy

ECD-16

Mercredi, 3h

Chère grande petite,
Êtes-vous libres tous les deux ce soir? Si oui allez à 9 heures au Théâtre des Champs-Elysées (avenue Montaigne) mon mari dirige un peu (quelle écriture!). Vous trouverez le programme dans les journaux. Il y aura *deux* places pour vous dans la "loge de corbeille lettre B." J'y serai peut-être . . . mais plus bas.

Tendrement votre

Emma Claude Debussy
A long kiss to the dearest Gregory!

Wednesday, 3 o'clock

Dear grande petite,
Are you both free this evening? If yes, go at 9:00 to the Théâtre des Champs Elysées (Avenue Montaigne). My husband will conduct a bit (what handwriting!). You will find the program in the newspapers. There will be *two* seats for you in the "dress circle, letter B." I will be there, perhaps . . . but lower.

Tenderly yours
Emma Claude Debussy
A long kiss to the dearest Gregory!

ECD-17

Mardi—

C'est avec grand plaisir chère Madame, que nous viendrons dîner Samedi très heureux de passer quelques heures avec vous. Donc à bientôt pour vous deux mon très sympathique souvenir et des caresses de Chouchou à partager.

Votre
Emma Claude Debussy

Tuesday—

It is with great pleasure, dear lady, that we will come to dinner Saturday, very happy to spend a few hours with you. So until soon, for you both my very affectionate thoughts and caresses to share from Chouchou.

Yours,
Emma Claude Debussy

ECD-18

Mercredi soir—

Voilà chère amie, puisque vous n'avez pas pu y aller la dernière fois.

Mille tendres pensées
Emma C. D.

––––––––––

Wednesday evening—

Here you are dear friend, since you were not able to attend last time.

A thousand fond thoughts
Emma C. D.

ECD-19

[to Arthur and Marie Hartmann]

Lundi

Madame et Monsieur Hartmann,
Madame et Mademoiselle "Chouchou" sont tout à fait charmées du gentil envoi de "Uncle Arthur." Les oeillets sont délicieux et embaumés! Remerciements accompagnés de regrets et d'affectueux souvenirs pour vous et la chère grande petite que vous emportez—

Revenez vite!
ECD

––––––––––

Monday

Madame and Monsieur Hartmann,
Madame and Miss "Chouchou" were totally charmed by the nice present from "Uncle Arthur." The carnations are delightful and fragrant! Thank you's accompanied by regrets and affectionate remembrances for you and the dear grande petite whom you bring—

Come back soon!
ECD

ECD-20

[to Arthur and Marie Hartmann]

24 décembre [1917]

Merci chers amis pour l'exquis envoi de cette double photo.

Vous devez être ravis d'avoir ces deux amours et je souhaite de tout mon coeur que tous les quatre soyez en bonne santé. Pour l'humeur avec les temps actuels on ne peut guère la changer. Après ces deux ans de "convalescence" le cher maître est encore alité depuis le 6 novembre (!) et très affaibli quoiqu'allant mieux.

Avez-vous jamais reçu un petit ridicule paletot pour le bébé en septembre 1916? Chouchou et mon mari se joignent à moi pour vous envoyer tous leurs affectueux souvenirs.

Votre amie attristée,
Emma Claude Debussy

———————

24 December [1917]

Thank you dear friends for the exquisite present of that double photo.

You must be thrilled at having these two loves, and I wish with all my heart that all four of you are in good health. As for mood, with times being what they are, one can hardly change it. After these two years of "convalescence" the dear master is again confined to bed (since 6 November!) and very weak, although doing better.

Did you ever receive a silly little jacket for the baby in September 1916? Chouchou and my husband join me in sending you all the best.

Your sorrowful friend,
Emma Claude Debussy

ECD-21

[to Arthur Hartmann]

17 mai [1918]

Il faut m'excuser mon cher ami mais ma peine est si écrasante que je n'ai pas encore eu le courage de répondre à tous ceux qui ont eu la compatissante pensée de m'écrire.

Ne vous tourmentez pas. J'ai reçu toutes vos lettres et la dépêche qui les précédait aussi—et tant de sympathie devrait m'aider à supporter une telle douleur. Mais quand on perd un être semblable (et dont j'avais la joie infinie d'être aimée) à la grandeur de cette perte peut seule se mesurer mon malheur.

Je sais—il y a Chouchou que j'adore—et qui m'oblige à ne pas "déserter" l'avenir mais la chère petite ne peut rien remplacer. Et je pleure mon maître bien aimé non seulement pour tout mon bonheur englouti mais pour tout ce que l'on perd de beauté et de joie, lui parti!

Après cette affreuse guerre je vous verrai et je vous raconterai ces années douleureuses que je ne saurais oublier.

Maintenant il faut que je réponde à votre dernière lettre reçue tout à l'heure—j'ai tout de suite cherché le manuscrit que vous recherchez, mais sans le trouver.

Peut-être est-il chez Durand—je lui écrirai demain mais je sais qu'habitant Fontainebleau il ne vient que très rarement à Paris. Dès que je saurai sa réponse je vous écrirai aussitôt. J'espère que ce manuscrit n'est pas égaré.

J'ai reçu un télégramme de M. Varèse mais j'ignore son adresse pour le remercier. Pouvez-vous lui transmettre ma reconnaissance?

J'embrasse vos chers enfants et la grande petite qui doit penser à mon affliction sachant de quelle tendre vénération j'entourais cet être si précieux. C'est un désastre.

Excusez-moi je ne devrais pas écrire car je ne peux pas "régler" ma douleur.

Votre dévouée
Emma Claude Debussy

---

17 May [1918]

You must forgive me, my dear friend, but my pain has been so crushing that I have not yet had the courage to respond to all those who had the sympathetic thought to write me.

Don't worry—I received all your letters and the telegram that preceded them also—and so much sympathy should help me to bear such a sorrow. But when one loses such a person (and by whom I had the infinite joy of being loved) the size of this loss can only be measured against my unhappiness.

I know—there is still Chouchou whom I adore—and who constrains me from "abandoning" the future, but the dear little thing can't replace anything. And I weep for my beloved master, not only for all of my vanished happiness, but for all the loss of beauty and joy, gone with him.

After this awful war I will see you again and I will tell you about these painful years which I will never be able to forget.

Now I must respond immediately to your last letter—I went at once to look for the manuscript you seek but without finding it.

Maybe it is with Durand—I will write to him tomorrow, but I know that living in Fontainebleau, he comes only rarely to Paris. As soon as I know his response, I will write to you promptly. I hope that this manuscript is not lost.

I received a telegram from Mr. Varèse, but I don't know his address to thank him. Could you convey my gratitude to him?

I kiss your dear children and the grande petite who must think of my affliction, knowing with what tender veneration I surrounded this ever so precious being. It is a disaster.

Forgive me—I should stop writing because I can't "control" my sorrow.

Your devoted
Emma Claude Debussy

ECD-22

[to Arthur and Marie Hartmann]

Paris, Hôtel d'Albe
7 ou 8 Oct [1919][27]

Mon Dieu! Comment vous le dire c'est si affreux—et de l'écrire moi-même, quelle torture. Chouchou, ma douce et belle petite fille, ma lumineuse et adorée Chouchou—en quatre jours, elle est partie—! De la diphthérie, d'une méningite les docteurs ne savent pas—ne savent rien! Tout mon trésor toute ma vie—tout ce qui me restait de plus précieux que toute l'image vivante de son père—partie—Elle aussi.

Pleurez sur Elle—faite pour la vie avec toute sa jeunesse sa santé son intelligence.

Pleurez sur Elle—et ayez pitié de moi!

Votre amie désespérée
E. C. Debussy

———————

7 or 8 October [1919]

My God! How can I tell you—it's so dreadful—and to write it myself, what torture. Chouchou, my sweet and beautiful little girl, my radiant and adored Chouchou—in four days is gone. From diphtheria or meningitis—the doctors don't know—they know nothing. My whole treasure, my whole life, all that remained most precious to me—the living image of her father—gone, as well.

Weep for her—made for life with all her youth, her health, her intelligence.

Weep for her—and have pity on me!

Your despairing friend
E. C. Debussy

ECD-23

[from Chouchou's English Governess to Marie Hartmann, in English]

Hôtel d'Albe, Ave George V, Paris
Oct. 18, 1919

Dear Madame,

Madame Debussy asks me to write and thank you and Mr. Hartmann for your beautiful kind thoughts for her in her terrible grief. My poor Madame has just written to you and begs to excuse her not answering your letter at once. It's so very hard for her to write, her sorrow is so great. It is so cruel to have to part with her darling Chouchou. She had grown [into] such a lovely girl. Such a comfort and companion indeed. The light and joy of life for my poor Madame since the loss of Mr. Debussy. Now there seems nothing left. It's so sad and lonely for her. One can only pray to God to help and sustain her in her great sorrow. But such desolation is inconsolable. My poor beautiful girlie, I miss her too terribly so I know how hard it is for Madame. Probably Madame will write again as soon as she feels able. She sends all kind thoughts and thanks to you. Believe me, yours truly

Miss

ECD-24

Hôtel d'Albe, Av. George V, Paris

Madame A. Hartmann
923 Harvard Street
Rochester, New York, USA

15 janvier [1920]—Souvent, très souvent je pense à vous, chère Amie

et je voudrais venir vous le dire et le courage me manque—j'ai trop de peine—je n'en peux plus.

Cette petite était ma seule raison de vivre le maître bien-aimé parti. Maintenant la mort est la seule chose que j'envie. Car cette vie avec le désir inapaisé de les rejoindre est une torture—c'est bien naturel. La solitude et le silence que je recherche me rendent encore plus révoltée contre la Destinée—car ce dernier malheur ne devait pas arriver. Je ne suis pas résignée. Je suis vaincue par la Fatalité.

Ma chère petite Chouchou si pure si bonne si intelligente, si tendre et qui renfermait tant de souvenirs précieux, tant d'amour échangé, je ne la verrai plus!

Oh! Je ne veux pas continuer à vous parler d'Elle, ni de tout ce que son départ peut me causer d'inexprimable détresse . . . je vous ferais trop de peine!

Merci d'avoir pensé à moi en ce jour de Xmas qui n'existera jamais plus maintenant!

Embrassez vos chers enfants pour moi, et gardez pour vous et votre mari les très fidèles et affectueuses amitiés

d'Emma Claude Debussy

---

15 January—Often, very often I think of you, dear friend, and I would like to come tell you so, and yet I lack the courage—I am in too much pain—I can't go on.

This little one was my only reason for living—with the beloved Master gone. Now death is the only thing that I want. For this life with the unquenched desire to reunite with them is a torture—it's only natural. The solitude and the silence that I seek make me even more disgusted with Fate—for this last calamity shouldn't have happened. I am not resigned to—I am conquered by Fate.

My dear little Chouchou, so pure, so good, so intelligent, so delicate, and who contained so many precious memories, so much shared love, I will never see her again!

Oh! I don't want to go on talking to you about her, nor about all that her leaving will cause me in grief beyond words . . . I would cause you too much pain.

Thank you for thinking of me on this Christmas day which, now, will no longer exist for me.

Kiss your dear children for me, and keep, for you and your husband, the faithful and affectionate best wishes of

Emma Claude Debussy

ECD-25

Villa Etchola, Saint-Jean-de-Luz (Bas Pyr.) [Basses Pyrénées]

Madame A. Hartmann
Houghton, New York, USA
Ce 25 août 1920

Quelle charmante surprise chère amie, que l'envoi de votre photo avec vos enfants . . . et sans aucune flatterie, votre fils a l'air de votre frère. Je ne l'aurais pas reconnu seul. La gentille petite que je n'ai jamais vue, vous ressemble infiniment. Que d'années passées déjà—et si terribles pour moi—sans aucun espoir d'allégement! Je me demande pourquoi la Destinée s'obstine à me laisser vivre . . . pour quoi faire? Je ne suis bonne à rien désormais sans Eux!

Depuis un mois je suis dans ce petit coin délicieux où le temps, le ciel, la mer, les fleurs, tout est exquis! Mais pour moi seule . . . comme c'est dommage!

Il fait froid paraît-il à Paris à Dieppe et dans les autres plages normandes. Ici c'est inouï! J'y resterai jusqu'au 15 octobre et après, définitivement, il faudra que je me décide à m'installer (!) à Paris—24 rue Vineuse XVIème—tout à côté du cimetière où reposent mes pauvres amours!

Ne viendrez-vous pas à Paris? Lorsque je serai un peu habituée à mon appartement et que je saurai où (peut-être) trouver une page ou quelques lignes du maître bien aimé je ne manquerai pas d'envoyer ce pieux souvenir à votre mari.

De ma chère petite Chouchou adorée je n'ai que des photos prises par moi—je sais que vous l'aimiez. Je vous en enverrai si vous ne venez pas.

Les très affectueuses mais très tristes pensées de votre pauvre vieille amie

Emma Claude Debussy

---

25 August 1920

What a charming surprise, dear friend, the gift of your photo with your children . . . and without any flattery, your son looks like your brother. I wouldn't have recognized him by himself. The pretty little girl whom I've never seen looks very much like you. How many years have gone by already—and so terrible for me—with no hope of relief! I wonder why Fate insists on letting me live . . . to do what? I'm good for nothing hereafter without them.

For a month I have been in this delicious little corner [of the world] where the weather, the sky, the sea, the flowers, everything is exquisite! But what a shame it is to be here by myself.

It seems that it's cold in Paris, Dieppe, and the other Normandy beaches. Here it's extraordinary! I will remain here until 15 October, and after that, for sure, I must decide to settle in Paris—24 Vineuse Street, 16th—just beside the cemetery where my poor loves rest.

Aren't you coming to Paris? After I've gotten used to my apartment and I am able (perhaps) to find a page or a few lines of the beloved master, I will not fail to send this precious souvenir to your husband.

Of my dear adored little Chouchou, I have only some photos taken by me—I know that you loved her . . . I will send you some if you cannot come.

Very affectionate, but very sad thoughts from your poor old friend

Emma Claude Debussy

ECD-26

[to Arthur Hartmann]

3 janvier 1921

Cher ami,

Mademoiselle Hélène Dufau est dans vos parages pour quelque temps.[28] Je serais heureuse que vous lui fassiez connaître gens et choses intéressant son art, car elle est venue seule. Vous prendrez grand soin d'elle, n'est-ce pas? Pour votre charmante femme et vos chers enfants mes tendres souvenirs.

Très cordialement vôtre
Emma Claude Debussy
Pourriez-vous me donner l'adresse de Lady Sapier? (Speyer, peut-être . . .)[29]

----

3 January 1921

Dear friend,

Miss Hélène Dufau will be in your part of the world for a while. I would appreciate it if you would make her acquainted with people and things concerning her art since she is there alone. You will take great care of her, won't you? My fond remembrances to your charming wife and your dear children.

Very cordially yours,
Emma Claude Debussy
    Would you please give me the address of Lady Sapier? (possibly Speyer . . .)

ECD-27

[to Arthur Hartmann]

Hôtel d'Albe, Avenue George V
11 février [1921]

Mon cher ami,

Il y a un mois à peu près, j'ai écrit à votre femme à l'adresse exacte que mentionne votre lettre. Est-ce que la mienne ne lui est pas parvenue? Cela m'étonnerait—car mon adresse était inscrite "au dos" et dans ce cas elle aurait dû m'être retournée. Elle peut essayer de la réclamer quoiqu'elle ne contienne que de la tristesse et de la douleur—comme tout ce qui est et sera ma vie désormais.

Il y a plusieurs mois—j'avais lu un de vos articles sur mon mari. En France on ne permet pas la publication des lettres—surtout intimes— quand il y a des personnes vivantes de la famille du défunt—on a pensé que vous ne le saviez pas car cela a étonné tout le monde—mais je ne crois pas qu'il s'agisse de l'article ni de la photo dont vous me parlez dans votre lettre—ce qui sera donc nouveau pour moi.

Mon mari avait la trop modeste habitude de déchirer tout ce qui n'avait pas la chance de lui plaire. Aussi ai-je très peu de pages inachevées—presque toutes sans suite et par conséquent jamais signées. À part les manuscrits qu'il me destinait spécialement tous les autres appartenaient à son éditeur. Je ne crois pas que les photographies "officielles" comme les appelait le pauvre cher grand maître, puissent vous intéresser—et elles sont toutes d'avant la maudite guerre. Pendant les trop rapides années vécues auprès de lui, j'ai souvent pris des instantanés—je vous en enverrai.

Le buste de mon mari a été confié au peintre et sculpteur Henri de Groux—mais je ne sais s'il est terminé et j'ignore où il sera placé.

J'ai le poignet droit cassé (le gauche aussi, mais le premier m'interdit toute longue lettre et celle là).

Je voudrais bien savoir si votre femme a ma pauvre lettre?

Paix et bonheur pour vous et les vôtres.

La très malheureuse
Emma Claude Debussy

———————

11 February [1921]

My dear friend,
    It was about a month ago that I wrote to your wife at the exact address mentioned in your letter. Did mine not reach her? This would surprise me—because my address was written on the back and, in that case, it should have been returned to me. She can try to claim it, although it contains only sadness and pain, like all that is and will be my life from now on.
    Several months ago I had read one of your articles about my husband. In France it is not permitted to publish letters—especially intimate ones—when there are family members of the deceased still living. Evidently, you didn't know, because this surprised everyone—but I don't believe that it is the same article or photo that you are telling me about in your letter—which will therefore be new to me.
    My husband had the overly modest habit of tearing up everything which didn't happen to please him. So I have very few unfinished pages— almost all of them abandoned and, as a consequence, never signed. Aside from the manuscripts which he destined specifically for me, all the others belong to his publisher. I don't believe that the "official" photographs, as the poor dear great master called them, could interest you— and they are all from *before* the cursed War. During the all too swift years lived with him, I often took snapshots—I will send you some.
    The making of the bust of my husband has been entrusted to the painter and sculptor Henri de Groux—but I don't know if it is finished and am unaware of where it will be placed.
    I have a broken right wrist (the left as well, but the former prohibits me from any long letter and this one).
    I would really like to know whether your wife has my poor letter?
    Peace and happiness for you and yours.

The very unhappy
Emma Claude Debussy

ECD-28[30]

Hôtel d'Angleterre—Saint-Jean-de-Luz—Basses Pyrénées

Lundi 29 août 1921

    Il faut me pardonner chère amie. J'ai perdu la mémoire, la vue, et beaucoup, beaucoup d'autres choses. Je n'en parle pas, car à côté de mes autres affreux malheurs il me semble que rien ne peut compter!

J'ai aussi reçu le livre—que votre mari me pardonne de ne pas lui avoir répondu encore une fois! J'ai été heureuse d'avoir de vos nouvelles et d'entrevoir la possibilité de votre retour à Paris, mais sans vous décourager bien au contraire—mais pour que vous preniez vos précautions—tâchez de retenir un appartement à l'avance, car ils sont toujours de plus en plus rares et chers!

Ici je suis à l'hôtel, mais j'y suis très mal, à part la vue sur la mer que j'adore. J'y resterai jusqu'au 15 octobre puis je retournerai dans mon triste appartement qui n'est toujours pas terminé.

Mademoiselle Dufau[31] habite à 6 kilomètres d'ici à Guéthary—endroit délicieux—où elle a une villa merveilleuse dans un jardin de féerie avec une vue sur la montagne et sur la mer de toute beauté! Je la verrai probablement et lui transmettrai vos compliments.

La musique? Souvent jouée, rarement bien, *Pelléas* massacré!—alors que souhaiter?? Je ne veux pas vous parler de ma peine—si affreuse, si lourde—je trouve que, malgré tous mes maux, j'ai une santé de fer pour résister à tout ce qui est arrivé et aux soucis incessants qui ont suivi ces catastrophes.

Pour la photo de mon amour de Chouchou je n'en ai que faites par moi en 1918—ici à Saint-Jean-de-Luz—le soleil lui avait fait presque fermer les yeux. Elle devenait plus jolie . . . si intelligente, si sensible jouant du piano, sans travailler, d'une façon si personnelle, avec un son tendre et compréhensif. Pourquoi me l'avoir donnée, pour me la reprendre. C'était toute ma vie après l'affreux départ de son Père . . . et maintenant je suis toute seule. Je sais, j'ai d'autres enfants et deux "petites" petites-filles—charmantes—mais ce n'est pas la même chose! Je n'ai pas besoin de vivre et je reste toujours là. . . . Pourquoi faire? Supporter tous les ennuis imaginables, moraux, physiques, matériels . . . alors, à quoi bon?

Cette vie à l'hôtel (les maisons à louer étaient d'un prix plus que doublé cette année) est stupide. Je prends tous mes repas toute seule! Je passe presque toutes mes soirées toute seule. Dans cet hôtel je ne connais personne et mes amies demeurent un peu loin pour mes mauvaises jambes. J'ai toujours la pauvre triste Miss[32]—comme un fantôme dévoué—mais dont la vue, la compagnie et le secours sont très peu efficaces.

Je crois que je vous ai assez ennuyée avec toutes mes plaintes.

Embrassez vos enfants pour moi. Transmettez toutes mes amitiés dévouées à votre mari et croyez-moi très sincèrement et fidèlement votre vieille amie

Emma Claude Debussy

Monday, 29 August 1921

Forgive me, dear friend. I have lost my memory, my eyesight, and many, many other things. I don't want to talk about them, because next to my other horrible misfortunes nothing seems to matter!

I have also received the book—may your husband forgive me for not having answered him again! I was glad to hear from you and to know that you might return to Paris. I don't mean to discourage you, quite the contrary—but in order that you take precautions—try to reserve an apartment in advance, because these apartments are getting harder and harder to find and more and more expensive!

Here, I am at the hotel and it is miserable, except for the view of the sea which I love. I will stay here until 15 October, then I will go back to my gloomy apartment, for which I always keep the lease.

Mademoiselle Dufau lives six kilometers from here at Guéthary—a charming place—where she owns a wonderful country house in an enchanting garden with a view of the mountain and of the sea in all their beauty! I probably will see her and will give her your regards.

The music? Often played, rarely played well, *Pelléas* massacred!–what can we expect?? I don't want to tell you about my suffering, which is so horrible and heavy. I do find that, in spite of all my troubles, I have an iron constitution to cope with whatever happens and with the endless worries which have followed these disasters.

For a picture of my beloved Chouchou, I have only the ones I took in 1918—here at Saint-Jean-de-Luz—the sun almost made her eyes close. She was growing more beautiful . . . so intelligent, so sensitive, playing the piano effortlessly, in such a personal manner, with a tender and intelligent sound!! Why was she given to me only to be taken away again?? She was my whole life after her father's terrible passing . . . and now I am all alone. I know, I have other children and two charming little grand-daughters—but it is not the same thing! I have no reason to live and I just stay here. . . . For what? Why put up with all the conceivable moral, physical, and material annoyances? What's the use?

This life at the hotel (the rent for the houses has doubled this year) is stupid. I take all my meals alone. I spend most of my evenings alone. I don't know anybody in this hotel and my friends live a little far for my bad legs. The sad, poor Miss is still with me—like a devoted ghost—whose understanding, companionship, and assistance are not all that helpful to me.

I am sure I have bored you enough with all my moaning.

Give your children a kiss for me. Give your husband my warmest regards.

Most sincerely,
Your old friend,
Emma Claude Debussy

ECD-29

[to Arthur Hartmann]

Mardi 12 juin 1923

Ce que je deviens, mon cher ami? Moins que rien! Quoique mes amis me disent le contraire sans cesse—mais on ne me persuade pas facilement.

La vie, si lourde à supporter de toutes les façons, n'a pas manqué un seul jour de me couvrir de soucis—parfois il me semble que, si petite, je vais être engloutie—mais petite boule que je suis, je flotte! Et en vieillissant je me ratatine dans les peines. C'est un tableau séduisant n'est-ce pas?

Comment vous conseiller de venir à Paris, où on ne trouve pas à se loger même à des prix fabuleux? Et la vie ne diminue pas . . . au contraire. Pourtant je serais si heureuse de vous revoir tous!

Quand penseriez-vous venir? S'il faut que je cherche quelque chose pour vous et que j'aie la même chance que pour moi vous ne serez guère satisfait! J'ai un appartement où je suis perdue—les circonstances qui me l'ont fait prendre—déserter et enfin habiter, seraient trop longues à vous raconter—mais on l'a encore beaucoup augmenté et je n'ai plus qu'un an ½ à pouvoir y rester. Je ne trouve rien!!

Si je vous parlais de ma santé ce serait encore un volume. Mais avec l'affreux double chagrin qui m'habite je trouve que j'ai une santé de fer pour n'être pas morte. La chère musique du maître bien-aimé est mon plus doux refuge mais cela ne peut en rien me consoler—ni de sa disparition ni de l'absence de mon amour de petite fille—on m'a tout pris—et vous qui les avez connus tous les deux pouvez comprendre mon irrémédiable chagrin quoique je puisse paraître.

Mais je vous parle beaucoup trop de moi.

Les journaux doivent vous mettre au courant des très nombreux concerts actuels—il faut que je m'arrête, j'ai ce soir très mal à mes pauvres yeux.

Enfin je mets ici mes souvenirs affectueux pour vous et les chers vôtres.
E. C. Debussy

Jeudi matin 15 juin[33]

Je viens fermer ma lettre, mon cher ami, qui ne vous aura guère intéressé, ne contenant que des tristesses.

"Pelléas" est à moitié "enterré"—car à l'Op. Comique, Mme. Carré ne veut pas quitter le rôle et elle n'est pas capable de le chanter se livrant à l'opérette ou à la grrrande comédie (La Dame aux Camélias!!).[34] Dans toute la saison on a donné deux fois Pelléas où toutes les places sont enlevées dès qu'on l'affiche—mais je me demande même comment on ose le présenter avec de vieux décors fanés et des interprètes de 20ème ordre. La musique est si belle qu'elle résiste à une telle interprétation mais vous avouez que c'est criminel d'abîmer un tel chef d'oeuvre.

Votre accompagnateur virtuose, Ciampi, a épousé Yvonne Astruc—qui j'ai peu entendue—mais on dit qu'elle a un très beau talent.[35] Et en ce moment il y a une avalanche de virtuoses mais ils ne sont pas tous remarquables.

Quand viendrez-vous?

Le livre de "Monsieur Croche" est épuisé et comme toujours on attend l'autre édition. Je vais tâcher de vous en donner un à moi.

Tuesday, 12 June 1923

What am I becoming, my dear friend? Less than nothing! Although my friends tell me otherwise constantly, I am not easily persuaded.

Life, so heavy to bear in every way, hasn't missed a single day of covering me with worries. Sometimes it seems to me, being so small, that I will be swallowed up—but little bubble that I am, I float! And in growing old, I am shriveling up under the difficulties. Not a pretty picture, is it?

How can I advise you to come to Paris where lodgings can't be found, even at incredible expense? And the cost of living is not going down . . . quite the contrary. Nevertheless, I would be so happy to see you again!

When are you thinking of coming? If I have to look for something for you, and I have the same luck I had for myself, you would hardly be satisfied! I have an apartment where I am lost. These circumstances which forced me to take—abandon and finally live in it—would be too long to tell you, but they have again greatly increased and I have no more than one and one-half years that I can stay here—I am finding nothing.

If I told you about my health, it would be another book—but with the awful double sorrow in which I live, I find that I have an iron constitution not to have died. The dear music of the beloved master is my sweetest refuge but that can in no way console me—either for his loss or for the absence of my darling little girl—everything has been taken from me—and you who have known the both of them can understand my incurable grief, no matter how I may appear.

But I speak too much of myself to you.

The newspapers ought to bring you up to date on the very many concerts at present—I must stop. This evening my eyes hurt me terribly.

Finally, I send my love to you and your dear ones. E. C. Debussy

Thursday morning, 15 June

I now turn to finishing my letter, my dear friend, which will hardly interest you, since it contains only sadness.

Pelléas is half "buried" since at the Opéra Comique Madame Carré does not want to leave the role and she isn't capable of singing it, indulging in operetta or "grrrand" comedy (*La Dame aux Camélias*!!). In the whole season *Pelléas* was given twice—and all the seats were snapped up the minute the poster went up—but I wonder how they can ever dare to put it on with a jumble of old sets and less than third-rate performers. The music is so beautiful that it holds its own against such a performance but you will admit that it is criminal to spoil such a masterpiece.

Your master accompanist, Ciampi, has married Yvonne Astruc, whom I have seldom heard, but they say that she is very talented. And right now there is an avalanche of virtuosos but they are not all remarkable.

When will you come?

The book of "Monsieur Croche" is *sold out* and as always one is left waiting for the next edition. I am going to try to give you one of mine.

ECD-30

[to Arthur and Marie Hartmann]

M. et Mme. A. Hartmann
Houghton, New York, US

30 décembre 1923[36]

Mille mercis chers amis pour votre charmant souvenir qui m'a beaucoup touché. Je suis malade et couverte de ventouses![37] Quelle horreur! Je me demande ce que j'attends pour mourir.

Bonheur et santé pour vous et vos chers enfants.

A quand?

Fidèlement,
E. C. Debussy

---

30 December 1923

A thousand thanks, dear friends, for your kind, thoughtful letter which greatly touched me. I am ill and covered with cupping glasses! What a horror! I wonder what I'm waiting for to die.

Happiness and health for you and your dear children.
Until when?

Faithfully,
E. C. Debussy

ECD-31

[to Arthur Hartmann]

Golf Hotel, Saint-Jean-de-Luz

Monsieur Arthur Hartmann
Houghton, New York, US
21 sept 1924

Mon cher ami,
    Votre lettre me rejoint ici où je trouve un peu de calme chaque année
depuis que je suis "seule" car vivant avec des ombres, même au milieu
de la foule ou d'amis très chers, je me sens *"seule."* Et dire merci pour
vous, vous ne savez pas ce que cela est réellement—je serais ingrate si je
ne disais pas que les gens sont bons et affectueux avec moi, m'ayant
suivie depuis tous mes affreux malheurs—mais ils sentent aussi que
pareille plaie ne se cicatrise pas, c'est impossible—je ne veux pas me
laisser aller sur ce sujet pénible car je reste brisée après. Le maître bien-
aimé est venu ici en 1917—il adorait la mer, mais il aurait été trop énervé
en habitant tout à fait près, et l'hôtel n'était pas possible dans l'état où il
se trouvait. Nous avions une villa pleine de roses et avec une vue sur les
montagnes et une rivière exquise—et deux fois par jour, avec une voiture,
je le conduisais, le matin, sur la plage et le soir sur les falaises qu'il adorait.
Il a tout de même prêté son concours (!!) à deux concerts de charité—
avec quelle fatigue! Un à Biarritz avec Poulet[38] et Boskoff—l'autre ici à
St. Jean—toujours avec Poulet et Koubitzky! Vous devinez quelle pouvait
être mon angoisse pendant l'exécution de la sonate, il me semblait chaque
fois qu'il n'irait jamais jusqu'au bout!!! Et quel retour à Paris, c'était
dramatique, pénible—mais trop long à vous raconter.
    Personne ne peut obtenir le livre de Salvy—les conférenciers sont
obligés de l'emprunter aux quelques rares élus d'autrefois pour le
consulter—on ne peut pas en vouloir à Salvy qui a déjà supplié
Dorbon l'éditeur d'en tirer d'autres exemplaires il promet mais n'en
fait rien.
    Pour M. Croche c'est la même chose—Dorbon l'a cédé à Gallimard
(92ème reine française 35 rue Madame je crois!). Mais le volume ne paraît
jamais et il n'en reste pas!

Dès que je saurai quelque chose au sujet du livre de Salvy je vous le dirai.

Oui, on joue *La fille aux cheveux de lin* et d'autres *Préludes* il me semble lorsque c'est bien—à n'en souffre pas mais j'entends des choses au *Cinéma* quelquefois c'est proprement joué mais d'autres . . . quelle torture!

Vous êtes gentil de m'avoir envoyé ces petites photos—vos enfants paraissent charmants—embrassez-les tendrement pour moi ainsi que votre chère, très chère femme. Si je vous racontais tous mes ennuis *ruineux* de logement depuis la mort de mon mari ce serait inouï! Et maintenant encore malgré un homme d'affaires honnête—pour ne pas être "dans la rue" je vais payer une fortune et sans mon fils qui m'aide beaucoup je ne pourrais ni être ici ni vivre à Paris—même avec des soucis—Et qu'est-ce qui m'attend au retour? Depuis 1918, les procès, les comptes arriérés avec Durand de bien avant notre mariage . . . tout—tout m'est tombé "sur le dos"! Je n'en peux plus cher ami.[39]

Pour vous et votre femme mes souvenirs affectueux et fidèles.

Emma Debussy
Répondez-moi à Paris
   J'adore votre "français"

———————

21 September 1924

My dear friend,

Your letter reached me here where I find a bit of peace each year since I've been "alone," for living with shadows, even amidst the crowd or with dear friends, I feel "alone." And to give thanks for you, you don't really know what that is—I would be an ingrate if I didn't say that people are good and caring with me, having stayed with me through all my terrible troubles—but they also sense that such a wound doesn't scar over—it's impossible—I don't want to let myself go over this painful subject because I am crushed afterward. The dear master came here in 1917—he loved the sea, but he would have been too nervous living right by it and the hotel wasn't possible in his condition. We had a villa full of roses and with a view of the mountains and an exquisite stream—and twice a day, with a car, I would drive him, in the morning on the beach, and in the evening on the cliffs which he adored. In spite of everything, he helped out with two charity concerts—with such fatigue! One at Biarritz with Poulet and Boskoff—the other here at St. Jean—always with Poulet and Koubitzky! You can guess how distressed I could be during the playing of the sonata—it seemed to me each time that it would never end!! And what a return to Paris, it was dramatic, painful, but too long to tell you about.

Nobody can get Salvy's book—the lecturers must borrow from among a few rare chosen copies of long ago in order to consult it—one can't hold it against Salvy, who has already begged the publisher Dorbon to print more copies—he promises, but does nothing about it.

. For M. Croche, it's the same thing. Dorbon transferred it to Gallimard (92nd reine française, 35 rue Madame I think!). But the volume has never appeared and there are none left.

As soon as I know anything about Salvy's book, I will tell you.

Yes, *La fille aux cheveux de lin* is played as well as other *Préludes*; it seems that when played well, they are bearable, but I hear things in the *cinema,* sometimes played properly, but at other times . . . what torture!

It was nice of you to send me the little photos—your children look delightful—kiss them tenderly for me as well as your dear, dear wife. If I told you all of my *disastrous* troubles with housing since the death of my husband, it would be unbelievable. And now, again, in spite of an honest business manager—in order not to be "on the street" I must pay a fortune, and without my son who helps me a lot I could neither be here nor live in Paris—even with [financial] worries—and what awaits me on my return? Since 1918 the legal proceedings, overdue accounts with Durand from well before our marriage . . . all—all has fallen "on my back"! I can't go on, dear friend.

For you and your wife, my affectionate and faithful thoughts.

Emma C. Debussy
Write to me in Paris
   I love your "French"

ECD-32

[to Arthur Hartmann]

Monsieur Arthur Hartmann
315 West 79th Street
New York City, US
Paris, 15 mars 1926

Cher ami,

Vous me feriez le plus grand plaisir en vous intéressant au jeune musicien virtuose (1er Prix de piano) porteur de ces lignes. Je suis sûre que vous apprécierez ses dons et son talent. Le maître le connaissait lorsqu'il était enfant et lui trouvait des qualités remarquables. Persuadée que vous serez un guide affectueux pour Daniel Ericourt je vous en remercie mille fois à l'avance.[40]

Mes tendres souvenirs autour de vous et croyez moi très sincèrement vôtre,

Emma Claude Debussy

––––––––––

Paris, 15 March 1926

Dear friend,

It would give me great pleasure if you would interest yourself in this young virtuoso musician (first prize for piano) who is the bearer of these lines. I am sure that you will appreciate his gifts and his talent. The master knew him since he was a child and found remarkable qualities in him. Persuaded as I am that you will be an affectionate guide to Daniel Ericourt, I thank you a thousand times in advance.

My fond remembrances to you. Very sincerely yours,

Emma Claude Debussy

ECD-33

[to Arthur Hartmann]
Paris, 24 rue Vineuse, 16e
26 août [1926]

Mon cher ami,

Je viens un peu tardivement vous remercier de l'aimable accueil que vous avez fait à mon jeune ami Daniel Ericourt qui est enchanté de la situation qu'il va avoir grâce à vous[41]—ayant trouvé le moyen de pouvoir retourner en Amérique. Car maintenant plus que jamais il est très difficile de gagner sa vie, quand on a embrassé la carrière d'artiste, mais aussi parfois impossible d'avoir le nécessaire pour aller trouver un emploi.

Après ce discours fort ennuyeux pour vous qui devez entendre cela souvent je viens vous demander des tas de choses *1o.* de vos nouvelles— car il y a très longtemps que vous ne m'avez pas écrit—*2o.* Quand pensez-vous venir à Paris? *3o.* Croyez-vous que je vous adresse un jeune virtuose (24 ans je crois) 1er prix de piano à 16 ans—élève de Diémer[42]—très musicien jolie sonorité—connaissant toute l'oeuvre du maître et jouant par coeur les 72 morceaux qui composent la partie pianistique—croyez-vous qu'il ait quelque chance de trouver à gagner sa vie en Amérique—

car ici les pianistes russes ont envahi la place—se soutiennent et se refroidissent gonflés d'orgueil du succès obtenu.

Il y en a qui sont merveilleux—le virtuose en question, qui s'appelle M. F. Gaillard (nom bien français!).[43] Il joue également et toujours par coeur, les oeuvres de Ravel, de Darius Milhaud, etc.

Je ne voudrais pas l'engager à partir pour qu'il aille se casser le nez— j'attendrai donc votre réponse avant de lui dire de prendre le bateau.

Pour des raisons matérielles, j'ai dû rester à Paris cet été—les hôtels, les taxes sont d'un tel prix que j'ai abandonné tout séjour à la mer ce qui est mortellement triste pour moi car tous mes amis parents sont partis et je suis très seule . . . avec mes peines.

J'espère que votre femme et vos enfants sont en bonne santé! Embrassez-les pour moi. Et croyez cher ami à ma fidèle et profonde amitié.

Emma Claude Debussy

---

6 August [1926]

My dear friend,

I am a bit late in thanking you for the kind welcome you showed my young friend Daniel Ericourt, who is thrilled about the position which he will have, thanks to you—having found a way to be able to return to America—because now, more than ever, it is difficult to earn one's living when one has embraced the career of an artist, but also sometimes impossible to have what's needed to go find employment.

After this discourse, very boring for you who must hear it often, I come to the point of asking you several things. First, your news—for it has been a long time since you have written to me. Second, when are you thinking of coming to Paris? Third, can I refer to you a young virtuoso (24 years old I think), first prize in piano at 16 years old, a student of Diémer—very musical, pretty tone—knowing the *entire* work of the Master, and playing *by heart* the 72 pieces which comprise his works for piano—do you think he would have any luck at earning a living in America—for here the Russian pianists have invaded the place—they keep themselves going—and they grow cold puffed up with pride from the success they have achieved.

There are some who are remarkable—the virtuoso in question, who is called M. F. Gaillard (a very French name!). He plays equally as well and always by heart the works of Ravel, of Darius Milhaud, etc.

I would not like to invite him to leave and have him find all doors closed to him—so I will await your response before telling him to set sail.

For material reasons, I have to stay in Paris this summer . . . the hotels and rates are of such a price that I have given up my stay at the seaside, which is deathly sad for me because all my close friends have left and I am very alone with my sorrows.

I hope that your wife and your children are in good health. Kiss them for me, and be assured, dear friend, of my deep and abiding friendship.

Emma Claude Debussy

ECD-34

[to Arthur Hartmann]

Monsieur A. Hartmann
315 West 79ᵗʰ Street
New York City, USA
Lundi 13 décembre 1926

Mon cher ami,
    La berceuse du roi Lear a toujours existé—mais n'était pas éditée. J'ai écrit à M. Jean Jobert éditeur 44 rue du Colisée (8e) pour qu'il vous réponde au sujet de ce que vous demandez.
    Le morceau inconnu et trouvé est de 1901—et écrit pour 2 pianos. Soyez persuadé que si je trouve la moindre "note" à votre intention, je vous en avertirai tout de suite.
    Ne viendrez-vous jamais à Paris? Embrassez votre femme et vos enfants pour moi.

Sincèrement à vous
Em Claude Debussy
    Avez-vous lu "M. Croche antidilettante"?
    Il a paru une seconde fois[44]

Monday, 13 December 1926
My dear friend,
    The berceuse from *King Lear* has always existed—but it wasn't published. I have written to the publisher, Mr. Jean Jobert, 44 rue du Colisée (8ᵗʰ), to have him respond to your request.
    The piece that was unknown and found is from 1901—and written for two pianos. Be assured that if I find the least "note" dedicated to you, I will let you know immediately.

Aren't you ever coming to Paris? Kiss your wife and children for me.

Sincerely yours,
Emma Claude Debussy
   Have you read M. *Croche antidilettante*?
   It has been published a second time.

ECD-35

[to Arthur and Marie Hartmann]
[Christmas card]

   M. et Mme. A. Hartmann
   315 West 79ᵗʰ Street
   New York City, USA
   20 December 1926

   [printed] Happy Christmas and a happy year to follow.

   [signed] With best wishes from
   Emma Claude Debussy

ECD-36

[to Arthur Hartmann]

   26 décembre 1928

Pardonnez-moi, grand ami de répondre aussi tardivement à votre lettre, mais je suis si occupée par mille choses pas toujours intéressantes, mais auxquelles je ne puis me soustraire—que les heures, les jours, les mois, passent sans apporter le loisir de faire ce que l'on désirerait et il n'y a place que pour les soucis de toutes sortes et la maladie. Voilà ma charmante existence!—et je vous assure que je n'exagère rien!

J'ai été ravie d'avoir la jolie petite photo de vos "trois enfants"—car la grande petite "a l'air" de la soeur aînée exactement!

J'ai eu le plaisir de faire la connaissance de votre neveu.⁴⁵ Il a eu autant de peine, je pense, à comprendre mon "anglais" que moi son "français"—mais nous nous sommes quittés bons amis tout de même.

Il va faire un beau voyage!

C'est tout ce que j'aimerais—mais seule ce n'est pas possible—et puis tout est trop cher pour moi maintenant! Connaissez-vous Ed. Varèse? Il est à Paris maintenant. Sa musique a-t-elle de la valeur? Il a un air mystérieux et machiavélique.

Donnez-moi bientôt de vos nouvelles. Pourquoi êtes-vous si loin?!!

Embrassez votre chère femme et vos chers enfants pour moi. Tous mes voeux pour 1929 . . . et la suite!

Sincèrement à vous
E. Cl. Debussy

---

26 December 1928

Pardon me, great friend, for responding so late to your letter—but I've been busy with a thousand things, not always interesting, but which I can't avoid. How the hours, the days, the months pass without bringing the leisure time to do what one would like, and there is room only for all kinds of worries and illness. Such a charming existence I have! And I assure you that I exaggerate nothing.

I was thrilled to have the pretty little photo of your 'three children"—for the grande petite "looks exactly like" the older sister.

I had the pleasure of meeting your nephew—he had as much trouble, I think, understanding my "English" as I did his "French"—but we left each other as good friends all the same.

He is going to have a fine journey.

That's just what I'd like [for myself]—but, being alone, this isn't possible—and besides, everything is too expensive for me now. Do you know Ed. Varèse? He is in Paris now. Does his music have any value? He has a mysterious and Machiavellian air.

Send me your news soon—why are you so far away?

Kiss your dear wife and dear children for me. All my best wishes for 1929 . . . and beyond!

Sincerely yours,
E. Cl. Debussy

ECD-37

[to Arthur Hartmann]

Golf Hotel, Saint-Jean-de-Luz, B. P.
Mercredi

Mon cher ami,

Je ne suis ici que depuis avant hier, pas complètement installée—car j'y viens pour deux mois. Mais je réponds immédiatement à votre lettre

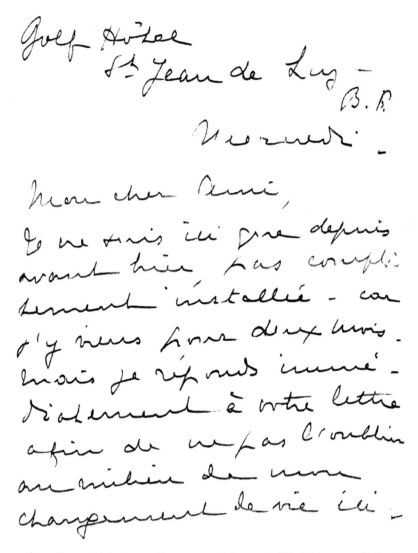

Letter from Emma Debussy to Hartmann, 5 August 1929. Hartmann Collection, Free Library of Philadelphia. Used by permission. Page 1.

afin de ne pas l'oublier au milieu de mon changement de vie ici. Vous me parlez d'un projet de composition pour le violon datant de 1910! Lorsque mon bien-aimé mari a dû être opéré en décembre 1915—il est resté des heures à déchirer tous ces bouts de papier si précieux, où quelquefois il jetait une pensée musicale. Les petits carnets avaient cessé depuis avant la guerre mille fois maudite—car elle précipite les événements cruellement!

Vous me parlez d'un projet
de composition pour le
violon datant de _____
Lorsque mon bien aimé
mari a dû être opéré
en Décembre 1915 — il en
reste des heures à déchi-
rer tous ces bouts de
papier si précieux, où
quelquefois il y avait —
une pensée musicale —
Les petits carnets avaient
cessé depuis avant la

Letter from Emma Debussy to Hartmann, 5 August 1929. Page 2.

Claude ne m'a jamais parlé d'une chose spéciale vous étant destinée—quoiqu'en 1915 il ait composé des quantités inouïes malgré son mal—des études—des sonates—des mélodies—sans parler du merveilleux St. Sébastien qui avait précédé tout cela.

De temps en temps il reprenait "La chute de la maison Usher" mais pour la laisser très peu de temps après. Si jamais je trouvais dans un cahier quelconque ce dont vous me parlez je vous en avertirais immédiatement soyez-en sûr.

J'ai eu la visite de votre ami M. Salzédo mais je n'ai pas eu le plaisir de l'entendre.[46] Il n'aurait guère encouragé le cher Maître à aller en Amérique où d'après lui la cuisine est horrible. Cela seul aurait suffi à l'en étriquer.

Hélas! Toutes ces suppositions ne servent à rien. Je suis comme chaque arrivée dans ce pays où mon mari est venu en 1917—et mon amour d'enfant en 1918—et je les vois dans tous ces chemins sur ces falaises, partout—pour ma très grande douleur—car rien au monde ne peut atténuer une peine aussi cruelle!

Ne viendrez-vous jamais à Paris? À Fontainebleau où il y a un conservatoire américain pour tout l'été?

Je me figure vos chers enfants, mais ils changent si vite et quelquefois si complètement. Embrassez-les tendrement pour moi ainsi que votre chère femme.

Ecrivez—et croyez à mes sentiments fidèles et dévoués.

Emma Claude Debussy
5 août 1929

———————

Wednesday

My dear friend,

I've only been here since the day before yesterday, not completely settled in—for I've come here for two months. But I am responding right away to your letter so as not to forget about it in the middle of my life change here. You spoke to me about a plan for a composition for the violin dating from 1910! When my beloved husband had to be operated on in December of 1915, he spent hours tearing up all those precious little bits of paper, where sometimes he jotted down a musical thought. The little notebooks had ended some time *before* the accursed war—because it cruelly precipitated events.

Claude never spoke to me about anything special intended for you—although in 1915 he composed an extraordinary amount in spite of his illness—etudes—sonatas—melodies—not to mention the marvelous *St. Sébastien* which preceded all of that.

From time to time he would pick up again *La chute de la maison Usher* only to leave it again shortly after. If ever I find in some notebooks that which you are talking about, rest assured that I will let you know immediately.

I was visited by your friend Salzédo, but I did not have the pleasure of hearing him. He would hardly have encouraged the dear Master to go to America where, according to him, the cuisine is horrible—that alone would have been enough to dissuade him from going.

Alas! All these suppositions are useless. I am like any other newcomer to the country where my husband went in 1917—and my beloved child in 1918—and I see them on all these roads, on the cliffs, everywhere, to my great sorrow—because nothing in the world can lessen such a cruel pain.

Won't you ever come to Paris? To Fontainebleau where there is an American conservatory for the whole summer?

I can picture your dear children, but they change so quickly and sometimes so completely. Kiss them tenderly for me, as well as your dear wife.

Please write. Cordially,

Emma Claude Debussy
5 August 1929

ECD-38

31 août [1929?]

Chère Amie,
   Après avoir reçu votre belle triple photo je vous ai écrit à Houghton—simplement—peut-être était-ce insuffisant comme adresse et ne recevez-vous pas ma lettre? Vous pouvez dans tous les cas la réclamer.

En fidèle affection,
E. C. Debussy

---

31 August [1929?]

Dear friend,
   After receiving your beautiful triple photo I wrote to you in Houghton—just that—perhaps it was insufficient as an address and you didn't receive my letter? In any case, you should be able to claim it.

With faithful affection,
E. C. Debussy

ECD-39

[to Arthur Hartmann]

15 avril 1931

Mon cher ami
   Vos quelques lignes, reçues à l'instant, me tourmentent. Où est votre femme? Où sont vos enfants?
   Je ne comprends pas votre solitude.
   Tout le monde est pauvre—autour de moi—et la vie devient de plus en plus coûteuse.
   Donnez-moi de vos nouvelles. Je souhaite vivement qu'elles soient meilleures.

Affectueuses pensées
Em Claude Debussy

———————

15 April 1931

My dear friend,
   Your few lines, just received, worry me. Where is your wife? Where are your children?
   I don't understand your solitude.
   Everyone around me is poor, and life becomes more and more costly.
   Send me your news. I fervently hope that it is better.

Affectionate thoughts
Em Claude Debussy

ECD-40

[to Arthur Hartmann]

15 août 1932

Mon cher ami,
   Votre lettre me rejoint au "Mourillon" près de Toulon—sur la Côte d'Azur et de feu aussi—car il y fait une chaleur tropicale—il y a quatre ans que je n'ai pas quitté Paris et le docteur à voulu que j'aille où il fait "sec"—c'est peut-être sain—mais bien désagréable—je n'ai pas eu les moyens d'aller dans un bon hôtel alors le manque de confort s'ajoute au

manque d'air car les vents variés n'apportent pas un changement dans la température actuelle—Ma fille et les siennes sont à Cannes—mais je n'ai pas de voiture pour aller les voir et j'attendrai sa visite—

Pour le monument (auquel on a daigné penser en 1928) il y a plus d'argent qu'il n'en fallait—il paraît qu'il y a cinquante mille francs qui restent et on doit les donner pour le monument de Fauré—je pense que celui de mon mari à St.-Germain-en-Laye, sa ville natale, est compris dans la somme reçue par souscriptions.[47]

Je suis navrée de vous savoir toujours souffrant et seul—Votre femme ne m'a jamais écrit—et votre séparation m'a peinée et surprise—Je serais contente de savoir que vous allez mieux—écrivez-moi bientôt—

J'étais malade et alitée lorsque Paderewski a donné son concert au profit du monument—

Croyez, cher ami à mes affectueuses et fidèles pensées

Emma Claude Debussy

"Le Prieuré de Lamalgue"
Toulon—Mourillon

———————

15 August 1932

My dear friend,

Your letter caught up with me at "Mourillon" near Toulon—on the Côte d'Azur, also the coast of fire—the heat here is tropical—I have not been out of Paris for the past four years and the doctor wanted me to go someplace "dry"—it is perhaps healthful—but very unpleasant—I don't have the means to stay in a good hotel, so the lack of comfort adds to the lack of air due to the fact that the varying winds bring no change to the actual temperature—my daughter and her family are in Cannes—but I do not have a car with which to visit them and I am waiting for her to come see me.

As for the monument (that they deigned to think of in 1928), there is more money than was needed—it seems that fifty thousand francs remain, and they ought to be contributed to Fauré's monument—I think that my husband's in St.-Germain-en-Laye, his birthplace, was covered by the sum received through subscriptions.

I am heartbroken to know you are still alone and suffering—your wife never wrote to me—and your separation surprised and grieved me— it would make me happy to know that you are doing better—write to me soon—

I was sick and bedridden when Paderewski gave his concert to benefit the monument—

Believe, dear friend, in my affectionate and faithful thoughts

Emma Claude Debussy

"The Priory of Lamalgue"
Toulon—Mourillon

PART THREE

Other Writings of Arthur Hartmann

Charles Martin Tornov Loeffler

Music Education Then and Now

In view of what music education has become today, with thousands of scholarships squandered and violinists graduating with but a limited—one might more truly say only a sectional—knowledge of the literature of their instrument, it is, I think, of interest to see what any violinist of my generation knew and had to know. In my particular case, it must be remembered that I had been a child prodigy and had already studied and played such works as the concerti of Rode, Kreutzer, de Bériot, Spohr, Mendelssohn, Beethoven (!), Molique, Bazzini, Vieuxtemps, and Lipinski, the now obsolete C-Major concerto of Saint-Saëns, the *Romantique* of Godard (with the composer in Paris), and a horde of other virtuoso pieces.

I no longer remember precisely with which etudes and concerto I started my work with Loeffler. But I do remember that if that first lesson was far from being a happy thing, it was not entirely disagreeable.[1] He took everything to pieces, every bit and shred was criticized and analyzed both from the instrumental and the musical viewpoint. Fingerings, bowings, motives, phrases, sections, structure—everything and all came in for minute criticism followed by detailed explanation, and he did this during the better part of an afternoon without once having taken a violin in hand. This, I must say, was staggering and of profound value to me for the rest of my life, and I think that I should here record that during the two years or so that I worked with Loeffler, never did I hear him play, either in public or in giving me instruction. There was but one exception, and this will be related later in its proper place. Loeffler of course did play in public on rare occasions, usually in presenting one of his own works with the Boston Symphony Orchestra. But I aver again the peculiarity of my having had a teacher who never once gave me the living example in any kind of demonstration and whose tone I had never heard. I was unquestionably sure that his "technique"—that is to say, his left hand—had the distinction of any of the then famous violinists of the French School, but as to his tone I had a peculiar feeling that it was feeble and as colorless as his hair.[2] Loeffler had to earn a living, and as circumstances drove him into the orchestra, almost from the start he had come to hate it all bitterly.

I was terribly unhappy already in that first lesson, for I kept asking myself until I thought tears would run from my eyes, "Why does he always yawn?!" Every point that he explained I immediately understood and executed. Things technical as well as musical, not shown me by living example but at times by a few words only, I seized upon with eager instinct and tried at once to remedy or eradicate the defect. Not only in the ways suggested but perhaps in trying to understand what he was explaining, I stumbled onto even other possibilities of changes of position or combinations of bowings, but I suddenly wanted to scream! "Why?" I asked myself again and again, "Why does he *yawn* when I'm trying so hard! Why does he yawn in such an objectionable manner, without even covering his mouth, with letting that disgusting rattle of a sound come out of his open throat! Why does he always sit there squinting at me, always critically and so personally sneering?" After about two hours of this he gave me a sign to stop. In silence he looked at me with squinted eyes narrowly drawn together, and while he kept fingering the beard over his chin he seemed to be reflecting on something. Presently he said, in an absolutely colorless manner, "You know, Osser, I'll tell you somesing. I'll call you Osser" (he was incapable to pronouncing the Anglo-Saxon *th*) "because I am not only the older man but also your teacher. You were born too late—there are no more Sarasates and Ysaÿes and Wieniawskis—but I think that some day you'll play so that even my humble self will approve and perhaps find some pleasure in it." Bowing to him with flushed face, I did not know in my inner conflict whether the man's mean encouragement meant more to me than the cruel and humiliating way in which he gave it. Another pupil arrived. We were not introduced to each other. I packed my instrument in the same silence in which he unpacked his, and bowing to Loeffler I turned toward the door. In that peculiar voice of his he cooly said exactly these words: "Und wenn Sie mich auf der Strasse sehen, so nehmen Sie den Hut ab!"[3] I was dumbfounded and offended and in my perplexity made him a slight bow and fled from the place. Reaching the street I became wild with fury, and from my heart I cursed, cursed aloud in that forgotten, quiet little street! This was my first unforgettable—and shall I say unforgivable—lesson with that man, and I must add that all my music which I studied with him bears the markings of fingerings, bowings, etc. in my handwriting and not in his.

A Lesson without Violin Music

Loeffler had a small apartment on Charles Street where he gave his lessons. It was in a small, narrow old house on the second floor and consisted of a large room facing the street and a small one in back of it which was connected to a small bath. In the small room was an iron cot, a table, a trunk, and many French books. The large room had his grand piano, a large rattan sofa, two chairs, and, over the narrow mantle of an old-fashioned chimney, several unframed photographs. As I've said, he used this place only to work in, for his home was with the Fay family—who doubtlessly owned the house—in the same street and within the same block, if I remember correctly.[4]

One afternoon (for the Boston Symphony Orchestra rehearsed every morning) not many weeks after I had started working with him, I went for my lesson. In answer to my knock I heard a muffled "Come in," and opening, as the door did, directly into that living room, I found it empty. Through an opened door I for the first time saw the adjoining little bedroom and Loeffler, fully dressed, lying on the bed. Ignoring my spoken greeting and my bow, he got up in a listless manner to a sitting posture and remained thus, moodily looking out on the back yard. Unpacking the violin box on the rattan seat, I stood there waiting patiently in silence. Finally I sat down, only to jump up immediately as I heard his first step. He entered the large room preoccupied with a mood, his hand on his face, and lifelessly ambling to the piano began to play small bits on odd pages of a large manuscript before him. I had not yet moved from the spot where I stood, and I listened with eagerness and fascination.

Turning his head slightly, he said, "Come here, you old duffer," and with a gesture signified I was to sit on the long piano bench beside him. He soliloquized aloud, mixing his languages and his oaths, asking himself how this or that place would sound and taking small groups of chords and changing notes. Suddenly cursing himself and the entire universe that he had but two hands, he told me to "play the third line from the top." I played but a few notes when he mumbled, "Miserable beggar," (which, of course, in his peculiar way of speaking sounded something like "Mis'rahbel buggah") "that's a clarinet! It plays a tone lower than written." He repeated that a clarinet, "eine B-Klarinette" plays a tone, "a whole tone," lower than written and pointing to where we were to start said, "Now play with me." Quaking with fear I told him that I could not play the piano, that I only knew where the notes are to be found but had no knowledge of fingering. "Then bring over your lousy fiddle," he said, "and start from here." I did what I had to do, what was somehow expected of me to be able to do immediately. The passages in question were often not merely sustained notes, but also at times had running figures, and after a few things, tried over a few times, he stopped, lost in thought. And thus it was I received my first lesson in transposition as well as in instrumentation! He did not by so much as a gesture or look acknowledge the terrific effort I had made to read a note by one name and immediately articulate it by its actual sounds, substituting A for B and thus down the entire alphabet, reading every letter one lower, somewhat like: Uif dbu kvnqfe pwfs uif nppo (= The cat jumped over the moon).

Thoughtfully turning some pages of his score, he came to a place at which he for a time gazed in silence. Turning to me he remarked, quite casually, that a clarinet in A sounds a minor third lower than written. Pointing to the place, he asked me to play those measures while he played other lines in the score. Somehow I found it easier to transpose a third below than a second. He then began a long talk on the difficulties of orchestral writing. He commented that one of the hardest things to do was to read—simultaneously of course—a group consisting of bassoons in the tenor clef, the bass clarinet in the bass clef, trumpets in one key, and two groups of horns in two different keys, and got out scores to illustrate his points.

Before I left he had me play snatches of things written in the tenor clef, the bass clarinet in the F and G clefs, and piccolo parts in their actual register. My violin music remained in the box-cover during that lesson.

His Appearance and Some of His Peculiarities

Loeffler was tall, very tall beside me. He had exceedingly long legs and arms, a splendidly proportioned torso—very broad shoulders but a rather thin and flat chest—and was lean as a greyhound. His head and brow were interesting. Though scarcely forty, he was very bald, and the thin, sandy-colored fringe of hair—and of his beard too—and the transparency of his skin and veins made him appear to me, especially at night, as a very old man.[5] His nose was large, long, thin, bony, and anemic. It had that peculiar pointedness of a critic's pen and seemed to have lengthened with peering and sniffing in the dusty and foul-smelling places of the Catacombs. Projecting from his thin face, his deeply set eyes and his flat cheeks with the closely cropped straw-colored hair of his beard and moustache, he presented to me the picture of a stork, and somehow I always thought of him as "the old stork." His walk too was different from that of anyone I've ever known. Perhaps from excessive horseback riding it had become truly a gait. It resembled a long, slow lope as he rose on his toes from one exceedingly long step to another. Once, in glancing up at him, I caught a glimpse of his mouth and the peculiar clusters of his teeth. The upper lip made a point close to his nose, by which his front teeth were always revealed, with the corners of his mouth turned down, and I thought, "You do well to wear a moustache, for you've got a mean mouth." His hands were interesting, the fingers artistic and the nails long and shapely. And, of course, he was always meticulous about his person and appearance and an aesthete without comparison.

It was in Boston that I donned my first long trousers. Notwithstanding, I had already elsewhere experienced my first passionately consuming love with a woman almost ten years my senior. Though I never got to know many people in Boston, I found "love" in a never-ending succession of women who, invariably being older than myself, knew what they were doing. These secretive escapades in my lonely and wretchedly unhappy turmoils were totally unknown to anyone, nor have I, until now, ever made mention of them. Hence what I could not understand was Loeffler's asceticism and his complete lack of feelings or thoughts towards anything feminine.

Apart from the flatness of his lips and something so "untouched" about his mouth, it was his hands to which my thoughts and attention always reverted. I am not making these observations and deductions in retrospect, for these things were too terribly true to me then and have consequently remained indelibly fixed. It might have been childish to be always trying to explain the anemia of his hands, yet it became a fixation until I finally became convinced that no real blood flowed in them. It was a watery and acrid serum, I felt sure, as if from the ulcer of morbidity, and not the ichor of classical mythology—that ethereal fluid which ran, instead of blood, in the veins of the gods.

His Voice

Is it possible for paper and printed words to convey the sound, the timbre, and the inflections of the human voice? His is so thoroughly in my ear that in imitations to people who have known him, all have exclaimed over the exactness of it. I find that when I have quoted a sentence by Loeffler which I have dictated to myself aloud it is *his* voice which I am yet hearing. Unconsciously my face immediately takes on that longish look; my mouth is twisted into a crooked curve (like the up-bow mark in violin music). It is a bitter mouth, downward my eyes narrow, and there is a strange sort of windiness which my lips emit at certain words. Voice, like the tone of the artist-individual, is the expression of one's true personality, and that of Loeffler had neither vibrancy nor vitality. Its color was moribund, it was neither high nor low. There was no declamation in it, there were no lines, no fire or climaxes, and in moments of greatest hate and anger it went cold and foul with low, slow cadences.

As a matter of fact, it was not easy to understand him, for he did not enunciate clearly; he rolled his syllables together, and on analysis I find that he had a queer jumble of accents. Carl Engel, in that outstanding article, claims, "Loeffler spoke with a decided German, and not French, accent."[6] I have already said that he was incapable of pronouncing the English "th." When he spoke in French, his "r"s were smoothed or blurred over in a manner which scarcely left a recognizable sound. It was certainly not the French "r," nor was it the harsh Germanic "errrr." If he spoke in German, there was a slightly perceptible sharpening of a "d" into a "t," of a "b" to a "p," and in French there were ever present the mixtures of inflections with contradictory ones. His way of using the letter "l" might more nearly be described as akin to the Pole's way of pronouncing it, a thing almost impossible to acquire, as any Pole will assure. He pronounced "i" as a Dane pronounces the "y" or practically as the German "ü." The "e," on the other hand, inclined more towards an "i."

To clarify this jumble of things, let me give a few practical illustrations. I can give no better one than the manner in which Loeffler pronounced the word "talent" when speaking English. The "French" in him—which he always claimed to be by birth ("Alsatian, and by blood, on his mother's side")—would, or should, have spoken it "tal*an*" The "German" in him would have said "tal*ent*" with the accent on the second syllable. The "American" in him should have spoken it "*tal*ent." Loeffler however pronounced it "*tahl*ent," with a decidedly long and slow accent on the first syllable, the second scarcely discernable and the "e" rolling upwards towards an "i" and the final "t" barely audible. Thus Miss Fay's name—Elise—was always uttered as "Uh*luss*" with a sharp accent on the second syllable and with hissing "esses." There was always that peculiar windy force in back of, for instance, this name, as if pushed forth by an effort. His habitual way of addressing any comments to me was by starting with, "I'll tell you Arthur," but it sounded somewhat like, "Atéyaossa." Later, in Medfield during the summer, he would say to me, "I'll tell you Arthur, we'll now go for a long walk, mushroom-hunting," and this would undoubtedly be spelt thus: Atéyaossa weealnow go fowalongwalk, mushroomhauntink.

Les Veillées de l'Ukraine

Loeffler had written a suite of pieces for violin and orchestra, of which at least one, I think, *Les Veillées de l'Ukraine,* was after a novel by Gogol.[7] Kneisel[8] was to play it in Boston, with the Boston Symphony Orchestra, and I heard the performance—with Loeffler sitting on the outside instead of his usual place at the concert-master's desk.[9] I, of course, expressed overwhelming admiration for the work—for I knew this was expected—even though I am very sure I was incapable of understanding, at first hearing, what it was all about. Furthermore, knowing how he always froze the marrow in my bones, I went home and wrote him what I am sure must have been quite a wonderful letter.

At my next lesson, while completely ignoring my letter, Loeffler suddenly asked what effect the orchestration had made on me. Completely nonplussed and blushing with embarrassment, I told him I could never venture to have an opinion on such a thing. He eyed me with cold sarcasm and with a slow deep-toned sneer continued to goad me to talk and to say what I thought. I stumbled and stuttered helplessly, but he lashed me on. With all sorts of confused apologies I told him that there seemed to be too long stretches—distances in the orchestration—somewhere in the treble (at the same time making a gesture upwards) and furthermore that, and I couldn't help saying that, certain passages for clarinets in thirds were particularly odious to me for their color, or I might as well say their odor, for somehow they made me think of Brahms! At that time I hated Brahms violently and intensely, and my revulsion to the clarinet was none less, for I considered its tone both lewd and odoriferous. I blurted, "Pour moi, la clarinette c'est la putain de l'orchestre,"[10] thinking it might be more acceptable in French than in English.

Loeffler glanced at me rather suddenly and, I thought, more with curiosity to know what a youth of sixteen or seventeen years could know about such things, rather than at my expression. But then he had never known my father, who, as a good Hungarian, was picturesque in the way he could juggle the souls and all other things of saints and mortals in an endless variety of profanations and unimaginable situations. Incidentally, let me say that my hatred for "that whorish instrument" endured for about twenty-five years until suddenly one day I came to think of the clarinet, with its range covering practically that of the viola and violin combined and the varied tone-colors inherent to its different registers, as the most wonderful and useful of all the instruments in the orchestral family.

Fingering his closely cropped blond beard right over his chin, Loeffler sat there, with legs crossed, and continued to eye me in a very personal and disconcerting way. I had already noticed a small horizontal vein under one of his eyes which seemed to come into prominence because of its sudden blackness. This peculiar apparition was the usual sign for one of his brusque tempers which became absolute fits of devastating blasphemies. I was quaking with fear, but instead he started on a tirade against Kneisel, "who played everysing slower as anyone living" and who was a "Schusterfleck, ein Biergarten-musikant," ["shoemaker, a beer-garden musician"] "just like that stinking old Brahms!"

Yes, he, too, hated Brahms, but not the clarinet. However, it must not be imagined that I am accrediting Loeffler with this hatred of Brahms and my peculiar loathing—for it was nothing else—of the clarinet, for since the time that I can at all remember, things which with sudden violence reacted on me, on my imagination or solar plexus, at once became actual. They were immediately so realized as to become factual. Words, wines, sights, sounds, odors, foods, could stir me to extremes, and some of these excitements became fixed and associated with symbols of great beauty and attraction or, in revulsion, even with things utterly unmentionable. The "analyses" of "sunsets," "bird-calls" (literally taken down, in the case of some "composers"), "the murmur of the brook," and similar clichés could move me to silent appreciation and mild contemplation, but they could never drive me to extremes. Thus he spoke to me, and only now from Carl Engel's remarkable article do I learn that *already then* Loeffler had dedicated compositions to his fellow deskmate, that same Franz Kneisel.[11]

After a considerable pause, he said to me, "Do you know, Osser, I sink you understand me. I sink *you* would be the one to play zis work of mine, even if you are only a lausbub' and a pupil of mine, and don' forget to remember what kind o' compliment zis is from my 'umble self!" Thus "the louse" received right on the spot the manuscript from "my humble self" and was truly overwhelmed by the compliment. It was the violin part only (I doubt whether the score has ever been reduced for the piano[12]), and with nothing further to guide him as to harmonies and orchestral weavings, this stripling was left to figure, and finger, it all out by himself.

In great excitement I took the manuscript home and soon enough found it to be a work teeming with technical difficulties. Here was a kind of violin writing which made me marvel at its inventiveness of an original kind of passagework and seemingly endless resourcefulness in matters purely instrumental. However, it did not take long—in spite of my admiration and my ambition to please him and, if possible, bowl him over with surprise—for me to know that I was beginning to "hate" this work, for I could find so few places where one could "sing." It was ingenious and original, but to me it was not red-blooded and warm and deep and, above all, alive!

There was, however, one tune—a Russian (or perhaps Little Russian or Ukranian) folk-song—which had a five-four meter and for a time intrigued me, though I very soon began to consider it rather naive. In this too I was on a par with the age in which I was living, for the *Symphonie Pathétique* by Tchaikovsky was still such a sensational thing. It was considered an extraordinary "stunt" for an orchestra to be able to play it and perhaps even more so for the conductor to be able to beat it. Music was usually written in either a two, three, or four-beat measure, and it was conducted very much like the symbols on a weather vane, that is to say "one" down to southwards, "two" towards the west, "three" towards the east, and "four" skywards. People actually argued as to how "five" could be signaled, and some claimed that the conductor gave the fifth beat by dropping his left arm. Hans Richter had performed this symphony by conducting the first few measures and then, folding his arms, let the orchestra continue without him. However, this is incorrectly put, as anyone knows who has played with Richter, for I well remember the fire of his eyes, his grimaces, the force of his concentrated gestures and the barely stifled grunts and "Schwein" and "Schusterfleck" which he distributed right and left, even during performance. I well remember Loeffler's amazement and enthusiasm as he came from a rehearsal one day and told me of a full-fledged March being introduced into a symphony in place of a Scherzo! It must have been around 1897—Tchaikovsky was dead but a few years, and the "Pathétique" was yet a great novelty.[13]

My next lesson followed within three days, and he seemed relatively benign. He made no comments, though he frequently pretended to yawn and stretch without even covering his mouth and often scratched his bald head with a real scratch. I had somewhere heard an old saying, possibly a New England one: "The way I was raised was with the Word and the blow . . . but the blow always came first," and thus I always played before him with a corner of my eye on his expected gesture or interruption. I was just rejoicing in his absence of comments when he suddenly sneered, "Hm! And where is my work! Hm, and you think you have talent when I know damn well you were born too late anyhow, but then," (with a pretended yawn and very wearily) "what's the use of anysing anyhow! And who cares a damn about composing!" Here he scratched his head, really and vigorously, and continued his monologue in a voice which was lugubrious: "I told Higginson, I said to him, I'm too poor to get my works played by the orchestra.[14] It cost me fifty dollars to get some parts copied and then what does the public know anyhow! You know, Osser, I played one of my works and had to work my goddam head and fingers to the bones just to learn what my 'umble self had written and what did the public know or give a damn, and when I made a stinking glissando, Melba said to Mrs. Jack Gardner, 'Isn't he marvelous'!"[15] Here an unprintable word and he spat on the floor!

He went on, telling me that his father was a Russian named Tornov ("He wrote books, too," he said with a gesture toward a shelf) and his mother a German named Loeffler, and that after his father's exile from Russia the family had taken the mother's name.[16] He told me too that he was the greatest Francophile in the world and that he hated everything Prussian.[17] He said he hated the climate and the people of Boston as much as he hated "the drill-master Gericke who played the rantings of Tchaikovsky with the same metronomic exactitude as he did the endless number of stupid symphonies by Haydn and Mozart."[18]

"Have you noticed, you damn buggah you, that Kneisel brings out an extra bow, two bows, one a bit heavier as ze ozer, for those few lousy measures in the stinking symphony by Schumann, and at the end of any emotional work the great 'corndoctor's' beard and hair remain parted exactly as before the concert and there is not even a crease or a crack in the very stiff shirt bosom of that German Kapellmeister?" He turned his back on me and staring into space for a few seconds dejectedly walked to the piano and began to play the Dies Irae. The morbidity of it all made me sense the catacombs as he turned around and with a gesture signified, "Get out, go home!"[19] Inevitably, at my next lesson three days later, I brought his manuscript and begged his indulgence if I tried to play it, to the best of my ability and as far as I was able to, for, as he well knew, it was not an easy work to perform. At various spots, I immediately stopped and apologized for the mistakes which had been the outcome of having first read it so drivingly, and, it being manuscript, I had somehow almost gotten a habit of playing notes different from what he had written. There were slight changes in the figurations or occasionally in passing notes. To my great surprise he not only was not displeased but also much interested. As he stood over me he often said, "Wie machen Sie das? Do it again, Osser," and taking a pencil, said, "Write it in." I explained that so-and-so, within that harmonic scheme, seemed to come to me more naturally, that it, so to speak, was more in my hand: "Es liegt mir besser, das habe ich mehr in der Hand." When I terminated, he put his hand on my shoulder quite affectionately and said, "Atéyaossa, you know what, I think I'll dedicate this to you," and taking pen and ink, inscribed my name! I was overcome with joy and red in my embarrassment, while he continued, now in his habitual voice which reeked with disdain and sarcasm, "*You* understand me, and one day, when you are no longer a pupil of mine, you play it with the orchestra and then let that Kneisel, with his slow vibrato, see what real violin-playing is like, and that Taktschläger understand a rubato and *color it,* goddam."

Thereupon he asked me to go to the St. Botolph Club with him that evening and have dinner.[20] It was all too much to believe or understand, and while I was vainly trying to show my joy and appreciation, he repeated his invitation with exactly these words: "Ich möchte daß Sie mit mir in den Klub kommen, weil ich will, daß Sie sehen sollen, wie ich dort von Allen *verachtet* bin!"[21] Have mortal ears ever heard a more bitter and revealing confession? His unhappiness touched me as anyone's always has, and to get away from it I asked if I might play his composition all again, for it certainly needed much work yet. I continued playing as heretofore, but when I at last reached the place which had something like red blood in it for me, I found him stalking towards me. This time, however, there was no menace in his slow lope as he stopped my bow arm very gently and said: "Listen, Ossa old boy, for so far you understand me. If you keep on burning yourself up like that, *or* you'll be dead or you'll be in your grave before you are twenty. Listen, Ossa, so far you understand me, but now I'll tell you." And in a low voice he said, very, very slowly, "I want that place there to sound real lousy." He was unquestionably a great artist and a "précieux," for one should not play the Sonata by Fauré with the same kind of tone and vibrato with which one interprets the Tchaikovsky Concerto.

He was equally master of English, German, and French. There were, however, two habits which seemed ineradicable. He would say "or this or that," from the French "ou ceci ou cela," instead of "either this or that." And when he said, "You remind me on Wieniawski," it was his German thinking: "Sie erinnern mich *an* Wieniawski." If, in writing English, he persisted in spelling "remarquable" in the French manner and Janvier for January, I felt already then that it was but one of his many affectations. In dress too, notably in stocks and cravats, he had rather foppish tastes, while he persistently called my attention to "the unconsciousness of my humble self" and had a mean delight in telling me that I was "born too late and much too self-conscious."

How I Became a "Violist"

One day Loeffler said to me that he had just gotten some music from Paris and would like to play it. "I know a talented young fella here, and I'll give him the piano part to look over." Having said this, he added in that tone of voice which perhaps naturally was not any too pleasant but which was an irritant to me when he tinged it with taunting sarcasms, "I'll get some players together within a few days, and as you think you have a tone, you'll get a chance to show it. You play viola!"

"But, Mr. Loeffler," I gasped, "I have never played the viola! I have never had one in my hands, and I know nothing about it."

"Well," he said with characteristic unpleasantness, "you've seen one and you know it's larger than a violin. It has four strings and is tuned in fifths, only its top string is A and not E."

He stopped abruptly and watched me with cold, critical, squinting eyes while he scratched the beard over his chin, a habit I had quite gotten used to expect. Closing my eyes hard, which drew my pursed mouth and face into knots, I thought hard for a moment. I thought in fifths backwards—"A–D–G–C"—and then exclaimed, "Then its lowest string is C in the cello register?" He made no reply, but he also did not contradict.

Instead he continued thus: "And, by the way, it is not written for like the violin, but this sign" (drawing it on whatever was before him) "is the viola clef, and this note as you read it as a violinist sounds here" (striking it on the piano) "on the viola. And now let's see whether you still think you have tone. I'll give you the music right now, and I'll lend you my viola. It's a Guarnerius, and that's more than I would do for the first viola of the orchestra. In a few days I'll tell you—as soon as I can arrange an evening with the pianist—and now go home and take these with you."[22]

He handed me the viola parts to the Fauré (G Minor) and d'Indy Piano Quartets—nothing less!—and that's how I learnt to play the viola, note by note, with the travail known to but few men. I learnt both works so painfully and thoroughly that I knew them from memory. I knew even the long stretches of pauses from memory, and fortunate indeed it was for me that I did. For within a week, when I came on the appointed evening to his rooms, I found that Loeffler himself was going to play the violin, his brother Erich the cello,[23] and a young man he introduced as "Gephart" the piano. It was the same Heinrich Gebhard who long since achieved such a distinguished position in Boston, but whom I have never met since that evening.[24]

I am not the least ashamed to confess that I almost wept as I begged Loeffler to put his hand over my heart and feel its thumpings, I was so terrified. He looked at me without the slightest sympathy while I begged, in my terror, to be allowed to run home, run away, anywhere. I was so mortified that I assured him if I ever got out of that room, I'd give up violin playing and music forever, that I was too weak to hold as big an instrument as the viola, that I had no idea how the composition was to go or sound, and thus on. He cut me short by telling me that I should be ashamed of myself for being such a baby and that, if I wanted to learn anything, now was my chance. And I took my place in the quartet and played blindly, practically from memory and, of course, with many blunders, false entrances, and some wrong notes for which I was duly jeered and cursed at.

That was the only time that Loeffler, in my presence, ever had a violin in his hands during the two years that I worked with him. Of course, my condition that evening did not permit my listening to him or anyone else in the ensemble with too great attention, for I was concentrating on counting time during their solos. That Loeffler must have had a prodigious and highly individualized violin technique is, in my opinion, beyond any question. But I am equally certain that, while his tone was refined and pure, it was neither large nor warm. It had no sensuous beauty or emotional vitality, for *those* qualities were simply left out of his nature.

On the question of tone and the art of bowing, I never tired of hearing his praises of Ysaÿe and Sarasate. Thus, unconsciously, I was shaping all my thoughts and ideals towards these two masters whose arts could not be compared because of their widely separated extremes, but with whose passings some of the subtleties and finesses of violin playing have also disappeared. There is not a violinist living today who can even approximate either of those immortals. At least that is my feeling about the art in general.

Besides all this, I had the inestimable advantage of hearing Loeffler make comparisons between the German, French, and Belgian schools, for he had been not only a pupil, but an outstandingly favored one of Joachim, Léonard, and Massart. From the two latter descended all the most eminent violin artists (including Kreisler) that the world had heard until that group of Russian prodigies appeared. Then too, from the time he was about sixteen, he told me, he had been obliged to earn his living and sat at the same desk with the somewhat older concertmaster César Thomson in the private orchestra of a Baron who maintained them in his villa at Lugano.[25] Thomson (born Liège, 17 March 1857; death at Bissone in August 1931 variously given as having occurred on 16, 22, and 24) was a pupil of Vieuxtemps, Léonard, Wieniawski, and Massart, and I am proud to claim fiddlistic lineage with the purest strain of what I am convinced is yet the greatest and only enduring method, the Franco-Belgian school.

The Viola d'Amore

Having thus "taken up the viola" (for was it not hurled at me?) I began to seek music for it, and finding little, I played all etudes and Bach and parts from quartet and orchestral scores. Listed on the back of some viola music, I saw *Hebrew Melodies by Jos. Joachim, after Lord Byron.* Naturally I not only had to get these compositions at once but also read the poems *Hebrew Melodies* by Byron! What, therefore, more natural than when Loeffler one day showed me a thing he was working on, his setting of the Psalm "By the rivers of Babylon we sat down and wept" that I should find myself walking around with ideas of writing music to Byron's "Oh, weep for those that wept by Babel's stream." Of the endless things conceived and sketched in those days, this is one of the few which I ultimately published, for mixed chorus and orchestra.[26] The Loeffler composition was for three-part female chorus with two violas d'amore, two violas da gamba, oboe d'amore, flute in G, harp, and organ, and I now learn from Carl Engel's invaluable article that said composition was published by G. Schirmer, Inc. in 1907 as Opus 3: *Psalm 137, By the Rivers of Babylon,* for four-part chorus of women's voices with accompaniment of organ, harp, two flutes, and violoncello obbligato.[27] I herewith add the last item from the complete listings of Loeffler's works: "There is apparently but one composition of Loeffler's which was published in Europe, before his coming to America: it is a Berceuse by M. Loeffler-Tornov, issued by Hamelle in Paris, in 1884."[28]

I wondered why he so often went to the piano, played a few chords or passages, and expected an exclamation or comment from me immediately. If I was confused and could not at once formulate an expression of an opinion (who could, unless they gushed forth hypocritical ecstasies?), he would lose his temper and abuse me. "Why don't you say it—why don't you say something you mis'rahbel elender Lausbub,'" and in my deep hurt I would shut myself away from him for weeks and pray that he never again showed me anything.

However, there were yet other things I was to learn from this extraordinary and much-feared man. For gradually I became sure that he was not playing unfinished scraps of things for me merely to judge how these effects reacted on others, but he also wanted an opinion, and that from me. How painfully and with what self-torture he sought for musical effects and sonorities, how willfully he "created" a theme no one living knows better than myself, for I heard them, over and again, from their embryo to every new change of an added note or some changed into different positions.

The viola da gamba line in his *Psalm 137* score somehow did not appeal to me enough to even inquire as to what differentiated it from its successor, the violoncello. But the very name of viola d'amore, "Love's viol," stirred me keenly! I begged for some information, and he said: "It has seven strings, with sympathetic strings under the bridge and is tuned—go look out of that window and see if you hear," and he struck a chord while my back was turned. Immediately, almost automatically, I commented, "D Major, but would you mind, Mr. Loeffler, to please strike that chord again?" and he obliged. Whereupon I said, "I wanted to make sure of the lowest note. At first I thought it was a 'D,' but now I hear it is an 'A.'" Slowly accounting for the intervals of the seven strings, I named them on my finger tips and said, "Then it is tuned in fourths and one third," and haltingly named each open string.[29] He barely nodded assent and that was all, at least for the time being and so far as he was concerned. But when I went to my room, I immediately drew a plan of the "keyboard" of that instrument and within a week or two, without ever having seen or heard a viola d'amore, I brought him a Romance, with a cadenza of course!

It was a sickly, mushy sort of thing, which always stayed in D Major, with a sort of middle section in F-sharp Minor and an occasional change to A Major. In the tuning of the strings I had ample double-stops and arpeggi, that is to say in D Major, but I did not know how playable real double-stopping might or could be in other tonalities. I took this manuscript to him, and he forthwith took it to the piano and started playing it. With comments scarcely fitting for an adolescent's ears, he laughed at its "passion and servant-girl's night off" and wound up with, "Atéyaossa, if you keep on as dissipated, or you'll be dead by twenty-one or you'll be in your grave." At least I had gained a year, for but a fortnight ago I was to be "or dead" by my twentieth year.

He yawned at me lazily with open mouth as he handed me my manuscript and said, "Come home with me and I'll lend you my viole d'amour, and then you can learn to play your junk on it."[30] We went to his home, and he handed me one of his instruments, for he had two. This one was by Johannes Udalricus Eberle, who worked at Prague toward the end of the seventeenth century [sic].[31] And thus I "learnt" to play the viola d'amore, going wild with fury for days at a time. Because of the great number of strings and their proximity, I found my fingers playing on one string, but my bow on quite another. I found such ecstasy in the seraphic beauty of its tone, however, that arpeggiating across the open strings was ravishing enough for a time. Presently I found its natural harmonics and the room reechoed with enchanting effects. Didn't Meyerbeer gain additional fame, at least to the extent of being quoted in all books on instrumentation, through the use of a straight D Major chord (the open strings of the viola d'amore) being broken into a slightly melodic idea in his *Les Huguenots*?

I had possession of the instrument for some months, but finding so little time for the practical use of it, neglected it utterly and virtually forgot its existence. One day, however, Loeffler suddenly asked me to return it to him at my next lesson. My horror can be imagined when I opened its case and saw that, due to steam heating, the instrument had opened and cracked in many places and that the upper part of its back, having come unglued, had actually curled! I rushed with it to the violin maker Jacob Thoma, father-in-law of Franz Kneisel, and in terror heard him tell me that the entire instrument would have to be taken apart and, in fact, slightly cut down to make all the warped pieces fit together again! I implored Mr. Thoma to be extremely careful, yet to rush the work on this job, as Loeffler had already demanded his instrument back. For the next few lessons I managed to strike my forehead and exclaim: "How stupid! I'm sorry, but again I have forgotten the viola d'amore," but ill-fortune would have it that after a rehearsal one day Loeffler should go to Thoma's shop and there recognize the whoops of his instrument hanging on pegs, the scroll on another and the back and belly on Thoma's work table! I was sincerely penitent and understood Loeffler's rage, for he was completely right and I ignorant of what steam heating can do to fine furniture as well as musical instruments.

Thus it happened that the instrument I had "learnt to play" through him was one which *he* never heard me play. I continued to dream about its harmonics and on a chart to try to figure out changes of position, and one day in London I became the possessor of a viola d'amore of my own.

A few years afterwards I earnestly set about acquiring every available piece of music, printed or manuscript, written for that instrument. I was finally fortunate in obtaining a copy, in its first edition, of the first Method written for it (Ariosti, circa 1688). I worked assiduously with articles and transcriptions, in hopes that I might be instrumental in helping to revive interest in that beautiful-toned, idyllic instrument. Once I played it publicly in the big hall of the Berliner Philharmonie in a concert for the benefit of the Berlin Philharmonic Orchestra's pension fund, at which time my accompanist was the equally young Artur Schnabel.[32] Occasionally I played it at the home of George Eastman in Rochester. I stood at the small platform near the huge organ, at the head of the stairs and out of sight of his guests, and in self-intoxication listened to the tones echoing through the large spaces of silence-haunted corridors of the mansion of that unfortunate man. I spent a part of a summer in writing a Method for it, based on different kinds of tunings, and of course I found no publisher for my work. Finding that nothing I could do could achieve any step towards dragging this instrument from obsoletion, my Method and my interest were willfully thrown into that great limbo of forgetfulness from which, by sheer determination, there is for me no return! I have had to school myself to do this in many tragic catastrophes and to consider a door, once closed, practically never to be opened again.

As for the viola, apart from that one deplorable experience with Loeffler, I continued the practice of reading the clef, so far as the limitations of the lowest note (the open G string) of the violin allowed. Thus I would sight read, just for myself, many a Kreutzer Etude as if actually the alto or C clef were there in place of the treble or G clef. A few years later I found this very profitable when I began to avidly learn chamber music and found I could be a "handy man" with such artists as Ysaÿe, Kreisler, Arbós, Rivarde, Nachez, and yet others in exchanging the violin for a viola. Those experiences past, I lost all interest in the instrument, and during the countless years when I played chamber music almost exclusively I never once took the instrument in hand. There remains a confession to add, and it is this: after years of habit of score-reading at the piano, I find that I can more readily play the alto clef on the piano than I can on the viola.

Conclusion

Underneath "my humble self" were some very natural vanities and satisfactions, not the least of which was his pride in his horsemanship. When he finally found, or tortured, something into the bizarre, the uncanny, or the startling, he would repeatedly tell me, "And maybe you don't think I didn't shake hands with myself and all over again, all day long!" But his natural expression at such times was gleefully to exclaim: "Oh Ossa, maybe old Foote and Chadwick won't have a sore ass when they try to figure out this one!"

Whenever I came into his presence, I was immediately aware that here was an "homme du monde," yet to whom nothing seemed of any value except to achieve something of his own in Music. He was always morbidly quiet when not bitterly against everyone or lost in melancholy introspection. There were two things which constantly ate at his vitals: the mystery of Death and the unattainable quest for Beauty and its Expression.[33] In retrospective moods he spoke to me of his youth, telling me about his father quite confidentially. He told me his real name was Tornov, and though he signed, at times, Charles M. T. Loeffler, he always preferred Ch-Martin, hyphenated thus (and to which I mentally added "dans la manière française sans doute et pour ainsi dire!"[34]).

He told me his father had been connected with the Department of Agriculture of Russia, or was, at one time, Minister of said Department; that he had been sent to study the subject and conditions in Hungary; and that as a child he (Loeffler) had lived for several years in Hungary, as he had in Russia. He recounted that his father had written several books, and with a wave of his hand toward his bookshelf, I think he added that one was on equestrianism and that he, like his father, knew horsemanship since childhood.

In a monotonous voice he continued, as if talking to himself, "I wrote a sort of concerto for the violoncello, and Nikisch said to me he considered it the best-orchestrated piece he had ever seen.[35] I don't believe in the concerto or the symphony. That is all left behind with Beethoven. It is only the 'Komposters' of this lousy country who go to that stupid country of German swine and learn the Schumacherei—alles schablonenhaft [stereotyped, mechanical, according to pattern]—minuets and marches and no imagination, no feeling for harmonies, no sense of colour. Everything *or* Rheinberger *or* Jadassohn *or* Reinecke. Verdammtes Gesindel [rabble, mob, riffraff]! All Bismarcks, all Prussians, alle Schweine! I call my work for cello 'fantastique,' and I remember the theme came to me when I was a child and my brother died. It was one of the earliest tragedies that I knew. My father died in exile—he was killed in a duel.[36] He fought two in one day—on a boat—right here—not far from the Statue of Liberty. I hate Germans, all Schweinehunde. You know, Ossa, there is not very much in life that is of any importance: first you are born and next you die. Then comes when or your father or your mother dies, and that makes four. If you marry and have a child and it dies, that makes five. The other day my doctor said to me, he said, 'Why don't you smoke,' and I said, 'Why should I smoke when it gives me no pleasure. Sometimes three or four cigarettes a day and then for weeks I don't care.' 'Why don't you take a little wine with your meals,' the Gottverdammter Schusterfleck bored me next. 'Because,' I said to him, 'wine must be good for me to take, and it is not easy in this country, and beer stinks, like Germans, and so I take a glass of milk at night and Gustave Kahn to bed with me.' So he says to me," continued Loeffler, "'then why don't you get married,' and I told him, 'because I don't want to run a Bordell in my own house.'"

I openly laughed while I looked at this unhappy man who, in one sentence, had told me so much of himself!

Letter from Loeffler to Hartmann, 22 January 1901[37]

112, Charles St.
22 Janvier 1901

My dear Arthur,

Before all do not feel angry towards me for not having written you before this. I have indeed received all your letters, but your first ones were so short, hasty, and uninteresting that to reply to you in the same vein would have meant my relating to you for example that in the evening when tired I have been going to bed lately, getting up in the morning, managing to gulp down in American haste three meals a day, getting through the customary lessons at higher prices, cursing Christian and Jew now by wholesale, etc., etc. Then there was really an abundance of lack of time to write not only to you, dear boy, but even my mother and sister. Now that I have done my duty toward them, I have reserved this evening for you, not to blow you up however but to thank you for your kind letters lately and for remembering me at Xmas. I received (probably through Mr. Curran[38]) a lovely matchbox for which receive my appreciative thanks, please.

I am delighted that you are studying with Mr. Pitt[39] whom I admire and cherish personally. He is a first rate man for you, as I told you at the time, besides being an eminently gifted composer. Make the best of your chances with him.

As to Ysaÿe I have feared that you would not see much of him although he plays often in London but he is so busy with his own affairs. However, you will have a hack at him in a few weeks, and I am thoroughly glad of it for all concerned for he is great, in fact the only great artist I know at present. Without ever having seen him conduct I know that he is a great conductor also. With my *La mort de Tintagiles* I have had bad luck. The copyist fell ill and kept me waiting for score and parts until now. The thing will be given in about two to three weeks when I shall dispatch the whole business to Ysaÿe. You will be so kind as to tell him about all this. The thing is dedicated to him, and I wish to God he would like it enough to give it. The day when I hear that he has given a thing of mine because he liked it, I shall mark with red pencil in the calender of my life, and we shall both of us, you and I, pass a happy day—for you, old boy, must take part in my happiness as an artist because you understand me, and I really believe that you care for your old friend.[40]

If the Symphonic Poem goes well and is artistically a success I will cable you. The thing for female chorus etc. called *L'archet* is going to be given in private at Montgomery Sears's 4th or 5th of March and in public some few days later.[41] I wish you were here to play the viola part! I shall write you about all this later.

By mere hazard the other day I was shown a dictionary published by the Schirmers in N. York, where to my surprise I found a rather long article on myself and my work. You know me not to be a vain person, yet I cannot deny that I was pleased with this attention on the side of the editor! Such is human weakness! Hélas!

What you wrote me about Rimsky-Korsakov's *Fantasie* was interesting.[42] I knew the thing—thought nothing of the composition and used that one theme (which is national) called "Thème russe." Ysaÿe found the arrangement of Korsakov more Russian, therefore played it. I shall now place instead of this theme another one (not unlike it) and when I have done that then I shall give Ysaÿe and you both a copy of it. The "Nuit de mai" is dedicated to Ysaÿe.[43] I would in the meantime send you the thing as it is but I have no Piano score to it!

You have not told me a thing about your work in composition, nor your violin playing, yet you know that that interests me most!!! Are you working hard? Also should I like to know how people use you in London! Are the Wieniawskis nice to you?[44] And Mr. Pitt and how about the Ortmans? Are you well located? How is Ortmans's health and his fingers?[45]

The other night I went again to the Café Boulevard on 2nd Avenue in N. Y. and heard the Hungarians play. They laid themselves out for me, I can assure you! After my arrival it began Hungarian and stayed Hungarian until the end in spite of public demonstration which demanded "Walking down the Street" and other rot. Arthur, it was grand! With you there it would have been perfect. I also discovered that some of those wonderful slides of Wieniawski's are of Zigeuner origin. There is for example that wonderful thing called by the Tziganes "der Liegenrutscher," or goat slide, which is a marvel. I have forgotten now the Hungarian word for it—it sounds so damn outlandish. Wieniawski used it a lot in his cantilenas. Ysaÿe, you, and myself seem to be the only violinists that seem to know it and use it. (I beg Ysaÿe's forgiveness for having managed to couple my name to his in the same and beforegoing sentence). (This is in spirit!). Oh, vanity, most human of weaknesses! Again I have succumbed!

The Zigeuner are a Godsend to me! Every month I take a good large dose of it while in N. Y. How talentless, mechanical, uninteresting, and stupid most other playing sounds after such people! It is of course only of one kind but in that so great! In this band were remarkable the violinist, cellist, and the cimbalom player. The cellist probably is the greater genius, for never have I heard such fantasies on any instrument before in my life. The cimbalom ranked second probably to no other artist on that instrument, and what invention in effect— what imagination! The violinist, with not more technique than is necessary to murder and butcher a concerto by Mendelssohn, is so to say a Wieniawski or Ysaÿe minus their technique, yet can one listen to him I should think forever. I feel like Baudelaire now—"J'ai mille ans de souvenirs."[46]

Hugo Becker has played with us with great public success.[47] He has sung, but not to me as others, but he played all the notes and damn those. He is never the less one of the best such as they are. *This is of course strictly confidential!*

H. Bauer played also here, very excellently![48] Gabrilowitsch did not sing to me—had success—played all the notes![49] Kneisel played his Brahms Concerto.[50] Adamowski the Dvořák one, was not in best voice.[51] Next comes Otto Roth.[52] As he now sits behind me I can tell you that he still has *it*! I mean the vibrato maledetto! God bless him though. He wears good cloth! The conductor [Gericke] also wears those.

So there is Longy left with his heavenly oboe[53] and a couple more like Kneisel and Schroeder[54] to console you. Yet do I feel like a caged up animal, somewhat isolated, as you may know and imagine! I do not feel with most of this playing and composing! And in the evening when I have been fed for the third time I lay down in this cage called Boston and dream of those with whom I should as an artist love to be, to find sympathy or encouragement. I also miss you, but hope and think that you are better off over there.

I now must beg of you to send me at once M. Ysaÿe's Brussels address, as I need it badly and doubt whether he still lives Avenue Brugman 46. If convenient enclose someday a gunmetal G (No. 2 Albert Gave) and an E–A–D same size and oblige me greatly.

Now, old boy, I must finish. Remember your aim: you must become a great artist. Work hard. Have a good time yet do not neglect your work. Don't do a thing that you would be ashamed of to relate to your friend. Remember me before all to Mr. Pitt, Mesdames Wieniawski, Ortmans. You will hear from me again shortly.

Keep me in memory as I do you.

Your old friend
C. M. T. Loeffler

Eugène Ysaÿe: Colossus of the Violin

Sharp Contradictions in Art and Personality of Belgian "Giant Oak"[1]

Ysaÿe—the Gargantuan—the Sublime—Emperor of Extravaganza! Everything about him was on the "gigantesque," and all the Hollywoodian hyper-super-terrifics would have fitted him with the naturalness of his own epidermis! In physical stature as in musicianship, mental power, greatness of heart, and, if it must be added, in uncontrollable anger and childishness and pettiness of moral fiber, he was always the Colossus. The French have a saying, well known to all gifted people, the good "Bohemiens," "to be a great artist, one must be a 'grand cochon,'" and this equally applies.

His playing was noble one moment and reeking with sensuality the next—beautiful, ideal, poetic, unmatched in grandeur and delicacy and tenderness, and, within the next few measures, unequaled for boisterous roughness, untrammeled vehemence, the most unbridled gypsified capriciousness of tempi, accents, and nuances, and of an extravagance that often made me put my hat before my face in my efforts to restrain open laughter! He was truly Rabelaisian and again as delicate as a brush stroke by Hokusai. It is neither unkind nor a lack of veneration for the dead and the living to make passing mention of the fact that his personal life was that of an extremist, and that some of his experiences and practical jokes (not always of the most refined nature) would, if recounted, bring roars of merriment and protests of incredulity. Truly, Ysaÿe was unique and should have lived to be at least one hundred years old, for this giant oak at sixty years had more vitality than four men of half his age.

Conflicting Elements in Ysaÿe's Nature

I heard him play more often than all the other great violinists put together, and though I never heard him play *one* work exactly as written, I still maintain that he was the greatest violinistic genius since Wieniawski! The apparent contradiction is explained—and justified—by the tremendous and conflicting elements of his nature and individuality. I have seen him conduct (and rehearse from memory) the "Eroica" and "La Cinquième" (as he and all French musicians call it), and, just then, it was my positive conviction that there was no greater conductor living.

I have never heard greater, more profound or revealing interpretations, and surcharged with his physical magnetism, the performances were nothing less than bomb-like in their overwhelming vitality. In the year 1900 (I think it was) I lived in London, in the home of René Ortmans, violinist and ultimately a conductor, a compatriot of Ysaÿe and a lifelong friend, their bond dating from their boyhood days together. Joachim, with his associates forming the celebrated Joachim Quartet, had given an annual series of concerts in London "since time immemorial," as I think one might well say, and that season, Joachim having fallen ill, Chappell suddenly found himself without a quartet organization. Whatever the reasons, the "Ysaÿe Quartet" was engaged for some twenty concerts, throughout the fall and winter. This so-called Ysaÿe Quartet consisted of the great violinist and three colleagues, fellow teachers in the Brussels Conservatory of Ysaÿe's former days.[2] Ysaÿe's all-around musicianship had, of course, long ago given him familiarity with the chamber music literature, yet I doubt if even the most perfervid admirer (such as myself) could have claimed for this "quartet" the homogeneity of an ensemble when the first violinist had, since decades, dotted the maps of Europe and America as a violin virtuoso, interspersed with appearances as guest conductor as well as conductor of the "Orchestre Ysaÿe" in Brussels.

The concerts took place on Monday afternoons (I think) and also on some Saturday evenings, and it happened more often than not that Ysaÿe was appearing, as violinist, somewhere in England or on the Continent, a day or two before, and would be doing so again within the following few days. There were many concerts, I know, that were done without any rehearsing, besides which, his associates came over from Brussels for each concert (or weekend) and returned there immediately after. Because of his many appearances in the British Isles that year, Ysaÿe had taken rooms somewhere in Duke Street, London, and—again if I correctly recall—this was not exactly an "elegant" neighborhood. In these two rooms were large straw hampers full of music (orchestral parts to violin concerti), stores of linen, huge Turkish towels, enormous briar pipes in their enormous étuis, and, to top it all, he was then wearing a fur coat and a huge, round fur cap. It is, however, not with proper recognition to their importance to Ysaÿe to mention the pipes casually among other indispensable items, for these more properly belonged at the head of the list.

Ysaÿe's Briar Pipes

After playing a concert, Ysaÿe invariably walked from the dressing room entirely out of the building and only on reaching the curb would ask, "Eh bien—my bass! Who's got my bass?" He knew that he was surrounded by friends and cronies and that some one was bringing his enormous double case. But I, for one, have never known him to ask, "Where did I leave my pipe?" whereas I did know that no gift could give him greater pleasure than a briar pipe in the shape and size for which he had a great partiality. These pipes were five inches deep and two inches in diameter. The stem was so carved out of the same enormous block of briar as to be very close to the pipe itself. With the curving amber or hard rubber mouthpiece then attached, these beautiful pipes suggested nothing so much as a miniature bassoon. There were, of course, individual becushioned and lined boxes for these, and when Ysaÿe, on coming to the dinner table, would deposit his pipe étui and the tobacco pouch at its side, the size of them together fully equaled the modern girl's overnight bag.

One night at Pagani's, surrounded by a half dozen musicians, he had been recounting his experiences; as the party finally broke up, he said to Ortmans: "René, you will be kind enough to come and wake me up tomorrow at eleven." He shook hands all around, and it seems to me that almost invariably he shook hands with his left and not with his right hand. I lived with the Ortmans somewhere out in West Kensington, and the trip down to Duke Street meant the better part of an hour—just "to awaken him at eleven o'clock." Ortmans insisted that I go with him, and reluctantly I consented. Arrived at his rooms, we found him not only awake but sitting on a chair in his vast nightgown, pipe in mouth, and playing away for dear life. He told us to disregard him, for he had to do some work as he was playing in Glasgow (which he pronounced Glozgov) the following evening and had to play a concerto he had not played in quite some time. To my inexpressible joy, it was the rarely heard Concerto in F by Lalo, which I knew, though I had never heard it played.

An Informal Performance

I leaned against a piece of furniture while he, with closed eyes and the huge pipe dangling from the right side of his mouth, was pouring forth his wealth of marvelous tone, staggering me with his mastery of the bow and ease of the left hand. However, there was another thing which dumbfounded me, and it was that in the pages of passagework there were scarcely two consecutive measures which contained the notes exactly as they had been written! Perhaps the composer, who doubtlessly had been an intimate friend of Ysaÿe's, had made a revision of that work, for the passages were different from the printed notes. Reaching a spot where the orchestra interrupts with loud chords, Ysaÿe relaxed for a moment, lowered his violin, and, opening his eyes, winked at me. Then, in a high-pitched, thin voice, imitated the "meow" of a cat, relighting his pipe, he turned to me and said, "Meow . . . eh bien cochon, ça va, hein?" He saw that I was transfixed with joy, and as I made no response he guffawed: "Well, say something! It went well, didn't it? What do you think?" I was too confused to be able to find the right words, and dreading to contradict him, I blurted the words which accomplished precisely that! I answered, "Oh, it is marvelous, only it isn't quite right. It isn't that . . . it isn't accurate!"

"What!" he roared like a bull which had just been stabbed, and putting fiddle and pipe down, took his long hair in each fist and bellowed, "René, René, did you hear that? René, this cochon has the effrontery to tell me that it wasn't right!" While he stood there, a fistful of hair in each hand, I begged his friend Ortmans to try explain to him that it was all, of course, marvelous, genial, overwhelming, and staggering because he was not playing the actual notes in the pages of figurations, as published by Lalo. It was in vain I tried to tell him that I knew I had been very much out of order to make the comments that I had, that I did not know the French language sufficiently to pick quickly the right forms and words with which, with due apologies, to express my astonishment that a page of artistically woven figurations, so characteristic of Lalo, could have been so similar and yet dissimilar sufficiently to confound me, and so on. But he was too stunned and infuriated to pay any attention to Ortmans's and my explanations, and, still tearing at his hair, he stood over me menacingly while he kept on repeating: "So you *know* the work—*you* know it? Do you hear that, René? This cochon here knows the Lalo, when I have played it before he was born."

Volatile Temperament

But suddenly his mood changed, and with thorough glee at my red-faced humiliation he roared, "René! Now you are going to see something! This cochon is going to play the Concerto in F of Lalo for me!" He winked his eyes, slapped his thighs, and seizing his fiddle and bow thrust them at me with terrific imprecations and ordered me to play the pages containing the passagework in question!

This was an encounter I had not expected, and paralyzed with terror as this infuriated Goliath towered over me, I begged, actually begged tremblingly, to be forgiven and to be allowed to run from that room. But it was useless, for he kept thrusting fiddle and bow toward me and with terrific oaths ordered me to begin. He straddled a chair, turning it around so that his arms rested on its back, his enormous bare legs and thighs exposed to view, and smoking his pipe. I started the concerto, unprepared as I was to play it. He watched me steadily, and when I reached the passages in question, he closed his eyes, squeezing them together very hard, as if to impress something on his brain. Presently he stopped me by holding up his hand, and opening his eyes he said to me in a normal, quiet voice: "Play that place over again, a little more slowly." Once more the eyes closed, were tightly squeezed, the head nodding. "And now continue," he said, and again all this had to be repeated. When I terminated the first movement, he turned to Ortmans and said in a matter-of-fact voice: "Eh bien, he is right. I must look through the score a little after lunch," and approaching me, he gave me a slap on the back and said, "Hm, c'ést un brave! He has talent. We will have lunch together, won't we, cochon?"

Pulling his nightgown over his head, he told me to continue with the two remaining movements while he dressed. His clothes were strewn all over the place, and I can now visualize him sitting there, pausing in the midst of pulling on a sock or his trousers, while with closed eyes he was again making a mental record of something in the music at a particular point. This experience is not recounted to show that although unprepared and under such demoralizing conditions I did manage to play the concerto with such a colossal violinist and artist watching every finger move and bow stroke, but that Ysaÿe, only one day before rehearsing and playing it publicly with orchestra, conceived the work as an entity and thus had woven things (scarcely less genial than those of Lalo himself) around the music, harmonies which he knew were in the background of the score, just as he, through habit, always filled in harmonies in the single-voiced or melodic phrases. This complete musicality of feeling I never knew of in any other violinist, nor the ability to create fullness of sonority through transposition into various registers and—of course—in any and all positions of the violin. It was like Saint-Saëns's gift and musicianship to be able to play any work of Bach which he knew in any key whatsoever! This is what I should call musicianship-plus.

Ysaÿe the Violinist

Ysaÿe had the rare power, at times, to inspire himself to such sublime heights that from no other artist have I seen the vistas of majesty, grandeur, and nobility so revealed. It is an experience of a lifetime to see an artist "of the other world" so feel the meaning of a simple line in the slow movement of the Beethoven Violin Concerto that, utterly unconscious of the orchestra, the lights, and the thousands of listeners before him, he stands there with tears streaming down his cheeks, and this I have seen more than once! And in the next movement he would sentimentalize with ridiculous mawkishness in one place only practically to double the tempo in another.

Ysaÿe's Grimaces While Playing

It was one of my "parlor tricks" to imitate his manner of "falling upstairs" as he came onto the podium and more especially to mimic his great variety of grimaces while playing. These were an inseparable part of his great artistry, born of absorption and intensity of emotions. But, be it said, when the real feeling was not present, the grimaces were, and perhaps to an even greater extent, for Ysaÿe was not only a born actor but also knew the value of gestures, expressions, and poses! Often it was downright funny to see him frantically whipping himself into trying to produce a trill with fingers that were exhausted beyond his will and control—to see him, in a cantilena place, assume the poses and grimaces of his inspired "moments of communing," and to know, as soon as one listened without looking, that his playing was lusterless, full of freakish absurdities, cleverly faked in passagework, and interspersed with a chain of unexpected momentary lapses of memory from which he always masterfully extricated himself. These lapses of memory were not entirely due to the fact that he never practiced, though he had an enormous repertoire, but also more generally because he knew every work so completely that he would lose his part in the whole and might very likely emphasize something in the horns or in the strings or in the reeds.

Right here is where mention should be made of a phenomenal manifestation of this extraordinary artist, one so fantastic that only those who have witnessed and heard it can fully believe, and furthermore never cease to marvel at. Ysaÿe was the violin itself, and, so far as I have ever heard, the only one to whom the violin sufficed as a medium of expression of all music. Thus, he accomplished the unbelievable, for with his huge pipe hanging out of the right corner of his mouth, with fiddle tucked sideways against his shoulder and bow, he would accompany any concerto, giving the fullest harmonies and the most complete effects of the various elements in the orchestration. Similarly, he would play any symphony or overture and could as well play the waltzes of Waldteufel or the latest jazz.

Ysaÿe the Chamber Musician

When it came to chamber music, I was less inclined to find things "genial," for his erraticism and fiddleistic virtuosity always made me laughingly think of a mountain climber leaping from cliff to cliff while his three associates were risking neck-breaking jumps after him and apprehensively wondering where the next slip would occur. Even with music before him, he might make those "musical lapses," and when his bow trembled, you could hear his grumbled "Allez, allez!" and the tempo was changed immediately and the succeeding measures "speeded up." Ysaÿe and Pugno were generally accepted as "the ideal combination for sonatas,"[3] but musicians remember with amusement that when Ysaÿe had the theme in the "Kreutzer" Sonata, he became majestic, grandiose, sublime, and ridiculous from beat to beat, and when his partner took it up, it was at least one-third faster, while Ysaÿe blinkingly made the most grotesque sudden crescendi and vanishings within a measure and often within a beat! (Reverting to my "parlor stunts," when

I was so disposed I would give an imitation of how he interpreted the Schumann Piano Quintet when he played the viola to my first violin. Where he had the solo in the "Funeral March" movement, he would invariably broaden the tempo, and as soon as he was through, he would urge me and the others on, from beat to beat. This imitation of Ysaÿe's tone, comments, and blasphemies, the manner in which he would murmur "à moi!" and "trop fort" and "attends donc, cochon," his grimaces, his urging, urging with his whole body while everyone could hear "allez, allez, eh bien, va donc!" has always caused uproarious laughter.)

My opinion of most of these quartet performances I have already given, and perhaps, at the best, they might have been considered as excellent "sight-reading." One day, after a performance of the Second Quartet of Opus 18 by Beethoven (which was extremely erratic), in answer to the applause, Ysaÿe returned to the platform alone. Suddenly a pianist appeared on the steps leading onto the stage in old St. James's Hall, and they played as an encore the "Obertass" Mazurka by Wieniawski! Inevitably I went back-stage, with Ortmans, and long before reaching the "Green Room," we could hear Ysaÿe's voice, roaring with happiness. In the crowded room, we saw him kissing and embracing every woman. Again taking the widow and daughters of Henri Wieniawski in his arms, he roared, "N'est-ce pas—I told you that when I have the happiness of seeing you in one of my con-certs, I'll play something especially for you!"

Ysaÿe the Conductor

I no longer recall whether it was at the end of that season or a year or two later when I was playing in London that Ysaÿe was engaged as conductor in, I think, a three-day festival. At one concert I played Ysaÿe's tenderly poetic *Rêve d'Enfant* (then virtually unknown) and played it quakingly, for Ysaÿe himself sat in the audience, right there under my nose. Arbós[4] had asked me to use his Guarnerius, for "he wanted to hear how it sounds in a hall," and with Arbós sat a wonderful fiddler, Achille Rivarde,[5] a second Sarasate, in my estimation, of whose passing I just read while penning this tribute! The old contact with Ysaÿe was renewed, and with his permis-sion—or rather at his invitation—I attended some of the rehearsals to-gether with my old friend Ortmans.

Ysaÿe's manner of conducting, as was to be expected, was replete with interesting, individual, magnetic, and amusingly contradictory elements. At times he did not conduct at all, was absolutely immobile. At others he would indicate to one section of the orchestra to listen to what, for in-stance, the flutes were playing. His beats, at times, were tiny or did not cover an area of more than an inch in any direction, and then suddenly like a lion he would spring with both arms in the air, the right foot raised, and when his "mane" fell all over his face and collar, it looked truly like three paws midair. These were his gestures at concerts as well as in rehearsing.

Once, dissatisfied with the spiccati the violins were playing in a Schumann Symphony, he stopped them in high dudgeon, while in a complaining voice he kept repeating, "Mais non, mais non, mais non!" and seizing a violin from under the chin of the player nearest him, meant to demonstrate what kind of spiccato he wanted. However, the strange bow did not respond to him immediately, and in that attentive silence, he stopped suddenly, scratched his head, and exclaimed, "Where is Ysaÿe?" and the orchestra roared and applauded.

His manner of starting a rehearsal was extremely funny. In a series of rolling-uphill falls he would reach the conductor's little platform, waving his greetings to the band. Then seizing a rather small baton, he would stand there blinking hard, when suddenly he would touch the iron enclosure around himself as if it were charged with an electrocuting current, for he jumped back away from it in the same instant. Then with terrific strength he hurled shoulders, arms, and clenched fists into the air and voilà, we had the first beat to "Betovans Sankiem." In that same work, in the transition from the third to the last movement (where the tympani has the motive and steady pulsations), both hands were held in the air, on a line with his face, without any beat whatsoever, which, of course, held the orchestra to a pianissimo without any nuance whatever, while his facial expressions were conveying what he felt. However, two or three measures before the entrance of the Finale, he had quietly dropped his left arm and had gotten his right arm, very slowly, completely across his body and far past his left shoulder. The crescendo was now made by his bringing the right arm across his body, in a straight line, and as he was shaking with the intensity of what he wanted, he accomplished this in a series of jerky little motions and with such terrific physical strength that when he suddenly raised his arm for the opening melody, the flexible little baton broke into a good dozen bits of wood about an inch or two long. These the orchestra eagerly gathered, and crowding around him, he was made to autograph each one.

As I have said, I think there were three concerts during which I saw him conduct from memory the two mentioned Symphonies by Beethoven, as also those by Franck and Chausson, the *Istar* by d'Indy, the overture *Lénore* by Duparc, the entire *La mer* by Paul Gilson, and "Brünnhilde's Immolation" from *Götterdämmerung*, with a "Brünnhilde" of course. His vitality and energy were absolutely inexhaustible, for after one of these concerts, he told me "stick around" as there was yet a rehearsal to start at about 11:30 (P.M.), an extra one for the next afternoon's performance. He took about two fingers of whiskey (for just then he was "on the water wagon"), and the orchestra having been reassembled he started with undimmed fire in his tiger-like leaps and, at times, devastating profanities. After going through one composition, he yelled into the wings, "Saint-Saëns," and sure enough that marvelous little man with the unique parrot-proboscis emerged and approached Ysaÿe. The latter rose from his seat and seizing Saint-Saëns under the arms lifted him to his own height and kissed him on both cheeks. Then with a wide wave of his left arm he made the presentation: "L'orchestre philharmonique . . . Saint-Saëns!" Thereupon the latter stepped down to the platform which had been extended and which was slightly lower than the stage, and Ysaÿe resumed his seat, his back completely turned on the soloist. And without ever once turning around, they rehearsed Saint-Saëns's Fifth Piano Concerto, "Africa."[6]

In all these things Ysaÿe was a self-made musician, a natural one and born with a tremendous instinct, enthusiasm, and understanding of music. On the other hand, I think no one would gainsay the fact that as a conductor, generally speaking, and more particularly as a disciplinarian, he was utterly beyond serious consideration. For with him it was always the extremes, and when the fires from the mounts of inspiration could not be commanded, the gestures and extravagances became parodies, and the "bigness" became one vast, meaningless space of emptiness. I must not fail to mention the night, about fifteen years ago, when the late Spiering had a "stag" at his home and at which were present Auer, Kreisler, Ysaÿe, and a score of other musicians. Towards the end of the evening, I was urged to do my imitations, which consisted of the personal characteristics and peculiarities of style, tone, bowings, fingerings, manner of holding the instrument, and entrances, of a number of famous fiddlers of the past and present, today, alas, almost all of them gone. The game consisted in the audience's guessing the name of the artist from the time of his entrance through his gait, his bows, tunings, and so on. I did Sarasate, Kubelik, and the great "Fritzey" himself. Finally, taking my courage in both hands, I ended the show with an imitation of Ysaÿe himself, and his roars could be heard above the din of the others.

I might add that in listening to the few performances of his unaccompanied Sonatas, which in recent years have appeared on programs at intervals, one might become persuaded into believing them of greater value if the great actor-artist himself were presenting them, for I sadly miss his grimaces. And in termination I crave to repeat that in Ysaÿe were incorporated the heart and soul of the violin. This instrument sufficed him as a medium for the expressions of every human tenderness and greatness of thought and emotions, as it did also in the reproductions of an orchestral palette. To me he remains the synonym for violin!

Memories of Masters of the Bow: An Impression of Joachim's Last Years

His Personality and Prejudices—Playing the Formidable *Hungarian Concerto* for Its Composer—Musical Experiences with Ysaÿe[1]

Equipped with a letter of introduction from no less a personage than Ysaÿe, in which he presented me as "un artiste du premier ordre," I went to Berlin with the purpose of becoming a pupil of the great Joachim. Arrived there, I sent it, together with one of my own in which I told the Meister that all my life it had been my goal to have the privilege some day of his advice when I should be sufficiently advanced in violin playing. I begged him now to appoint a time when I might come and play for him his own *Hungarian Concerto,* hoping that my playing merited being accepted as a pupil by him whom my father had always called "az Ur Isten" [Mister God Almighty]!

A Time of Venerable Figures

It is utterly impossible for the present generation even to imagine what music-study in those days in Germany meant, for they are totally lacking in veneration towards any teacher and live in an atmosphere that is far removed from the calm and old-world culture, notably that of the time of that venerable and historic figure, Joseph Joachim. During the seven or eight years of my residence in the Prussian Capital, Richard Strauss, Muck, and Blech were all active as conductors at the Royal Opera House, with Weingartner conducting the Opera House concerts and Nikisch the Philharmonic. Joachim was Director of the Royal High School for Music, with Haliř, Wirth, Moser, and others as sub-teachers of the violin, and Humperdinck and Bruch in the composition department. Busoni, Scharwenka, Hekking, d'Albert, Godowsky, Carreño, and yet a score of great and celebrated artists made Berlin their home, and with six or eight concerts nightly, by artists from all over the world, it was the usual thing to hear three or four of the great violinists, and an equal number of celebrated pianists and singers, within any fortnight. New York City today has become the same kind of music world center, yet living is so incomparably different that to explain the manifold reasons therefor and the effects thereof would require an especial dissertation of its own.

The name and position of Joachim, not only in Germany but in the entire world of music, was immutably placed together with those of Mendelssohn, Schumann, and Brahms, and he was the acknowledged embodiment of the highest achievements in the progressive developments of the music of the German School since Beethoven's days! He was on a pedestal as violinist, composer, conductor, quartet player, and teacher, and this homage was given him to the day of his death. Of course, from earliest childhood, I had learnt all the available details of his life history and achievements, and my father's usual expression, "Joachim? O az Ur Isten!" (Joachim? He is Mister God Almighty!) was the summing-up of all.

After an interim of days, I received a notice from a secretary to the effect that Herr Prof. Dr. Joseph Joachim would receive me at his home on such-and-such an afternoon at three o'clock. Strangely enough, I have, since that very day, forgotten the name of the street, the house, and its apartment number, expecting to recall that it was somewhere "Im Westend" or near Charlottenburg. The maid led me into a room and asked me to wait a few moments as the Herr Doktor was occupied in the room adjoining. I immediately noticed a large, framed photograph of Beethoven on one wall and on that directly opposite, one of Brahms and, by Jove, in the corner of the room was a large wooden music stand and on it, opened at the spot—the Ciaconna of Bach! I was startled, for I must say the impression was far from a pleasant one. "Great grief," I thought, "hasn't the world changed at all?"

Just then the doors opened and there stood Joachim, dressed in the typical ample double-breasted Prince Albert coat of that epoch, even as I was. He was a venerable, tall man, of great dignity and calm, and looked more like a surgeon and a philosopher than a musician. "Guten Tag," he said. "Sprechen Sie Deutsch, oder möchten Sie lieber Französisch oder Englisch sprechen?" I answered, in German, that it was immaterial as to which of these languages, and thus we continued in German. The room I now was in was the Salon, with a grand piano near the window. He gave me an "A" as I placed the piano part to his monumental *Hungarian Concerto* on the piano rack, and I noticed that the maid in cleaning that day (I assume) had carelessly thrown the rug so that one side had curled over the soft pedal, and I also noted, at the end of my performance, that Joachim had not noticed this, for he never used the left pedal and, as a matter of fact, most of the time accompanied with his right hand, his left falling into his lap except occasionally when he gave the bass notes to a chord.

When I reached the first "Tutti," which yet leaves two-thirds of the first movement to be done, "Na!" he exclaimed as he rose from the bench, "Na! Sie sind ja ein ganz koloßaler Kerl!" [Well, you are truly a most prodigious talent!] and moving the rim of his glasses up and down while looking at me earnestly, he slowly approached and kissed me on both cheeks! My feelings can perhaps best be imagined—the terrific strain, the nervousness of days and weeks in anticipation, the months of hard work in final polishing-off of a gigantic work first studied some years previously, the inadequate accompaniment which really hindered more than helped, Joachim watching me more than the music before him and through force of habit giving a beat with his hand where he missed playing the notes in the accompaniment. Flushed, grateful, and excited, I asked whether I might continue, and he answered, "Ja—bitte, bitte," adding, "You see for yourself just how I play piano—but just finish the movement," which I did, while he watched me even more during the succeeding eight pages than he had during the preceding four.

Hungarian Concerto Described

I may here comment that the concerto has sixty-three pages of piano score, thirty-one for the violin, and that properly interpreted, this work takes *fifty minutes and no less*! Apart from its highly original way of writing for the violin, it requires extraordinary physical and nervous endurance because of its vehemence of accents, glissandi octaves, stretches, and a kind of repeated figuration of three notes—all of which can very easily tie the player's hand in cramps. It is yet, in my opinion, the most unviolinistic work created by a violinist, and its technique is the twin to the Brahms Concerto, which it preceded by at least a quarter of a century.[2] In this work Joachim has documented for all time the greatness of his musicianship and given a portrait of his gigantic personality as a violinist and man of noble sincerity. This—to me—autobiographical masterpiece, created in his early twenties (if I correctly recall),[3] is one so individualistic, so taxing of every resource of the player, that I have not the slightest fear of contradiction in claiming that no violinist living, however great, would undertake a performance of it, uncut, without fear and intensive preparation, for it is the kind of violin technique which requires refurbishings so that it does not "go out of the fingers" entirely; and the nervous expenditure is greater than that needed for an entire recital plus encores.

There are yet other factors which have driven this unique work into oblivion—only the violinist can realize what extraordinary fiddle problems the performer is grappling with, which have no particularly exciting effect on the audience. Added to which, the orchestration is drab and undramatic and is, in my judgment, in many spots downright bad!

Joachim's Personal Characteristics

There was great calmness in Joachim, and though he was then an old man, his voice was deep and vibrant, though without any enthusiasm. When I finished the first movement, he rose from the piano bench and asked:

"Mögen Sie Tee?" to which I bowed my thanks. He rang for the servant, ordered her to prepare tea and bring it in and, turning to me, added, "Until then you can have played the slow movement." That terminated, we went to the adjoining room and had tea while he asked me many questions. He didn't smoke, nor did I, in those days. I soon noticed he had a habit of raising and lowering his eyeglasses while observing or talking to me, and I asked him whether he still spoke Hungarian. He answered that he had so completely forgotten it that he no longer understood a single word of it, and in this he was not unlike Liszt and many others. He wanted to know how I had come to know Ysaÿe, and I told him that I had been living in London, in the home of an old friend and colleague of his, René Ortmans, who ran a sort of chamber music school in his house, and that, as Ysaÿe and many other artists came there often, I had many times had the privilege of playing quartets and piano quintets with him, sometimes as violist to Ysaÿe's leadership and at others as first violinist with Ysaÿe taking the viola part. I told him furthermore that I had always wanted to study with Ysaÿe and that he finally told me that in the summer, when he was through with his endless concerts and travels, I could come to the small village in Belgium where he went (Wideumont, I think, was its name) and then "on verra." I had gone and spent many weeks there, during which time I played for Ysaÿe once—many hours on end and parts of at least a half-dozen concerti, to which he supplied fabulously complete accompaniments with his fiddle tucked under his chin! The rest of the time, Ysaÿe went fishing, while in the evenings he demonstrated extraordinary gifts in acting out charades with his family and friends and a few other fiddlers who were hanging around in hopes of doing some serious work.

Joachim's Advice about Careers

With exultation I asked him when I could have the honor to begin work with him, and his answer was: "That is quite impossible. I have already told you that you are a talented fellow—extraordinarily so. Furthermore, I cannot accept you as a student in any case, for I am not allowed to teach privately, and as for taking you into my class? Tja, du lieber Gott! you wouldn't fit there at all, for a violinist such as you already are should let the world hear of him—and the things you lack will come with life itself and experience in public performance and the development of your career. No, no, go ahead and follow your career—you will make your way, have no fear!"[4] I could scarcely express my joy and gratitude, yet begged him to try to realize that since earliest childhood it had been one of my great ambitions to some day be worthy of the privilege of studying with him, and now that I was at last in his presence and encouraged by his high praise, would he not tell me what there was about my playing that he did *not* like? He answered: "I've told you twice what I think of you as a fiddler. Apart from which, you are endowed with a warm, musical nature and fiery temperament. Your phantasy leads you once in a while to rubatos, and in the slow movement, here and there, you did things with which I am not completely in accord—wenn auch die Paar Stellen, hie und da, mir nicht direkt misfallen haben." I jumped, ere he had terminated, to fetch the music, and returning to the table, requested him to indicate the places, but he interrupted with "nicht jetzt." As I saw no other opportunity, I begged, "Aber, verehrter Meister," but he returned impatiently, "Nein, nein—nicht jetzt. Jetzt hab' ich den Bauch voller Musik," which in plain English means, "Now I've got a bellyful!"

His Musical Prejudices

He thereupon asked me what I played—what was my repertoire. My exact answer was: "Tja, honored Master, I believe I may claim to say, without the slightest mock modesty, that I play, just simply, everything!"[5]

"Hm," he grunted amusedly, "everything! What do you call everything?" And as the names came to me, offhand, I answered, with a vague gesture, "Saint-Saëns, Lalo, Vieuxtemps, Wieniawski."

"Kenn' ich nicht," he interrupted, "aber sagen Sie 'mal, spielen Sie das Konzert von *Brahms*?" That "don't know them" had so startled and infuriated me that I answered his question with a curt "Nee!" which in German is slang for "nein." Whereupon he haughtily said, "Na, dann sagen Sie 'mal, Menschenskind, was spielen Sie denn eigentlich?!"[6] Speechless, I stared, hurt and disillusioned. It was futile to wish I might have disbelieved my ears, but inside me the shock was real, for with one blow the god had fallen from his pedestal and lay in shattered fragments all around and within me. I might have answered: "Bach, Beethoven, Brahms, Bruch, Corelli, Mozart, Viotti," and through another dozen names (or even the entire alphabet, starting with Alard and ending with Zarzycki), but I had somehow instinctively answered with the names of violinist-composers, for I have always considered Saint-Saëns and Bruch "violin-composers" through the immense influence of Sarasate and his actual collaboration in their compositions for the violin. Thus for Joachim to have put his old colleagues Vieuxtemps and Wieniawski aside with a "don't know them," meaning "don't recognize them in music," was an insult to gods whom I revered and shall worship to the end of my days!

Joachim, of course, like most great personalities, had his prejudices and hatreds, and I must say that I respected his convictions, albeit without admiring them, for he was consistent in these to the end of his days. In his early youth he broke friendship with Liszt because he could not see the "Tendenzmusik" to which the latter was inclining, and when, on his seventy-fifth birthday, a group of his pupils presented him with the full-size orchestral score of *Die Walküre* and had the three volumes gorgeously bound in green with a dedication and their names in gold-letterings, this septuagenarian sat down and wrote each of the sixteen admirers a longhand letter in which he forbade them to come within his presence because of the affront they had given him, knowing his hatred of Wagner.

The "German School" of Joachim's Day

Something horrible and devastating had happened, and I felt that, inevitably, the interview was at an end, while inwardly I rejoiced that my path, whatever it might become, lay in a direction away from that of Joachim. It was not to learn the "German School" of violin playing that I had come to him, for I had never been able to admire either their tone production, their inartistic and matter-of-fact fingerings, their revolting slides by which, in changes of position, the auxiliary note was always audible (this crutch-and-pulley by which they finally got from one place to another), the remnants of a Spohr tradition of slow "vibrato" in which the oscillations were almost counted. As to the so-called German School in matters of phrasing and bowing, I never could view the latter with anything but ridicule, for everything was calculated from the wrist and even from the fingertips of the right hand. The arm was held close to the body, and the ideal way to attain this was to practice with a book (the thinner and smaller, the better) under one's arm. Thus the four strings presented four platforms at different angles, and grace, legato, and suavity were as absent from the melodic line as they were to the beholder of such exhibitions. This "practicing with a book under one's arm" is no invention with the aim to ridicule, and in stating the simple summing-up of that school, in which thousands (once) believed, the many detrimental things are unavoidably and immediately apparent. It was not the school that I had wanted, but the guidance, the advice, and the contact with such a great personality as Joachim, and this, evidently, was not to be.

Very grateful for his kindness and his tremendous encouragement, I finally left and began reliving each moment of that unforgettable afternoon. Plans, dreams, hopes were in a turmoil in my brain, for instead of entering a Conservatory as a pupil, Joachim had told me, as Ysaÿe had before him, to go out, tackle the world, and make myself be heard from. And in my loneliness and tremendous exultation, I celebrated accordingly!

An Impression of the Joachim Quartet[7]

Next morning, at exactly two minutes before ten, the side door at the Königliche Hochschule für Musik was opened, and Joachim, attired as on the previous afternoon in the large double-breasted redingote, gave me a sign to enter and slip into the seat left vacant for me. My excitement was intense, and I noted everything about him and his three bewhiskered colleagues. Their manner of tuning and Joachim's finishing his with a G Major chord (and scratchy, I immediately thought, and also exactly *why* that chord?). The violin of Halíř seemed unusually small and appeared to be resting on a beer barrel. Wirth seemed both cross-eyed and pigeon-toed, and his slides and bowings caused me to smile. The spectacle of Hausmann playing the cello without its resting on a peg at first intrigued me, and when I saw him drop it, or rather slide it, from his knees to his feet, stare at the music during the pauses and then suddenly "Zip" when he "yanked it back" to playing position, I became amused.

And throughout it all, I kept asking myself whether I was actually sitting there and hearing the historic and world-famous Joachim Quartet, when this playing was so dry, so lifeless, leathern, scratchy, and out of tune! The monotony of it all, doubtlessly combined with too much festivity of the night preceding, finally brought about a catastrophe—I had fallen asleep and was brought to by the applause of the adoring audience! I was shocked and ashamed of myself, and the stabbing looks of those about me plainly let me feel that I should really be thrown out of the auditorium. Sobered in every way, I told myself that this was my one opportunity to hear this Immortal playing quartet, that tickets were not to be had at any time, and that perhaps Death itself would intervene ere another concert took place, and thus rigorosly chastened, without and within, I pulled myself together and at the next number—the Second Rasumovsky—paid attention with every fiber of me. Again the round of observations: the scratchy chords at the opening, the distasteful slides in the phrases immediately following in each instrument, the jarring accents of string crossings, the "feeble-old-man tone" of Joachim, the rawness of the viola, the leathery dryness and tympani-like pizzicati of the cello, and ere I knew it, the same disaster overtook me—I was sound asleep and probably snoring. The concert terminated, I returned to the Hotel, wrote Joachim a letter in which I expressed profound gratitude and admiration, and begged him for a photograph of himself. And this he sent me some days later.

Life in Berlin

Berlin became my home about two or three years after that, and I lived, played, and taught there for seven or eight years. Through my friendship with the owners of the large hall, the Philharmonie, I had free access to their box to any and all concerts, and thus I made it a point never to miss a Joachim quartet concert, when not absent on some concert tour or other. Curiously enough, during all my years of living in a beer-drinking country,

I drank French wines, and when I moved to Paris I'd go to a large brasserie on the Avenue de la Grande Armée and bring home a large carafe of Munich Spatenbräu! Never an extremist in drinking, except when in company, never touching alcohol during the day, and often for weeks and months on end, I made it a point to have tea with my light evening meal (for in those days concerts began at 7:30 P.M. in Berlin and in many cities even at seven o'clock) before going to hear Joachim. And every time, without fail or exception, I found myself getting drowsy and finally falling off to sleep!

At the end of the concert season of 1906–1907 there was a Joachim concert, and I went, saying inwardly (as I did each time), "Perhaps it will be his last and I want to be there, and perhaps some day pupils will ask me how Joachim played, and I want to be able to tell them," and so on. And so, at six in the evening, I actually took a cold shower, dressed in my "smoking jacket," and seated myself in the rear of the box. Midway in the program my friends would nudge me every once in a while and whisper, "Du! Du! Du schläfst ja!"

Joachim, of course, was a monumental figure and in his day one of the greatest of violinists, and my experiences detract nothing from his playing, nor, should I add, prove anything about me.

Joachim's Death

On the afternoon of 15 August 1907, I was in my home in Berlin giving an American girl a lesson. The sultriness was intense, and presently a terrific thunderstorm with rain broke over the earth. Terrified by it all, I commented to the young woman, "What a storm, eh? What a time for Joachim to die, just like Beethoven!" The lesson terminated and the storm died. I took my hat and went for a walk. Passing a small music store not far from my house, I glanced into the window and there saw the proprietor beckoning to me. Entering, I at once noticed his bloodshot eyes, his tear-stained face. "What is it? What's the matter with you?" I asked with sudden concern. He choked, sobbingly, "But didn't you hear? Joachim died this afternoon!" and leaning against the wall, he wept unrestrainedly.

I waited for several days, knowing that hundreds of people were streaming to his house to see the Grand Old Man before burial. And one day I, too, presented myself in Charlottenburg and asked the maid if I might enter. I found myself quite alone in the large rooms and heard the maid say, "There is a gentleman here who asks to see the Meister." Presently a lady appeared and asked me, "Were you a pupil of my father?" "No, Madame," I answered quietly, but also without adding any polite words of regretting not to have been. "Your name?" she asked curtly, and I gave it. She inclined her head and with her left hand invited me to advance. And finally I stood at the foot of the casket and gazed long at that calm face, those crooked and twisted fingers, those large tufts of hair protruding from the top of his nose and near his ears, and fervently I prayed: "O, great God Almighty, if only I could take up where he left off, and carry on!" The room was piled high with wreaths from Emperors, Kings, Academies, Artists, and Pupils. I approached closer, and leaning over him gazed at him long—long—all alone with the great, dead Joachim! Then I bowed to him and backed out of the room.

Edvard Grieg

On one Scandinavian concert tour [1905] I made a partnership with the Italian pianist Ernesto Consolo, despite which we remained loyal and affectionate friends to the day of his death.[1] Of course he was a delightful fellow and outside of music was better educated than the average pianist. We were to "do" (as the American saying goes) eighteen concerts in something like twenty-one days, in Sweden, Norway, and Denmark, and Consolo was looking to it all with considerable excitement, as it was to be his first (though my second or third) acquaintance with those countries and people.

I knew that if one played Norrköping one would also play Nyköping, but also, inevitably, if one played Lund it would be followed—or preceded— by Malmö; that one would consume considerable quantities of Swedish Porter in Göteborg and Cederstöm's Caloric (Svenska) Punschet in Stockholm. The ceremonial was to order a quart bottle and a large pot of black coffee simultaneously, and once the "Skål" was pronounced the liquor was consumed with the utmost gravity, to its last drop, all the while keeping your eyes steadily on those of your partner (male or female, a thing I found hard to do in the latter case without winking, if ever so slightly), following it by a deep bow and a gesture to show the emptied glass to one's companion. Then, from the other hand, several sips, or an entire demitasse, of black coffee were taken down, for the Swedes—as the Finns— argued that the Punsch being one type of poison and the coffee another, each counteracted the effects of the other, and thus the tune could go on merrily all night, a thing I experienced often and always to my abiding remorse. My memories of Swedish punch are that it affected me as no other strong alcoholic drink ever had. With all others my head remained perfectly clear and the stimulation made my thoughts come quicker than I could possibly rush words to express what was already being driven away by new avenues or ideas; whereas with the punch my spirits rose equally to fantastic flights, my words came in torrential flow, but when I tried to rise from the table my legs, from my knees down, were leaden and refused to come to life.

Arrived at the beautiful city of Stockholm, we stayed at the Grand Hotel, directly opposite the Royal Palace, with the statue of Sweden's national poet Rydberg before it.[2] Immediately I told the porter to order a hot bath for me—28° Celsius—for in those days I carried paperbound books and would sit idly in a steaming-hot bath for a good half-hour while I read a few chapters of some kind of literature. The porter looked at me in astonishment and in good German asked me to be good enough to give myself the trouble to follow him to the front door and out of the entrance of this magnificent hotel. Once on the sidewalk, he raised his arm and pointing to a large building at the very next corner said, "Sir, would you be good enough to note that sign with the letters B-A-D? That, Sir, is the bath establishment, and you will get far better baths there than what we can arrange here." Accordingly, I proceeded to the corner and on entering saw the ticket office, with a woman seated behind the enclosure to sell tickets and make change. In bad Swedish I told her I would gladly like to purchase a ticket for a bath, to which she retorted with one of those inhaled "Jo-då!" which sound like a gasping choke and asked "Which class, first or second?" Surprised and amused, I felt like chancing "a first-class bath" and paid the price asked.

If there yet be travelers to Sweden who have not had a bath in one of their sumptuous establishments, this episode will be almost as much a shock as it was to me at my first as at my twenty-first experience. My surprise can well be imagined when I relate that once I was in the tub, the door was opened by a key from without, and turning around, I saw a buxom young woman entering with an enormous wooden bucket on her arm. It is not for the sake of making a story that I say she was beautiful, really beautiful, for she was of the type that abounds there—tall, blonde, strongly built, and looking like a country dairymaid. However, I was not only embarrassed but also horrified, and making frantic gestures at her I supplemented them by almost screaming at her to "Go away, get out, go away!" in a good half-dozen languages. With an amused expression she calmly approached the side of the enormous tub and depositing her large wooden bucket on the floor, folded her arms, threw back her head, and openly laughed at me! "Satan!" I yelled, "You old Satan!" knowing no other oath, and one which, incidentally, is Norwegian, I think.[3]

Laughingly she retorted, "But I am not old!"

"How many years?" I asked eagerly, and don't forget that she was very beautiful.

"Eighteen," she answered in a voice in which was the ring of veracity, good health, and happiness. I have always known how to say "I love you" in at least ten languages and when telling her this, with arms stretched towards her, she answered by bending down and reaching into the bucket brought forth an enormous mop dripping with warm soapsuds, and squashing this over my head proceeded to bathe me. And bathe me she did, as a mother does a babe, and when it was all over she held an enormous towel before her and uttered the routine phrase "Step out, if you please" after which, without so much as a glance over her shoulder she left the room only to return somewhat later with a shoe-buttoner, as she must have noticed that I was wearing button shoes.

In Finland I found that women entered the bath-room in the hotels and thus the only variety, from city to city, was that I was washed one day by a sturdy country lass and the next by a toothless hag of sixty-five. But I had learnt to never declare my "love" for any of them, for I did not much relish those suds in my eyes.

The Students at Uppsala

There are two reasons why the concert at the University at Uppsala, Sweden, remains memorable. Firstly, the festivities with the students after the concert had so satiated me with Swedish punch that never since have I tasted another drop of it; and secondly, that in such a lamed condition, I was—unconscious of it—going towards one of the most glorious experiences any artist could wish for! We left early the following morning and spent the entire day on trains, going from the University town directly to Kristiania, as the capital of Norway was then called and where we were to debut that very evening.[4]

It is one thing to moralize and another to refuse to accept the invitation of the faculty and students of the University of Sweden. True, we knew we had a concert ahead of us and should have quietly retired, but the University too knew that we could not leave that night, as there were neither boats nor trains. My mistake was that I had not reckoned with the true Scandinavian temperament, for these races live only at night, when, under strong alcoholic stimulus, their fires come to the fore. Then this real, temperamental nature is hard to be equaled even by the southern races, who have the reputation for passionate outbursts. We could not foresee that there would be speeches, and that I too would be fired to the mad courage to attempt one, and in a language which I assumed they would accept as Swedish! I had picked up some phrases—in theatres and travels—and I can faithfully record that, with glass in hand, I said, "Tak! Mange, mange tusend Tak! [Thanks! Many, many thousand thanks!] This night I cannot speak any language but *Swedish*! (Applause). This night, I *am* Swedish!" (More applause and roars). Then raising my glass, but lowering my voice impressively, I uttered the phrase which I had heard in a Norwegian play, this time merely changing the name of the country: "God preserve old Sverige!" (Wild cheers and more "poison").

The public which regards a concert as an "entertainment" has no conception of the fatigues and nervous drains under which the artist tours; and in the larger of the important small towns of America, the "thrill," the "kick" is relished by the upper strata if some Society Dame has managed to corral the artist as jest-of-honor at a "Party" to which she invites all her friends, knowing their envy and hatred for her "cleverness" in again having achieved social eminence through the publicity attached to the celebrity of the moment. Is there an artist who at one time or other in his career was not obliged or advised by his manager to accept hospitality in the home of a totally strange woman-president of a See-sharp-but-be-natural Club? By way of contrast—still in the way of moralizing—it might be asked, are the aftereffects of a night even such as that, spontaneously spent with delightfully cultured and temperamental people, any more devitalizing than is the demoralization and anger of the innocent victim when he finds that his hostess has invited the entire Club to a reception *before* the concert, she having ascertained from the management that immediately after the concert the artist has to entrain for a distant city? However resenting this "trap," he is compelled to stand around, with a cup of coffee in one hand and a plate of ice cream in the other, and is supposed to be able, even thus, to consume both and smile and talk inanities. After about two hours of being drained by a hundred more people, he dresses and finally mounts the platform, robbed of his reserve of nervous energy and wishing his manager, in accepting this "hospitality" for him, had also agreed to play in his stead.

A Previous Visit to Kristiania

Consolo belonged to that guild of players who carried a mute-clavier when traveling and all day on the train, while I was treated to the click-click-click of those toneless keys as he tried to work the alcohol out of his joints by double-thirds, augmented fourths, and cavalcades of octaves from the wrists, I told him of my earlier experiences in the city we expected to reach around six o'clock that evening.

On that previous tour I had met the composer Johan Halvorsen (related by marriage, I understood, to Grieg), who was the first conductor at the National Theatre in Kristiania.[5] This theatre, where opera and drama alternated, faced a small public park or Square, and before its entrance there stood on pedestal enormous, full-length, bronze figures of Ibsen and Bjørnson (and this, mind you, during their lifetimes), each in characteristic pose. Ibsen stood with hands clasped behind him, his head down, mouth firmly set in what might be called "pessimistic" thought. His friend and relative Bjørnson (for the son of one of these great poets and writers married the daughter of the other[6]) stood in great contrast in a posture natural to him, looking up and smiling in a mood of cheerful "optimism." At the right-hand corner of that Square was a small hotel, the Hotel Westminster, and there Grieg and his wife, when they came from their mountain retreat near Bergen and spent a part of the winter months in the capital, had a suite of two rooms. It is not overstating that this suite was never available to anyone unless the management positively knew from the Griegs that they would not be in the capital at any time of that year, and that my affectionate old friend Sinding had to await the demise of his earlier colleague ere he could "inherit" those "historic" rooms.[7]

Having met Halvorsen in the café of the National Theatre, he invited me to his house with the purpose of wanting to show me some of his compositions. First he presented me with a few copies of some of his published works, including orchestral scores, then showed me several small violin pieces, in manuscript, and finally showed me his violin, a Sanctus Seraphin, commenting that he had never heard it played in a hall.

My theories then were—and yet are—that "tone" is the most individual and revealing expression of an artist's personality. It represents the quintessence of all he thinks and feels, of his musical culture, and, above all, the art of expressing imagery and the quality of *colors*! Naturally, a fine instrument is an asset, as its capabilities of response to sensitivity makes it easier for the player to achieve his ends with less effort, but, everything summed up, it is the artist who creates "tone" and not the instrument. Even on a poor instrument the characteristics of the player—warmth and vibrancy or the lack of them—will become apparent, and an artist will be able to produce better tone, both in quality and substance, than the type of player to whom everything is a matter of science and physical manipulation.

Halvorsen was a typical man of the soil, huge, heavy, and peasant-like in appearance and bearing. As he sat there, affectionately gazing at that small-modeled Seraphin, he sighed heavily: "Yes, I have never heard this violin in a concert hall, for, of course, since these years of conducting, I have neglected the violin and given up solo playing entirely." Immediately I offered to play his violin at my concert the next day, if only for one number, and delightedly he exclaimed, "Na-na! Så! Ja-så! Na!" expressions which are equivalent to "Well-well! Indeed! Is that so!" and such. "I'll tell you what I'll do, Hartmann," he continued. "Tomorrow night is Madama Butterfly. I'll have the concertmaster conduct part of the second act and I'll come over and hear you play at about nine o'clock. I'll bring the violin to your hotel tomorrow morning after rehearsal."

I said to him, "Herr Kapellmeister, if you'd lend me the manuscript of that one composition of that series, I'll learn it tonight, rehearse it with my accompanist tomorrow, and give it as an encore immediately after I shall have played on your violin—providing you stand in the back of the hall and applaud vigorously! We'll do it like this: on my first return to the stage, I merely bow" (and I carried out the pantomime) "but if you help bring me back a second time, I'll play your composition and announce it from the stage!"

With many jovial wallops on my back he agreed to this little conspiracy and this is exactly what happened the following night. The composition pleased enormously, as might be expected from a Norwegian audience applauding a little piece by its native son, however I felt sure there was something more. For there was something so haunting and native in that *Chant de "Veslemøy"* that, once published, it played its way into the hearts of many audiences of various nationalities and tastes. I have a souvenir of it all in the photograph of Halvorsen inscribed in slightly misspelled German. I should like to add that some time later I repeated that experience of publicly playing an instrument totally unknown to me when, in London, the late Arbós[8] (who many years afterwards became the conductor of the Madrid Philharmonic Orchestra) wanted to hear his [Guarnerius] del Gesù fiddle played in a hall.

Kristiania, 1905[9]

Finally arrived at Kristiania, we had but little time in which to get to our hotel and dress hastily. As soon as we entered the room backstage, memory again became alive, and I continued to relate to the champing Consolo that, in that room, some admirers had presented me with a "Hardanger" or Hardanger fiddle. This is the national instrument of Norway and has been played since time immemorial by the peasant folk. It is a violin with modified flatness yet peculiarly raised "f"—or sound—holes, is richly inlaid with pieces of mother-of-pearl, and has highly decorative scrawls on its back. Its head, or scroll, resembles the carved bow of a Viking ship and is of very ornate design. Its further peculiarities are that it has an extremely low and flat bridge (an influence which Ole Bull, in his great charlatanism, could not get away from) and has four wire, so called "sympathetic," strings which pass through holes in the lower part of the bridge, as the viola d'amore has seven. Furthermore, while it is tuned as the violin with the exception of substituting an A for the low G string, its D string, though made of gut, has a thin wire loosely and curiously in a zig-zag manner woven over it (precluding any shifting or change of positions), giving the instrument a very rasping and mandolin-like sound, though played with a bow. The fingerboard was also not supplied with frets, and any great virtuosity is quite unimaginable. Unforgettable is the evening when, at the National Theatre, I heard Halvorsen's music to *Kongen Kristian* in which the entire violin section of sixteen players used Hardangers with the composer himself sitting in the conductor's chair, directing the orchestra with his fiddle bow when not playing the Hardanger. The name itself derives from the section around the Hardanger Fjord, one of the few fertile valleys of Norway, and Halvorsen had published a collection of old Norse peasant dances for this instrument which are called Slåtter (the circle of the "a" gives it the pronunciation of "Slutter"[10]).

We were very nervous (where is the artist who is not and does not remain so to the end of his days?), for each concert (notably in a capital) is the-one-and-only, another challenge, a battle in which the player must overcome anew, or "win," as the saying goes, his public and either make a reputation or add to it if he already has something of a start of one. In the latter case there is also the responsibility of doing things that are detrimental, and then his bit of a favorable reputation finds itself on the downward grade with press and public. Hence the lamed condition in which we found ourselves that night was both a worry and, let it be confessed, a humiliation to us; and while Consolo was massaging his fingers, I yet had the slight advantage of having my own instrument with me, whereas the pianist makes acquaintance with a totally strange piano only when he is on the podium. Chatting ceaselessly, I asked Consolo, "Don't you remember that colored picture I have in Berlin? *The Norwegian Wedding* by Tidemand with the Hardanger leading the procession?"[11] Consolo, who had been raised in England, spoke the language excellently, in fact with a slight Cockney accent, answered by wishing the whole thing were gotten over with and that henceforth he'd stick to mild wines and Asti spumante. With fiddle in hand, I started dancing around him while I asked: "I sigh old top and all that sort o' thing ye knaow, an' 'ow would yer like to 'ave a coupla Norwegian Slutter?" for the talk of the Hardanger had revived my memories of Halvorsen's Album.

Grieg had largely utilized folk dances in his compositions, and with the excitement of a discovery, I suddenly remembered that in the very sonata we were about to play there occurs a part of one of the "Slåtter" to be found in the Halvorsen collection. Waltzing around Consolo, I played it in its entirety, adding the cadences and open fourths which Grieg had omitted. Parodying all this and coming at Consolo from all sides, I was stealing up on him from behind while without pause I kept repeating that "Grieg" dance when suddenly I stopped as if struck by lightning! The door had opened and there stood a small, slightly hunch-backed man with a shock of gray hair—"Grieg!" I almost screamed.

"Ja," he said in a peculiar intaking breath resembling a gasp,[12] and I could not believe my ears or trust my eyes, for I was still too dumbfounded to be able to move or think.

Rooted to the spot, in dumbfounded and petrified amazement, I could not think of anything to do or say, and again I exclaimed "Grieg! Mein Gott!"

"Ja, ja," he said asthmatically, as he approached, "Ja, der bin ich."

"Meister," I exclaimed, holding out my arms, the violin in one hand, the bow in the other, and with bowed head before him I said in a voice deep with penitence, "Verzeihen! Bitte, Meister!" I felt humiliated at having been caught parodying his sonata and on top of it all to have been so knocked over by surprise as to have been unable to address him even with the civility of "Mister Grieg."

Shaking hands with Consolo and myself, Grieg told us that he seldom found himself in Kristiania so late in the year for he usually spent his winters in Kopenhagen and on the continent and that (turning to me) he was curious to hear me play, for, he said, he had heard considerable talk of me. In turn, we thanked him for the great honor he had done us in coming to the concert and complained of the fatigues of travel, of concerts in daily succession, and, above all, of our friends of only the evening previous, the students of the University at Uppsala. "Na-na-na-na," he said with a deprecating gesture as he started for the door, and amicably adding, "Ich bin sehr gespannt" ["I am very eager"], he left the room.

"Caro mio ben!" I exclaimed desperately, "We'll die! We'll surely die, but not tonight! We'll die tomorrow or the next day, but tonight *we play,* per Bacco, we play as we never have before!" And with fierce earnestness we clasped hands and walked out before the audience. In the front row sat Grieg with several of his friends, and we made a deep bow to him personally and then one to the public as at a court concert in other parts of Europe, for in those days Norway had put up the Storthing [Parliament of Norway] and was in the midst of her fight for separation and independence from Sweden.[13]

I had no idea whether our interpretation of his music was the right one from any angle whatsoever, but I knew that so far as my feelings and convictions carried me it was the only way in which I could play it. I had, of course, heard a number of violinists play the Grieg Sonatas, and while I readily admit that they too must have acted from convictions, I must state without circuitous argument that my own interpretation was my own and since then has remained immutably so.

The stupid custom, which originated in Germany, of suppressing one's emotions and refraining from applause until one has choked down three or four separated and totally unrelated movements of a sonata or symphony had, fortunately, not yet spread in any lati- or longitudinous directions, and thus after the first movement there was applause in which, of course, Grieg joined. After the second movement Grieg's "Bravos" and exclamations of "Extraordinary" and his enthusiastic gesticulations could be seen and heard by all, and when, at the termination of the Sonata, he stood up, wildly applauding and waving his arms, the success of the evening was complete. He came back at the end of the concert exclaiming "Wonderful . . . extraordinary" and added, "We have dinner together tomorrow—two o'clock—but I'll telephone you at ten in the morning," and precipitously avoiding the people crowding into the room he disappeared from view.

A Dinner Party with Grieg

At ten minutes preceding ten o'clock the next morning, the hotel porter approached our rooms to say that Herr Grieg had just telephoned and wished us to be informed that he would be ten minutes late. I never forgot this indication of his breeding, this punctilious correctness to details which I have often noted in other first-class minds, in individuals who have accustomed themselves to the discipline of constructing a work and then of writing an orchestral score with the utmost neatness and clarity. They had learnt to know that a misplaced note, a mere dot, if put on the wrong line, might produce a terrific clash of the cymbals.

We awaited Grieg's arrival downstairs (we stayed at the Grand Hotel), and after shaking hands, he reached into his overcoat pocket and presented me with the photograph which I reproduce together with its glowing tribute written on back. Despite my wild joy at this unsolicited gift and such enthusiastic praise, I felt abashed and pained to see that he had brought Consolo nothing at all. Consolo, however, in that same instant was telling Grieg that he, of course, played the Concerto, and Grieg immediately retorted by asking whether by any chance Consolo had the score of the work with him. Receiving a reply in the affirmative, Grieg asked Consolo to go fetch it and leave it with him as he had some changes in orchestration from the printed pages and would like to write them in, and turning to me said that we would all dine together at two o'clock that day and gave us the address. It turned out to be a small, low building, somewhere near the outskirts of the city, it seemed to me, where he had reserved the parlor floor and where an extraordinary dinner had been ordered. In the party were Grieg and his wife, the famous Nina, Halvorsen and his wife, Bjørnson and his wife, a son of Ibsen (Einar) and his wife Ellen Gulbransen, the then-famous opera singer, and yet two or three others.

Most of the ladies wore full décolleté gowns and many men were in full evening suits . . . at 2 P.M.! It would be as futile as it is unnecessary to attempt to recall what the conversations were in a company of such minds and personalities, but what is worthy of recording is that a truly great musician practically never talks about music! He may and does inject a comment here and there in his conversation which is a meaningful observation or a revealing musical deduction, a philosophical conclusion, or the expression of a religious sentiment which he, as a musician, expresses in musical terms or even by quoting, by singing, a musical phrase which depicts or illustrates. It is only the small-minded and limited musician, or the narrowed and ungifted pedagogue or theorist, or the "successful virtuoso," the one-sided technician or instrumentalist, who is so obnoxious in steering the talk to his favorite harangue on musical vivisection, a revolting exhibition of a shameless egocentric whose clashing and antagonistic vibrations I can sense even from an adjoining room and whose actual company forebodes nightmares and a sluggish liver for at least two days.

Starting with the typical Smørgåsbord—those Scandinavian "butter breads" or appetizers consisting of endless varieties of roe, of sardines and sardellen, of many kinds of sausages and pressed meats, of fried eggs, luscious little hot balls of meat, black goat's cheese, everything sped on its way by intermittent little glasses of Arrac or the Danish Aquavit—we at last proceeded to the large table where soup was followed by the national fish dish, the cod, with an excellent Sauterne. Then came an enormous Châteaubriand with sauce Béarnaise and pommes soufflées with a Bordeaux Château. This was followed by "Ryper," the wild black quail which is always served with the Norwegian "lingon"-berry and sated by a deep

Burgundy. In its place of etiquette now belonged the Omelette Souflée with a château sauce and the champagnes, of course. There were toasts and speeches in Norwegian and German, in Italian, French, and English. It was the typical banqueting or festivities program of those days and often the almost daily dining (in the late evening hours) of the well-to-do classes of Scandinavia or the continent.

Ere quitting the table to have coffee and cognac in the adjoining room, I was rather startled to have someone tap me on the shoulder while at the same time my name was whispered into my ear. Turning slightly, I saw it was Grieg, who at the same time was making me some mysterious signs and reaching into his hip pocket, from which he extracted a small bottle which contained a perfectly clear fluid. "Here, Hartmann," he said enthusiastically, "Here is something that I have brought especially for you. I drink it on rare occasions only, and I brought just a little along, just for us two. Hold your glass . . . the small one will do . . . for of this one must not drink too much . . . and now, Skål Hartmann, du Teufelskerl [you devil of a fellow], and God preserve you!" I gulped it with him, and by my soul I yet believe it was white, unadulterated alcohol with a peculiar flavoring added! It was dynamite, and I feared what might happen the next moment. It exploded in Grieg, for running around the table to his place he started banging it and above the din was yelling to the waiter, "Postkarten! Postkarten! Pen and ink!" and seizing them from the tray of the approaching waiter, he wrote on one, "Tausend begeisterte Grüße an die Frau des herrlichen Geigenmeisters Hartmann! Edvard Grieg,"[14] and across the table asked me for my Berlin address. Then he gave it to the waiter to mail, telling him to first bring it over to me.

Grieg's First Anecdote

We were sitting apart from the others, in the adjoining salon—Grieg and his quaint and equally famous wife, Nina, Consolo, and myself—when Grieg started reminiscing over his coffee and cigars. I give two anecdotes which I consider worthy of record, for I have never heard or read of them elsewhere. The sequel to the first I do not give, for it has long ago passed into history, but what preceded that memorable visit to Liszt I was hearing for the first time.[15]

"Some time after our marriage," he started, "we were planning a trip to Rome, and I decided to break the journey by a stop in Leipzig, where I wanted to show my former teacher Reinecke the Piano Concerto I had at last completed.[16] Reinecke, as you know, was then director of the Leipzig Conservatory and conductor of the Gewandhaus concerts. I made a bundle of the orchestral score and, with a letter on top, left it at the Conservatory. In that letter I told Reinecke that I had married and with my wife was on

my way to Italy but had made this stopover for the sole purpose of showing the Meister the Piano Concerto which I had completed, the score of
which I was taking the liberty herewith of leaving for his kindly inspection.
Three days went by without a sign of any kind from Reinecke, and then
came a note saying he would by very pleased to have me come, with my
wife, on Thursday—yet two days off!—and have coffee at his house at four
o'clock. Now, you understand," continued Grieg with considerable heat,
"that meant that we had been sitting in a hotel room for five days, and in a
town which had never been particularly sympathetic to me. I had already,
more than once, regretted that stop, for I was yearning for the warmth of
Italy and, besides, I had high hopes of meeting Liszt and—if my courage
did not fail me—of showing him my work. What little packing we had to
do was all completed so we could get the night train out of Leipzig as soon
as the visit to the Reineckes was through.

"The professor and his wife received us with mild but marked affability,
though lukewarm and tinged with a peculiar restraint which at once made
me unpleasantly self-conscious." Imitating the impersonal and rather con-
descending tone of Reinecke's conversation, Grieg continued: "'So, so! Well,
well! Na, indeed! And so you have gotten married! Well, well! And where
did you get yourself this charming bride? And now doubtlessly on your
honeymoon to Italy! Well, well, Italy! Ah yes, Italy is beautiful . . . its skies
and its climate . . . do have more coffee . . . Bellagio, Como . . . oh, please
another small piece, won't you? Not even a tiny piece of this crumb cake?
Oh, please, do take some!' I was painfully annoyed and could not quite
fathom what lay behind this tone of playfulness, yet however impatient I
was to hear him veer the talk to my manuscript, I could, of course, not
broach the subject.

"We had to drink more coffee and eat more cake while he, as if humor-
ing a youngster, continued his childish banter: 'And so you have married,
and the former Leipzig student has brought his young bride—and a neat
little person she is—to call on his old teacher. Well, well! Now, but that is
frightfully nice of you, really very, very nice indeed!' and he swallowed
large gulps of coffee with a sound that was an added irritation to me."

As if suffocating with rage, Grieg suddenly jumped from his chair and
began pacing around us. Laughingly I interposed, "Having made Italy and
marriage his subject, already given the masculine and feminine themes, I
suppose the good old Reinecke began to expostulate on the first movement
of the sonata form with many, highly original episodes and transitions
thrown in in the shape of time-tables, change of trains, and . . ."

"Bravo!" exclaimed Grieg, enthusiastically slapping me on the back.
Then abruptly stopping before me, he exclaimed, "What did you say? No!
Quite the contrary! The good old Herr Professor Reinecke took the varia-
tion-form, and after he had tortured every bit of essence from the theme, he
dissected it, motif by motif down to one or two notes until these two, like

dried bones, rattled together!" This, of course, called for copious drinking after which Grieg continued: "I exchanged glances with my wife, and, she seeing I was suffering acutely, we both rose to take our departure, my anger and humiliation almost driving me insane!" He choked in his asthmatic way, excited as he was by the hatred of those memories and the quantities of alcohol we all had been imbibing during the afternoon.

His eyes flashing lightning as he struggled for breath, Grieg resumed: "I thought that surely this last gesture of ours would bring up the matter of my score. But no! We were actually allowed to bow our way out, with many good wishes from the Reineckes for a happy journey and not a mention of, not an allusion to, my piano concerto! They accompanied us to the front door and at last we stood outside, looking at each other helplessly! I felt so weak I could hardly walk down the stairs, but suddenly a fury seized me, a mad rage against myself even more than against Reinecke, and ere my courage should fail me I ran back up the stairs and gave the bell a violent pull. 'My manuscript!' I would demand in an outraged scream. Not another word, just 'My manuscript!' I would shout. But Reinecke himself opened the door! He had not yet had time to have traversed the antechamber. Suddenly I felt weak, all my timidity overcame me, and with half-uttered words hemmed in my throat I painfully stammered, 'Ach, forgive me, Verehrter Meister, but at the time I left my letter, I took the liberty of leaving my manuscript, a package, so to speak, and . . .' 'A package?' he echoed vaguely, as if trying to recall, 'quite so, ein packetchen, please remain where you are, just for a momentchen, if you please, and I'll run and fetch it. I know just where I placed it, just a second.' He disappeared and, returning with it immediately, said, 'So, here we are, and Glückliche Reise and much, much happiness to you.'"

Grieg's sixtieth birthday was celebrated by the dedication of a bust of him in the Leipzig Gewandhaus. Was it put face to face with that of Reinecke? . . .

Grieg's Second Anecdote

Shortly after Grieg had married his cousin, Nina, in Kopenhagen on 11 June 1867, the twenty-five-year-old composer started working on his Piano Concerto, which immediately found an enthusiastic admirer in his fellow countryman, Edmund Neupert.[17] Grieg dedicated the work to Neupert, who gave its first performance at an orchestral concert in Kopenhagen on 3 April 1869. Grieg's second anecdote referred to a somewhat later performance at the hands of Neupert, with the composer as conductor. Having, at last, obtained a grant from the Norwegian government—to which end Liszt's endorsement had helped—the young couple started on a journey to Italy in the fall of 1869.[18] On the way, two concerts took place in the hall of the Casino, in Kopenhagen, and it was at the second of these that Neupert performed and Grieg conducted the Concerto.

"The concert took place in Kopenhagen," Grieg related, "with the orchestra of the Association, which is that of the Royal Opera. *I* was to conduct, and you can imagine, Hartmann, how I felt!" With mimicking, comic gestures he continued, "Can you imagine *me* as a conductor?! By the time the concert was to start, I was so nervous I did not know where I was, believe me! Neupert and I came out together, he of course first and I a little behind him. I made a slight, nervous bow and, hastily mounting the conductor's small platform, raised my arm and, turning toward the tympani, signaled him to begin.

"Now, I don't know whether you remember that the concerto begins with a crescendo tympani roll followed by a crashing chord of the orchestra and the soloist, who, from that point, starts the work. Well, I meted out four beats and the orchestra came in with the chord, but no soloist! In terror I turned around and saw Neupert nervously struggling to unbutton his gloves and extricate his perspiring fingers. In those days it was customary for soloists to appear on the stage wearing white kid gloves, and in my frantically nervous state I had simply forgotten to allow time for this little ceremonial."

The Second Kristiania Concert

The party broke up around five o'clock, and Consolo and I hastened to the hotel to try to find a quarter-hour's relaxation, were such a thing at all possible after a day of such memorable exultation and excitement. For notwithstanding this unexpected meeting and dinner, we had another concert that very evening, with, of course, an entirely different program. Yes, that is a part of an artist's nervous equipment which puts him apart from all his fellowmen—the will and ability to resuscitate an energy which lies at the lowest state of exhaustion; or that especial technique to command his imagination to at least a glow, if not to a fire, before a public which is largely ignorant and completely apathetic to the personality and art of the performer!

As we appeared on the stage, to our surprise and momentary distraction we again saw the Griegs and practically the entire party of the afternoon occupying the first two rows. The surprise was because we certainly would not have presumed to ask a musician of Grieg's caliber whether he cared to hear more music, and we had regarded the eventful day and its preceding evening as our first and last meetings with the great national tone poet. In a country where poets and musicians have seen monuments erected to them *during* their lives (as Saint-Saëns and others had experienced elsewhere) it is assumed that wherever they choose to indicate a preference they are

welcome, and I recall that while playing, with half-closed eyes, I was comparing the living Grieg—directly in front of me, right there in the first row—
with the bust of a younger Grieg which was in that hall together with those
of Svendsen and other Norwegians.[19] But the fact remains that again I knew
within me, and with the suddenness of a blow of an overwhelming force,
"Tomorrow I die! Yes, tomorrow, but not now! Now I have to *live,* even if
I die by the effort tomorrow!" for one is never unaware of the personality
of a great individual, nor could one ever be. However, this second concert
in the presence of Grieg had already the great and rare warmth of sympathy and admiration; it meant making music, fortunately this time without
the terrific ordeal of interpreting (to the very best of one's convictions) a
work by a living composer in his presence.

Upon the concert's termination, Grieg came back alone, dressed in street
clothes as he had been all day, and inquired where our next concert was to
be. We replied that we were leaving the following morning at eleven, returning directly to Stockholm for our third and final concert there. How
deeply were we moved, when reaching the railway station next morning,
to see that picturesque couple, Edvard and Nina Grieg, awaiting us! A
heavy snow had fallen all through the night and it was yet coming down in
pieces the size of my thumb. To see these two dwarf-like figures standing
there, bundled in furs, woolen mufflers, and galoshes, their gray hair seemingly a part of the huge batches of snow which fell around two dear faces
from which shone warmth and kindliness, playful vivacity, and spring eternal, was to make me feel again that in these two living roots of Norway my
heart too pulsated with love and understanding. For had not I, too, heard the
deep sonorities of the majestic Fjords; on the decks of their tiny steamers had
I not in countless hours of vast silences become selfless with the mysteries of
their eternal mountains; at dusk and dawn had I not seen the faces of the
imperishable gods; and through the depths of noble granite had I not heard
the troglodytes making merry below? These mysteries had been my actual
and soulful experiences and now, before me, was standing the man whose
heart, brain, and soul had given all this to the world in his music! I did not
know how to tell him all this, ere we parted, for my heart was overflowing
with emotion. But I also knew that feelings require no oratorical effusions.

He inquired what our next Stockholm program was to be, and we answered, "The one we had played at our first Kristiania concert," that is to
say, containing his G-Major Sonata.

"Oh, but that is very bad!" he exclaimed in a most startled manner.
"That is terrible. . . . It might even be catastrophic for you!" he went on
with abrupt, angry gestures. "You surely must know what the political
situation is and how long our Storthing has been fighting that Norway
obtain her independence from Sweden! And to play Norwegian music in
Sweden now is surely very ill-advised! I'm very sorry, but by Jove, that is a
great mistake. Your manager should have known better!"

The train now steaming in, Grieg accompanied us to the outer platform. The snow fell on us silently, in heavy, large flakes. The moment had come, and, deeply overcome, I deposited my large, heavy, two-fiddle case by my side on the snow, and, removing my hat, I stood before him. "Master," I said, while amazedly I saw him take his large, round fur cap from his head with both hands (Grieg was then 62!). As I stood humbly before this great spirit, affectionately watching the snow drop tenderly on his white hair, my heart spoke, and impulsively I cried, "Dear Master, I shall *never* forget you, never, never! You have been so good to me—so wonderful, so warm—I can never ever describe my gratitude. I shall never forget you! God preserve you," and with fervor and solemnity I said, "Gud bevare gamle Norge!" ("God preserve Old Norway!")

He kissed me on both cheeks and shaking hands said to me (in German, of course), "Adieu Hartmann, much fortune and success! You play my Sonata as if you had composed it. God be with you, for you've got the Devil in your belly![20] And don't forget to send me your photograph!"

We stood at the windows waving to those diminishing figures and spent the rest of that day in silent gazing out of the carriage windows, for our emotions and memories of that marvelous and strange meeting were too vivid, too deep for words. And each had the realization that something had happened that came but once and to few, to very few of our fellow mortals.

Separation of Norway and Sweden

Arrived at Stockholm, we again stayed at the hotel which is directly opposite the Royal Palace, and this time, by a strange and fortunate coincidence, were given rooms facing the street, the large Square, and the statue of Rydberg. Glancing out of the window the dark morning of the day of our concert, I noticed an ever-growing crowd of the populace gathering in the square below. Running to Consolo's room, adjoining, I dragged him to his windows, and with curious wonderment we stood there watching. Silently the crowd grew ever denser, and after telephoning downstairs to ascertain the meaning of this, we too watched in grave silence. At about eleven o'clock, or perhaps it was noon, as the bells tolled, the windows to the balconies of an upper story of the Palace were thrown open, the King appeared and saluted the bare-headed populace standing below in poignant silence. In another moment, in utter silence, the old flag which symbolized Sweden and Norway was lowered, and standing at rigid salute (we, too, in the hotel room), the new flag, that of Sweden alone, was hoisted, and the multitudes dispersed in solemn, proud but mute sorrow. Again we had been partners in events of great significance, and numbed by the great moment, we smiled at each other with faint irony while simultaneously we exclaimed, "And tonight we are to play *Grieg's* music here!" It was to be the last number on the program, and we realized we'd have to face it, for there was, as yet, no communication from our manager, nor, as a matter of fact, any sign of him.

The concert went very well with our opening Sonata, followed by Consolo's number (the *Symphonic Variations* by Schumann, I think) and mine, the Ciacona of Bach. Thus far the evening had been a very successful one, and we were a-tremble to know what reception, or surprise, the audience had reserved for us with the Grieg Sonata. Summoning every bit of courage we were capable of, we returned to the platform and started the work. At the end of the first movement the applause was tremendous; ditto at the second; and at the termination of the work we were recalled again and again! The audience did not leave, the clapping did not subside, many crowded around the stage (as was customary, more or less, in various countries of Europe), and as it was a Sonata recital and not an individual one, we finally returned to the stage and repeated the last movement of the Grieg Sonata! Excitedly hastening from the hall, we sent Grieg a telegram somewhat as follows: "Enormous success . . . compelled to repeat last movement of your Sonata . . . Homages from Consolo and Hartmann."

In 1905, my essay on the Bach Chaconne having appeared in the *Allgemeine Muzik Zeitung* of Germany, I took the liberty of sending Grieg a copy.[21] I quote his amiable reply:

Kristiania, 17/11/05, Hotel Westminster. Please accept my heartfelt thanks for the beautiful picture as well as for the article on Bach's Ciacona, which I read with great interest. Now I understand *why* your interpretation of this piece was so wonderful! I hope we shall meet again some day. Best regards from my wife. Very truly yours, Edvard Grieg.[22]

On 4 September 1907, the news of the passing of that great and beautiful person hit me with the grief of a personal loss, and at once I busied myself trying to obtain a concert hall. In Berlin's overcrowded concert life this was no longer possible, but there was a pianist, a mediocre individual, who was willing to cede me his reservation on the condition that we combine in the three Sonatas as a memorial to Grieg. It was not exactly the person I would have cared to have as a partner, but, after all, the fundamental thing was a public tribute, even if, in these memorial concerts, we were by no means the only ones to pay homage to his music. Mine, however, was also personal.

Was Grieg a great composer? Yes, a thousand times yes! This small man, slightly hunchbacked and possessing but one-eighth of *one* lung, had the willpower of a giant; the fiery temperament and imagination of all the

Seven Hells (as also the temper of a fiend); the poetry and the soul of a race of great people and of a country unique in its beauty and grandeur, its passion and tenderness; and his heart embraced all mankind. His national-ism was so passionately true that this microcosm appealed to all the Cos-mos—regardless of race and nationality—and I believe that what he gave the world, when he wrought with beauty, remains indestructible.

Appendix A

The *Minstrels* Manuscripts

A-1. Facsimile of Hartmann/Debussy Concert Program, 5 February 1914
A-2. Facsimiles of the *Minstrels* Manuscripts

Introduction

We are including in Appendix A two manuscripts of the transcription for violin and piano of Debussy's *Minstrels*: a Debussy autograph dated 17 January 1914 at the Sibley Music Library of the Eastman School of Music and an undated (circa 1944) Hartmann autograph at the Free Library of Philadelphia. For Arthur Hartmann, these were two extraordinary documents of a musical friendship. They bear witness to his joy in knowing Debussy, but they also reveal the conflict and sorrow Hartmann had experienced.

Hartmann first met Claude Debussy on 6 October 1908. Hartmann had earlier attended a performance of *Pelléas et Mélisande* in Paris and had been deeply moved by the music. He had written to Debussy for permission to make transcriptions of his music. This initial meeting was for the purpose of showing the fruit of Hartmann's labor. With Debussy at the piano, Hartmann played his violin transcription of *Il pleure dans mon coeur* from the song cycle *Ariettes oubliées*. After several hearings Debussy gave his enthusiastic approval. In Hartmann's own words:

> Thoughtfully turning toward me he said: "There is only one little place," and pointing to it continued, "You see this? Well, this is yours and you put it in the violin, and this is mine, and in the piano part, and instead, I would ask of you to permit me to change that so that *I* become the violin and *you* the piano, this way, we will become more . . . this way," and he made a gesture of clasping his hands tightly, with fingers interlaced, and then he impulsively held out his hand to me in our first and long handclasp![1]

Thus began a collaboration which would produce two more transcriptions, *La fille aux cheveux de lin* (1910) and *Minstrels* (1914), both from Debussy's *Préludes,* Book I, for piano. On 5 February 1914, Debussy and Hartmann gave a public performance of all three transcriptions at the Salle des Agriculteurs.

La fille aux cheveux de lin was instantly popular, frequently presented in recitals by Fritz Kreisler, Jascha Heifetz, Nathan Milstein, and many other violinists. Measures 24–27 are especially remarkable: to the original parallel piano chords in this *sans lourdeur* passage, Hartmann added the melody from the opening, played in delicate violin harmonics. It was a stroke of genius, a stunning effect reminiscent of an earlier Hartmann masterpiece, his iridescent setting of Edward MacDowell's *To a Wild Rose.*

The history of *Minstrels* is not so peaceful. In his memoir Hartmann indicated that Debussy had asked him for the manuscript of the transcription so that the work could be published in Debussy's name. Hartmann states that Debussy's reason for such a request was his strained financial circumstances.[2] Debussy argued that if Hartmann published the transcription under his own name it would bring him nothing and Debussy only minuscule royalties at a later date; however, the transcription could be profitable for the composer if published under his own name.[3]

In a letter of 2 January 1914 [CD-22], Debussy told Hartmann he was working on *Minstrels,* presumably working from the original Hartmann manuscript (we are not aware of the existence of this manuscript). Debussy's 17 January 1914 autograph manuscript is inscribed: "Transcription pour piano et Hartmann." In the Debussy manuscript, four measures in the violin part (mm. 28–31) were crossed out and replaced with simpler material. When the transcription was published (Durand 1914), these same four measures were further simplified. There are additional differences between the manuscript and the publication.

Hartmann gave an amusing account of how he reminded Debussy about the posters for their upcoming recital in which notice was given of the three Hartmann transcriptions. Debussy replied: "Moi, je m'en fiche des affiches." ("Who cares about the posters!"). The printed program from this recital reads "Trois Transcriptions par Arthur Hartmann" (see facsimile of printed program, Appendix A-1). Apparently this confusion about the authorship of the transcription did not go unnoticed. *Musical Courier* editor Leonard Liebling reported on 7 December 1916:

> Hartmann is a real adapter, as he proved when he made the charming violin version of MacDowell's *To a Water Lily* and the exquisite Debussy transcriptions. Some of the latter are credited to Debussy himself, for reasons best known to the publisher. Hartmann is not aware that we know this, and that is why we take malicious delight in publishing it.[4]

As late as 7 June 1929, violinist Jacques Thibaud and pianist Alfred Cortot performed the *Minstrels* transcription in London with the credit given to Hartmann.[5] Whatever the name on the published transcription, evidence points to Hartmann as the originator of the transcription, followed by collaboration with Debussy.

The *Minstrels* episode notwithstanding, Hartmann was grateful for the inspiration and friendship of this great musician. At the beginning of their friendship Hartmann confessed: "I was so impressed that I thought of Debussy constantly, when I play Bach or Beethoven or Mozart I found myself wondering what Debussy would have done under similar inspiration."[6] Ten years later, even after having given Debussy the *Minstrels* transcription, Hartmann was still speaking of "a friendship which years of intimacy have only strengthened and deepened in devotion and affection."[7] Debussy likewise was solicitous of Hartmann's friendship. On 24 June 1916, he wrote to Hartmann about "preparing to write the sonata for violin and piano, for which you must be quite impatient" (see facsimile of part of the letter [CD-23], pp. 126–28). Alas, it was the violinist Gaston Poulet who gave its first public performance in Paris on 5 May 1917, with the composer at the piano, Hartmann having long since left Paris. More than ten years after Debussy's death, Hartmann wrote to the composer's widow to inquire about any Debussy manuscripts for a composition for the violin. Sadly, Emma Debussy replied on 5 August 1929 [ECD-37]: "Claude ne m'a jamais parlé d'une chose spéciale vous étant destinée" ["Claude never spoke to me about anything special intended for you"] (see facsimile of part of the letter, pp. 166–67). In fact, Hartmann already had in his possession the only indication of any composition intended for him, the Capriccioso theme for the *Poème* for violin and orchestra, inscribed by Debussy on 13 May 1910 in Hartmann's autograph book [CD-6]. The *Poème* itself was never written.

In truth, however, the violin sonata, the last finished work by Debussy and his only work for violin, may possibly be regarded as being written with Hartmann in mind. Debussy had not composed any work for violin before he met Hartmann. In his letter of 3 August 1910, Debussy thanked Hartmann for the "renseignements 'violonistiques'" ("'violinistic' information") from the essay on the Bach Chaconne [CD-14]. But some of the earliest and most lasting inspiration for the violin sonata seems to have come from the Hartmann transcriptions, especially *Minstrels*.[8] It is reasonable to believe that Debussy's skills to compose for the solo violin were significantly enriched through his friendship and musical collaboration with Hartmann.[9]

Hartmann's devotion to Debussy was lifelong. In the early 1940s, in addition to writing the memoir "Claude Debussy As I Knew Him," Hartmann revisited the Debussy transcriptions. In 1943 Edition-Musicus of New York published a new and "freely transcribed" version of *Il pleure dans mon coeur,* with an even greater "interlacing of fingers," as Debussy had so charmingly characterized the continuous exchange of musical material between violin and piano. Hartmann applied the same technique to another Debussy work, a transcription of the song *Beau soir* (published by G. Schirmer in 1943). Not surprisingly, Hartmann also returned to *Minstrels.* The memories of 5 February 1914 must have lingered in Hartmann's mind. It was the scene of one of his great artistic triumphs, and the *Min-*

strels transcription was surely the high point of that evening for him. In a review of the recital Louis Laloy found *Minstrels* to be the finest of the three Hartmann transcriptions, especially "des pizzicati glissés où tient en raccourci tout le continent noir" ("those gliding pizzicati where the whole dark continent is held in miniature").[10] In revising the *Minstrels* transcription, Hartmann made these treasured pizzicati even more prominent, turning the violinist into an "authentic" minstrel, a banjo player.

A-1. Facsimile of Hartmann/Debussy recital program, 5 February 1914.

SALLE DES AGRICULTEURS
:: 8, Rue d'Athènes, 8 ::

JEUDI 5 FÉVRIER 1914
à 9 heures précises du soir

CONCERT

donné par

— Arthur —

Hartmann

avec le concours de M.

Claude

Debussy

PRIX DES PLACES

Fauteuils parterre, première série · · · 10 fr.
Seconde série · · · · · · · · · · · · · · · 7 —
Galerie, premier rang · · · · · · · · · · · 5 —
Autres rangs · · · · · · · · · · · · · · · · 3 —

BILLETS EN VENTE :

SALLE des AGRICULTEURS, 8, r. d'Athènes;
DURAND, 4, place de la Madeleine ; MAX
ESCHIG, 13, rue Laffitte et 48, rue de Rome ;

Représentant : C. KIESGEN
8, RUE DE MILAN — TÉLÉPHONE : Central 44-45

PROGRAMME

✤

Sonate en *sol mineur* (Op. 13), pour Piano et
Violon . . . . EDVARD GRIEG
  Lento doloroso, Allegro vivace.
  Allegretto tranquillo.
  Allegro animato.

MM. *CLAUDE DEBUSSY* et *ARTHUR HARTMANN.*

Concerto en *mi majeur* . . . . J.-S. BACH
  Allegro.
  Adagio.
  Allegro assai.

M. *ARTHUR HARTMANN.*

Ciaconna, pour Violon seul . . . . J.-S. BACH

M. *ARTHUR HARTMANN.*

**Trois Transcriptions par Arthur
Hartmann** . . . . CLAUDE DEBUSSY
  Il pleure dans mon cœur.
  La Fille aux cheveux de lin.
  Minstrels.

M. *ARTHUR HARTMANN.*
Au Piano : *l'AUTEUR.*

a) **Adagio et Allegro** . . . . A. CORELLI
b) **Sarabande** . . . . GEMINIANI-NACHÉZ
c) **Moïse** . . . . N. PAGANINI

M. *ARTHUR HARTMANN.*

✤

Au Piano d'accompagnement : *M. EUGÈNE WAGNER*

✤

PIANO BECHSTEIN

A-2a. Debussy's Autograph Score of the *Minstrels* Transcription, Inscribed to Hartmann, 17 January 1914.

[1] Title page. Sibley Music Library, Eastman School of Music, University of Rochester. Used by permission.

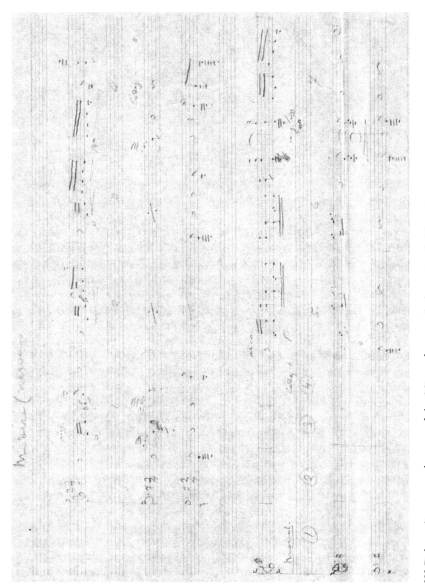

[2] Debussy's autograph score of the *Minstrels* transcription, mm. 1–11.

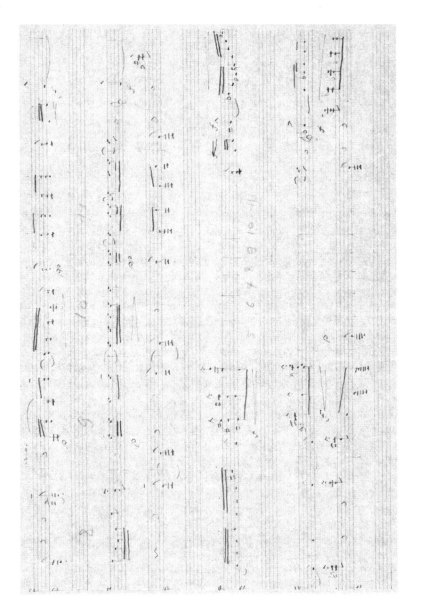

[3] Debussy's autograph score of the *Minstrels* transcription, mm. 12–27.

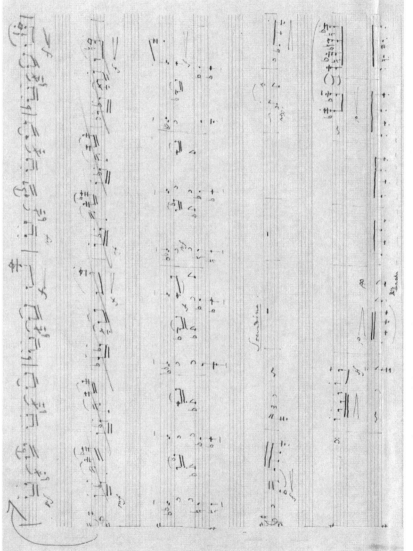

[4] Debussy's autograph score of the *Minstrels* transcription, mm. 28–38.

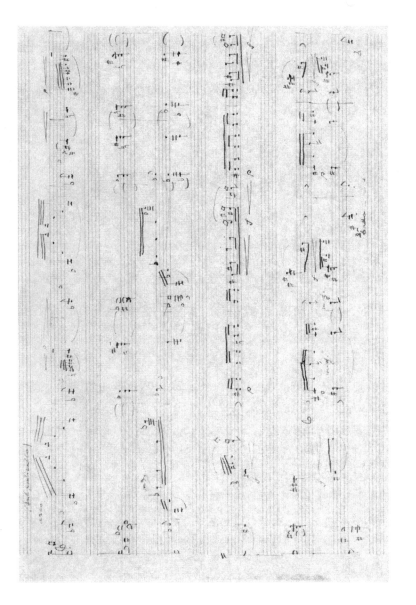

[5] Debussy's autograph score of the *Minstrels* transcription, mm. 39-48.

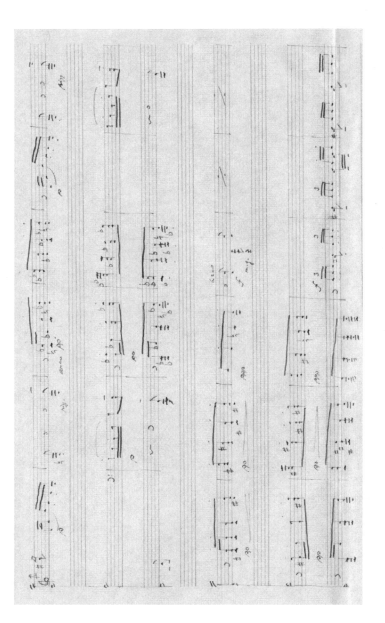

[6] Debussy's autograph score of the *Minstrels* transcription, mm. 49–60.

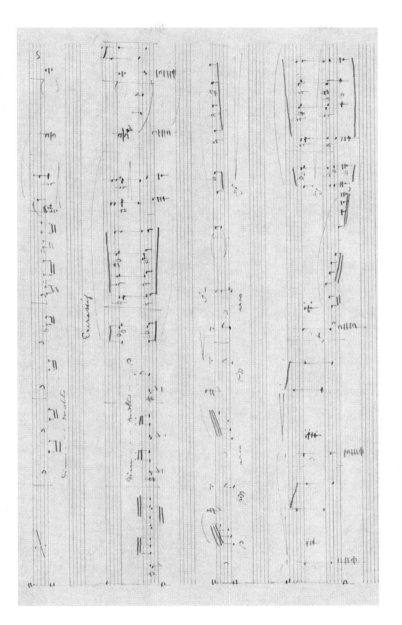

[7] Debussy's autograph score of the *Minstrels* transcription, mm. 61–72.

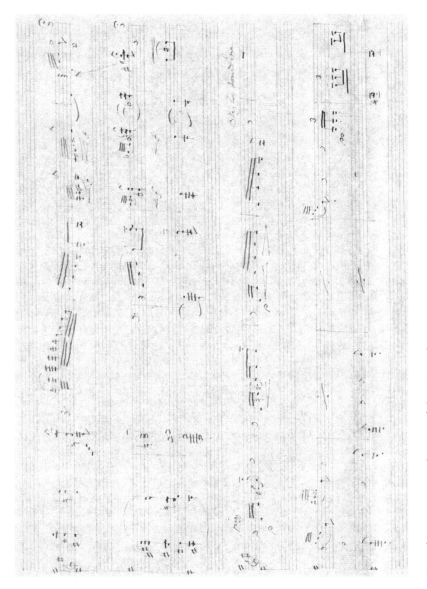

[8] Debussy's autograph score of the *Minstrels* transcription, mm. 73–82.

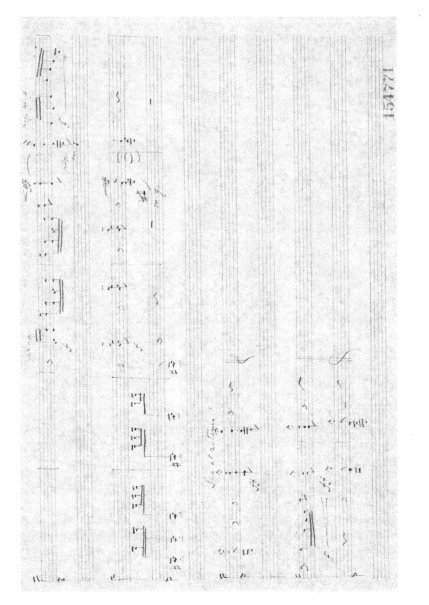

[9] Debussy's autograph score of the *Minstrels* transcription, mm. 83–89.

A-2b. Hartmann's Manuscript Score of the Transcription of Debussy's *Minstrels*, Undated (circa 1944).

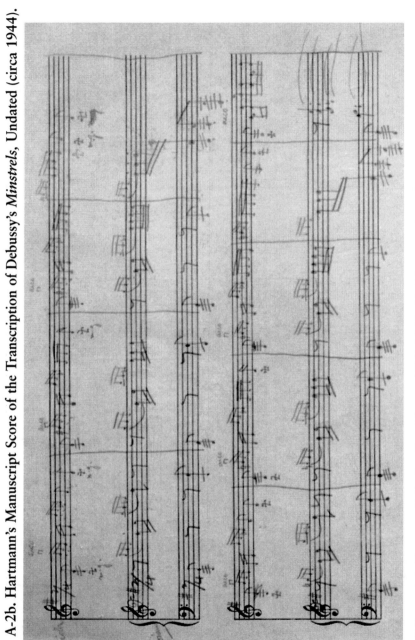

[10] mm. 1–9. Hartmann Collection, Free Library of Philadelphia. Used by permission.

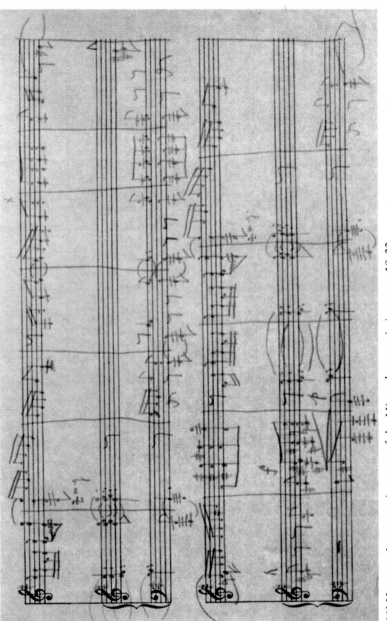

[11] Hartmann's manuscript score of the *Minstrels* transcription, mm. 10–22.

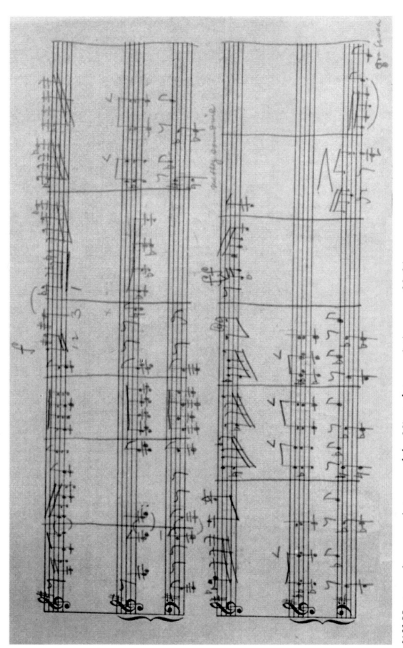

[12] Hartmann's manuscript score of the *Minstrels* transcription, mm. 23–34.

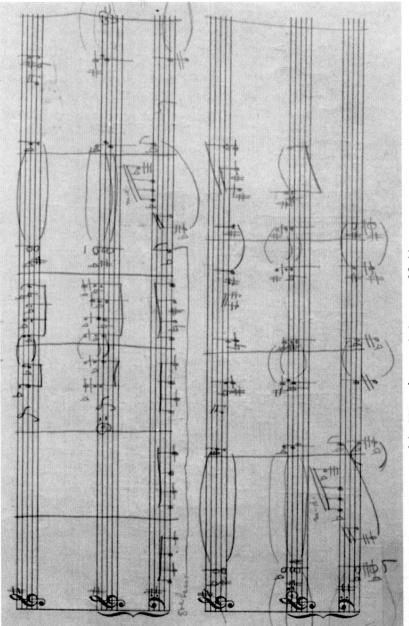

[13] Hartmann's manuscript score of the *Minstrels* transcription, mm. 35–44.

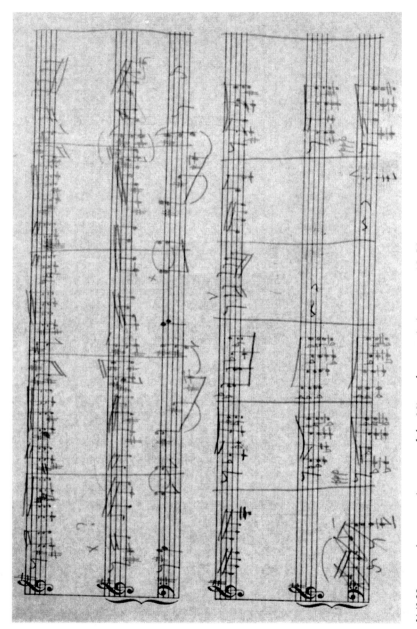

[14] Hartmann's manuscript score of the *Minstrels* transcription, mm. 45–55.

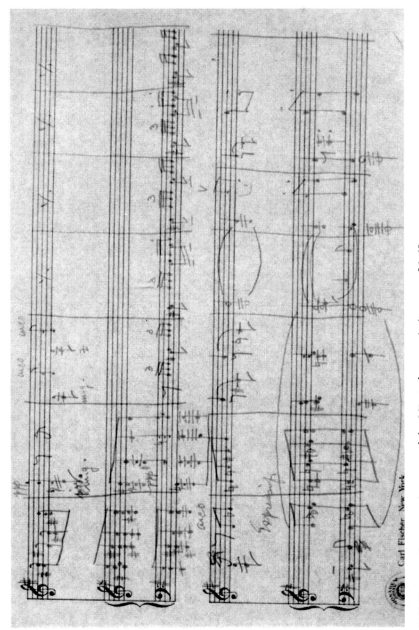

[15] Hartmann's manuscript score of the *Minstrels* transcription, mm. 56–68

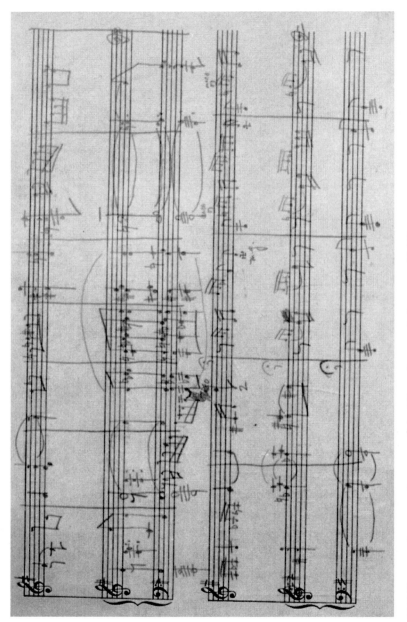

[16] Hartmann's manuscript score of the *Minstrels* transcription, mm. 69–79.

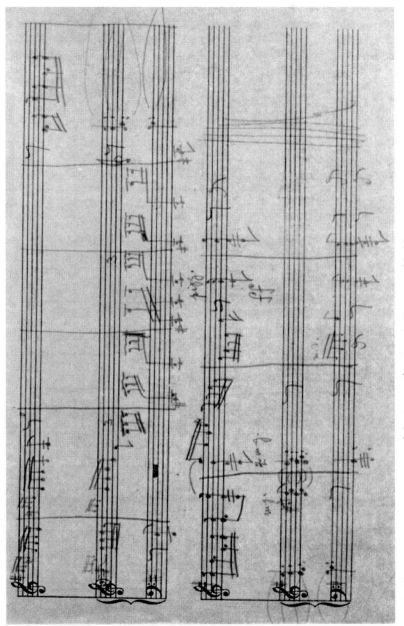

[17] Hartmann's manuscript score of the *Minstrels* transcription, mm. 80–89.

Appendix B

Three Letters from Debussy to Pierre Louÿs

Letter #1. 23 August 1895

Letter #2. 21 April 1898

Letter #3. Lundi Matin ("Cher Pierre, Peux-tu faire?")

Introduction

In 1929 Hartmann purchased from a dealer on Rue de Clichy in Paris two autograph letters from Debussy to Pierre Louÿs, one dated 23 August 1895, and one undated. These letters must have been a source of comfort to Hartmann during his time of severe illness and exhaustion. On 9 April 1931, he obtained from Frank H. Ginn of Cleveland, Ohio, a photostat copy of another letter, dated 21 April 1898. These letters add significant details to the letters of Debussy and Louÿs published in *Correspondance de Claude Debussy et Pierre Louÿs (1893–1904)*, edited by Henri Borgeaud (Paris: Librairie José Corti, 1945).

The letter of 23 August 1895 addresses several matters of interest. Annoyed by Debussy's excessive intrusion into the libretto for the opera *Cendrelune*, Louÿs had already told him on 12 May to write it himself: "Ecris TOI-MÊME *Cendrelune*" (Borgeaud, *Correspondance de Debussy et Louÿs*, 54). Yet, on 21 August, Louÿs still wanted to know when to begin working on it (Ibid., 59). Debussy's response: this is the time.[1] The Louÿs novel mentioned in the letter was being published at the time in serial form in *Mercure de France* under the title *L'Esclavage,* and later in a single volume as *Aphrodite*. Debussy also alluded to three Nocturnes for violin and orchestra, a work intended for Eugène Ysaÿe. There is no trace of this work, although it may have been an earlier version of the Nocturnes for orchestra of 1897–99. Of historical significance is Debussy's statement: "*Pelléas* est terminé depuis le 17 août." David Grayson points out that the 17 August date is confirmed by Debussy's own annotation on the short score of Act II and also in a letter to Henry Lerolle.[2]

A portion of the 21 April 1898 letter was published by Borgeaud, pp. 110–11. The published portion begins with "Je t'assure que j'ai besoin de

ton affection tellement je me sens seul et désemparé." There are large dele-
tions from the original text, and the published version ends with "Il y aurait
là une spéciale coquetterie dont tu ne peux qu'approuver la charmante
ironie." The complete text of the letter gives greater insight into Debussy's
emotional distress and his need for encouragement from Louÿs. David
Grayson observes that Debussy was depressed over the lack of success in
getting *Pelléas* performed.[3] On 5 May Louÿs responded in an assuring tone
and encouraged him to make every effort to have *Pelléas* performed.[4]

Although the original letter and envelope are presumed lost, we are happy
to report that the photostat copy of the letter in Philadelphia is now matched
with a copy of the envelope in Paris. Denis Herlin, who is preparing a
publication of the complete correspondence of Claude Debussy (a project
which he had undertaken with the late François Lesure), has in his possession a copy of the stamped envelope with the following in Debussy's handwriting: "Monsieur Pierre Louÿs / Le Caire [crossed out] / Égypte [crossed
out] / 147. Bd Malherbes [*sic*] / Paris."[5] As in the previous letter, Debussy
here showed great interest in his friend's literary works. He made suggestions concerning the preface Louÿs was writing for René Peter's *La tragédie
de la mort* (Paris: Mercure de France, 1899). Debussy also alluded to an
announcement he had read in *Le Journal* about a new Louÿs novel entitled
Une femme de quinze ans. This novel was eventually published under the
title *La femme et le pantin*, first in serialization in *Le Journal* from 19 May
to 8 June 1898 and then in a single volume by Mercure de France on 20
June 1898.[6] Again he cherished hopes that Louÿs would write the
Cendrelune libretto; but the libretto never materialized, and the project
was abandoned.

The subject of the brief undated letter is certainly not extraordinary:
Debussy needed money, in this case, 20 francs. Throughout Debussy's correspondence there are many references to his financial needs. For example,
in a 14 May 1897 letter he asked Pierre Louÿs for 50 francs to be sent to
Gaby Dupont (Borgeaud, *Correspondance*, 94).

Letter #1

vendredi. 23 août—95

Et d'abord qu'est ce que c'est que cette conduite de vil clown?

S'en aller sans rien dire, sans agiter le parlementaire mouchoir, enfin agir
de façon que Claude vint se casser misérablement le nez rue Chateaubriand
et s'en retourna furieux, jurant d'ignorer à jamais le nom de Pierre Louÿs!
Je ne veux du reste pas sonder toute cette indifférence et je vous pardonne
en faveur de *Cendrelune*.

· · · · ·

(ça, c'est des injures!)

Pelléas est terminé depuis le 17 août. Rien ne fut dérangé dans l'ordre des choses pour cela la terre ne trembla pas, on remarqua seulement un parti-pris chez les baromètres à jouer à la hausse mais on est pas sûr que l'incident cité plus haut en ait été la cause!

Si tu veux travailler à *Cendrelune* c'est indubitablement le moment, pourtant je peux te donner encore quelques temps si cela t'arrange ayant l'intention de finir les trois *Nocturnes* pour Violon et Orchestre. Agite toute cette histoire avant de t'en servir et dis moi ce que tu penses faire?

Il me semble regrettable que ton roman ne soit pas fini à temps et le célèbre coup de collier est nécessaire.

La chaleur ne me permet pas d'en dire plus long!

Ton
Claude Debussy

Friday, 23 August 1895

And first of all what is this conduct of a vile clown?

Leaving without saying a word, without waving the flag of truce, acting in such a way that Claude went and broke his nose miserably on Chateaubriand Street and returned furious, swearing to forget the name of Pierre Loüys forever! I do not want to probe all this indifference and I forgive you because of *Cendrelune.*

. . . . .

(These are such insults!)

Pelléas was finished 17 August. Nothing in the order of things was disturbed, it was not an earth shaking event. We only noticed that the barometers had set their minds on rising, but we do not think the incident mentioned above was the reason.

If you want to work on *Cendrelune,* this is the time to do it, but I can give you more time, if you wish, because I want to finish the three *Nocturnes* for violin and orchestra. Think about all of this and tell me what you want to do.

It seems unfortunate to me that your novel will not be finished on time and that a strenuous effort is necessary.

Because of the heat, I cannot say any more.

Yours,
Claude Debussy

Letter #2

jeudi 21 avril, 98

Mon cher Pierre,

J'avais mérité ta lettre, et plus encore que tu m'ensevelisses au fond d'un tiroir mais, j'aurais aimé que tu répondes à la mienne, je t'assure que j'ai besoin de ton affection tellement je me sens seul et désemparé, rien n'a changé dans le ciel noir qui fait le fond de ma vie, et je ne sais guère où je vais, si ce n'est vers le suicide, dénouement bête à quelque chose qui méritait peut-être mieux, et cela sera par lassitude de lutter contre d'imbéciles impossibilités en outre méprisables.

Tu sais donc combien ton amitié m'est chère et comme il me serait pénible d'en avoir perdu si peu que ce soit, écris-moi je t'en prie, dis-moi les choses les plus dures mais que je te sache encore avec moi. Tu me connais mieux que personne, et toi seul peux t'autoriser à me dire que je ne suis pas tout à fait un vieux fou.

Comme tu peux le penser, ta lettre a ravi René Peter et lui a donné en outre des désirs nombreux qui légitimait ta gentillesse envers lui.

Ne pourrais-tu pas, tout en conservant les termes, changer la forme de ta préface? Qu'elle ne soit plus une lettre charmante mais un document pour l'histoire littéraire de ce temps.

Verrais-tu un inconvénient à dire ce que tu penses (par exemple) du vers libre étant donné la forme employée dans la pièce de R. P., il y aurait là une spéciale coquetterie dont tu ne peux qu'approuver la charmante ironie.

Puis, cette pièce qui n'est ni "rosse," ni "tranche de vin," serait peut-être un excellent prétexte à développements contradictoires dont je te laisse le soin de distiller le plus sûr poison.

Ce serait pour toi l'occasion d'un voyage dans un pays où tu es maître et dont bénéficierait celui qui montera derrière toi dans le même train.

Tu peux faire tout cela et puis aussi tout ce que tu voudras, ce que j'en dis est tout à fait anecdotique et je tiens surtout à ne pas t'embêter plus longtemps avec cette histoire.

As-tu un peu pensé à la petite *Cendrelune?*

Qu'est-ce que c'est que "la femme de quinze ans" qu'annonce *le Journal?*

J'attends une lettre de toi avec impatience et te prie de croire à mon entière amitié.

Ton Claude

———

Thursday, 21 April 1898

My dear Pierre,

   I deserved your letter, and moreover, you are burying me at the bottom of a drawer. But, I would have loved to have you respond to mine. I feel so lonely and helpless I need your affection. Nothing has changed in the dark sky which overshadows my life, and I don't know where I am headed if not toward suicide, a stupid ending to something which should have been better, mainly on account of my weariness to fight against the imbecile and despicable impossibilities.

   You know how much I treasure your friendship, and how much pain it would cause me if I were to lose ever so little of it. Write to me, I beg you, say the harshest things but let me know you are still with me. You know me better than anyone, and you are the only one who has the right to tell me that I am not completely an old fool.

   As you can imagine, your letter has delighted René Peter and has given him many inspirations that do justice to your kindness toward him. While preserving the content, could you not alter the form of your preface? Rather than just a charming letter, let it be a document for the literary history of our time.

   Would you have any objection to giving your thoughts (for example) on free verse, since it is the form used by R. P. in this work. It would have that special touch whose charming irony you undoubtedly approve. Then, this work, which is neither fish nor fowl, would perhaps be an excellent place to develop conflicting ideas whose most effective poison I leave to you to concoct. This would be an opportunity for you to take off to a land where you are the master, and where those who come on your train would be blessed.

   You can do all that and whatever you wish. I am just talking off the top of my head and will stop boring you with my gibberish.

   Have you given any thought to the little *Cendrelune*?

   Who is "the fifteen year old woman" announced in *le Journal*?

   I am eagerly waiting for a letter from you. Most cordially,

Your Claude

Letter #3

Monsieur Pierre Louÿs
147 Boulevard Malesherbes

Lundi Matin

Cher Pierre,
   Peux-tu faire l'impossible pour m'envoyer 20 francs demain matin mardi à la première heure? Je suis horriblement gêné et traqué. Maintenant je n'en suis pas moins ton

Claude

Monsieur Pierre Louÿs
147 Boulevard Malesherbes

Monday Morning

Dear Pierre,
   Could you do the impossible by sending me 20 francs tomorrow morning, Tuesday, as early as possible? I am terribly embarrassed and strapped. Now I am no less your

Claude

Arthur Hartmann

ରେ ———————————————— ଙ

Catalogue of Compositions
and Transcriptions

A. Original Compositions

Cat. No.	Title[1]	Manuscript[2]	Published	Remarks
Orchestra				
A1	Caprice on an Irish Poem: Scherzo-Caprice	24 November–2 December 1931		Poem by H. T. Blunt
A2	Eljen: Hungarian Rhapsody for violin and orchestra	June 1909	Julius Hainauer 1907	
A3	Hymnus Hungaria	Undated		Also referred to as "In the Orient"
A4	Impressions from the Balkans 1. Idyll 2. Bacchanal	1. 20 June 1905 2. 20–23 August 1908		
A5	My Jean	15–17 September 1949 (sketches) 1–3 October 1949	Carl Fischer	
A6	Scherzo & March	1934	Carl Fischer	
A7	Suite 1. Serenade 2. Solitude 3. Insects	1. Undated 2. 17 August 1915 3. 13–25 September 1934		
A8	Timar: A Symphonic Poem	1899	W. Bessel 1910	Based upon M. Jokai's novel *Der Goldmensch*
Orchestra with Voice				
A9	Arab Love Song	August 1924		For tenor and orchestra; text by F. Thompson

Cat. No.	Title[1]	Manuscript[2]	Published	Remarks
A10	At the Mid Hour of Night, op. 22	15—21 September 1911	H. W. Gray 1947	Text by T. Moore
A11	Barbara: A Melodrama, op. 23	August 1911 (Library of Congress)	Gamble Hinged 1914 (piano edition)	For narrator & orchestra; text by A. Smith; re-scored in New York City, March 1947
A12	Oh! Weep for Those That Wept by Babel's Stream, op. 20	1 December 1924	Gamble Hinged 1911 (piano-vocal edition)	Text by Byron, from *Hebrew Melodies*
Chamber Music[3]				
A13	An Dante Gewidmet	Undated		For viola d'amore & piano
A14	Andantino	Undated		For viola d'amore & piano
A15	Hymnus Impressions of Byron's *Hebrew Melodies*	Undated		For string quartet
A16		Undated		For viola & piano
A17	Little Suite for Two Violins in the First Position		T. Presser1925	
A18	String Quartet, Adagio [second movement only], op. 18		W. Hansen 1932	*Pro Musica* 5 (1932), 57–62
A19	Up from Earth's Centre	Undated		For voice, viola d'amore & piano; text by O. Khayyam
Violin Solo				
A20	Cadenza for Beethoven's Violin Concerto in D[4]	Undated		

Cat. No.	Title[1]	Manuscript[2]	Published	Remarks
A21	Ungarische Kadenz for F. W. Ernst's Violin Concerto[5]	Undated		
Violin & Piano				
A22	Around the May-Pole	Undated	O. Ditson 1929	
A23	Badinage		Gamble Hinged	
A24	Barbara		John Church	
A25	Bogdan		Carl Fischer 1912	Dedicated to Viva Liebling
A26	A Cradle Song			
A27	Cradle Song, op. 32, No. 2	Undated	T. Presser 1923	
A28	Danse Grotesque		John Church	
A29	Eljen: Hungarian Rhapsody		Julius Haineuer 1907	
A30	Esprit de Ravioli-Polah	August 1923		Dedicated to André Polah, "Souvenir of an unforgettable evening"
A31	From My Sketch Book 1. Autumn (In Hungary) 2. Seven O'clock (A Cradle Song)		Carl Fischer 1912	
A32	Galop of the Wooden Horses	Undated		
A33	Grief	Undated		
A34	Guitarre	Undated		

Cat. No.	Title[1]	Manuscript[2]	Published	Remarks
A35	Hungarian Dance	12 April 1895	J. W. Jost 1895	Piano accompaniment by Martinus Van Gelder
A36	An Indian Romance	Undated		
A37	Jazz	Undated		
A38	Kossuth Lajos		John Church	
A39	Lullaby		John Church	
A40	Meditation: Berceuse Slav	Undated		
A41	The Merry-go-round	Undated		
A42	A Negro Croon		Breitkopf & Härtel 1916	Orchestrated by W. Happich, 6 March 1920 (MS)
A43	Nyiregyházi Emlék		Undated	
A44	The Old Gypsy	Undated		
A45	On-Between-Above and Below the Lines	Undated		
A46	Pan and Thalassius		John Church	
A47	Prayer		Breitkopf & Härtel 1916	
A48	Rhapsodische Skizze		O. Junne 1906	
A49	A Sad Story	Undated		
A50	Six Character Sketches		O. Ditson 1918	

Cat. No.	Title[1]	Manuscript[2]	Published	Remarks
A51	Six Pieces for Violin and Piano in the first position, op. 28 1. Swing Song 2. Indian Summer 3. The Love-Letter 4. Waltz 5. Caprice 6. Dance of the Aborigines	9 March 1915	O. Ditson 1916	
A52	The Smugglers	Undated		
A53	Solitude	17 April 1915		
A54	Souvenir		Carl Fischer 1912	
A55	En Sourdine	Undated		
A56	Spagnuola	17–28 January 1950		MS includes orchestration indications
A57	Suite in Ancient Style 1. Aria 2. Sarabande Varia 3. Gavotte 4. Finale		Carl Fischer 1915	
A58	Szäll A Madár: Ungarische Rhapsodie No. 2		O. Junne 1906	
A59	Szomozúság: Ungarische Rhapsodie No. 1		O. Junne 1906	
A60	Tango		G. Schirmer 1906	

Cat. No. Title[1]	Manuscript[2]	Published	Remarks
A61 Ta ga		G. Schirmer 1906	
A62 Three Compositions for Violin & Piano 1. La Coquette 2. L'Amour 3. La Tzigane		Harms 1927	
A63 Tiny Suite for Tiny Fiddlers 1. The See-Saw 2. The One-finger Waltz 3. March of the A-B-Cs	G. Schirmer 1923		
A64 To Lillian		John Church	
A65 Tristesse		O. Junne 1906	
A66 Two Dances 1. Caprice 2. Valse		G. Schirmer 1924	
A67 A Waltz (C Major)	Undated		
A68 Yearning		John Church	
Keyboard Music[6]			
A69 At the Garden Gate	Undated		
A70 Evening Song	Undated		
A71 From Babyland: Scenes From the Life of the Wee One, op. 21	Undated		

Cat. No.	Title[1]	Manuscript[2]	Published	Remarks
A72	Lovers' Dialogue	Undated		
A73	Maestoso	Undated		
A74	Melody of Love	Undated	O. Ditson 1929	
A75	A Miniature for the Piano 1. A Spring Time Frolic 2. A Summer Afternoon 3. Autumn 4. Desolation		Carl Fischer 1913	
A76	Prière à Notre Dame		Breitkopf & Härtel 1916	For organ
A77	Regrets . . .	22 June 1921		
A78	Six Preludes for the Piano, op. 29 1. Paysage Russe 2. In an Old Monastery Courtyard 3. Danse Roumaine 4. "Tania" 5. An American Prelude		O. Ditson 1916	Contract with O. Ditson (1915) lists only five preludes; published as *Six Preludes*
A79	Tempo di Valse	Undated		
A80	Three Hungarian Poems	12 February 1911/ 24 July 1921	John Church	
A81	Three Moods			
A82	Three Poems 1. Soliloquy 2. Meditation 3. Threnody	1. Undated 2. Undated	Breitkopf & Härtel 1921	No. 2 dedicated "to the memory of my best friend, A. D. C."; marked as No. 1 on manuscript

Cat. No.	Title[1]	Manuscript[2]	Published	Remarks
A83	The Willow Waltzes	Undated		
Chorus				
A84	Allah	August 1918		For four-part male chorus & optional piano; text by S. A. Mahlmann, translated by H. W. Longfellow
A85	Bring Her Again, O Western Wind	1918	T. Presser 1933	For male chorus & piano; text by W. Henley
A86	An Indian Cradle Song, op. 30a	23 February 1917	Clayton Summy	For three-part female chorus
A87	Invictus	14 June 1916	T. Presser 1933	For male chorus & piano; text by W. Henley
A88	A Madrigal, op. 30b	11 July 1915		For three-part female chorus; text by F. Truesdell
A89	May Day Song, op. 27a		O. Ditson 1914	For four-part female chorus; text by F.B. Money-Coutts
A90	Nun verlass ich diese Hütte	Undated		For four-part mixed chorus & piano
A91	Out of the Deep	Undated		For four-part mixed chorus & piano
A92	Rainbow Showers at Sunlight Falling	Undated		For four-part mixed chorus
A93	Sister, Awake, op. 27b		O. Ditson 1914	For four-part female chorus & piano; text by T. Bateson
A94	Through the Lonely Halls of the Night	Undated	Gamble Hinged 1911	For male chorus; text by B. Taylor

Cat. No.	Title[1]	Manuscript[2]	Published	Remarks
A95	When Love Has Drawn His Little Bow	11 July 1915	Gamble Hinged	Madrigal for three-part female chorus & piano; text by F. Truesdell
Solo Voice and Piano				
A96	At the Garden Gate	Undated		Text by T. Bateson
A97	Arab Love Song	Undated		Text by F. Thompson
A98	Baby Tears, op. 26a		Carl Fischer 1914	Text by F. Bowles
A99	The Ballad of Reading Gaol	September 1906		For narrator and piano; text by O. Wilde
A100	Ballade		*Songs with Piano*, Gamble Hinged 1911	Text by Davenport; dedicated to Chas. W. Clark
A101	Ballade for a baryton voice and pianoforte, op. 25	15 June 1913		Text by F. Doyle
A102	Ballade: An Irish Tune	Undated		Text by H. F. Blunt
A103	Believe Me if All These Endearing Young Charms		T. Presser 1920	Text by J. Stevenson
A104	The Breath of an Evening Is Sweet with Dew	Undated		
A105	The Call	1912		Text anonymous
A106	A Child's Grace		*Songs with Piano*, Gamble Hinged 1911	Text by R. Herrick; dedicated "to my mother"

Cat. No.	Title[1]	Manuscript[2]	Published	Remarks
A107	Christ in Hades	August 1905		For narrator and piano; text by S. Phillips
A108	Closer	Undated		For soprano & piano; text by J. B. Miller; dedicated to Marie Hartmann
A109	Cradle Song	[1911]?		Text by Tennyson; dedicated "for my son Gregory Kemenyi"
A110	A Dream	Undated		Text by O. Custance
A111	Evening Song	Undated		Text by T. Bateson
A112	Floridy am de lublest place	Undated		Text anonymous
A113	A Fragment	18 April 1912	*Songs with Piano*, Gamble Hinged 1911	Text by R. Le Gallienne; dedicated to Mrs. Fred'k Stevens
A114	From the Cloudland of Dreams			Text by F. Truesdell
A115	Here a Little Child I Stand	12 January 1911		Text by R. Herrick
A116	Ich fühle deinen Odem	Undated		Text by Mirza-Schaffy
A117	Ich stand in dunkeln Träumen	Undated		Text by H. Heine
A118	I Loved a Lass	13 January 1911	*Songs with Piano*, Gamble Hinged 1911	Text by G. Wither; dedicated to Madame Jeanne Jomelli
A119	In a Gondola		*Songs with Piano*, Gamble Hinged 1911	Text by R. Browning; dedicated "to my mother (Mrs. Harriet C. Tucker)"
A120	Is It a Rose?	21 August 1925		Text by F. Bowles; dedication "to bless my little girl's 9th birthday"

Cat. No.	Title[1]	Manuscript[2]	Published	Remarks
A121	Lennavan-Mo. (Lullaby)	Undated		Text by F. Macleod
A122	Life's Garden	22 April 1918		
A123	A Little Work, A Little Play	13 August 1915		Text by G. Du Maurier
A124	A Love Song: The Night Has A Thousand Eyes	Undated		Text by F. W. Boundillon
A125	Love's Logic	3 June 1914		Text by F. Truesdell
A126	Lovers' Dialogue	Undated		Text by T. Bateson
A127	Madrigal	Undated	Boston Music 1914	Text from F. Davison's "Poetical Rhapsody"
A128	Mater Dolorosa	10 May 1911		Text by W. Barnes
A129	My Love in Her Attire	Undated		Text by F. Davison
A130	My Yesterday	24 June 1912		Text by F. Truesdell
A131	Out Fishin'	Undated		Text by E. Guest
A132	Requiem	3 March 1911	Gamble Hinged 1911	Text by R. L. Stevenson; dedicated "to the memory of my mother, died Feb. 12, 1911"
A133	The Robin	Undated		
A134	Sleep, Beauty Bright		White-Smith	
A135	A Slumber Song		*Songs with Piano,* Gamble Hinged 1911	Text anonymous; dedicated to Chas. W. Clark

Cat. No.	Title[1]	Manuscript[2]	Published	Remarks
A136	Soliloquy	Undated	Gamble Hinged 1912	Dedicated to Oscar Seagle
A137	There is a Lady Sweet and Kind	10 May 1911		Text by T. Ford
A138	Three Poems from *An Old New England Child's Book of Verse* 1. Come, My Love 2. I Love the Flowers 3. I Love to See a Noble Dog	23 August 1916		Cycle for soprano (or mezzo-soprano) and piano
A139	Three Songs, op. 24 1. The End 2. Cherry Ripe 3. Mem'ry's Garden	1. 20 April 1913 2. 22 April 1913 3. Undated	Carl Fischer 1915 (Nos. 1 & 2 only)	1. Text by R. Le Gallienne; dedicated to Kathleen Brooks Chard 2. Text by R. Herrick; dedicated to Kathleen Brooks Chard MS has different order of movements
A140	Two Together		*Songs with Piano*, Gamble Hinged 1911	Text anonymous; dedicated to Mme. Schumann-Heink
A141	A Valentine		White-Smith 1913	Text by F. Truesdell; dedicated "to my friend H. Nevill-Smith"
A142	Und bist du weiter nichts für mich geblieben	Undated		Dedicated to Siegmund Leipziger
A143	. . . und Gott sprach	6 November 1904		Text by C. Sylva
A144	When I Am Dead, My Dearest	Undated		Text by C. Rossetti
A145	When I Walk with You, op. 26c		Carl Fischer 1914	Text by F. Bowles; dedicated to Mrs. F. N. Snyder
A146	Wo ich bin mich	Undated		Text by H. Heine

Cat. No.	Title[1]	Manuscript[2]	Published	Remarks
A147	Ye Awakening	Undated		Text by G. du Maurier; dedicated to Arthur G. Burgoyne
A148	You are So Fair	27 April 1913		Text by F. Truesdell
A149	Zwei Lieder 1. Ins All 2. Letztes Gebet		Mitteldeutscher Musikverlag 1907	Text by and dedicated to Queen Elizabeth of Romania (C. Sylva)

B. Arrangements/Transcriptions

Cat. No.	Title	Composer	Manuscript	Published	Remarks
Orchestra					
B1	Andante & Scherzo	A. Borodin	Undated		
B2	Bei Männern, welche Liebe fühlen (from *Die Zauberflöte*)	W. A. Mozart		Breitel & Bach	
B3	Hungarian Rhapsodie No.18: Adagio	F. Liszt	June 1910		
Chamber Music					
B4	Adagio molto espressivo	L. van Beethoven	Undated		For viola d'amore & piano; from Sonata for violin and piano, op. 30, no. 1, II
B5	Berceuse de Yeremushka	M. Mussorgsky	Undated		For string quartet

Cat. No.	Title	Composer	Manuscript	Published	Remarks
B6	Four Well-Known Melodies for Two Violins	Various		T. Presser, 1924	For two violins and piano
B7	Gondoliera	M. Moszkowski		G. Schirmer 1921	
B8	Little Horseman	P. Tchaikovsky	[27 December 1917]?		For string; from Album pour enfants, op. 29, no.3 [4][7]
B9	Rákóczi March	Traditional Hungarian	Undated		For string quartet
B10	Sarabande	J. S. Bach	Undated		For viola d'amore & piano or organ; from French Suite No. 5, BWV 816
B11	Sérénade	S. Rachmaninov		O. Ditson 1929	For string quartet, from op. 3, no. 5
B12	Tableaux d'une Exposition 1. Promenade 2. Il Vecchio Castello 3. Tuileries 4. Bydło 5. Ballet des Poussins dans leurs Coques 6. Samuel Goldenberg und Schmuyle 7. Promenade 8. Limoges-Le Marché	M. Mussorgsky	Undated (incomplete)		For string quartet; movements are in the order they appear on manuscript.
Violin & Piano					
B13	Adagio	W. A. Mozart		Breitkopf & Härtel 1920	
B14	Adagio and Allegro	A. Corelli	Undated	T. Presser 1915	

Cat. No.	Title	Composer	Manuscript	Published	Remarks
B15	Afton Water	Old Scotch melody	Undated	Undated	
B16	À la Lune	H. Kjerulf		Undated	
B17	À la Viennoise (In Viennese Style)	J. Brandl		G. Schirmer 1929	
B18	À la Viennoise: nach Motiven von Eduard Gärtner	I. Friedman	Undated	Universal-Edition 1926	
B19	Albumleaf	E. Grieg		G. Schirmer 1921	
B20	Alla Mazurka	A. Nemerowsky		Breitkopf & Härtel 1916	
B21	Andante and Gavotte Gracieuse	W. A. Mozart		Breitkopf & Härtel 1920	
B22	Andante religioso	F. Thomé		T. Presser	
B23	Andantino molto grazioso	W. A. Mozart		Breitkopf & Härtel 1920	
B24	Angel's Serenade	G. Braga		T. Presser 1922	
B25	Arabian Melody	A. Glazunov		W. Bessel	
B26	Aria	I. Shishov	Undated		
B27	Arietta (quasi Gavotta)	T. Lack		Breitkopf & Härtel 1920	
B28	Aurore (Aurora)	G. Fauré		G. Schirmer	

Cat. No.	Title	Composer	Manuscript	Published	Remarks
B29	Autumn Song	P. Tchaikovsky		G. Schirmer 1920	
B30	Badinage	L. Lacombe		O. Ditson 1928	
B31	Barcarolle	G. Fauré		G. Schirmer 1945	From Fauré's op. 70
B32	Beau Soir (Evening Fair)	C. Debussy		G. Schirmer 1943	Dedicated to Harry and Frances Adaskin
B33	Believe Me, If All Those Endearing Young Charms	J. Stevenson [British folk melody]		T. Presser 1920	
B34	Berceuse	S. Barmotine		T. Presser 1917	
B35	Berceuse	G. Korganov		G. Schirmer 1923	
B36	Berceuse	P. Tchaikovsky		Universal-Edition 1925	
B37	Biroulki	A. Liadov		O. Ditson1928	
B38	The Birth of the Harp	S. Taneiev		G. Schirmer 1928	
B39	Bist du bei mir	J. S. Bach [G. H. Stölzel]	Undated		
B40	The Butterfly (Le Papillon)	C. Lavallée	Undated		MS has been crossed out with pencil
B41	Camille	J. Kern		T. Presser 1928	
B42	Capriccetto	A. Cipollone		Undated	

Cat. No.	Title	Composer	Manuscript	Published	Remarks
B43	La Chanson des Abeilles (Song of the Bees)	E. Filipucci		Carl Fischer 1945	
B44	Chanson Triste	P. Tchaikovsky		G. Schirmer 1920	
B45	Chant d'Automne	A. Gretchaninov		Breitkopf & Härtel 1916–1918	
B46	Chant du Pêcheur	M. Balakirev		Breitkopf & Härtel 1916–1918	
B47	Chinatown	J. Rodgers		T. Presser 1928	
B48	Christmas	P. Tchaikovsky		Breitkopf & Härtel 1916	
B49	La Cinquantaine	M. Gabriel		T. Presser 1916	
B50	Clair de Lune	E. MacDowell		A. P. Schmidt 1935	
B51	La Cour de la Marquise	J. Exaudet		Edition Musicus 1945	Also arranged for flute and piano and oboe and piano
B52	Cradle Song	E. MacDowell		Julius Hainauer 1907	
B53	Cradle Song	M. Reger			
B54	Cradle Song	N. Rimsky-Korsakov		C. F. Summy 1926	
B55	Cradle Song	A. Spendiarov		W. Bessel	
B56	Dance Arabe	P. Tchaikovsky	Undated		

Cat. No.	Title	Composer	Manuscript	Published	Remarks
B57	Danse Russe	P. Tchaikovsky		Universal-Edition 1924	
B58	Deserted	E. MacDowell		A. P. Schmidt 1935	
B59	Dorian Mazurka	M. Mussorgsky		W. Bessel	
B60	En Prière	G. Fauré		Edition Musicus 1945	Also arranged for clarinet and piano, flute and piano, and oboe and piano
B61	L'Espiègle	P. Tchaikovsky		G. Schirmer 1920	
B62	Estrellita	M. Ponce		T. Presser 1928	Copyright letter designates piece for *Etude*, June 1925, 486
B63	Evening Song (Abendlied)	R. Schumann	Undated	Breitkopf & Härtel 1916	
B64	Exaltation	B. Karagitscheff			
B65	La Fille aux cheveux de lin	C. Debussy	1910	Durand 1910	
B66	The Flight of the Bumblebee	N. Rimsky-Korsakov	Undated	W. Bessel 1925	
B67	Florian's Song	B. Godard		T. Presser 1919	
B68	From Youth's Happy Day	R. Radecke		T. Presser 1919	
B69	Gavotte	C. von Gluck		G. Schirmer 1921	From *Iphigenia in Aulide*
B70	Gavotte	M. Marais		A. P. Schmidt 1928	

Cat. No.	Title	Composer	Manuscript	Published	Remarks
B71	Gavotte	W. A. Mozart		Breitkopf & Härtel 1925	
B72	La Gioja	F. Plotenyi		Breitkopf & Härtel 1920	
B73	Gitanerias (The Gipsy)	M. Grever		G. Schirmer 1927	
B74	Golden Wedding Minuet	G. Korganov		T. Presser 1923	*Etude*, November 1923
B75	Gopak: Little-Russian Dance	M. Mussorgsky		W. Bessel	
B76	Hebrew Song	M. Mussorgsky		W. Bessel 1926	
B77	Hejre Kati (Pretty Katy)	J. Hubay			
B78	Hobgoblin	E. Grieg		G. Schirmer 1928	
B79	Home, Sweet Home	H. Bishop		T. Presser 1923	
B80	Humoresque	P. Tchaikovsky	Undated	Breitkopf & Härtel 1916	
B81	Hungarian Hymn	F. Erkel		Breitkopf & Härtel 1916–1918	
B82	Il pleure dans mon coeur	C. Debussy		Fromont 1908	
B83	Il pleure dans mon coeur	C. Debussy	1943	Edition Musicus 1944	Revised version
B84	In Crimea	M. Mussorgsky			Advertised by W. Bessel, but never appeared

Cat. No.	Title	Composer	Manuscript	Published	Remarks
B85	In the Gondola	G. Korganov		Breitkopf & Härtel 1916	
B86	Italian Cradle Song	A. Cipollone		T. Presser 1916	
B87	Italian Song	P. Tchaikovsky		T. Presser 1917	
B88	Júrame: Spanish Tango	M. Grever		T. Presser 1922, G. Schirmer 1926	
B89	Just A Little Waltz	C. Cadman		T. Presser 1926	*Etude*, July 1926
B90	Kobold	E. Grieg		1928	
B91	Largo	W. F. Bach	Undated (Library of Congress)	Breitkopf & Härtel 1916–1918	J. S. Bach's BWV 596; attributed to W. F. Bach
B92	Little Horseman	P. Tchaikovsky	Undated		From Album pour enfants, op. 29, no.3 [4]
B93	The Little Sandman	Rhenish folksong		T. Presser 1920	
B94	Long Ago	E. MacDowell		A. P. Schmidt 1935	*Etude*, August 1921
B95	Lullaby	A. Naumann		T. Presser 1926	
B96	Matouska Goloboushka	Russian folksong		Breitkopf & Härtel 1920	
B97	Mazurka	F. Chopin		T. Presser 1921	
B98	Mazurka	R. Glière		Undated	

Cat. No.	Title	Composer	Manuscript	Published	Remarks
B99	Mazurka	M. Glinka		Breitkopf & Härtel 1916–1918	
B100	Mazurka	A. Ilyinsky		Breitkopf & Härtel 1920	
B101	Mazurka	G. Korganov	21 April 1916	Breitkopf & Härtel 1916–1918	
B102	Mélodie	R. Glière		Breitkopf & Härtel 1916–1918	
B103	Menuetto et Allegro	F. J. Haydn		T. Presser 1924	
B104	Mi Teresita	T. Carreño		T. Presser 1918	
B105	Midsummer Lullaby	E. MacDowell		Breitkopf & Härtel 1917	
B106	Minstrels	C. Debussy	Undated [c. 1944]		
B107	Minuet	A. Scarlatti		Breitkopf & Härtel 1920	
B108	Minuet	J. Exaudet	Undated	G. Schirmer 1928	
B109	Minuet	F. J. Haydn		G. Schirmer 1923	
B110	Minuet in D	W. A. Mozart		A. P. Schmidt 1928	
B111	Minute Waltz	F. Chopin	Undated	G. Schirmer 1928	
B112	Moon Dawn	R. Friml		T. Presser 1923	*Etude*, December 1923

Cat. No.	Title	Composer	Manuscript	Published	Remarks
B113	Moto Perpetuo	C. Böhm		T. Presser	
B114	Le Moulin	G. Pierné	Undated		
B115	Nell	G. Fauré	Undated		
B116	Neapolitan Dance Song	P. Tchaikovsky		T. Presser 1917	
B117	The Nightingale	A. Glazunov		W. Bessel 1926	
B118	Nocturne	G. Fauré		G. Schirmer 1922	
B119	Nocturne	J. Hofmann		T. Presser 1925	*Etude*, April 1925
B120	Nocturne: C-Sharp Minor	P. Tchaikovsky		Universal-Edition 1924	
B121	Nocturne in F Major	P. Tchaikovsky		Universal-Edition 1924	
B122	Notturno	E. Grieg		G. Schirmer 1928	
B123	The Old, Old Love!	R. de Koven		T. Presser 1917	*Etude*, December 1917
B124	Oriental Romance	N. Rimsky-Korsakov		Breitkopf & Härtel 1924	
B125	Orientale	N. Amani		T. Presser 1918	
B126	Pantomime	W. A. Mozart		Breitkopf & Härtel 1925	
B127	Papillons	O. Olsen		Undated	

Cat. No.	Title	Composer	Manuscript	Published	Remarks
B128	La Partida (The Farewell)	F. M. Alvarez		G. Schirmer 1920	
B129	Petite Berceuse	E. Schütt		T. Presser 1916	
B130	Playera: Spanish Dance	E. Granados		T. Presser 1917	
B131	Poem	Z. Fibich		T. Presser 1920	
B132	Poupée Valsante	E. Poldini		Breitkopf & Härtel 1916	
B133	Prayer from *Moses in Egypt*	G. Rossini/N. Paganini		T. Presser 1915	Based on a theme from Rossini's opera *Mose in Egitto*
B134	Princesita	J. Padilla		G. Schirmer 1927	
B135	Rákóczi March	Traditional Hungarian		T. Presser 1917	
B136	Rêverie	E. Schütt		T. Presser 1920	
B137	Revery of the Young Peasant	M. Mussorgsky		W. Bessel 1926	
B138	The Robin Sings in the Appletree	E. MacDowell		Breitkopf & Härtel 1917	
B139	Romance	C. Cui		O. Ditson 1928	
B140	Romance	R. Glière		Breitkopf & Härtel 1916–1918	
B141	Romance	N. Rimsky-Korsakov		G. Schirmer 1928	

Cat. No.	Title	Composer	Manuscript	Published	Remarks
B142	Romance	J. Svendsen		T. Presser	
B143	Romance in E-flat Major	A. Rubinstein		T. Presser 1919	
B144	Romance in F Minor	P. Tchaikovsky		G. Schirmer 1922	
B145	Romance sans Paroles	G. Fauré		G. Schirmer 1945	
B146	La Roxelane	F. J. Haydn	Undated		
B147	A Russian Festival	L. Ornstein		Breitkopf & Härtel 1918	
B148	Serenade	C. Gounod	Undated		
B149	Serenade	A. Rubinstein		T. Presser 1924	*Etude*, January 1925
B150	Serenade	F. Schubert		T. Presser	
B151	Sérénade levantine	A. Alféraki	9 April 1916	Breitkopf & Härtel 1916–1918	
B152	Sirens	J. H. Rogers		T. Presser 1923	*Etude*, November 1924
B153	Slumber Song; Berceuse	A. Gretchaninov		T. Presser 1922	*Etude*, June 1922
B154	Slumber Song	W. Taubert		T. Presser 1919	*Etude*, October 1919
B155	Snowflakes	N. Rimsky-Korsakov		1928	
B156	Song of the Volga Boatmen	Traditional		T. Presser 1920	

Cat. No.	Title	Composer	Manuscript	Published	Remarks
B157	Songs My Mother Taught Me: Gypsy Melody	A. Dvořák		T. Presser 1919	
B158	String Quartet	I. Friedman	Undated		
B159	Sylvia	O. Speaks		G. Schirmer 1932	
B160	Tabatière à Musique	I. Friedman	13 January 1925	Universal-Edition 1926	
B161	Tambourin	J. P. Rameau		T. Presser 1918	
B162	Tango	I. Albéniz		T. Presser 1923	*Etude*, February 1924
B163	A Tear	P. Fuentes		Undated	
B164	Thou'rt Like Unto A Flower	A. Rubinstein		T. Presser 1919	*Etude*, October 1919
B165	To a Humming Bird	E. MacDowell		A. P. Schmidt 1916	
B166	To a Wild Rose	E. MacDowell		A. P. Schmidt 1907	Original edition
B167	To a Wild Rose	E. MacDowell		A. P. Schmidt 1907	Simplified edition
B168	To Slumber-Land	A. Kopylov		G. Schirmer 1922	
B169	Toccata	S. Vasilenko		Leeds Music 1945	
B170	Trees	O. Rasbach		G. Schirmer	
B171	Troïka	P. Tchaikovsky		Universal-Edition 1924	
B172	Une Larme (A Tear)	M. Mussorgsky		G. Schirmer 1927	

Cat. No.	Title	Composer	Manuscript	Published	Remarks
B173	Valse	P. Tchaikovsky		T. Presser 1917	
B174	Valse Posthume (F-Sharp Minor)	F. Chopin	Undated	O. Ditson 1930	
B175	Viennese Refrain	[J. Brandl] old folk song		T. Presser 1925	*Etude*, February 1925
B176	Wiener Tanz, No. 1	I. Friedman	Undated	Universal-Edition 1925	
B177	Will O' the Wisp	E. MacDowell			
B178	With Sweet Lavender	E. MacDowell		A. P. Schmidt 1935	
B179	Yo no sé (I know not)	M. Grever		G. Schirmer 1927	
B180	Zwei Wiener Tänze	I. Friedman	Undated	Universal-Edition 1916	
Piano Solo					
B181	Dance	G. Egnazarov	Undated		
B182	Fountains	S. Tañeyev	Undated		
B183	Hungarian Melodies 1. A macskának négy lába van (The cat has four legs) 2. A mióta szeret m vagy (Since you are my sweetheart) 3. A mely kis lány sokat	Traditional Hungarian		T. Presser 1918	Dedicated "To mamuska—my baby girl"

Cat. No.	Title	Composer	Manuscript	Published	Remarks
	szeret (Which little girl loves much)				
4.	Este van már, szerelmesek napja (It is dusk, of a lover's day)				
5.	Szitnya, Léva, Csábrág				
6.	Húzzad csak, húzzad csak keservessen (Play on, play on [bitterly])				
7.	A korcsmabán (In the tavern)				
8.	Csicsó néni (Aunt Csicsó)				
9.	Ez a kis lány jaj be czifra (This little girl, my how fancy)				
10.	Mikor én még legény voltam (When I was a free lance)				
11.	Régi nóta (An old song)				
12.	Régi Népdal (Old Folksong)				
13.	Falu végén czifra csárda (At the village end a fancy tavern stands)				
14.	Márosszéki piros páris (The red apples of Márosszéki)				
15.	Elmehetsz már angyalom (You may go [now], my angel)				
16.	Nincsen annyi tenger csillag az égen (There are not so many countless seas of stars)				
17.	Kurucz tábori dal (Kurucz camp song)				
18.	Haj! Rákócki! Bercsényi! (Ho! Rákócki! Bercsényi!)				

Cat. No.	Title	Composer	Manuscript	Published	Remarks
	19. Sárga csizmás Miska verbunkos (Yellow-booted Nick's recruiting song)				
	20. A híres Chlopiczky nóta (The famous Chlopiczky song)				
	21. Nem loptam én életemben (Never in my life have I stolen)				
	22. F ldre hull a mandulafa virága (The almond-tree blossoms fall to the ground)				
	23. Két lánya volt a falunak (Two maidens had the village)				
	24. Rongyos csárda két oldalán ajtó (A ragged tavern with doors at the sides)				
	25. Sárga ugorkának z ld a levele (Yellow cucumbers have green leaves)				
	26. Az én torkom álló malom (My throat is a standing mill)				
	27. Panaszkodik az esti szél (The plaint of the evening wind)				
	28. Szakitanék veled rózsám (Could I but forsake you, my rose)				
	29. Lassú csárdás (Slow tavern dance)				
	30. Elfelejtettem a neved (I have forgotten your name)				
	31. Hová t ntél? (Where have you vanished?)				
	32. Az én lelkem feketébe lt zik (My soul is garbed in black)				
	33. Volt nekem egy darusz r				

Cat. No. Title	Composer	Manuscript	Published	Remarks
paripám (I had a crane-coloured, long-maned horse)				
34. Megátkoztam csalfa szíved (I have cursed your deceiving heart)				
35. Bár merre jár (Wherever my glances go)				
36. Nem parancsol nekem senki (Nobody bosses me)				
37. Míg a tóban halak lesznek (So long as there will be fish in the pond)				
38. Rózsasz ll édesebb (Red grapes are sweeter)				
39. Régi népdal (Ancient folk-song)				
40. Eszem azt a kis kezedet (Oh, I eat that tiny hand of yours)				
41. Vékony héja van a piros almának (The pink apple has a thin skin)				
42. Lassú magyar táncz (Slow Hungarian dance)				
43. Édes anyám, nagy a bajom (Dear Mother, great is my trouble)				
44. Pálfy huszár (The hussar Pálfy)				
45. Mit integetsz a kend del? (To whom do you beckon with your kerchief?)				
46. Mit integetsz a kend del? (To whom do you beckon with your kerchief?)				

Cat. No.	Title	Composer	Manuscript	Published	Remarks
	47. Hármat füttyentett (Thrice the train whistled.) 48. Hej! fosztóka, kukorica fosztóka (Ah, vagrant, little corn thief) 49. Be szomorú ez az élet (Oh, how sad is this life) 50. Messze hallik (Twilight bells) 51. Húzd ki czigány a vonódot egészen (Pull the entire bow, Gypsy)				
B184	Valse Caline	R. Brogi	August 1911	Carl Fischer	
Chorus					
B185	Good-Night	A. Rubinstein	Undated (sketch)	Gamble Hinged 1911	For male chorus & piano; text by Byron; dedicated "to the Apollo Club of St. Louis and Mr. Charles Galloway, conductor"

Notes

Preface

1. François Lesure, "Correspondance de Claude Debussy et de Louis Laloy (1902–1914)," *Revue de Musicologie* 48 (1962): 40.

2. "Hartmann and Debussy: Hartmann Talks to the *Musical Courier* Interviewer about the Composer of 'Pelléas et Mélisande,'" *Musical Courier,* 4 November 1908, 23. This article is included in our biographical chapter on Hartmann.

3. Letters from Claude Debussy to Arthur Hartmann are identified throughout the volume by the abbreviation "CD" and a cataloguing number (e.g., CD-1); letters from Emma Claude Debussy to Marie Hartmann and Arthur Hartmann by "ECD" and a cataloguing number. All letters from Claude Debussy and Emma Claude Debussy are included in Part 2, "Letters from Claude and Emma Debussy to Arthur and Marie Hartmann," and are arranged there by their "CD" and "ECD" numbers.

4. A selection from one of the letters, dated 21 April 1898, appeared in *Correspondance de Claude Debussy et Pierre Louÿs (1893–1904)*, ed. Henri Borgeaud (Paris: Librairie José Corti, 1945), 110–11.

Arthur Hartmann: A Biographical Sketch

1. Alfred Bendiner, *Music to My Eyes* (Philadelphia: University of Pennsylvania Press, 1952), no pagination.

2. Alfred Bendiner, *Translated from the Hungarian* (New York: A. S. Barnes, 1967).

3. Ibid., 20. Sigmund Hartman was naturalized 13 April 1892 in New York, where Arthur was studying at the time. Note from unidentified author regarding Hartman's naturalization, Hartmann Collection, Free Library of Philadelphia.

4. Contrary to information in older music reference books, almost all of which state that he was born in his father's hometown of Máté Szalka in Hungary. See "Inventing 'Hartmann'" in the present biography.

5. S. B. Fleisher is likely Simon B. Fleisher, father of Philadelphia music patron Edwin A. Fleisher (1877–1959) who founded the Fleisher Collection of Orchestral Music at the Free Library of Philadelphia.

6. "Violinist's Marriage Sad Blow to Father," *Philadelphia North American,* 31 August 1903.

7. Arthur Hartmann claims to have played Pierre Rode's Violin Concerto No. 8 at the age of 6 in Philadelphia. H. Nevill Smith, "Arthur Hartmann in Berlin," unidentified clipping from Hartmann's scrapbooks, Hartmann Collection, Free Library of Philadelphia.

8. Born in Amsterdam, van Gelder (1854–1935) began his piano studies at the age of six under the guidance of his father. At twelve he became a theory and composition pupil of Frans Coenen and showed enough ability to be sent to the Cologne

Conservatory to study with Ferdinand Hiller. He made his New York debut in 1877 and soon thereafter moved to Philadelphia to teach at the Musical Academy.

9. The article "Arthur Hartmann," *Musical Courier,* 22 July 1896, 22a, states: "When Paderewski heard him in Érard Hall, London, June 1892, he pronounced him to be 'the coming Paganini.'" The article also quotes the *London Times:* "At the concert in Princes' Hall last evening, an extremely clever violinist was introduced in the diminutive person of Master Arthur Hartmann, the little American genius, whose performance of Tivadar Nachez's *Danses tziganes* electrified the audience and made us ask ourselves if we had at last found another Paganini." It includes further endorsements from Sir Charles Hallé, Princess Elizabeth Soltykoff, and Mark Twain, among others.

10. Hartmann's meeting with Nachez is confirmed by the entry dated 28 June 1892 in his childhood autograph book. A *Musical Courier* article about Hartmann's 1892 European performances in Europe states that Arthur played Nachez's *Danses tziganes* for the composer by special request. "Arthur Hartmann," *Musical Courier,* 22 July 1896, 22a.

11. "Le 4 Juin 1894. Mon cher Monsieur, En rentrant de voyage, j'ai trouvé votre lettre que m'a fait grand plaisir. Je suis charmé d'apprendre que mon ami Saint-Saëns vous ait bien accueilli et vous ait donné rendez-vous à Londres où j'espère vous vous ferez entendre avec succès, car j'ai été très intéressé par votre jeu. Vous avez la justesse, le rythme et d'autres qualités de virtuose; je fais donc les voeux les plus sincères pour qu'une belle carrière s'ouvre devant vous, et si je peux y contribuer, je suis à votre disposition pour vous recommander chaleureusement. Veuillez agréer, cher Monsieur, l'expression de mes meilleurs et dévoués sentiments Alex. Guilmant. à M. Arthur M. Hartmann, *jeune violoniste!*" Hartmann Collection, Free Library of Philadelphia; translation by Regine Johnson.

12. In an interview for the *Rushford (N.Y.) Spectator,* 26 October 1911 ("A World's Master Violinist"), Hartmann claimed that he played Mendelssohn's Violin Concerto under Walter Damrosch in Carnegie Hall when he was 7 and that, soon after, he played Saint-Saëns's Violin Concerto No. 2 in C Major (Op. 58) in Paris and London and also "in Vienna under Hans Richter." The performance of the Saint-Saëns concerto is confirmed by a letter from the composer to the young violinist praising him for his execution and musical sentiment in playing this concerto. Letter from Camille Saint-Saëns to Arthur Hartmann, 8 June 1896, private collection of Karen Hartmann Kleinmann.

13. "8. Juni, 1894. Lieber Herr Hartmann! Ich habe Ihren Sohn Arthur spielen gehört und finde, daß er ein außergewöhnliches Talent für die Violine besitzt; von ihm ist zu hoffen, daß er einst ein Meister dieses Instrumentes werden wird. Mit bestem Gruße Ihr Hans Richter." Hartmann Collection, Free Library of Philadelphia; translation by Regine Johnson.

14. Quoted in "Arthur Hartmann," *Musical Courier,* 12 August 1896, 11.

15. Arthur D. Curran was a wealthy Boston coal merchant whose assistant was evidently a Mr. Leipziger.

16. Writ of Emancipation, 13 July 1897, Hartmann Collection, Free Library of Philadelphia. Sigmund Hartman was furious at Arthur's action in this regard, and the relationship between father and son disintegrated. The Hartmann Collection, Free Library of Philadelphia, contains eight letters from Sigmund to Arthur, written between 1903 and 1917, in which Sigmund complains about Arthur's ingratitude

and about being cheated by people who have misled his son and betrayed him (Curran and Leipziger). Sigmund repeatedly recounts all that he did for Arthur and chides Arthur for not even sending money regularly to support him in his old age.

17. "Arthur Hartmann's History," *Violin World*, 15 September 1906, 5. The article further reports that this "rich Boston music lover" not only "adopted" Hartmann but gave him a Stradivarius violin "worth $10,000." Evidently, Hartmann was the beneficiary of another such extravagance when, in 1906, a rich Philadelphia violin collector gave Hartmann a Guarnerius violin after hearing him play the Tchaikovsky Concerto with the Philadelphia Orchestra. Unfortunately, this instrument was stolen on the train between Houston and El Paso during the night of 3–4 January 1907, when Hartmann was on his first extensive American tour. "How Hartmann Earned His Violin," *Musical Courier*, 11 February 1907, 33; "Valuable Violin Stolen on Train," *Los Angeles Herald*, 6 January 1907.

18. Despite the somewhat negative portrayal of Loeffler in his essay, Loeffler seems to have developed a respect for Hartmann and the two did develop a friendship, as evidenced by Loeffler's letter to Hartmann after the latter had moved to London, 22 January 1901 (included at the end of Hartmann's essay on Loeffler in the current volume). This letter is in the Hartmann Collection, Free Library of Philadelphia.

19. This manuscript is in the Hartmann Collection, Free Library of Philadelphia.

20. Letter from Loeffler to Hartmann, 12 June 1905, Arthur Hartmann Collection, Sibley Music Library, Eastman School of Music.

21. Philadelphia Orchestra program notes, 15 December 1906.

22. "Arthur Hartmann's History," *Violin World*, 15 September 1906, 58. The veracity of this statement is doubtful. Sigmund Hartman's letter to Curran's agent, Leipziger, on 6 August 1902 does not refer in any way to a mental disorder on Curran's part. It rather implies that there was a falling out between Arthur and Curran which led to Arthur's departure for Europe. In light of Arthur's strong personality, this seems to be a more feasible course of events. Letter from Sigmund Hartmann to Mr. Leipziger, 6 August 1902, Hartmann Collection, Free Library of Philadelphia.

23. René Ortmans (1863–1949), French violinist, conductor, and composer who studied at the Paris Conservatoire and with Eugène Ysaÿe.

24. See Hartmann's memoir, "Memories of Masters of the Bow: An Impression of Joachim's Last Years," in the present volume.

25. "Arthur Hartmann's History," *Violin World*, 15 September 1906, 58.

26. He, in turn, set several of her poems to music, including ". . . und Gott sprach," "Ins All," and "Letztes Gebet."

27. Arthur Walter Kramer, "Enigma of Hartmann's Nationality," *Musical America*, 3 July 1915, 36.

28. Hartmann himself wrote at least two articles to this effect: "The Tragedy of European Study," *Musical Courier*, 15 April 1908, 39; and "America versus Europe," *Musical Monitor and World*, July 1914, 1.

29. In an interview appearing in "Music and Musicians," in the *Illustrated Buffalo Express*, 28 May 1911, Hartmann elucidated: "Prior to 1770, our family name was Kemenyi . . . but the Emperor Josef compelled the Hungarians to change or Germanize their names. Kemenyi means 'of the hard man,' so the German equivalent was Hartmann, which we have borne ever since."

30. Pictures of Hartmann also appeared on the covers of the 28 December 1904 and 5 December 1906 issues of the *Musical Courier.*

31. Letter from Camille Saint-Saëns to Arthur Hartmann, 8 June 1896, private collection of Karen Hartmann Kleinmann.

32. Two letters from Jenö Hubay to Arthur Hartmann, 26 May 1907 and 20 June 1920, are extant in the private collection of Karen Hartmann Kleinmann.

33. See W. Henry Hill, Arthur F. Hill, and Alfred E. Hill, *Antonio Stradivari: His Life and Work* (New York: Dover, 1963 [1902]), which lists "Mr. Hartmann" as the owner of a Stradivarius violin dated 1735. [Editors' note.]

34. This article, entitled simply "Arthur Hartmann," was attributed to the Danish critic and composer Fini Henriques, *Musical Courier,* 27 May 1903, 13. Henriques protested vehemently to the Danish consul in New York that he had not written a word of this shamelessly flattering article and demanded an apology. From Berlin, Hartmann had to cable Marc Blumenberg, the *Musical Courier* publisher, to notify him that an inexplicable misunderstanding on the part of his agent had taken place. Blumenberg's defense, "Insulting a Profession," appeared in the *Musical Courier,* 26 August 1903, 15. Sigmund Hartman wrote an angry and sarcastic letter to Henriques blaming him for the negative publicity that resulted from the incident. Letter from Sigmund Hartman to Fini Henriques, 18 November 1903, Hartmann Collection, Free Library of Philadelphia.

35. Leonard Liebling, one of Arthur's oldest friends and editor of the *Musical Courier,* congratulated Arthur on all the free publicity his marriage had generated.

36. The *North American* ran another (humorous) article on this subject on 10 September 1903, in which they corrected the statement that Sigmund Hartman's collar was paper. They quote in full Sigmund's letter of 1 September 1903 to the *North American,* in which he expresses pleasure with the previous article in general, but argues that his collar was celluloid and not paper. Sigmund had even submitted the collar in question to corroborate his statement. "Hartman's Collar Really Wasn't Paper," *Philadelphia North American,* 10 September 1903.

37. "Violinist's Marriage Sad Blow to Father," *Philadelphia North American,* 31 August 1903. Sigmund's distrust of his son's marriage might also be explained by the breakup of his own marriage a few years earlier, when his wife Pepi established her own residence a few blocks from the cigar store. Sigmund's letters to Arthur housed in the Hartmann Collection, Free Library of Philadelphia, contain frequent invectives against marriage in general and his wife in particular.

Arthur later made Sigmund agree not to give any more newspaper interviews regarding his son. Sigmund signed a notarized statement to this effect on 7 July 1905. This document is in the Hartmann Collection, Free Library of Philadelphia.

38. Béla Bartók, in a letter to his mother on 29 October 1903, mentions visiting the Hartmanns in Berlin. *Béla Bartók Letters,* ed. János Demény (New York: St. Martin's Press, 1971), 33.

39. Sigmund's change of heart apparently resulted from a letter sent from Lutie to the Hartmans in Philadelphia, in which she begs the family to "treat me as your own." Sigmund wrote in response: "With an open heart, I say to my new and dear daughter: January 1, 1891, the Almighty suddenly took my highly talented daughter [Gizella]. So suddenly, the Almighty made up for my loss. I shall love you, dear Lutie, just as much as my late Gizella." Letter from Sigmund Hartman to Arthur and Lutie Hartmann, 17 September 1903, Hartmann Collection, Free Library of Philadelphia.

40. Harold Morrill Murray (he used his mother's maiden name instead of Hartmann) took his own life on 4 October 1935 in Vienna; on 20 November 1940, Arthur Hartmann wrote a heartfelt letter to his former wife requesting a photograph of his son as an adult. Hartmann Collection, Free Library of Philadelphia. A number of legal documents relating to Harold and his death are extant in the private collection of Karen Hartmann Kleinmann.

41. Arthur Hartmann, "The 'Ciaconna' of Bach," *Musical Courier,* 21 September 1904, 14–15. In August and September 1922, the *Musical Courier* published Hartmann's six articles under the title "Bach's Sonatas for the Violin." The fourth article, published 31 August 1922, updates and expands his original article on the Chaconne.

In an unpublished essay Hartmann mused, "To be called a great Bach-player has always stood for an extraordinary achievement. Yet, why should this be so? Is Bach's music harder to understand than that of Vivaldi or Corelli or Mozart or Debussy? That its execution, we refer specifically to the unaccompanied violin works, poses problems of some instrumental difficulty, chiefly through polyphony, we grant; yet surely not of the kind to merit extolling the executant into the extraordinary." "The Bach Bogey," unpublished essay, 1914, Hartmann Collection, Free Library of Philadelphia.

42. Letter from Edvard Grieg to Arthur Hartmann, 17 November 1905, Hartmann Collection, Free Library of Philadelphia.

43. Letter from Claude Debussy to Arthur Hartmann, 3 August 1910 [CD-14], Hartmann Collection, Free Library of Philadelphia.

44. See "Arthur Hartmann: Catalogue of Compositions and Transcriptions" at the end of the present volume. Hartmann elaborated upon his views on transcriptions in such articles as "When Transcriptions Are True Art Works" *Musical America,* 31 March 1917, 13; and "Arrangements—Derangements—Transcriptions," *Musical Courier,* 10 January 1918, 6.

45. Letter from Marian MacDowell to Arthur Hartmann, 25 July 1907, Arthur Hartmann Collection, Sibley Music Library, Eastman School of Music.

Twelve additional letters from Marian MacDowell to Arthur Hartmann are extant in the private collection of Karen Hartmann Kleinmann. The letters, dating from 13 November 1906 to 9 April 1913, document the permissions for the transcription, repeatedly relate Marian MacDowell's gratitude for Hartmann's transcription and for his performances of MacDowell's music, and record the ongoing friendship between the two.

46. Letter from Victor Talking Machine Company to Haensel & Jones, 16 April 1907, Hartmann Collection, Free Library of Philadelphia.

47. Even while vacationing, Hartmann wrote several articles about himself. One described how he escaped a rabid dog by running into a chapel, seizing the heavy wooden crozier, and beating the dog to death! Arthur Hartmann, "'Violin Demon,' Seeking Sanctuary from Mad Dog, Slays Beast beside Church Altar, Thereby, in Eyes of Brittany Peasants, Performing Miracle," reprinted in *Rochester (N.Y.) Herald,* 10 September 1922.

He also published a brief account of how he rescued his Stradivarius from a fire, as well as a photograph of himself with composer Arthur Nevin "discussing the complexities of Debussy" while smoking in a garden (dated 17 September 1908). One photograph shows him wearing "Tolstoyan" sandals as "symbols of asceticism." Unidentified news clippings from Hartmann's scrapbooks, Hartman Collection, Free Library of Philadelphia.

The grandest anecdote of them all was published on 12 August 1908 in the *Musical Leader*: "Arthur Hartmann, the famous violinist, is a guest this month at the Château St. Yves, Finistère, one of the most beautiful localities in France. Recently, he celebrated his twenty-seventh birthday there, and a typical French alfresco fête was given in his honor by his hosts, a procession, Watteau minuet, lawn banquet, fireworks, and dance helping to wind up the occasion. All the peasantry for miles around assisted at the occasion, and . . . broke into cheers when they saw the host approach Hartmann, [who] sent for his Stradivarius violin. Standing on the veranda of the château, . . . Hartmann played 'In God's own auditorium,' as a French newspaper describes the scene, 'with the deep, dark heavens as a ceiling and the softly slumbering forests as the walls. The night was still and balmy, and the romantic looking fiddler, with his expression half tender, half demoniacal, attuning his soul and his melodies to the witchery of the scene around him, made a sight— and an entrancing sound—not likely to be forgotten. . . . Among them was the present scribe—an uninvited guest—who happened to be strolling past the château gates, and was first interested, then attracted, then held spellbound by the weirdness of the scene and the irresistible fascination of the great artist's tone and temperament. It is doubtful whether he ever played better for king or crowded house than he did that night, for his throbbing and crazily enthusiastic audience. At the end, the ardent villagers carried Hartmann around on their shoulders and crowned him with an emblem made of oak leaves in lieu of the laurel, which the spokesman declared was the violinist's just due.'"

48. Letter from Claude Debussy to Arthur Hartmann, 6 September 1908 [CD-1], Hartmann Collection, Free Library of Philadelphia. The letter is misdated 6 XI 08 rather than 6 IX 08 (Debussy's second letter to Hartmann is dated 17 September 1908).

49. Letter from Claude Debussy to Arthur Hartmann, 17 September 1908 [CD-2], Hartmann Collection, Free Library of Philadelphia.

50. William Crane Carl (1865–1936), American organist and teacher, studied with Guilmant in Paris. He founded the Guilmant Organ School in New York in 1899 and was one of the founders of the American Guild of Organists.

51. Debussy worked on his opera *L'histoire de Tristan*, to a libretto by Gabriel Mourey, during the years 1907–9. The work was never completed.

52. "Hartmann and Debussy: Hartmann Talks to the *Musical Courier* Interviewer about the Composer of 'Pelléas et Mélisande,'" *Musical Courier*, 4 November 1908, 23.

53. "Won in three days; married in three weeks. The heroine of this charming adventure is Miss Marie Tucker, the foster child of Mrs. Stevens, of Buffalo, whose husband is at the head of the American Locomotive works. When Mrs. Stevens came abroad last month her unfailing companion, as usual, was Marie Tucker. One of the fellow passengers was Arthur Hartmann, the violinist, known from one end of the United States to the other as a virtuoso. The second day out he met the beautiful Buffalo girl, loved her at first sight, and told her so. Within three days she had promised to marry him." Vance Thompson, *New York American*, 25 December 1909. Marie was born in Houghton, N.Y., on 28 April 1881.

54. In the margin of the passage recounting the première of *Ibéria* in his copy of Oscar Thompson's *Debussy: Man and Artist* (New York: Dodd, Mead, and Company, 1937), 169, Hartmann wrote: "I was there! A. H. (next day—Monday about 11:30 A.M.)."

55. In the original typescript of the 1940 memoir, Hartmann introduced Madame Debussy immediately after his second visit with the composer and then recounted a long anecdote about the dinner at the Hotel Majestic that actually took place in August 1910. Debussy had married Emma Bardac two years previously (on 20 January 1908). Writing years later, Hartmann claimed that Debussy's "delicacy" forbade any "intimations" of the composer's second marriage. Comparing the composer's biography to his own, Hartmann observed, "Debussy's private life was the exact parallel of my own but with every situation reversed." This may suggest that, just as Debussy had been unfaithful to his first wife, Lilly, Hartmann thought his first wife had been unfaithful to him.

56. Letter from Claude Debussy to Arthur Hartmann, 24 June 1916 [CD-23], Hartmann Collection, Free Library of Philadelphia.

57. Letters from Claude Debussy to Arthur Hartmann, 10 March 1910 [CD-5] and 17 March 1910 [CD-4], Hartmann Collection, Free Library of Philadelphia.

58. See also Marcel Dietschy, *A Portrait of Claude Debussy,* ed. and trans. William Ashbrook and Margaret G. Cobb (Oxford: Clarendon Press, 1990; French edition, 1962), 161.

59. Letters from Claude Debussy to Arthur Hartmann, 15 May 1910 [CD-7] and 27 July 1910 [CD-8], Hartmann Collection, Free Library of Philadelphia.

60. Letter from Marc Blumenberg to Arthur Hartmann, 13 May 1910, Hartmann Collection, Free Library of Philadelphia.

61. Letter from Claude Debussy to Arthur Hartmann, 27 July 1910 [CD-8], Hartmann Collection, Free Library of Philadelphia.

62. Entry in Hartmann's autograph book, Claude Debussy to Arthur Hartmann, 13 May 1910 [CD-6], Hartmann Collection, Free Library of Philadelphia.

63. Letter from Emma Debussy to Arthur Hartmann, 17 May 1918 [ECD-21], Hartmann Collection, Free Library of Philadelphia. Readers of the memoir will notice that Hartmann also frequently hinted or even begged the composer for a violin sonata. Debussy invariably, and at times brutally, rebuffed Hartmann for proposing a work in a Germanic form. Yet in his last letter to Hartmann on 24 June 1916 [CD-23], Debussy claimed, "I had worked like a whole plantation of slaves and was preparing to write the sonata for violin and piano, for which you must be quite impatient."

When Debussy completed his Violin Sonata, he dedicated the work, as he did the other sonatas finished during the war, to his wife. It seems Hartmann was offended that Debussy never offered him either the world première or even the American première of this long-awaited work. These were performed, respectively, by the young violinist Gaston Poulet with the composer (in one of his last public appearances, 5 May 1917), and by Eddy Brown accompanied by Louis Gruenberg (Carnegie Hall, 11 November 1917).

In 1929 Emma Claude Debussy sent Hartmann a copy of the sonata with the following inscription: "Au grand artiste à l'ami fidèle Arthur Hartmann, Affectueusement, Emma Claude Debussy 1929" ["To the great artist {and} faithful friend Arthur Hartmann, Affectionately, Emma Claude Debussy 1929"]. While there is no evidence that Hartmann ever performed the Debussy sonata publicly, the many markings on the violin part demonstrate that he spent a great deal of time studying the work. Hartmann's copy of the sonata is in the Hartmann Collection, Free Library of Philadelphia.

64. Letter from Claude Debussy to Arthur Hartmann [CD-9], undated [24 May 1910], Hartmann Collection, Free Library of Philadelphia.

65. On 8 November 1910 Debussy inscribed a copy of Hartmann's *La fille aux cheveux de lin* transcription to the violinist. Hartmann Collection, Free Library of Philadelphia.

66. Hartmann guarded his authorship of this transcription jealously (as he did his other transcriptions), always insisting that his name was mentioned in the program when it was performed. In letters dated 21 March and 6 April 1921, Kreisler assured Hartmann that he was playing the transcription often and enclosed programs to prove that Hartmann was being properly acknowledged. Letters from Fritz Kreisler to Arthur Hartmann: 21 March 1921, Arthur Hartmann Collection, Sibley Music Library, Eastman School of Music; 6 April 1921, private collection of Karen Hartmann Kleinmann.

67. See photograph of this poster at the beginning of "Claude Debussy As I Knew Him," p. 36.

68. Debussy rewarded Hartmann for each transcription: In the ink MS of the 1941 memoir, Hartmann wrote, "1st trans—brought me his photo/2nd trans—score of *Pelléas*/3rd trans—copy of *Minstrels* with dedication." (That is, for *Il pleure dans mon coeur*, Debussy gave Hartmann an autographed photograph, dated 6 October 1908; for the second transcription, *La fille aux cheveux de lin*, Debussy gave him the autographed orchestral score of *Pelléas*, dated 12 June 1910; and for the third transcription, *Minstrels*, Debussy gave him the manuscript of *Minstrels* in his [Debussy's] own hand, dated 17 January 1914 and inscribed "pour piano et Hartmann"). The 1941 memoir: Hartmann Collection, Free Library of Philadelphia.

69. In his personal copy of *Lettres de Claude Debussy à son Éditeur* (Paris: Durand, 1927), Hartmann corrected the date of the 4 January 1914 letter to 4 February 1914. In this letter, Debussy promised the manuscript of *Minstrels* to the publisher "tomorrow evening" at the recital.

For a more detailed discussion of the authorship of the *Minstrels* transcription, see the Introduction to Appendix A, pp. 229–32.

70. In a letter dated 5 January 1914, Debussy invited Laloy to his home for an evening of music. Describing the invited guests, Debussy wrote: "il y aura les Hartmann; lui est intéressant et joue prodigieusement du violon" ["The Hartmanns will be there; he is an engaging person and an extraordinary violinist"]. François Lesure, "Correspondance de Claude Debussy et de Louis Laloy (1902–1914)," *Revue de Musicologie* 48 (1962): 40. Laloy's review here clearly seconded Debussy's opinion of Hartmann.

71. A reference to François Couperin's *L'art de toucher le clavecin* (1716).

72. "Un concert d'un caractère tout particulier retint l'attention des musiciens soucieux de défendre un poète de l'harmonie actuellement persécuté par les pions. Louis Laloy a souligné toute l'importance et l'opportunité du geste de Claude Debussy tendant affectueusement à Edvard Grieg ses deux mains secourables, au moment précis où une redoutable suffragette accablait le doux petit vieillard de coups de

parapluie. Ma tendresse pour l'opprimé et son défenseur me fait un devoir de donner ici la parole à Louis Laloy, pour lui permettre de conclure harmonieusement son bel article de jeudi dernier:

'M. Arthur Hartmann est un maître à qui le violon obéit sans discuter. Son archet quand il s'est emparé d'une corde, y adhère comme s'il fût aimanté; ses doigts battent le manche d'un crépitement catégorique; le son, depuis les abîmes de la quatrième corde jusqu'aux cimes vertigineuses de la chanterelle, garde sa densité et son calibre les traits et les accords ne laissent jamais place à la moindre hésitation. On croirait que l'instrument lui appartient comme une partie de son corps dont il dispose par volonté, que la caisse vernie est le prolongement de son menton, et que les cordes sont les dernières ramifications de ses nerfs mis à nu. La Chaconne, de Bach, où les plus redoutables problèmes de la technique se trouvent aggravés de la nécessité du style, retrouve, grâce, à lui, la sublime pureté de la pensée qui l'inspira. Comme Paganini, à qui, d'ailleurs, il ressemble par quelque dissymétrie de sa personne, il est un peu sorcier.

'M. Claude Debussy, qui, par une exceptionnelle faveur, l'accompagne, est magicien. Ce n'est pas ici le lieu de déduire les différences entre la sorcellerie, qui dompte les esprits, et la magie qui les gagne. La puissance de la magie sera comprise de tous ceux qui ont une seule fois entendu ce piano surnaturel où les sons naissent sans chocs de marteaux, sans frôlements de cordes, s'élèvent dans un air transparent qui les unit sans les confondre et s'évaporent en brumes irisées. M. Debussy apprivoise le clavier d'un charme qui n'est à la portée d'aucun de nos virtuoses. Comme un de ses ancêtres spirituels, François Couperin, il pourrait écrire un *Art de toucher le piano*, qui, d'ailleurs, ne trahirait pas son secret aux profanes.

'La sonate en sol mineur de Grieg n'a pas déçu mes souvenirs: j'en aime encore la grâce, la fraîcheur, la tendresse, la bravoure coupée de refrains nostalgiques, enfin la sonorité toujours agréable et claire. Des trois morceaux de M. Debussy qui furent ce soir-là scindés entre le violon et le piano, celui qui s'est le mieux trouvé de l'opération est le troisième, *Minstrels*, où le violon se livre aux plus burlesques cabrioles, et particulièrement à des pizzicati glissés où tient en raccourci tout le continent noir.'"

73. Hartmann's last meeting with Debussy was on the composer's birthday, 22 August 1914, and Debussy's last letter to Hartmann is dated 24 June 1916. The Hartmanns' relationship with Emma Debussy did continue for many years after the composer's death, as evidenced by the many letters from Emma to both Arthur and Marie located in the Hartmann Collection, Free Library of Philadelphia. The last of these, to Arthur, is dated 15 August 1932. See "Letters from Emma Claude Debussy to Marie Hartmann and Arthur Hartmann" at the end of "Claude Debussy As I Knew Him" in the present volume.

74. *Documenta Bartókiana*, vol. 3, ed. D. Dille (Mainz: B. Schott's Söhne, 1968), 83. Translation by Regine Johnson.

75. Letter from Béla Bartók to Arthur Hartmann, 22 May 1914, Hartmann Collection, Free Library of Philadelphia. In response to Hartmann's interest in his violin compositions, Bartók wrote: "All I have for the violin is a rather 'ineffective' kind of 'Romance' (may be performed with orchestral accompaniment only) which perhaps I could bring along." This may refer to the first movement of Bartók's Violin Concerto No. 1, which was written in 1907, but not performed until 30 May 1958. Bartók revised this movement in 1907 as the first of his *Két portré* (*Two Portraits*), Op. 5.

76. Letter from Béla Bartók to Arthur Hartmann, 23 June 1914, Hartmann Collection, Free Library of Philadelphia.

77. Hartmann's autograph book, Hartmann Collection, Free Library of Philadelphia. Hartmann's notes also contain the following entry regarding Bartók's visit: "August [*sic*] 1914—Bartók turning up with a market basket full of round conical discs of Arabian Rhythms which he wanted to give to the archives of the Paris Conservatoire."

78. Hans Moldenhauer, *Anton von Webern: A Chronicle of His Life and Work* (New York: Knopf, 1979), 187–88.

79. Letter from Anton von Webern to Arthur Hartmann, 15 July 1914, Arthur Hartmann Collection, Sibley Music Library, Eastman School of Music.

80. Both Hartmann's working manuscript and a fair copy of the Giardini sonatas survive in the Hartmann Collection, Free Library of Philadelphia. Hartmann apparently never published his editions of the sonatas.

81. The trunk was eventually found and returned to Hartmann.

82. From "Paris in Peace and War," *Canadian Journal of Music,* October-November 1914.

83. Hartmann's colleagues at the Von Ende School included Alberto Jonas, Anton Witek, and Sigismond Stojowski. A list of Hartmann's students, published in 1916 in the *Musical Courier,* included Carl H. Tollefson, Gilbert Jaffery, Nicholas Garagusi, Frank Havick, M. Rabinovitz, J. Rosenthal, Gustave Wille, S. Unglada, Benj. Wood, Arlene Ingham, Norman Kimball, Katherine Lewis, A. Sinigalliano, William Butler, Marcy Gordon, M. Gleissner, Charles Klein, Edward Malloy, M. Rasbury, Tom Gardner, Eben Smith, Rafael de Silva, John Taylor, and Dan Visanski. Unidentified *Musical Courier* clipping from Hartmann's scrapbooks, Hartmann Collection, Free Library of Philadelphia.

84. William Armstrong, "Arthur Hartmann: Violinist and Thinker," *Musician,* March 1915, 1. For further details of Hartmann's approach to teaching, see Frederick H. Martens's interview of Hartmann in *Violin Mastery: Talks with Master Violinists and Teachers* (New York: Frederick A. Stokes, 1919), 66–77, as well as the reprint of a lecture Hartmann gave to the New York State Music Teachers' Assocation, "The Educational Literature of the Violin," in "Music and Musicians" column, *Illustrated Buffalo Express,* 2 July, 9 July, 16 July, 23 July, 30 July, 6 August 1911. See also *Arthur Hartmann's Instinctive Method for the Violin* (New York, Belwin, 1926); the manuscript of this work is in the Hartmann Collection, Free Library of Philadelphia.

85. "An Obedient Soloist: How Arthur Hartmann as Boy Artist Observed Parental Mandate," *Musical America,* 26 February 1916, 31.

86. Quoted in "Huss, 'One of the Best of American Composers,'" *Musical Courier,* 21 March 1918, 40. See also Review of "Huss-Hartmann Matinee," 20 February 1918, in "New York Concerts," *Musical Courier,* 28 February 1918, 16; and Gary A. Greene, *Henry Holden Huss: An American Composer's Life* (Metuchen, N.J.: Scarecrow Press, 1995), 56–57, 60. Greene states that Huss and Hartmann performed the sonata once again at the Harvard Club on 3 August 1928.

In a letter to Hartmann dated 7 March 1918, Huss wrote: "G. Schirmer Co. are going to give me note of introduction to Victor Phonograph people. I hope we (you and I) will make a fortune out of the Andante." But it does not appear anything ever came of this. Letter from Henry Huss to Arthur Hartmann, 7 March 1918, private collection of Karen Hartmann Kleinmann.

87. Hartmann had petitioned Marian MacDowell for a recommendation to perform at the MacDowell Club as early as 1913. In a letter to Hartmann dated 9 April 1913, Marian MacDowell stated that she would write to the musical committee of the MacDowell Club in New York on his behalf, but had little hope of success as she felt she was largely without influence there. Letter from Marian MacDowell to Arthur Hartmann, 9 April 1913, private collection of Karen Hartmann Kleinmann.

88. Walter Morse Rummel (1887–1953), German-American pianist and composer. Rummel moved to Paris in 1909, where he met Debussy and became a leading interpreter of his piano music. Rummel and Hartmann evidently became friends during Hartmann's time in Berlin, at which time William Rummel, Walter's brother, studied violin with Hartmann. Arthur M. Abell, "Berlin," *Musical Courier,* 21 October 1908, 5.

89. Arthur Walter Kramer, "Enigma of Hartmann's Nationality," *Musical America,* 3 July 1915, 36.

90. Letter from Walter Morse Rummel to Arthur Hartmann, undated, Hartmann Collection, Free Library of Philadelphia.

91. Byron Hagel, "The Bystander," *Musical Courier,* 4 April 1918, 24.

92. Arthur Hartmann, "The Real George," unpublished essay, Hartmann Collection, Free Library of Philadelphia.

93. Elizabeth Brayer, *George Eastman: A Biography* (Baltimore, Md.: Johns Hopkins University Press, 1996), 322.

94. Ibid., 449.

95. One of Hartmann's pupils from the 1930s, John Celentano, has been on the faculty at Eastman School of Music since 1946. Professor Celentano, in a telephone interview conducted on 20 September 1999, confirmed the legendary account of his teacher playing Paganini's *Moto Perpetuo* in fingered octaves, but stated that Hartmann emphatically disdained any form of showmanship. Celentano remembered Hartmann as a violinist with an intensely beautiful singing tone and a profound understanding of the music literature, who demanded no less from his students.

96. César Saerchinger, "Berlin is Full of American Musicians," *Musical Courier,* 19 October 1922, 7.

97. Letter from Arthur Hartmann to Leonard Liebling, 17 January 1923. Quoted in Leonard Liebling, "Variationettes," *Musical Courier,* 8 February 1923, 22.

98. Both letters from Copland to Hartmann are in the Hartmann Collection, Free Library of Philadelphia.

99. In a letter to Hartmann on 3 January 1923, Bartók writes about financial arrangements for sonata recitals in Budapest and possibly Italy. Bartók also states that if Hartmann is able to secure a contract for any other tour (he suggests "Holland or Scandinavia, Switzerland, etc."), he would like to participate. Bartók does stipulate: "I don't wish to play my sonatas just anywhere but only where they are in demand, that is, where there is a feeling for them." As far as repertory, Bartók states that he would leave the choice to Hartmann, but asks the violinist to look at Ernest Bloch's Sonata No. 1 for Violin and Piano and at Karol Szymanowski's *Mity (Myths,* Op. 30): no. 1, *Zrod o Aretuzy (The Fountain of Arethusa)* and no. 3, *Driady i Pan (Dryads and Pan).*

Bartók's letter of 28 October 1924 laments the poor economic conditions in Europe that make Hartmann's proposed tour unfeasible. He does, however, inquire whether Hartmann will be in America in January 1926. Both letters are in the Hartmann Collection, Free Library of Philadelphia.

100. Letters from both Edgard Varèse (28 December 1925) and Carlos Salzédo (25 May 1927) to Hartmann are extant in the Hartmann Collection, Free Library of Philadelphia.

101. This likely refers to Hartmann's disappointment that the première of the Debussy Violin Sonata that he felt had been promised to him had been given to someone else.

102. *Documenta Bartókiana*, vol. 3, 123. Translation by Regine Johnson.

103. Hartmann was a friend of Szigeti at least in later years, as evidenced by two 1940 letters from Szigeti to Hartmann: 2 April 1940 (Hartmann Collection, Free Library of Philadelphia) and 12 November 1940 (private collection of Karen Hartmann Kleinmann). In the second of these letters, Szigeti wrote: "Will you give us the pleasure of dropping in on Wednesday evening around nine o'clock? Bartók and his wife will be with us, and it would be delightful if you could join us."

104. Quoted in "Artists Everywhere," *Musical Courier*, 12 November 1925, 50.

105. Review of Hartmann Quartet, 16 November 1925, in "New York Concerts," *Musical Courier*, 26 November 1925, 14–15.

106. "Impressive Debut of Hartmann Quartet," *Musical Courier*, 17 December 1925, 42. The *Musical Leader* further praised the participation of Dohnányi as "an authority as a composer and as an interpreter" and also noted that the Bridge quartet had "many moments of grace and beauty." Unidentified *Musical Leader* clipping from Hartmann's scrapbooks, Hartmann Collection, Free Library of Philadelphia.

Frank Bridge himself wrote Hartmann expressing his gratitude, as he had previously written in 1921 after Hartmann's performance of the same quartet at George Eastman's mansion. Both of these letters are in the Hartmann Collection, Free Library of Philadelphia. Another letter from Bridge, dated 21 May 1921, thanks Hartmann for the programs indicating performance of both the E Minor and G Minor quartets. This letter is in the private collection of Karen Hartmann Kleinmann.

107. Weiner had won the Coolidge Prize in 1922 for his second String Quartet and owed much gratitude to Hartmann, who had informed the composer in distant Budapest of the competition.

108. Hartmann had played Grainger's *Molly on the Shore* with the Kilbourn Quartet in Rochester in 1920. Three letters (4 January 1921, 9 March 1921, and 29 April 1921) and an inscribed photograph (undated) from Percy Grainger to Arthur Hartmann are extant in the private collection of Karen Hartmann Kleinmann. In the letters, Grainger thanks Hartmann for his performances of *Molly on the Shore* and also praises Hartmann both as performer and composer.

109. Review of Hartmann Quartet, 8 March 1926, in "New York Concerts," *Musical Courier*, 18 March 1926, 20.

110. The *Musical Courier* critic stated that the Casella concerto was "powerful if not beautiful. It is modern in the extreme—dissonant, unlovely, yet undoubtedly powerful. One may not like it, but admire it one must." "International Composers' Guild Introduces Two New Compositions to New York," *Musical Courier*, 18 February 1926, 5, 56. Olga Samaroff, in the *New York Evening Post*, 15 February

1926, called the concert an "undisputed success" and noted the presence of "such figures as Klemperer, Furtwängler, Prokofiev, [and] Goossens." Olin Downes, writing for the *New York Times*, 15 February 1926, wished that the Casella work had also been played twice: "On preliminary acquaintance there is the impression that this is one of Mr. Casella's finest compositions." Lawrence Gilman, in the *New York Herald Tribune*, 15 February 1926, pointed out that the Stravinsky "naturally overshadowed" the Casella and expressed the desire to hear the concerto "under less distracting circumstances."

111. After the divorce, Marie raised Gregory and Helen, living in New York City and Pasadena. She later lived in New York City with her sister, Elizabeth Cole Tucker, a professor of art at the Pratt Institute. When Elizabeth retired, the sisters moved back to their family home in Houghton, N.Y. Marie died there in 1959 at the age of 78.

Gregory became a physicist and mathematician, earning degrees from Queens College at Oxford and Brown University. Joining the Navy in 1941, he served as technical director of the U.S. Naval Ordnance Laboratory (now the Naval Systems Weapons Command) in White Oak, Md., from 1955 until his retirement in 1973. He died 8 April 1996 at the age of 84. Helen Hartmann Winn currently resides in Virginia. Private correspondence from George C. Hartmann, 15 October 2002; obituary of Gregory Kemenyi Hartmann, *Washington Post*, 11 April 1996.

112. Hartmann's autobiographical notes, Hartmann Collection, Free Library of Philadelphia.

113. "Famous Violinist Ill at Temple Hospital," *Philadelphia Record*, 1 February 1931.

114. Leonard Liebling, "Variations," *Musical Courier*, 28 February 1931, 25, 30.

115. Leonard Liebling, "Variations," *Musical Courier*, 30 May 1931, 25.

116. Hartmann did perform occasionally as a soloist with such groups as the Syracuse Symphony, conducted by Andre Polah, and the Trenton Symphony, conducted by Max Jacobs. These events, however, became increasingly less frequent as the years went by.

117. *Pro Musica* 5 (1932): 57–62. A review of the quartet in the *New York Times*, 13 December 1931, stated: "The International Society for New Music's recent recital in Berlin brought forth, among other things, the première of a String Quartet by Arthur Hartmann. The reviewer of the *Allgemeine Musikzeitung* described it as a 'noteworthy kaleidoscope of styles, now hottentottish with a Saxon cadence, now truly Saxon with a hottentottish accent.' Despite this somewhat astonishing characterization, the work seemed to possess great freshness, especially in the strong and expressive conviction of the slow movement, according to further comment." In "1932 Salzburg Festival: Stokowski and Richard Strauss to Conduct Orchestral Concerts—Foreign Notes," *New York Times*, 13 December 1931.

118. Pearl McCarthy, "Hartmann, Notable Violinist, Friend of Great Composers, Not Sorry to Leave Toronto," *Toronto Daily Mail and Empire*, 4 February 1933.

119. In the May 1932 issue of *Pan Pipes*, Gertrude Evans, the president of Sigma Alpha Iota, thanked Hartmann for his gift of photographs from the estate of Maud Powell and urged local chapters to present Arthur Hartmann musicales in his honor. "Gift of Maud Powell Collection," *Pan Pipes* (May 1932): 422–24.

Hartmann's long friendship and professional relationship with Maud Powell is documented in Karen A. Shaffer and Neva Garner Greenwood, *Maud Powell: Pioneer American Violinist* (Ames: Iowa State University Press, 1988). See also letter from Maud Powell to Arthur Hartmann, 23 July 1919, Arthur Hartmann Collection, Sibley Music Library, Eastman School of Music.

120. Arthur Hartmann, "Woodstock and the Woodstockians," *Musical Courier*, 5 December 1931, 10.

121. Arthur Hartmann, "Sidelights on Saint-Saëns' Essays," *Musical Courier*, 5 March 1932, 6, 16.

122. Unpublished essay, Hartmann Collection, Free Library of Philadelphia.

123. Hartmann, "La Plus Que Lente," *Musical America*, 25 December 1930, 10.

124. McCarthy, "Hartmann, Notable Violinist."

125. The present volume includes the articles on Joachim and Ysaÿe (courtesy *Musical America* Archives). Hartmann knew these great artists and gives the reader a sense of their personalities and his own response to their artistry. Although Hartmann heard Sarasate play once or twice, he did not have that personal relationship that enlivens the other accounts. See Arthur Hartmann, "The Perfect Virtuoso: Sarasate, the Wonder Worker, as Recalled by a Fellow Violinist," *Musical America*, 25 March 1940, 8.

126. Letter from Leonard Liebling to Arthur Hartmann, 11 February 1940, Hartmann Collection, Free Library of Philadelphia.

127. Letter from Joseph Szigeti to Arthur Hartmann, 2 April 1940, Hartmann Collection, Free Library of Philadelphia.

128. The manuscript is in the Hartmann Collection, Free Library of Philadelphia, and serves as the basis for Hartmann's Debussy essay in the present volume.

129. Arthur Hartmann, "A Tribute to Paganini on the Centennial of His Death," *Who Is Who In Music*, ed. Leonard Liebling (Chicago: Lee Stern Press, 1941), 250–51. Hartmann also served on the editorial board for this publication.

130. The first article, "A Compliment—and a Correction," *Violins and Violinists*, September 1946, 352–55, explains that in Doring's book *How Many Strads?* (Chicago: William Lewis & Son, 1945), Hartmann's 1735 Stradivarius had been mistakenly said to be owned by another Hartmann in Copenhagen. The second, "Re: J. B. Guadagnini Violins . . . Reminiscences," *Violins and Violinists*, December 1946, 475–77, concerns a 1752 Guadagnini that Hartmann acquired as part of the selling price for his Stradivarius. Doring's book, *The Guadagnini Family of Violin Makers* (Chicago: William Lewis & Son, 1949), contains a description and photograph of Hartmann's Guadagnini, 123–25.

131. Jean Riegger, "My Musical Memories" (1927). The manuscript focuses on Toscanini, under whom she had sung Beethoven's Ninth Symphony and *Missa Solemnis* several times. Hartmann made some attempt to edit it but eventually gave up. The manuscript is in the Hartmann Collection, Free Library of Philadelphia.

No relationship between Hartmann and Wallingford Riegger is documented, although they were both involved with the International Composers' Guild in New York.

132. Letter from Albert Schweitzer to Arthur Hartmann, 13 May 1950, Hartmann Collection, Free Library of Philadelphia.

133. See Bendiner, *Translated from the Hungarian*, 142–54. Bendiner, Arthur's

nephew, was responsible for the disbursement of Hartmann's estate. A number of letters regarding Hartmann's estate, including some by Bendiner and one written on 8 December 1973 by Gregory Hartmann describing items of the estate that he had received, are extant in the private collection of Karen Hartmann Kleinmann.

Claude Debussy As I Knew Him

1. Arthur Hartmann, "Claude Debussy As I Knew Him," *Musical Courier,* 23 May 1918, 6–9. A selection from this article appears in Roger Nichols, *Debussy Remembered* (London: Faber and Faber, 1992), 204–11. Hartmann's expanded memoir was written in 1941.

2. Hartmann's 1918 *Musical Courier* article gives the date as 15 June 1908.

3. This phrase, although not precisely translatable, may be understood as: "To be German, for the sake of the thing itself!"

4. *Louise,* opera by Gustave Charpentier (1860–1956), produced in Paris in 1900.

5. Translated by Hartmann in his pencil manuscript: "But my dear sir—we are today in 1940!"

6. Hartmann is referring here to Saint-Saëns's Violin Concerto No. 2 in C Major, Op. 58. This was the first Violin Concerto that Saint-Saëns composed (1858), but it was not published until 1879 after his Violin Concerto No. 1 in A Major, Op. 20 (composed in 1858, published in 1868). In a letter dated 8 June 1896, Saint-Saëns praised Hartmann for his performance of this concerto. Letter from Camille Saint-Saëns to Arthur Hartmann, 8 June 1896, private collection of Karen Hartmann Kleinmann.

7. The performance of *Pelléas* that Hartmann attended featured Maggie Teyte as Mélisande.

8. "On fait remonter l'origine de Douarnenéz (spécialités: sardines, thon, maquereaux) à la fondation, dans L'Île Tristan, d'un prieuré—Pendant la Ligue la petite ville fut détruite par le chef de bandes Fontenelle, qui s'établit solidement dans L'Île Tristan, d'où il ne put être délogé qu'après plusieurs années d'efforts par les troupes de Henri IV. Cette Île doit son nom au Chevalier de la Table Ronde dont le souvenir est inséparable de celui d'Yseult."

9. During his stay in Brittany, Hartmann himself became an object of this superstition. He tells this story in his article, "'Violin Demon,' Seeking Sanctuary from Mad Dog, Slays Beast beside Church Altar, Thereby, in Eyes of Brittany Peasants, Performing Miracle," in *Rochester [N.Y.] Herald,* 10 September 1922.

10. We have included in Hartmann's memoir only those letters which he himself inserted in the text, though in English translation rather than their original French. All letters from Debussy to Hartmann appear following the essay in chronological order. As Hartmann indicates in his text, this letter was actually written in September, not November. This letter is in the Hartmann Collection, Free Library of Philadelphia.

11. Hartmann Collection, Free Library of Philadelphia.

12. This photograph is published in Hartmann's article "Hartmann and Debussy: Hartmann Talks to the *Musical Courier* Interviewer about the Composer of 'Pelléas et Mélisande,'" *Musical Courier,* 4 November 1908, 23. From the inscription, we can determine the date of this first meeting as 6 October 1908.

13. This letter does not appear in *Lettres de Claude Debussy à sa femme Emma,* ed. Pasteur Vallery-Radot (Paris: Flammarion, 1957); however, Hartmann is mentioned in passing in Debussy's letters of 3 and 4 December 1910. An English translation of the 3 December 1910 letter is included in *Debussy Letters,* ed. François Lesure and Roger Nichols, trans. Roger Nichols (London: Faber and Faber, 1987), where "Hartmann" is identified as Debussy's former publisher, Georges Hartmann (1843–1900). Given his Hungarian descent and reputation as a storyteller, this more likely refers to Arthur Hartmann.

14. Since Hartmann married Marie Cole Tucker in Paris on 21 December 1909, we may date this second meeting with Debussy as occurring in January 1910.

15. A quotation from Fafner in Wagner's *Siegfried,* Act II, Scene 1.

16. It is unlikely that Debussy ever met Wagner in person. Debussy visited Bayreuth in 1888 and 1889 and admired Wagner greatly up to that point. He turned away from Wagner, however, in the early 1890s while seeking to define his own personal style.

17. "Ouf! Celui-là! Ce Wagner avec ces éternels motifs à chaque instant et qui n'en finissent pas! Aussitôt que quelqu'un sur la scène recommence une de ces interminables histoires, il y a quelqu'un dans l'orchestre qui présente sa carte de visite tout-de-suite . . . comm' un commis voyageur! Ah bon Dieu, ce qu'il est assommant . . . celui-là! Je l'ai vu une fois à Bayreuth ce Wagner-là, ah . . . ce qu'il avait des yeux . . . mon Dieu . . . des yeux *farouches* . . . épouvantables . . . terribles . . . tandis que Liszt . . . ah Litz . . . Litz c'était . . . comment vous dirais-je . . . Litz c'était la bonté même!"

Debussy and Liszt did meet three times in January 1886 while Debussy was residing at the Villa Medici as recipient of the Grand Prix de Rome.

18. 20 February 1910.

19. In the margin of the passage recounting the première of *Ibéria* in his copy of Oscar Thompson's *Debussy: Man and Artist* (New York: Dodd, Mead, and Company, 1937), 169, Hartmann wrote: "I was there! A. H. (next day—Monday about 11:30 A.M.)."

20. The anecdote, from Hartmann's papers, unfortunately breaks off at this point.

21. From Hartmann's manuscript notes: "As usual, Marie failed me, for while she knew every thought of mine and understood my emotional nature and temperamental extremes, she was always too unwilling to try to overcome her reticence with regard to expressing herself to others than myself. The depths of her misunderstanding and emotions she could not bring to expression or revelations before others, even to the point of having *me* answer the letters which Emma-Claude wrote her 'Chère grande petite.' Marie would correct my spelling and then perhaps sign 'Marie' under my name."

22. See letter from Emma-Claude to the Hartmanns, 7 or 8 October 1919 (ECD-22) and from "Miss" (Chouchou's English governess) to the Hartmanns, 19 October 1919 (ECD-23).

23. Hatmann is referring here to the story recounted on pp. 82–89 under "A Dinner Party," which actually occurred later, on 3 August 1910.

24. "Ah Seigneur! Sacré bon Dieu, il n'y a que lui! Quel homme que celui-ci, et puis, quel musicien. Grand Dieu! Nom de Dieu, quel DON de Dieu! Je ne parle même pas du violon, car il s'en fiche, de ça mais avec lui je ferais de la musique *toute ma vie*!"

25. Gabrielle Réjane (*née* Gabrielle Charlotte Réju, 1857–1920), silent film actress. Eugene Michael Vazzana, *Silent Film Necrology* (London: McFarland, 1995), 276.

26. See letter CD-23.

27. Regarding Debussy's proposed American tour, see also letters CD-7 and CD-8.

28. Inscribed 27 July 1910. Hartmann Collection, Free Library of Philadelphia.

29. Inscribed 21 May 1910. Hartmann Collection, Free Library of Philadelphia. While Hartmann combines the stories of Debussy's gifts of *Le promenoir des deux amants* and *Préludes* (Book I), they were actually on two separate occasions, as the dates of the inscriptions indicate (27 July 1910 for *Le promenoir des deux amants* and 21 May 1910 for *Préludes*). Chronologically, the *Préludes* gift fits at this point in the memoir, while *Le promenoir des deux amants* would come at a later point alongside Hartmann's discussion of *La plus que lente* (a copy of which was also inscribed to Hartmann by Debussy on 27 July 1910).

30. Hartmann Collection, Free Library of Philadelphia.

31. Arthur Hartmann Collection, Sibley Music Library, Eastman School of Music.

32. Hartmann Collection, Free Library of Philadelphia.

33. See also letter from Emma Debussy to Marie Hartmann upon the same occasion, ECD-1.

34. This anecdote presumably occurred in June 1910 when Toscanini was in Paris on tour with the Metropolitan Opera. This date is further substantiated by Hartmann's *Pelléas* score (the central theme of the conversation) inscribed by Debussy and dated 12 June 1910. Hartmann Collection, Free Library of Philadelphia.

35. On 2 April 1908 Toscanini had directed the Italian première of *Pelléas* at La Scala. Despite the Italian public's strong disposition against foreign operas, Toscanini went to great lengths to make the performance a success. He had invited Debussy to attend the preparations and the première, but the composer was not able to come. He wrote to Toscanini: "I put *Pelléas*'s fate in your hands, sure as I am that I could not wish for more loyal or more capable ones. For this reason as well, I would have liked to have worked on it with you; it is a joy which one does not often find along the path of our art." Quoted in Harvey Sachs, *Toscanini* (Philadelphia: J. B. Lippincott, 1978), 101.

36. See Hartmann's article, "The Czimbalom, Hungary's National Instrument," *Musical Quarterly* 2 (1916): 590–600.

37. Debussy did leave music for portions of the work, though he did not complete it. The extant music for *La chute de la maison Usher* consists of a twenty-one-page manuscript of the vocal score for the entire first scene and the beginning of the second and approximately twenty-five pages of sketch material. The surviving music covers a little less than half of the libretto, which Debussy did complete. See Robert Orledge, *Debussy and the Theatre* (Cambridge: Cambridge University Press, 1982).

In 1976, *La chute de la maison Usher* was reconstructed in two versions. One was by musicologists Carolyn Abbate and Robert Kyr, the other by Chilean composer, organist, and musicologist Juan Allende-Blin. Robert Orledge is presently reconstructing the work for the *Oeuvres complètes de Claude Debussy*.

38. Debussy inscribed a copy of *La plus que lente* to Hartmann on 27 July 1910. Hartmann Collection, Free Library of Philadelphia.

39. Hartmann is alluding here to the French pianist and composer Cécile Chaminade (1857–1944).

40. This score is extant in the Hartmann Collection, Free Library of Philadelphia.

41. Hartmann Collection, Free Library of Philadelphia.

42. Hartmann Collection, Free Library of Philadelphia.

43. Selection from letter CD-14, Hartmann Collection, Free Library of Philadelphia.

44. This is clearly a hyperbole on Hartmann's part, in which he is not considering Debussy's student days.

45. Louis Laloy, "La musique chez soi: Edvard Grieg (1843–1907)," *Comoedia,* 5 February 1914. In this article, Laloy writes eloquently of Grieg's mastery of harmony and cites for support César Franck's delight in performing works of Grieg. Laloy goes on to state that, in performing the Grieg sonata with Hartmann, "Claude Debussy today confirms the approval of César Franck" ("M. Claude Debussy confirme aujourd'hui l'approbation de César Franck").

46. Dreyfus was arrested in 1894 and finally exonerated and reinstated as an officer in 1906. See Jane F. Fulcher, *French Cultural Politics and Music: From the Dreyfus Affair to the First World War* (Oxford: Oxford University Press, 1999), esp. 155–56 and 170–94.

47. Actually, a month before Grieg's concert in Paris (19 April 1903), Debussy wrote an article in which he sharply criticized Grieg's compositions and misrepresented Grieg's statements about the Dreyfus Affair. See Finn Benestad and Dag Schjelderup-Ebbe, *Edvard Grieg: The Man and the Artist,* trans. William H. Halverson and Leland B. Stateren (Lincoln: University of Nebraska Press, 1988), 350–58.

Hartmann also represents Debussy throughout his memoir as being thoroughly opposed to things German—whether musical, cultural, or political—especially during the World War I period.

48. Debussy's debt to Durand had reached a total of 49,688.30 francs by 1914. Christophe Charle, "Debussy in Fin-de-Siècle Paris," in *Debussy and His World,* ed. Jane F. Fulcher, trans. Victoria Johnson (Princeton, N.J.: Princeton University Press, 2001), 288. In early 1914 Debussy traveled to Rome, Amsterdam, The Hague, Brussels, and London for the essential purpose of supporting his family. François Lesure, "Claude Debussy," *New Grove Dictionary of Music and Musicians,* 2nd ed., ed. Stanley Sadie (London: Macmillan, 2001), 7:100.

49. Emil Sjoegren (1853–1918). Friend of Arthur Hartmann in Paris, appearing at my home in a program of his . . . and my (!) compositions, and playing one of his sonatas with me. [This footnote is Hartmann's].

50. The "*sic*" at this point is Hartmann's own. Hartmann and Debussy played Grieg's Violin Sonata in G Major, Op. 13. There was a general confusion regarding the tonality of the Sonata, as both the concert announcement and the review in *Comoedia* label it as G Minor. The probable source of this confusion is that the Sonata's nineteen-measure introduction is in G Minor (Lento doloroso). After a seven-measure transition, the G-Major tonality of the Sonata is firmly established in measure 26 (Allegro vivace).

51. "Hotel König von Dänemark, Kopenhagen, 7/3/14. Sehr verehrter Hr.

Hartmann! Haben Sie vielen Dank für Ihren freundlichen Brief, der mir wirklich in die Hände kam als ich auf einige Tage in Kristiania war. Gleich darauf musste ich nach Berlin, deshalb bekommen Sie leider meine Antwort so spät. Schon von dem schwedischen Komponisten, Emil Sjoegren, hatte ich die fröhliche Nachricht bekommen dass Claude Debussy die C-moll (*sic*) mit Ihnen prachtvoll gespielt hatte, es hat mich aber sehr gefreut es von Ihnen persönlich zu erfahren. Dass Debussy Grieg liebt hatte ich schon früher von Percy Grainger gehört, kann es auch aus seinen Werken hören, die mir sehr lieb sind. Mit wiederholtem Danke Ihre ergebene Nina Grieg." Hartmann Collection, Free Library of Philadelphia.

52. This translation is Hartmann's. A more literal reading is found in the preceding translation of the entire letter.

53. Edward MacDowell studied at the Paris Conservatoire from 1876 to 1878. No relationship has been documented between MacDowell and Debussy, who had begun his studies there in 1872.

54. See Hartmann's Loeffler essay in the present volume.

55. Since Debussy was born on 22 August 1862, this episode apparently took place in June 1914 (Loeffler was born on 30 January 1861). Hartmann was in America in 1913 and returned to Paris in the Fall of 1913.

56. Though Loeffler and Debussy apparently never met, they did correspond (the Debussy letters are not extant). Loeffler clearly objected to Debussy's morals, but he greatly admired Debussy's music. In 1910, Loeffler stated, "Debussy is, or was, a genuine innovator. He expresses himself, it is true, within a small circumference, but in that little kingdom he is supreme. I think that he hears more than any of us in nature. At least he is more conscious of his sensations and more successful in expressing them." Quoted in Ellen Knight, *Charles Martin Loeffler: A Life Apart in American Music* (Chicago: University of Illinois Press, 1993), 147–48.

57. The third largest glacier of the country, in the Nordland, above the Arctic Circle, and possessing the distinction of being the only Glacier which extends down into the Sea and not into a lake, as the others do. [This footnote is Hartmann's]

58. This section is an excerpt from Hartmann's 1918 *Musical Courier* article, "Claude Debussy As I Knew Him." While Hartmann quotes only certain portions of the letter, it is reproduced here in its entirety.

59. Only days later, on 30 August 1914, the first German bombers flew over Paris. Hartmann and his family immediately fled the city. See Hartmann's account of their escape in "The Prologue: Some Very Choice Bits of Musical News," *Buffalo Express*, 3 and 4 October 1914, and "Paris in Peace and War," *Canadian Journal of Music*, October-November 1914. The latter of these articles is reprinted in part in Hartmann's biography in the present volume.

60. Hartmann Collection, Free Library of Philadelphia. A facsimile of part of this letter appears on pp. 126–28.

61. During the summer of 1915, Debussy composed in quick succession the Cello Sonata, *En blanc et noir*, the *Études*, and the Sonata for Flute, Viola, and Harp.

62. On Hartmann's son Gregory, see note 111 to "Arthur Hartmann: A Biographical Sketch," p. 303.

63. See CD-19.

Letters from Claude and Emma Debussy

1. This letter is housed in the Aldrich Autograph Collection of the State Historical Society of Iowa. On 15 August 1910 Hartmann donated more than forty autograph letters to the Museum at Des Moines, Iowa (now the State Historical Society of Iowa) after the University of Iowa had conferred an honorary doctor of music degree on him on 30 July 1909. "AH a Doctor of Music," *Pittsburgh Chronicle Telegram,* 31 July 1909. The fact that Hartmann did not have this letter in his files when he wrote the memoir in 1941 explains the discrepancy in the appointment time.

2. Given the contents of the letters dated by Debussy "10 III 10" and "17 III 10," it appears that at least one of the two is misdated. In the letter labeled "10 III 10" Debussy has received an answer from Pierné to his request, while in the letter labeled "17 III 10" Debussy has not yet sent the request to Pierné. Therefore, the "17 III 10" letter comes chronologically before the "10 III 10" letter, as we have rendered them here. Despite Debussy's disappointment, a concert program dated 18 December 1910 shows that Hartmann did eventually perform with Gabriel Pierné and the Association Artistique des Concerts Colonne. Hartmann played Mozart's Violin Concerto in E-flat Major, K. 268.

3. Entry in Hartmann's autograph book, Hartmann Collection, Free Library of Philadelphia. See Example 3, "Debussy's Entry in Hartmann's Autograph Book," p. 67.

4. This letter is apparently misdated. The discussion regarding Debussy's proposed American tour took place in May 1910, as evidenced by the letter from Marc Blumenberg to Hartmann dated 13 May 1910 and the letter from Debussy to Hartmann dated 15 May 1910 [CD-7].

5. There is a discrepancy over the date of the performance that Debussy mentions in this letter. Edward Lockspeiser, in *Debussy: His Life and Mind* (New York: Macmillan, 1965), 2:297, gives the date of 25 May 1910. But Roy Howat, in the Foreword to *Oeuvres complètes de Claude Debussy,* série I, vol. 5 (Paris: Durand, 1985), states that it was 5 May 1910. The complementary references to *La fille aux cheveux de lin* in the present (undated) letter and the following one (30 May 1910) seem to support the later date, thereby placing this letter on 24 May 1910.

6. Letter housed in the Arthur Hartmann Collection, Sibley Music Library, Eastman School of Music.

7. See also ECD-1, p. 000.

8. Debussy's father, Manuel-Achille Debussy, would die on 28 October 1910.

9. Hartmann hand copied this letter by Debussy before presenting the original to Hungarian-born violinist Edwin Bachmann (ca. 1890–1985). Bachmann played in a string quartet with Lajos Shuk, who had previously been a member of the Hartmann Quartet. He taught at Curtis Institute of Music from 1928 to 1932 and was principal second violin in the NBC Symphony Orchestra under Arturo Toscanini from its creation in 1937 to its disbandment in 1954. Bachmann's extensive music collection was acquired by the University of Texas at Austin in 1958. See Ronald Dale Clinton, "The Edwin Bachmann Collection at the University of Texas at Austin: Perspectives on the Solo and Chamber Music with Keyboard" (D.M.A. diss., University of Texas at Austin, 1983) and Bachmann obituary in *International Musician,* October 1985, 14.

10. It appears that this letter is misdated and was actually written on 2 August 1910.

Emma's letter referring to the same event (ECD-2) is labeled "Tuesday" and says that the dinner is the following day on Wednesday since they were not free on Thursday. 2 August 1910 was a Tuesday, which would have placed the dinner on Wednesday, 3 August, and Debussy's letter the same day as Emma's on Tuesday, 2 August.

11. On 4 May 1940 Liebling typed out the text of this undated Debussy letter that Hartmann had given to the *Musical Courier* editor as a souvenir.

12. Sent to Arthur Hartmann on his tour of Norway.

13. Christmas card, housed in private collection of Karen Hartmann Kleinmann.

14. Telegram sent to congratulate the Hartmanns on the birth of their son Gregory, 25 May 1911.

15. This letter is reproduced by kind permission of the Bayerische Staatsbibliothek, Munich, Germany, where it is housed. ("Autogr. Debussy, Claude" in Abteilung für Handschriften und Seltene Drucke).

16. Debussy is here referring to Russian-born conductor Serge Koussevitzky (1874–1951), at whose invitation Debussy conducted concerts of his works in Moscow and St. Petersburg in early December 1913. Lockspeiser, *Debussy: His Life and Mind*, 2:135.

17. 2 January 1914 was a Friday, not a Monday.

18. For issues of the authorship of the transcription of *Minstrels*, see pp. 97–99 and 229–32 in the present volume.

19. Inflammation of the rectum, known in English as either proctitis or rectitis.

20. Debussy's mother died on 23 March 1915.

21. In 1914, Hartmann wrote that not far from Balzac's house was "Maeterlinck's former home, with its large garden where he raised bees and carefully studied them before writing his famous essay, 'Bees.' The house is now inhabited by Walter Morse Rummel, the celebrated composer." Hartmann, "Paris in Peace and War."

22. Helen Elizabeth Hartmann would be born on 21 August 1916 at Houghton, New York.

23. All letters in this section to Marie Hartmann unless otherwise noted. All letters from the Hartmann Collection, Free Library of Philadelphia except ECD-28, which is from the private collection of Karen Hartmann Kleinmann. This letter is a reference to Arthur Hartmann's recital on 2 June 1910.

24. See CD-11, written by Claude Debussy to Hartmann upon the same occasion.

25. Denise Piazza, daughter of Mme. Rummel's sister Marguerite and her husband Henri Piazza. Denise was born in 1906, one year after Chouchou. In her memoirs she writes of studying piano as a child with her aunt (Mme. Rummel) and being made to play the piano for Debussy when he visited the Rummels. Denise Tual, *Au coeur du temps* (Paris: Carrère, 1987), 22, 28.

26. In regard to the Hartmann/Debussy concert, 5 February 1914

27. After Chouchou's death, 16 July 1919.

28. Hélène Dufau (1859–1939) was a French painter whose works were exhibited at the Salon des artistes français in Paris. See also letter ECD-28.

29. Debussy was invited to London by Lady Speyer in July 1914. He stayed with the Speyers at their home on Grosvenor Street where, on 17 July, he took part in a private concert of his works, including the Deux Danses for harp and *Children's Corner*. Lockspeiser, *Debussy: His Life and Mind*, 2:138.

30. Letter housed in private collection of Karen Hartmann Kleinmann.

31. See letter ECD-26.

32. Chouchou's English governess. See letter ECD-23.

33. 15 June 1923 was a Friday, not a Thursday.

34. Marguerite Carré (1880–1947), French soprano. The year of the present letter, 1923, was Carré's last singing in Paris.

35. This is a reference to French pianist Marcel Ciampi (1891–1980), who was known for his interpretations of Debussy, and his wife, French violinist Yvonne Astruc (1889–1980).

36. The postmark is 29 December 1923, so the letter is probably slightly misdated.

37. Cupping is "a therapeutic process, rarely used in modern medicine, in which glass cups, partially evacuated by heating, are locally applied to the skin in order to draw blood toward or through the surface." *American Heritage Dictionary*, 2nd College ed., s.v. "cupping."

38. French violinist Gaston Poulet (1892–1974), who also gave the first performance of Debussy's Violin Sonata with the composer (Paris, 1917).

39. By the time of his death, Debussy had amassed a debt to Durand of 66,080.30 francs. Charle, "Debussy in Fin-de-Siècle Paris," 289.

40. Daniel Ericourt (1903–98), American pianist and teacher of French birth, studied with Georges Falkenberg, Santiago Riera, Jean-Jules Roger-Ducasse, and Nadia Boulanger. Charles Timbrell, *French Pianism: A Historical Perspective*, 2nd ed. (Portland, Ore.: Amadeus Press, 1999).

41. The teaching position that Ericourt obtained in 1926 through Emma's letter and Hartmann's influence was at the Cincinnati Conservatory of Music.

42. Louis Diémer (1843–1919), one of the leading French piano teachers of his time, taught at the Paris Conservatoire for over thirty years, beginning in 1887.

43. Marius-François Gaillard (1900–1973) was one of the first pianists to make 78 r.p.m. recordings of Debussy. In 1928 he published an arrangement of Debussy's *Le printemps (Comte de Ségur)* (1882) for chorus and piano under the title *Salut printemps*. The same year he completed the orchestration of Debussy's *Ode à la France* (sketched 1916–17), of which he then conducted the première performance on 2 April 1928 at the new Salle Pleyel in Paris. Orledge, *Debussy and the Theatre*, 362. See also Louis Laloy, "La dernière oeuvre de Claude Debussy: l'*Ode à la France*," *Musique* 1 (15 March 1928): 245–49.

44. Hartmann's copy of the English translation of Debussy's *Monsieur Croche: The Dilettante Hater* (London: Noel Douglas, 1927) was a gift from Emma inscribed November 1927.

45. Alfred Bendiner.

46. Carlos Salzédo (1885–1961), French born harpist and composer, became an American citizen in 1923. Salzédo mentions conversing with Madame Debussy about Hartmann in his letter to Hartmann, 25 May 1927, Hartmann Collection, Free Library of Philadelphia.

47. A monument to Debussy near his last home on the Bois de Boulogne in Paris was unveiled in June 1932, and a second monument at St.-Germain-en-Laye on 9 July 1933.

Charles Martin Tornov Loeffler

1. This sentence seems to summarize the whole of Hartmann's studies with Loeffler. From Hartmann's essay it is clear that he was often intimidated by Loeffler's

demanding teaching style and annoyed by many of Loeffler's personal mannerisms. However, it is also evident that Hartmann developed a profound respect for his teacher, which Loeffler in time reciprocated. The personable nature of their relationship is reflected in the letter from Loeffler to Hartmann appearing at the end of the essay. Letter from Loeffler to Hartmann, 22 January 1901, Hartmann Collection, Free Library of Philadelphia.

2. Carl Engel states: "There was perhaps no violinist of his generation, except César Thomson, who so mastered the discipline of the left hand as Loeffler did." "Views and Reviews," *Musical Quarterly* 21 (1935): 368–75.

3. "And when you see me on the street, take off your hat."

4. Loeffler's friendship with the Fay family—which consisted of Temple Fay, his sisters Theresa and Elise, and their widowed mother, Mary Nielson Fay—began in 1882, when the family helped Loeffler settle in Boston. Both living on Charles Street, as Hartmann says, Loeffler became an intimate friend of the family and eventually married Elise in 1910. Ellen Knight, *Charles Martin Loeffler: A Life Apart in American Music* (Chicago: University of Illinois Press, 1993), 41.

5. Loeffler was born in 1861 and was therefore only about thirty-six years old when Hartmann began his lessons with him in 1897.

6. Hartmann refers several times in this essay to Carl Engel's "outstanding article." While Engel wrote four articles about Loeffler, it is clear that Hartmann is referring to the article "Charles Martin Loeffler," in the *International Cyclopedia of Music and Musicians,* ed. Oscar Thompson (New York: Dodd Mead, 1938), 1030–37. This particular citation is found on p. 1030. The other articles written by Engel about Loeffler are as follows: "Charles Martin Loeffler," *Chesterian* (March 1920): 168–72; "Charles Martin Loeffler," *Musical Quarterly* 11 (1925): 310–29; and "Views and Reviews," *Musical Quarterly* 21 (1935): 368–75 (cited above).

7. *Les veillées de l'Ukraine,* (d'après Nicolai Gogol), suite for orchestra, violin, and harp. Hartmann is here speaking of the revision of the work, whose original version had premièred on 20 November 1891 with Loeffler as soloist with the Boston Symphony Orchestra conducted by Artur Nikisch. The suite contains four movements, individual tone poems each based on stories by Gogol. Despite criticisms of its length and the similarity of the second and third movements, the work was a widely acclaimed success in both versions. Knight, *Charles Martin Loeffler,* 87–89.

8. Franz Kneisel (1865–1926), concertmaster and assistant conductor of the Boston Symphony Orchestra from 1885 to 1903 and founder of the Kneisel Quartet (the other original members were Emmanuel Fiedler, second violin; Louis Svečenski, viola; Fritz Giese, violoncello), which was extant from 1885 to 1917. Steven Ledbetter, "Kneisel, Franz," in *New Grove Dictionary of American Music,* ed. H. Wiley Hitchcock and Stanley Sadie (London: Macmillan, 1986), 2:644–45.

9. This performance took place on 24 November 1899 with Wilhelm Gericke conducting. Hartmann, for his part, records that the incident took place in 1897 when he was a "youth of 16 or 17." Hartmann studied with Loeffler when he was 16 and 17 years old, in 1897 and 1898 (perhaps beginning as early as the fall of 1896). There is no evidence that Hartmann was still a formal student of Loeffler's in November 1899, though he may have still been in Boston. Hartmann moved to Europe in 1900.

10. "To me, the clarinet is the whore of the orchestra."

11. Loeffler dedicated three compositions to Kneisel: Sextet for two violins, two

violas, and two cellos, completed about 1892 and premièred on 27 February 1893 by the Kneisel Quartet with Max Zach and Leo Schulz at Chickering Hall, Boston; *Les soirs d'automne*, the third of his *Quatre mélodies*, for voice and piano, on poems by Gustave Kahn, Op. 10, composed about 1899 and premièred on 10 May 1900 by Julia Heinrich and George Proctor at Green Hill, Brookline, Mass.; and *La villanelle du Diable*, based on a poem by M. Rollinat, Fantasie symphonique for orchestra and organ, Op. 9, composed during the summer 1901 and premièred 11 April 1902 by the Boston Symphony Orchestra, conducted by Gericke.

It is not clear that Loeffler always disliked Brahms, and he was certainly not always so opposed to Kneisel. In his letter to Hartmann in 1901 (found at the end of the present essay), Loeffler includes Kneisel among the performers who "console you." Letter from Loeffler to Hartmann, 22 January 1901, Hartmann Collection, Free Library of Philadelphia.

12. A manuscript reduction of *Les veillées de l'Ukraine* does exist. Knight, *Charles Martin Loeffler*, 294.

13. Tchaikovsky's Symphony No. 6 ("Pathétique") was first performed on 28 October 1893 and subsequently published in 1894. The composer died on 6 November 1893. The first performance of the "Pathétique" by the Boston Symphony Orchestra was on 28 December 1894. It was performed subsequently in the 1895, 1896, 1897, and 1898 seasons.

14. Henry Lee Higginson (1834–1918), founding patron of the Boston Symphony.

15. Dame Nellie Melba [Helen Porter Mitchell] (1861–1931), coloratura soprano; Isabella Stewart Gardner (1840–1924), patroness of music and art and close friend of Loeffler.

16. Loeffler's parents were actually German, both born in Berlin. "Loeffler" was the family name of his father, not his mother. His father, Dr. Karl Immanuel Loeffler (1821–84) published a number of books, including novels and volumes of poetry as well as books on agricultural and scientific subjects. Some of these books were published under the pen name "Tornow," which originated from the small town of Tornow near Landsberg, where Karl spent his childhood. Loeffler's sister, Mrs. Helen Gaffky, wrote to Engel: "As concerns the name Tornow, it belongs neither to my father nor my mother, but was a pseudonym of my father's, who as a scientist in his time published many books, partly under the name of Dr. Karl Loeffler, as well as under the name of Tornow; in your place, I should omit it entirely, since it did not belong to our family but was, as I said, a pseudonym of my father's, which we, too, had earlier adopted but have not carried for a long time." Engel, *International Cyclopedia*, 1031.

17. Loeffler retained a deep-seated antipathy toward things German throughout his life. See Knight, *Charles Martin Loeffler*, 1–13.

18. Wilhelm Gericke (1845–1925), Austrian conductor who served as conductor of the Boston Symphony Orchestra from 1884 to 1889 and again from 1898 to 1906. Gericke's arrival in Boston was difficult for conductor and orchestra alike, with twenty players losing their positions in his first season and being replaced mostly by young men from Central Europe or France. As Loeffler implies, one of the main complaints against Gericke was his ultraconservative and very German programming. However, under his direction the Boston Symphony Orchestra developed into a first-class orchestra, and upon his return in 1898, he was spoken of

as the "true maker" of the Boston Symphony Orchestra. Knight, *Charles Martin Loeffler*, 56–57; J. N. Burk, "Wilhelm Gericke: A Centennial Retrospect," *Musical Quarterly* 31 (1945): 163–87. See also M. A. de W. Howe, *The Boston Symphony Orchestra, 1881–1931* (Boston: Houghton Mifflin, 1931).

19. Though Loeffler could reportedly be a charming, gentlemanly companion in public, his moodiness and acerbic melancholy were familiar characteristics among his friends, as was his insecurity and feeling of being unappreciated. Knight, *Charles Martin Loeffler*, 38–40.

20. The St. Botolph Club was formed in 1879 for the promotion of "social intercourse among authors, artists, and other gentlemen connected with or interested in literature or art." Loeffler joined the club around the turn of the century and served as its vice president from 1921 to 1928. Knight, *Charles Martin Loeffler*, 232.

21. "I want you to come to the club with me, for I want you to see how everybody *despises* me there."

22. Loeffler himself was asked by his violin teacher Joachim to play viola in chamber music when an extra player was needed. Perhaps his own introduction to the instrument had come in a similar manner. Knight, *Charles Martin Loeffler*, 16.

23. Erich Loeffler arrived in America in 1883 and played violoncello with the Boston Symphony Orchestra until his suicide in 1909.

24. Heinrich Gebhard (1878–1963), American pianist, composer, and teacher who made his concert debut in Boston on 24 April 1896 and appeared thirty-five times with the Boston Symphony Orchestra in the years 1901–33. Gebhard premièred Loeffler's *A Pagan Poem* for piano and orchestra and subsequently played it nearly 100 times with U.S. orchestras.

25. Thomson entered the service of Baron Paul von Derwies in Lugano in 1873. Loeffler played in the Derwies orchestra in 1879–81, living at the baron's two estates, the Villa Valrose at Nice and the Château de Trevano near Lake Lugano. Of Thomson, Loeffler stated: "I never even took a single lesson of him, and yet I learned more from him (and through personal contact) in hearing him play in those glorious days of his and my youth in Lugano." Knight, *Charles Martin Loeffler*, 21–24.

26. Chicago: Gamble Hinged Music Co., 1911. The Fleisher Collection of the Free Library of Philadelphia holds the manuscript scores for this version as well as for a version for baritone and orchestra. The Hartmann Collection also contains the manuscript for Hartmann's *Impressions of Byron's "Hebrew Melodies"* for viola and piano.

27. Loeffler's *Psalm 137* was premièred on 28 February 1902 by the Choral Art Society directed by Wallace Goodrich, Church of the Messiah, Boston. It was published by Schirmer in 1907 both in full score and piano-vocal score. Knight places the time of composition for *Psalm 137* as about 1901, but has no problem with assigning an earlier composition date to the work as Hartmann's account implies. Knight, *Charles Martin Loeffler*, 274; Engel, *International Cyclopedia*, 1037.

28. Engel, *International Cyclopedia*, 1037. This was Loeffler's first publication. Knight, *Charles Martin Loeffler*, 11.

29. Spelling from top down, a viola d'amore tuned in D Major is D (just below the violin E string), A, F#, D, A, D, A (one note above the cello G string). The intervals, contrary to what Hartmann writes, are: fourth, minor third, major third, fourth, fifth, fourth.

30. The Hartmann Collection of the Free Library of Philadelphia includes the manuscript of a "Sarabande composed by Matheson (1681–1722), transcribed for viola d'amour et piano" by Loeffler inscribed to Hartmann by the composer. The composition is listed in Knight's catalog, *Charles Martin Loeffler*, 303, but this particular manuscript is not included.

31. Loeffler acquired this instrument in the fall of 1897 and presented it to Isabella Gardner in 1903. It remains on display at the Gardner Museum in Boston. Knight, *Charles Martin Loeffler*, 127. The Eberle brothers (Tomaso and Johannes) both made violas d'amore; they lived and worked in Prague during the eighteenth century.

32. Artur Schnabel (1882–1951) accompanied Hartmann in this recital on 8 January 1904 in the Beethovensaal, Berlin, with the pair performing the Andante and Minuet for viola d'amore and piano by Milandre (1720).

33. "[Loeffler] was ever torn between two 'idées fixes': beauty and death. They alone counted. Persistently he struggled to reconcile the two." Engel, *International Cyclopedia*, 1036.

34. "The French way, undoubtedly, and so to speak!"

35. *Morceau fantastique*, for cello with orchestra and harp (also known as the *Fantastic Concerto*), a five-movement work composed in 1893, which premièred on 2 February 1894 with Alwin Schroeder as soloist with the Boston Symphony Orchestra, conducted by Emil Paur. Knight, *Charles Martin Loeffler*, 297.

36. Loeffler's father died from a stroke on 6 November 1884 in Coblenz, Germany. He did visit the United States, but whether the two duels are anything more than a romantic fancy of Loeffler's is unknown. Knight, *Charles Martin Loeffler*, 58.

37. Sent to Hartmann while he was living with René Ortmans in London. Hartmann Collection, Free Library of Philadelphia.

38. Arthur D. Curran, the rich Boston merchant who had sponsored Hartmann's studies in Boston.

39. Percy Pitt (1870–1932), English conductor and composer, whom Loeffler had met during his time in London during the summer of 1900.

40. *La mort de Tintagiles*, dramatic poem after the drama of M. Maeterlinck, for orchestra and viola d'amore, Op. 6 (originally for 2 violas d'amore). In 1906, Hartmann appeared as soloist for *Tintagiles* in Europe (with Artur Nikisch conducting) at Loeffler's request. See letter from Loeffler to Hartmann, 12 June 1905, Arthur Hartmann Collection, Sibley Music Library, Eastman School of Music. Ysaÿe also performed the work with Felix Mottl in 1906. Knight, *Charles Martin Loeffler*, 149, 296.

41. *L'archet*, fantazia-légende for soprano solo, women's chorus with viola d'amore, Op. 26 (for SSAA, soprano, viola d'amore, and piano). Premièred on 5 March 1901 with Julia Wyman (soprano), Loeffler (viola d'amore), Heinrich Gebhard (piano), and the Cecilia Society conducted by B. J. Lang at J. M. Sears's home, Boston. The public première was not until 4 February 1902 at Symphony Hall, Boston. Knight, *Charles Martin Loeffler*, 274.

42. This paragraph is in reference to Loeffler's revision of *Les veillées de l'Ukraine*, done in the summer of 1899.

43. "Une nuit de mai" is the second movement of *Les veillées de l'Ukraine*, which Loeffler did separate as an independent composition but was never performed as such. The movement was originally dedicated to Pablo de Sarasate, but this dedication was removed in the revised version (1899). Knight, *Charles Martin Loeffler*, 90, 295.

44. Loeffler had met and played for Madame Wieniawski during his visits to London in the summer of 1900.

45. René Ortmans, violinist with whom Hartmann lived during his time in London.

46. The actual quotation from "Spleen (II)" of Baudelaire's *Les fleurs du mal* reads: "J'ai plus de souvenirs que si j'avais mille ans."

47. Hugo Becker (1863–1941), German cellist. Loeffler does not list soloists chronologically here, but they all appeared during the 1900–1901 season.

48. Harold Bauer (1873–1951), English pianist, who made his U.S. debut with the Boston Symphony Orchestra in 1900. Bauer and Hartmann toured together in Holland and Belgium twice in the early 1900s.

49. Ossip Gabrilowitsch (1878–1936), Russian-American pianist and conductor. His first American tour was in 1900, with subsequent visits during the years 1901–16.

50. Kneisel was soloist for the first American performance of the Brahms Violin Concerto. Ledbetter, "Kneisel," 644.

51. Timothée Adamowski (1857–1943), American violinist, who settled in Boston in 1879 and conducted several summer seasons of popular concerts by the Boston Symphony Orchestra (1890–94; 1900–1907). Adamowski played the Dvořák Violin Concerto (Op. 53) in Boston on 16 and 17 November 1900.

52. Otto Roth, violin, was a member of the Boston Symphony Orchestra from 1887 to 1920. The performance to which Loeffler refers was Roth's final solo appearance with the BSO (1901).

53. Georges Longy (1868–1930), French oboist who was principal oboe in the Boston Symphony Orchestra from 1898 to 1925.

54. Alwin Schroeder (1855–1928), German cellist who premièred Loeffler's *Morceau fantastique*. He was a member of the Boston Symphony Orchestra (on three separate occasions between 1891 and 1925) and also of the Kneisel Quartet.

Eugène Ysaÿe

1. Courtesy *Musical America* archives; originally published in *Musical America*, 10 November 1940.

2. The Ysaÿe Quartet was organized in 1886 and included Mathieu Crickboom, Léon Van Hout, and Joseph Jacob.

3. Raoul Pugno (1852–1914), French pianist, with whom Ysaÿe formed a duo in 1883.

4. Enrique Fernández Arbós (1863–1939), Spanish violinist and conductor.

5. Serge Achille Rivarde (1865–1940), American violinist.

6. Piano Concerto No. 5 in F Major ("Egyptian"), Opus 103 (1896).

Joseph Joachim

1. Courtesy *Musical America* archives; originally published in *Musical America*, 10 February 1940.

2. Joachim's *Konzert in ungarischer Weise*, Op. 11, was composed in 1861.

Brahms's Violin Concerto in D Major, Opus 77, was composed in 1878 and dedicated to Joachim, who also served as soloist for its première with Brahms as conductor. There are many markings in Joachim's hand in the manuscript of the Brahms concerto—suggestions for revisions in the violin part.

3. Joachim was born in 1831, and the concerto composed in 1861.

4. "Das ist außer aller Frage! Ich habe Ihnen schon einmal gesagt, Sie sind ein *Kerl*—ein ganz Kolossaler! Außerdem, als Schüler kann ich Sie überhaupt nicht annehmen, denn privatim darf ich keinen Unterricht erteilen, und Sie in meine Klasse aufnehmen? Tja, du lieber Gott! Da gehören Sie gar nicht hinein, denn ein Geiger wie Sie schon sind, der soll was von sich hören lassen—und was Ihnen noch fehlt, das bringt das Leben schon mit sich und die Erfahrungen im öffentlichen Spielen und Karriereentwicklung. Nein, nein, gehen Sie nur Ihrer Laufbahn entgegen. Sie werden sich sicherlich durchschlagen!"

5. "Tja, verehrter Meister, ich glaube, daß ich ohne irgendwelche falsche Bescheidenheit behaupten darf, daß ich überhaupt alles spiele!"

6. "Well, then do tell me, man, what is it then you do play?"

7. The members of the Joachim Quartet at this time were Joachim, Karel Haliř, Emanuel Wirth, and Robert Hausmann.

Edvard Grieg

1. Ernesto Consolo (1864–1931) was born in London and studied piano first with Giovanni Sgambati in Rome and later with Karl Reinecke in Leipzig. He made his British debut in 1904, after which time he rapidly became esteemed as a leading Italian pianist. Wilson Lyle, *A Dictionary of Pianists* (New York: Schirmer, 1984), 66.

2. Abraham Victor Rydberg (1828–95).

3. "Du gamla Satan!" This oath is, in fact, a Swedish one.

4. Krisitania was renamed Oslo in 1925.

5. Johan Halvorsen (1864–1935), Norwegian violinist and composer. He served as conductor of the Kristiania National Theater for the years 1899 to 1929.

6. Ibsen's son, Sigurd, married Bjørnson's daughter, Bergljot.

7. Christian Sinding (1856–1941), Norwegian violinist, pianist, and composer.

8. Enrique Fernández Arbós (1863–1939), Spanish violinist and conductor.

9. Hartmann here returns to the main stream of his story, the previous section having related experiences from an earlier tour.

10. Hartmann's instruction for pronunciation is poor, as the sound should be a short "o," as in the British pronunciation of "got."

11. This painting, entitled *Brudefærden i Hardanger,* was by Adolph Tidemand and Hans Gude. The 1849 occasion for which *Brudefærden i Hardanger* was painted was the catalyst event for the great push for independence from Sweden that finally came in 1905, and the painting became a symbol of the Norwegian national romantic period.

12. Grieg's attack of pleurisy in 1860 established the respiratory problems that troubled him for the remainder of his life.

13. Norway declared its independence from Sweden on 7 June 1905, after which time Sweden nearly went to war against Norway. It was not until September 1905

that Sweden recognized Norway's independence. Later in the present essay ("Separation of Norway and Sweden"), Hartmann relates his experiences, particularly regarding his performance of Grieg's music in Stockholm, on the day that Sweden recognized Norway's independence. On Grieg's political views, see Finn Benestad and Dag Schjelderup-Ebbe, *Edvard Grieg: The Man and the Artist*, trans. William H. Halverson and Leland B. Stateren (Lincoln: University of Nebraska Press, 1988), 371–77.

14. "A thousand enthusiastic greetings to the wife of the magnificent violin master Hartmann!"

15. Edvard and Nina Grieg traveled to Italy in December 1869, where they remained for four months. During this time Grieg met with Liszt in Rome on two separate occasions. At their first meeting Grieg played his Second Violin Sonata (G Major, Op. 13, 1867) and the minuet from *Humoresker* (Op. 6, 1865) for Liszt. The second meeting is the "memorable" one to which Hartmann refers, at which Liszt played at sight Grieg's Piano Concerto in A Minor (Opus 16, 1868). Grieg described Liszt's reaction in a version of a letter to his parents published in *Samtiden*: "There is one perfectly divine episode I cannot forget. Towards the end of the finale, as you will remember, the second theme is repeated in a great fortissimo. In the very last measures, where the first note of the first triplet of the theme—G sharp—is changed to G in the orchestra, while the piano in a tremendous scale passage traverses the entire keyboard, he suddenly stopped, rose to his full height, left the piano, and with mighty theatrical steps and raised arms strode through the great monastery hall, literally roaring out the theme. When he got to the above-mentioned G, he gestured imperiously with his arm and cried: 'g, g, nicht giss! Famos! Das ist echt schwedisches Banko!' He then went back to the piano, repeated the whole phrase, and concluded it." Quoted in Benestad and Schjelderup-Ebbe, *Edvard Grieg*, 137.

16. Grieg studied with Reinecke at the Leipzig Conservatory, where the latter began teaching in 1860. Reinecke also served as conductor of the Leipzig Gewandhaus Orchestra until 1895 and as director of the Leipzig Conservatory from 1897 until his retirement in 1902.

17. Edmund Neupert (1842–88), Norwegian pianist.

18. On 10 January 1868, Grieg submitted to the Ministry of Education his application for a stipend of 500 spesidalers. His stated purpose for the stipend was "by a visit abroad to secure time and leisure for creative work as well as an opportunity—through association with art and artists—to rejuvenate my mind and broaden my view of the ideal, which, under the circumstances in which I am living, can only become narrower." As part of his application, Grieg submitted letters of recommendation from such prominent musicians as Ignaz Moscheles, Johann Hartmann, Niels Gade, and—most significantly—Franz Liszt. See Benestad and Schjelderup-Ebbe, *Edvard Grieg*, 125–27.

19. Johan Svendsen (1840–1911), Norwegian violinist, composer, and conductor who, along with Grieg, represents the culmination of national Romanticism in Norway.

20. "Adieu Hartmann . . . viel Glück und Erfolg! Du spielst meine Sonate, als ob Du sie komponiert hättest! Gott sei mit Dir, denn Du hast den Deibel im Leib!"

21. Arthur Hartmann, "Die 'Ciacona' von Bach," *Allgemeine Musik-Zeitung* 22 (2 June 1905): 397–400.

22. "Hochverehrter Herr Hartmann! Empfangen Sie meinen herzlichen Dank für das schöne Bild sowohl wie für den Artikel über die Ciacona von Bach, welchen

ich mit grossem Interesse gelesen habe. Jetzt verstehe ich am besten, *warum* Ihre Interpretation gerade von diesem Stück so wundervoll war! Ich hoffe, wir werden uns noch einmal wiedersehen. Mit den besten Grüssen von meiner Frau wie von Ihrem sehr ergebenen Edvard Grieg." Hartmann Collection, Free Library of Philadelphia.

Appendix A

1. See p. 51 in the present volume.

2. Debussy's debt to Durand had by 1914 reached a total of 49,688.30 francs. Christophe Charle, "Debussy in Fin-de-Siècle Paris," in *Debussy and His World*, ed. Jane F. Fulcher, trans. Victoria Johnson (Princeton, N.J.: Princeton University Press, 2001), 288. In early 1914 Debussy traveled to Rome, Amsterdam, The Hague, Brussels, and London for the essential purpose of supporting his family. François Lesure, "Claude Debussy," *New Grove Dictionary of Music and Musicians*, 2nd ed., ed. Stanley Sadie (London: Macmillan, 2001), 7:100.

3. Hartmann's description of this exchange is found in the section "Minstrels and Its Authorship" of "Claude Debussy As I Knew Him" in the present volume, pp. 97–99.

4. Leonard Liebling, "Variationettes," *Musical Courier*, 7 December 1916, 21.

5. Claude Debussy, *Minstrels,* Jacques Thibaud and Alfred Cortot, Great Recordings of the Century, EMI Records, Ltd., 1989.

6. *New York Evening Mail,* 28 October 1908. From Hartmann's scrapbooks, Hartmann Collection, Free Library of Philadelphia.

7. Arthur Hartmann, "Arrangements—Derangements—Transcriptions," *Musical Courier*, 10 January 1918, 6.

8. The English pianist Denis Matthews sees the shadow of *Minstrels* lurking in the central movement ("Intermède") of Debussy's Violin Sonata. Liner notes to Claude Debussy, *Minstrels,* Jacques Thibaud and Alfred Cortot, Great Recordings of the Century, EMI Records, Ltd., 1989.

9. In 1929 Emma Claude Debussy sent Hartmann a copy of the Debussy Violin Sonata with the following inscription: "Au grand artiste à l'ami fidèle Arthur Hartmann, Affectueusement, Emma Claude Debussy 1929" ["To the great artist {and} faithful friend Arthur Hartmann, Affectionately, Emma Claude Debussy 1929"]. While there is no evidence that Hartmann ever performed the sonata in public, the many markings on the violin part demonstrate that he spent a great deal of time studying the work. Hartmann's copy of the sonata is in the Hartmann Collection, Free Library of Philadelphia.

10. Louis Laloy, Review of Hartmann/Debussy recital in Émile Vuillermoz, "La Musique au Concert," *Comoedia*, 9 February 1914. This review is included in full in "Arthur Hartmann: A Biographical Sketch" in the present volume.

Appendix B

1. See also Robert Orledge, *Debussy and the Theatre* (Cambridge: Cambridge University Press, 1982), 261–62.

2. David A. Grayson, personal communication, 13 June 2000. See also David A. Grayson, *The Genesis of Debussy's "Pelléas et Mélisande"* (Ann Arbor, Mich.: UMI Research Press, 1986), 154; and Maurice Denis, *Henry Lerolle et ses amis, suivi de quelques lettres d'amis,* (Paris: Duranton, 1932), 32, quoted in Grayson, *The Genesis of Debussy's "Pelléas et Mélisande,"* 56.

3. David Grayson, personal communication, 13 June 2000.

4. Edward Lockspeiser, "Neuf lettres de Pierre Louÿs à Debussy," *Revue de Musicologie* 48 (1962): 68–69.

5. Denis Herlin, personal communication, 6 June 2000.

6. Pierre Louÿs, *La femme et le pantin*, ed. Michel Delon (Paris: Éditions Gallimard, 1990).

Catalogue of Compositions and Transcriptions

1. All titles are as given by Hartmann, including the translation of non-English titles in parentheses.

2. All orchestral manuscripts (unless otherwise noted) are housed in the Edwin A. Fleisher Collection of Orchestral Music in the Free Library of Philadelphia. All other manuscripts (unless otherwise noted) are part of the Hartmann Collection, Free Library of Philadelphia.

3. All music for solo instrument with piano is included in the chamber music section, excepting works for violin and piano, which are listed under their own heading.

4. Ludwig van Beethoven, Concerto for Violin and Orchestra, Op. 61, Third Movement.

5. F. W. Ernst, Concerto for Violin and Orchestra, Op. 22.

6. All music for piano unless otherwise noted.

7. Hartmann used the published order by Jürgenson, not Tchaikovsky's original order.

Archival Sources

Bayerische Staatsbibliothek, Munich. Abteilung für Handschriften und Seltene Drucke.

Letter from Claude Debussy to Arthur Hartmann, 29 December 1913.

University of Rochester, Eastman School of Music, Sibley Music Library. Ruth T. Watanabe Special Collections.

Five autograph manuscripts inscribed to Hartmann, including Claude Debussy, *Minstrels* (transcription for violin and piano), and Edward MacDowell, *To a Wild Rose* and *Will o' the Wisp*.

Arthur Hartmann Collection (SC1995.4). 72 letters to Hartmann from various persons (including Béla Bartók, Claude Debussy, Alexandre Guilmant, Fritz Kreisler, Charles Martin Loeffler, Maud Powell, Marian MacDowell, Arnold Schoenberg, and Anton von Webern).

Free Library of Philadelphia, Music Department. Hartmann Collection.

Hundreds of letters to Hartmann from various persons (including Béla Bartók, Marc Blumenberg, Frank Bridge, Aaron Copland, Claude Debussy, Emma Claude Debussy, Edvard Grieg, Nina Grieg, Alexandre Guilmant, Sigmund Hartman, Leonard Liebling, Charles Martin Loeffler, Hans Richter, Walter Morse Rummel, Carlos Salzédo, Albert Schweitzer, Joseph Szigeti, Edgard Varèse, and Felix Weingartner). Three letters from Claude Debussy to Pierre Louÿs. Hartmann's scrapbooks of programs, clippings, photographs, and memorabilia. Hartmann's autograph book, including entries by Béla Bartók and Claude Debussy. Manuscripts and publications of Hartmann's various essays and articles, including his unpublished essays on Johann Sebastian Bach ("The Bach Bogey"), Claude Debussy, George Eastman, Edvard Grieg, and Charles Martin Loeffler, as well as Hartmann's autobiographical notes. Music manuscripts and publications by Hartmann, as well as Hartmann's copies of music by other composers.

Private collection of Karen Hartmann Kleinmann.

Christmas card with music inscription from Claude Debussy to Arthur Hartmann, 25 December 1910. Letter from Emma Claude Debussy to Marie Hartmann, 29 April 1921. Letters to Hartmann from Harold Bauer, Frank Bridge, Eugene Goossens, Percy Grainger (3), Sigmund Hartman, Jenö Hubay (2), Henry Huss, Fritz Kreisler, Marian MacDowell (12), Alexander MacKenzie (3), Daniel Gregory Mason, Camille Saint-Saëns, Joseph Szigeti, and Germaine Tailleferre. Various legal and financial documents from estates of Arthur Hartmann and Jean Riegger.

State Historical Society of Iowa. Aldrich Autograph Collection.

Letter from Claude Debussy to Arthur Hartmann, 2 October 1908.

Bibliography

"1932 Salzburg Festival: Stokowski and Richard Strauss to Conduct Orchestral Concerts—Foreign Notes." *New York Times,* 13 December 1931.

Abell, Arthur M. "Berlin." *Musical Courier,* 21 October 1908, 5.

"AH a Doctor of Music," *Pittsburgh Chronicle Telegram,* 31 July 1909.

Armstrong, William. "Arthur Hartmann: Violinist and Thinker." *Musician,* March 1915, 1.

"Arthur Hartmann." *Musical Courier,* 22 July 1896, 22a.

"Arthur Hartmann." *Musical Courier,* 12 August 1896, 11.

"Arthur Hartmann's History." *Violin World,* 15 September 1906, 58. Reprinted as "The History of Hartmann." *Musical Courier,* 26 September 1906, 44.

"Artists Everywhere." *Musical Courier,* 12 November 1925, 50.

"Autograph Album." *Musical America,* 29 January 1916, 21.

Bartók, Béla. *Béla Bartók Letters.* Edited by János Demény. New York: St. Martin's Press, 1971.

Benestad, Finn, and Dag Schjelderup-Ebbe. *Edvard Grieg: The Man and the Artist.* Translated by William H. Halverson and Leland B. Stateren. Lincoln: University of Nebraska Press, 1988.

Bendiner, Alfred. *Music to My Eyes.* Philadelphia: University of Pennsylvania Press, 1952.

——. *Translated from the Hungarian.* New York: A. S. Barnes, 1967.

Blumenberg, Marc. "Insulting a Profession." *Musical Courier,* 26 August 1903, 15.

Borgeaud, Henri, ed. *Correspondance de Claude Debussy et Pierre Louÿs (1893–1904).* Paris: Librairie José Corti, 1945.

Brayer, Elizabeth. *George Eastman: A Biography.* Baltimore, Md.: Johns Hopkins University Press, 1996.

Burk, J. N. "Wilhelm Gericke: A Centennial Retrospect." *Musical Quarterly* 31 (1945): 163–87.

Charle, Christophe. "Debussy in Fin-de-Siècle Paris." In *Debussy and His World,* edited by Jane F. Fulcher, translated by Victoria Johnson, 271–95. Princeton, N.J.: Princeton University Press, 2001.

Clinton, Ronald Dale. "The Edwin Bachmann Collection at the University of Texas at Austin: Perspectives on the Solo and Chamber Music with Keyboard." DMA diss., University of Texas at Austin, 1983.

"A Composer's Experiences: An Interview with Arthur Hartmann." *Canadian Journal of Music,* January 1916, 149.

Debussy, Claude. *Debussy Letters.* Edited by François Lesure and Roger Nichols; translated by Roger Nichols. London: Faber and Faber, 1987.

——. *Lettres de Claude Debussy à sa femme Emma.* Edited by Pasteur Vallery-Radot. Paris: Flammarion, 1957.

——. *Lettres de Claude Debussy à son éditeur.* Edited by Jacques Durand. Paris: Durand, 1927.

——. *Monsieur Croche: The Dilettante Hater.* Translated by B. N. Langdon Davies. London: Noel Douglas, 1927.

Denis, Maurice. *Henry Lerolle et ses amis, suivi de quelques lettres d'amis.* Paris: Duranton, 1932.

Devore, Nicholas, ed. *The Violinist's Dictionary.* New York: The University Society, 1926.

Dietschy, Marcel. *A Portrait of Claude Debussy.* Edited and translated by William Ashbrook and Margaret G. Cobb. Oxford: Clarendon Press, 1990 (French edition, 1962).

Dille, D. *Documenta Bartókiana,* vol. 3. Mainz: B. Schott's Söhne, 1968.

Doring, Ernest N. "A Compliment—and a Correction." *Violins and Violinists,* September 1946, 352–55.

———. *The Guadagnini Family of Violin Makers.* Chicago: William Lewis & Son, 1949.

———. *How Many Strads?* Chicago: William Lewis & Son, 1945.

———. "Re: J. B. Guadagnini Violins . . . Reminiscences." *Violins and Violinists,* December 1946, 475–77.

Downes, Olin. Review of Hartmann Quartet, 14 February 1926, *New York Times,* 15 February 1926.

Eberhardt, Goby. "Arthur Hartmann." *Musikalisches Wochenblatt,* 1 April 1909, 1–2.

Engel, Carl. "Charles Martin Loeffler." *Chesterian* (March 1920): 168–72.

———. "Charles Martin Loeffler." In *International Cyclopedia of Music and Musicians,* edited by Oscar Thompson, 1030–37. New York: Dodd Mead, 1938.

———. "Charles Martin Loeffler." *Musical Quarterly* 11 (1925): 310–29.

———. "View and Reviews." *Musical Quarterly* 21 (1935): 368–75.

Evans, Gertrude. "Gift of Maud Powell Collection." *Pan Pipes* (May 1932): 422–24.

"Famous Violinist Ill at Temple Hospital." *Philadelphia Record,* 1 February 1931.

Fulcher, Jane F. *French Cultural Politics & Music: From the Dreyfus Affair to the First World War.* Oxford: Oxford University Press, 1999.

Gilman, Lawrence. Review of Hartmann Quartet, 14 February 1926, *New York Herald Tribune,* 15 February 1926.

Grayson, David A. *The Genesis of Debussy's "Pelléas et Mélisande."* Ann Arbor, Mich.: UMI Research Press, 1986.

Greene, Gary A. *Henry Holden Huss: An American Composer's Life.* Metuchen, N.J.: Scarecrow Press, 1995.

Hagel, Byron. "The Bystander." *Musical Courier,* 4 April 1918, 24.

Hartmann, Arthur. "On How to Make a Good Student." *Musician,* undated, 276.

[———] (attributed to Fini Henriques). "Arthur Hartmann." *Musical Courier,* 27 May 1903, 13.

———. "The 'Ciaconna' of Bach." *Musical Courier,* 21 September 1904, 14–15. Reprint in *Musical Leader and Concert Goer,* 14 June 1906, 14–15.

———. "De 'Ciaconna' van Bach." *Weekblad voor Muziek* 12 (4 February 1905), 39–42.

———. "Die 'Ciacona' von Bach." *Allgemeine Musik-Zeitung* 22 (2 June 1905): 397–400.

———. "À Propos de la 'Chaconne' de Bach." *Le Guide Musical* 52 (7 January 1906): 3–6.

———. "Tragedy of an American Girl in Germany: Arthur Hartmann Writes of Young Musical Students Abroad." *Seattle Post-Intelligencer,* 24 November 1907.

———. "The Tragedy of European Study." *Musical Courier*, 15 April 1908, 39.

[———.] [Untitled]. *Musical Leader*, 12 August 1908.

[———.] "Hartmann and Debussy: Hartmann Talks to the Musical Courier Interviewer about the Composer of 'Pelléas et Mélisande,'" *Musical Courier*, 4 November 1908, 23.

[———.] "The Fable of a Fiddler." *Musical Courier*, 6 January 1909, 12.

———. "The Educational Literature of the Violin." In "Music and Musicians" column, *Illustrated Buffalo Express*, 2 July, 9 July, 16 July, 23 July 30 July, 6 August 1911. Reprint as "Violin Playing" in *The Violinist*, November 1911, 33–35; December 1911, 27–30; January 1912, 23–26.

———. "Musical Paris." *Canadian Journal of Music*, June 1914.

———. "America Versus Europe." *Musical Monitor and World*, July 1914, 1.

———. "The Prologue: Some Very Choice Bits of Musical News," *Buffalo Express*, 3 and 4 October 1914.

———. "Paris in Peace and War." *Canadian Journal of Music*, October-November 1914.

———. "Is America Musical?" *Canadian Journal of Music*, February 1915.

———. "Why All Chin-Rests Should Be Abolished." *Musical Times*, 1 February 1915, 105–6. Reprint in *The Violinist*, September 1915, 11.

———. "Important Novelties and Débuts." *Canadian Journal of Music*, March-April 1915.

———. "How to Play Bach." *The Violinist*, May 1915, 19.

———. "Who Is Arthur Alexander?" *Canadian Journal of Music*, December 1915, 127.

———. "The Czimbalom, Hungary's National Instrument." *Musical Quarterly* 2 (1916): 590–600.

———. "The Subtleties of Violin Art." *Musical America*, 4 March 1916. Reprint in *The Violin World*, 15 March 1916, 1.

———. "A Sermon on the Violin Concerto of Ludwig van Beethoven." *Musical Courier*, 2 November 1916, 33.

———. "When Transcriptions Are True Art Works." *Musical America*, 31 March 1917, 13. Reprint in *Canadian Journal of Music*, August 1917, 57.

———. "What Is True Vibrato?" *Canadian Journal of Music*, July 1917.

———. "Acquiring and Retaining a Repertoire." *The Violinist* (November 1917): 427–29.

———. "Arrangements—Derangements—Transcriptions." *Musical Courier*, 10 January 1918, 6.

———. "Claude Debussy As I Knew Him." *Musical Courier*, 23 May 1918, 6–9.

———. "Bach's Sonatas for the Violin." *Musical Courier*, August-September 1922. Part 1, 10 August, 6–8; Part 2, 17 August, 6; Part 3, 24 August, 7; Part 4, 31 August, 6–7, 10; Part 5, 7 September, 6; Part 6, 14 September, 6.

———. "'Violin Demon,' Seeking Sanctuary from Mad Dog, Slays Beast beside Church Altar, Thereby, in Eyes of Brittany Peasants, Performing Miracle," *Rochester Herald*, 10 September 1922.

———. *Arthur Hartmann's Instinctive Method for the Violin*. New York: Belwin, 1926.

———. "La Plus Que Lente," *Musical America*, 25 December 1930, 10. Reprint in *Woodstock Outlook*, 3 September 1932, 10–11.

————. "Woodstock and the Woodstockians." *Musical Courier*, 5 December 1931, 10.

————. "Sidelights on Saint-Saëns' Essays," *Musical Courier*, 5 March 1932, 6, 16.

————. "Homage to Henri Wieniawski." *Musical Courier*, 15 June 1935, 6.

————. "The Perfect Virtuoso: Sarasate, the Wonder Worker, as Recalled by a Fellow Violinist." *Musical America*, 25 March 1940, 8.

————. "Memories of Masters of the Bow: An Impression of Joachim's Last Years." *Musical America*, 10 February 1940, 17, 130, 138.

————. "Eugène Ysaÿe: Colossus of the Violin." *Musical America*, 10 November 1940, 5, 36, 38.

————. "A Tribute to Paganini on the Centennial of His Death." In *Who Is Who in Music*, edited by Leonard Liebling. Chicago: Lee Stern Press, 1941.

————. "Our Speeding Violinists: Modern Players Sacrifice Artistry for Agility." *Musical Digest*, May 1948, 24.

"Hartman's Collar Really Wasn't Paper," *Philadelphia North American*, 10 September 1903.

Hill, W. Henry, Arthur F. Hill, and Alfred E. Hill. *Antonio Stradivari: His Life and Work*. New York: Dover, 1963 (1902).

"How Hartmann Earned His Violin." *Musical Courier*, 11 February 1907, 33.

Howat, Roy. Foreword to *Oeuvres complètes de Claude Debussy*, série I, vol. 5. Paris: Durand, 1985.

Howe, M. A. de W. *The Boston Symphony Orchestra, 1881–1931*. Boston: Houghton Mifflin, 1931.

"Huss, 'One of the Best of American Composers,'" *Musical Courier*, 21 March 1918, 40.

"Impressive Debut of Hartmann Quartet." *Musical Courier*, 17 December 1925, 42.

"International Composers' Guild Introduces Two New Compositions to New York." *Musical Courier*, 18 February 1926, 5, 56.

Knight, Ellen. *Charles Martin Loeffler: A Life Apart in American Music*. Chicago: University of Illinois Press, 1993.

Kramer, Arthur Walter. "Enigma of Hartmann's Nationality." *Musical America*, 3 July 1915, 36.

————. "Spiering Honors Violinist-Composers." *Musical America*, 26 February 1916, 53.

Laloy, Louis. "La dernière oeuvre de Claude Debussy: l'*Ode à la France*." *Musique* 1 (15 March 1928), 245–49.

————. "La musique chez soi: Edvard Grieg (1843–1907)." *Comoedia*, 5 February 1914.

————. Review of Hartmann/Debussy recital in Émile Vuillermoz, "La Musique au Concert." *Comoedia*, 9 February 1914.

Ledbetter, Steven. "Kneisel, Franz." In *New Grove Dictionary of American Music*, vol. 2, edited by H. Wiley Hitchcock and Stanley Sadie. London: Macmillan, 1986.

Lesure, François. *Claude Debussy avant Pelléas, ou les années symbolistes*. Paris: Klincksieck, 1992.

————. "Correspondance de Claude Debussy et de Louis Laloy (1902–1914)," *Revue de Musicologie* 48 (1962): 40.

————. "Debussy, Claude" In *New Grove Dictionary of Music and Musicians*, 2nd ed., vol. 7, edited by Stanley Sadie. London: Macmillan, 2001.

Liebling, Leonard. "Variationettes." *Musical Courier*, 7 December 1916, 21.

————. "Variationettes." *Musical Courier*, 8 February 1923, 22.

————. "Variations." *Musical Courier*, 28 February 1931, 25, 30.

————. "Variations." *Musical Courier*, 30 May 1931, 25.

Lockspeiser, Edward. *Debussy: His Life and Mind*. 2 vols. New York: Macmillan, 1962, 1965.

Louÿs, Pierre. *La femme et le pantin*, edited by Michel Delon. Paris: Éditions Gallimard, 1990.

————. Preface to *La tragédie de la mort*, by René Peter. Paris: Mercure de France, 1899.

Lyle, Wilson. *A Dictionary of Pianists*. New York: Schirmer, 1984.

Martens, Frederick H. *Violin Mastery: Talks with Master Violinists and Teachers*. New York: Frederick A. Stokes, 1919.

McCarthy, Pearl. "Hartmann, Notable Violinist, Friend of Great Composers, Not Sorry to Leave Toronto," *Toronto Daily Mail and Empire*, 4 February 1933.

McVeigh, Simon. *The Violinist in London's Concert Life 1750–1784: Felice Giardini and His Contemporaries*. New York: Garland, 1989.

Moldenhauer, Hans. *Anton von Webern: A Chronicle of His Life and Work*. New York: Knopf, 1979.

"Music and Musicians" [interview of Arthur Hartmann]. *Illustrated Buffalo Express*, 28 May 1911.

Nichols, Roger. *Debussy Remembered*. London: Faber and Faber, 1992.

————. *The Life of Debussy*. Cambridge: Cambridge University Press, 1998.

Nichols, Roger, and Richard Langham Smith. *Claude Debussy: Pelléas et Mélisande*. Cambridge: Cambridge University Press, 1989.

Noppen, Leonard van. "Haunted." *Musical Courier*, 24 August 1916, 15.

"An Obedient Soloist: How Arthur Hartmann as Boy Artist Observed Parental Mandate." *Musical America*, 26 February 1916, 31.

Orledge, Robert. *Debussy and the Theatre*. Cambridge: Cambridge University Press, 1982.

Pesce, Dolores. "Edward MacDowell." In *New Grove Dictionary of Music and Musicians*, 2nd ed., vol. 15, edited by Stanley Sadie. London: Macmillan, 2001.

Review of Hartmann Quartet, 16 November 1925. In "New York Concerts," *Musical Courier*, 26 November 1925, 14.

Review of Hartmann Quartet, 8 March 1926, in "New York Concerts," *Musical Courier*, 18 March 1926, 20.

Review of "Huss-Hartmann Matinée," 20 February 1918. In "New York Concerts." *Musical Courier*, 28 February 1918, 16.

Sachs, Harvey. *Toscanini*. Philadelphia: J. B. Lippincott, 1978.

Samaroff, Olga. Review of Hartmann Quartet, 14 February 1926, *New York Evening Post*, 15 February 1926.

Saerchinger, César. "Berlin is Full of American Musicians." *Musical Courier*, 19 October 1922, 7.

Shaffer, Karen A., and Neva Garner Greenwood. *Maud Powell: Pioneer American Violinist*. Ames: Iowa State University Press, 1988.

Smith, H. Nevill. "Arthur Hartmann in Berlin." Unidentified clipping from Hartmann's scrapbooks, Hartmann Collection, Free Library of Philadelphia.

Thompson, Oscar. *Debussy: Man and Artist.* New York: Dodd, Mead, and Company, 1937.

Thompson, Vance. "Violinist Hartmann Wins a Beautiful Bride in Three Days." *New York American,* 25 December 1909.

Timbrell, Charles. *French Pianism: A Historical Perspective,* 2nd ed. Portland, Oreg.: Amadeus Press, 1999.

Tual, Denise. *Au coeur du temps.* Paris: Carrère, 1987.

Vallas, Léon. *Claude Debussy: His Life and Works.* Translated by Maire and Grace O'Brien. Oxford: Oxford University Press, 1933.

"Valuable Violin Stolen on Train," *Los Angeles Herald,* 6 January 1907.

Vazzana, Eugene Michael. *Silent Film Necrology.* London: McFarland, 1995.

"Violinist's Marriage Sad Blow to Father," *Philadelphia North American,* 31 August 1903.

"A World's Master Violinist," *Rushford (N.Y.) Spectator,* 26 October 1911.

Index

Arthur Hartmann (1881–1956), a celebrated violinist who performed over a thousand recitals throughout Europe and the United States, met Claude Debussy in 1908, after he had transcribed "Il pleure dans mon coeur" for violin and piano. Their relationship developed into friendship, and in February 1914 Debussy accompanied Hartmann in a performance of three of Hartmann's transcriptions of Debussy's works. The two friends saw each other for the last time on the composer's birthday, 22 August 1914, shortly before Hartmann and his family fled Europe to escape the Great War.

With the publication of Hartmann's memoir *Claude Debussy As I Knew Him*, along with the twenty-two known letters from Claude Debussy and the thirty-nine letters from Emma Debussy to Hartmann and his wife, the richness and importance of their relationship can be appreciated for the first time. The memoir covers the years 1908–1918. Debussy's letters to Hartmann span the years 1908–1916, and Emma (Mme) Debussy's letters span the years 1910–1932. Also included are the facsimile of Debussy's *Minstrels* manuscript transcription for violin and piano, three previously unpublished letters from Debussy to Pierre Louÿs, and correspondence between Hartmann and Béla Bartók, Nina Grieg, Alexandre Guilmant, Charles Martin Loeffler, Marian MacDowell, Hans Richter, and Anton Webern, along with Hartmann's memoirs on Loeffler, Ysaÿe, Joachim, and Grieg. A biographical sketch of Hartmann's career, gleaned from the Hartmann collections of the Sibley Music Library and the Free Library of Philadelphia, reintroduces a musician who was known and treasured by many of the leading composers and performers of his time.

CPSIA information can be obtained at www.ICGtesting.com
Printed in the USA
LVOW052055010213

318128LV00008B/351/P

"Intriguing and meticulously produced." —*Times Literary Supplement*

"This is a fine account of a remarkable life story, just as well paced as any of Hartmann's own literary endeavors . . . a delightful book: the sort that leads you captivated from page to page." —*The Musical Times*

"The editors . . . have contributed appreciably to the ever-evolving image of De[ ] and his circle." —*Music and Letters*

"A treasure of a book." —Jessica Duchen, author of *Gabriel Fauré* (Phaidon)

SAMUEL HSU is a pianist and professor of music at Philadelphia Biblical University.

SIDNEY GROLNIC, now retired, was a librarian in the music department of the Free Library of Philadelphia, where he served as curator of the Hartmann Collection.

MARK PETERS is associate professor of music at Trinity Christian College.

R UNIVERSITY OF ROCHESTER PRESS

668 Mt. Hope Avenue, Rochester, NY 14620–2731, USA
P.O. Box 9, Woodbridge, Suffolk IP12 3DF, UK

www.urpress.com

ISBN 978-1-58046-364-5

90000

9 781580 463645